DYING FOR THE CAUSE

Kerry's Republican Dead

Tim Horgan

MERCIER PRESS
IRISH PUBLISHER - IRISH STORY

MERCIER PRESS
Cork
www.mercierpress.ie

© Tim Horgan, 2015

ISBN: 978 1 78117 278 0

10 9 8 7 6 5 4 3 2 1

A CIP record for this title is available from the British Library

This book is sold subject to the condition that it shall not, by way of trade or otherwise, be lent, resold, hired out or otherwise circulated without the publisher's prior consent in any form of binding or cover other than that in which it is published and without a similar condition including this condition being imposed on the subsequent purchaser.

No part of this publication may be reproduced or transmitted in any form or by any means, electronic or mechanical, including photocopying, recording or any information or retrieval system, without the prior permission of the publisher in writing.

Printed and bound in the EU.

DYING
FOR
THE CAUSE

DEDICATIONS

For Ruth, without whom much would not have been possible and little worthwhile. God's greatest gift to me.

Martin Moore would like to dedicate his work in this book to his daughter and young author, Fiona. She lost her battle with a long illness at the young age of sixteen before the world could see her many talents and charms, which her friends and family had enjoyed during her short life.

The author's royalties have been donated to the National Graves Association. The objectives of the Association have always been:

- To restore, where necessary, and maintain fittingly the graves and memorials of our patriot dead of every generation.
- To commemorate those who died in the cause of Irish freedom.
- To compile a record of such graves and memorials.

The Association is not in receipt of, nor have they ever applied for, state funding of any kind. They depend entirely on voluntary donations from nationally minded people, at home and abroad, and on annual subscriptions from Associate members.

Contents

Acknowledgements	11
List of Abbreviations	14
Preface	15
Introduction	19
1st and 9th (Tralee) Battalions, Kerry No. 1 Brigade	**27**
John Conway	31
Daniel Daly	33
Thomas Drummond	36
Eugene Fitzgerald	38
Jackie Fleming	40
Michael Flynn	43
Tom Flynn	46
Daniel Foley	48
Patrick (Percy) Hannafin	50
William Harrington	52
Tommy Hawley	54
Con Healy	57
Frank Hoffman	59
Seán Moriarty	62
Billy Myles	64
George Nagle	66
James O'Connor	69
Jerry O'Sullivan	71
John O'Sullivan	73
Paddy Reidy	75
Michael Ryle	76
Michael Sinnott	78
Jim Walsh	80
2nd (Ardfert) and 3rd (Lixnaw) Battalions, Kerry No. 1 Brigade	**82**
Thomas Archer	86
James Barry	89
John Cantillon	91

Edward Greaney	93
James Hanlon	96
Reginald Hathaway	98
Seán Houlihan	101
Jack Lawlor	103
Timothy 'Aero' Lyons	105
William McCarthy	108
Jim McEnery	110
Tom McGrath	113
Michael McGuire	115
Michael Nolan	117
Daniel O'Driscoll	119
George O'Shea	121
Patrick O'Shea	123
Tim Tuomey	126
4th (Castlegregory) and 5th (Dingle) Battalions, Kerry No. 1 Brigade	**128**
Thomas M. Ashe	131
John Casey	133
James Cronin	135
Maurice Fitzgerald	137
Thomas Greaney	139
Paddy Kennedy	140
Daniel 'Bob' McCarthy	142
Michael McKenna	144
Thomas Moriarty	146
Tom O'Sullivan	148
Timothy Spillane	151
6th (Listowel) and 8th (Ballylongford) Battalions, Kerry No. 1 Brigade	**153**
Eddie Carmody	156
Paddy Dalton	158
Patrick Foran	161
Michael Galvin	163
Pat Hartnett	166
John Lawlor	169
John Linnane	171

Jerry Lyons	174
Michael (Bob) McElligott	178
Charles O'Hanlon	180
Paddy Walsh	183
Daniel Scanlon	187
Jack Sheehan	189

1st (Castleisland) Battalion, Kerry No. 2 Brigade; 7th (Castleisland) Battalion, Kerry No. 1 Brigade — 192

Michael Brosnan	195
Patrick Buckley	197
John Daly	200
Tom Fleming	203
Patrick Kenny	205
Bertie Murphy	207
Dan Murphy	210
Michael O'Connell	213
Denny O'Connor	215
Jer O'Leary	218
Jack Prendiville	221
John Savage	224
Richard Shanahan	226
James Walsh	229

2nd (Firies) Battalion, Kerry No. 2 Brigade, and Ballymacelligott Company — 233

Jim Baily	237
Denis Broderick	240
Michael Brosnan	242
John Browne	244
Robert Browne	247
Mossie Casey	249
John Clifford	251
Jack Flynn	253
Paddy Herlihy	255
Richard Laide	257
John Leen	259
John McMahon	261

Thomas McLoughlin	263
Jack Reidy	265
Maurice Reidy	267
3rd (Kenmare) Battalion, Kerry No. 2 Brigade	**269**
Con Looney	271
Timothy O'Shea	274
Denis Tuohy	276
4th (Killarney) Battalion, Kerry No. 2 Brigade	**278**
Dan Allman	281
Stephen Buckley	284
Jerry Casey	286
Patrick Casey	288
James Daly	290
John Kevins	293
Patrick McCarthy	297
Timothy Murphy	299
Daniel O'Donoghue	301
Jeremiah O'Donoghue	303
5th (Rathmore) Battalion, Kerry No. 2 Brigade	**306**
Jeremiah Carey	309
William Cronin	310
Laurence Hickey	312
Michael McSweeney	313
Andrew Moynihan	315
Patrick O'Connor	317
Michael O'Sullivan	319
Tadhg O'Sullivan	322
John Sharry	324
6th (Killorglin) Battalion, Kerry No. 2 Brigade	**327**
Michael Ahern	331
William Conway O'Connor	333
Jack Galvin	335
Frank Grady	338
Patrick Murphy	341
Joe Taylor	343

Séamus Taylor	346
Kerry No. 3 Brigade	**348**
Dan Clifford	351
Michael Courtney	353
Eugene Dwyer	355
Con Keating	357
Jeremiah 'Romey' Keating	360
Tadhg Keating	362
Patrick Lynch	364
Dan Shea	366
John Tadhg O'Sullivan	369
Willie Rearden	371
John Sugrue	373
Dying for the Cause Elsewhere	**376**
Thomas Ashe	377
Charlie Daly	382
Dan Enright	386
Tom Healy	389
Jim Hickey	391
Charlie Kerins	393
Michael Mulvihill	397
Seán O'Leary	399
Maurice O'Neill	402
Michael Rahilly (The O'Rahilly)	405
Tim O'Sullivan	409
Jack O'Reilly	412
Thomas Russell	414
Liam Scully	416
Paddy Shortis	419
'The Others'	**421**
William Brosnan	422
Giles Cooper	423
Brendan Doherty	425
Liam Hegarty	427
Thomas Leane	430

Michael Lynch	431
Charles Monaghan	432
William O'Brien	434
John O'Connor	436
Thomas Prendiville	440
Donal (Dan) Sheehan	442
Austin Stack	444
Timeline of Events in Kerry	447
Bibliography	456
Index	458

Acknowledgements

History, especially local and family history, is received, remembered and passed on. To the following listed below and to many others, I am deeply indebted for being entrusted with their stories and for the assistance that they afforded me in my attempts to record those in Kerry who 'died for The Cause'. I hope that your history has become our history and that the memories of these brave Kerry people will endure for many generations to come and perhaps become an inspiration to those who follow us.

I wish to thank especially Martin Moore, whose foresight and interest allowed many of the stories and photographs of these men to be preserved from the generation which lived through the 1916–1923 period. His generosity with his extensive archive of images and documents has greatly enhanced this publication and for that I am greatly indebted to him. His attention to detail has allowed many of the stories contained within this book to be an accurate part of our sad but glorious history, rather than being denigrated as half-remembered myths.

There are a number of people without whose assistance this work could not have been undertaken. Mattias Ó Dubhda from Cloghane, whose enthusiasm for this project ensured that fallen Volunteers from his native Corca Dhuibhne would not be forgotten. His idealism and commitment to 'The Cause' remains undimmed in spite of his many years. George Rice, whose recollections, research and advice regarding those men who fought in South Kerry under his father, General John Joe Rice, was invaluable and generously given. Stephen Kelleghan of Ballinskelligs, whose information concerning the dead of the Kerry No. 3 Brigade is greatly appreciated. He also provided several of the photographs of the South Kerry Volunteers. Stephen's technical and photographic expertise allowed many of the other photographs in the book be enhanced to a level where they could be reproduced. Denis Fleming and Donie O'Sullivan, who helped with events in Kilcummin, and Mícheál Walsh of Knocknagoshel, have ensured that the memories of those who fought in these areas will not be forgotten. Tomás and Mai O'Hanlon provided tireless help in my research in the Rathmore area.

Thanks also to: Sr Alma Moynihan, Boston (Vol. Andrew Moynihan); Ann Deenihan, Ballinclogher (Vol. Patrick O'Shea); Seán Seosamh Ó Conchubhair, Tralee (Vol. Michael Nolan); Peggy and Brendan Crowley, Dublin (Vol. Timothy Murphy); Dan O'Donoghue, Killarney (Vol. Daniel O'Donoghue); Mary Lehane, Cahersiveen (Vol. Dan Shea); Nora Barrett, Tralee (Vol. Jack Reidy); Una Kavanagh, Killarney (Vol. Patrick McCarthy); Margaret Read, USA (Vol. Con Looney); Richard Colligan, England (Vol. Con Looney); Peggy Murphy, Killorglin (Vol. Patrick Murphy); Mary Brosnan, Killarney (Vol. Daniel O'Donoghue); Maura O'Brien, Killarney (Vol. Michael O'Sullivan); Liam Scully, Tralee (Vol. Liam Scully); Adrian Breathnach, Cork (Vol. James Walsh, Currow); Michael Scanlon, Ballybunion (Vol. Daniel Scanlon); Julie McEvoy McCarthy, Kilfenora (Vol. Tom Flynn); Margaret Cagney, Dublin (Vol. Daniel Daly); Noreen Finn, Castlegregory (Vol. James Cronin); Frank Kevins, Currans (Vol. John Kevins); Liam Canny, USA (Vol. Daniel Foley); Phil O'Shea, Waterville (Vol. Michael Courtney); Aidan Larkin, Dublin (Vol. John O'Connor); Michael O'Shea, Ballycleave (Vol. Michael Ahern); Margaret Doherty Houlihan, Currow (Vol. Brendan Doherty); Kate Cremins, Cullen (Vol. William Cronin); Seán Harnett, Listowel (Vol. Pat Hartnett); Jimmy O'Connell, Castleisland (Vol. Michael O'Connell); Con Moynihan, Killorglin (Vol. Andrew Moynihan); Imelda Murphy, Listowel (Vol. Thomas Archer); Breandán Ó Cíobháin, Ventry (Vol. Maurice Fitzgerald); Michael O'Hanlon, Listowel (Vol. Charles O'Hanlon); Nora Mai and Séamus Fleming, Currow (Vol. Jer O'Leary); Dan Brosnan, Tralee (Vol. Michael Brosnan, Ballymac); John Laide, Gortatlea (Vol. Richard Laide); Brian Caball, Tralee (Vol. Maurice Reidy).

Tom Harrington of Clashmealcon, Cecilia Lynch of Ballyduff, John Quirke of Derrymore, Batt Riordan of Firies, Jerry Savage of Ballymacelligott, Jack Godley of Ballymacelligott, Catherine McGillycuddy of Glencar, Mícheál Mac Giolla Cuda of Glencar, Batt Cronin of Toureencahill, Josie Hickey of Rathmore, Donal Hickey of Gneeveguilla, Tommy O'Connor of Ardfert, Jerry Flynn of Ballymacelligott, Matt Leen of Tralee, Morna Williams Clifford of Tralee, Seán O'Mahony of Dublin, John McCarthy of Killarney, Fr Tom Hickey of Ballyferriter, Fr James Linnane of Listowel, Peggy Goggin of Kelly's Height, Dan King of Tralee, Máire Collins of Abbeyfeale, Dan Casey of Dunloe,

Acknowledgements

Fr Teddy Linehan of Tralee, Seán Stiophán Ó Súilleabháin of Rathmore, Eileen Daly of Gneeveguilla, Maureen and Noreen Ahern of Killorglin, the Joyce family of Ballycleave, Peggy and Thomas Clifford of Dooks, Michael Lynch, Archives Dept, Kerry County Library, Mary Murphy of An Gleann, Ray Bateson of Dublin, Con Moynihan of Killorglin, Dr Norrie Buckley of Killarney, Dr Conor Brosnan of Dingle, Con Crowley of Rathanny, Pádraig Garvey of Cahersiveen, William Goggin of Ballinskelligs, Kay Looney of Kenmare, Rachel and Helen Horgan of Crossroads, Dr Pádraig Óg Ó Ruairc of Clare, Dr John Rice of Ballymacelligott, Tim Galvin of Tralee, Luke Keane of Knocknagoshel, Sinéad Cotter and Justin Flynn of The Spa, James 'Sonny' Egan of Garrynagore, Ray Bateson of Dublin, Kitty Galvin of Tralee, Martin O'Dwyer of Cashel and John Houlihan of the National Graves Association also helped immeasurably.

I would like to thank Mary Feehan and all the team at Mercier Press for their encouragement, advice and their dedication to giving the people of Ireland the history of Ireland.

I would like to express my gratitude to my parents, Eileen 'Dodie' Horgan and my later father Declan Horgan, teacher and Republican. Among their many gifts to me was a love of my country, a pride in its history and a belief that one day it would be truly free. To my children, Ciara, Meadhbh, Declan and Tadhg, whose words of encouragement, assistance with computer problems and company on my many journeys made the whole project much easier. Finally, none of this could be possible without the encouragement, forbearance and generosity with her time of my wife, Ruth.

List of Abbreviations

BMH	Bureau of Military History
GHQ	General Headquarters
IRB	Irish Republican Brotherhood
O/C	Commanding Officer
RIC	Royal Irish Constabulary
V/C	Vice-Commanding Officer
WS	Witness Statements

PREFACE

On 27 September 1922, during fierce fighting for control of the town of Killorglin, IRA Volunteer Con Looney was shot and fatally wounded. As his young life ebbed away, his final words were recorded by his comrades: 'Give my rifle to my brother, my love to my mother and tell them I am dying for the cause.' His rifle was brought back to his brother and perhaps his mother's grief was eased a little by his last declaration of affection. And he did die for 'The Cause' – the cause of Irish freedom. With the passage of time, as his comrades died and the generations changed, the story of Con Looney faded in all but the memories of his family and *An Dream Beag Dilís*, 'The Faithful Few'.

The men and women who fought for Ireland's freedom were not conscripted to do so, nor were they paid for their services. They were volunteer soldiers driven only by an ideal which had been handed down to them by generations past and that ideal was the unquenchable belief that the Irish people should live in freedom, unfettered by foreign domination. In the course of their brief lives not force of arms, not lonely prison cells, not inhuman torture, not material inducements and ultimately not even death could separate these volunteer soldiers from that ideal.

Ironically, however, it was this idealism that proved to be the catalyst that hastened their memory on its journey into a national amnesia. While soldiers fight wars, it is politicians who get to guide the subsequent histories. Such histories are often based on the requirements considered expedient for their current political needs. Unrealised ideals become embarrassments and so must follow the well-worn path of apathy to antipathy and eventually to ridicule. The volunteer soldiers who died for the cause of freedom could not and cannot be separated from the beliefs that inspired them and so it was deemed necessary to consign these men and women to the national amnesia along with their ideals. Thus it is a sad fact that within a couple of generations the nation that they fought and died for has shamefully forgotten these heroes. It is the aim of this book to go some way towards preserving the memory of the lives, deaths and ideals of these men of Kerry who died for 'The Cause'.

During the twentieth century over 150 Kerry men died in the fight for Irish freedom. Many were killed in action but others were executed or died while in captivity as a result of brutality or neglect. Some had their physical or mental health broken, ending their young lives prematurely, but theirs was no less a sacrifice than had they fallen in the heat of battle. A final, definitive list of those who died for 'The Cause' defied any clear criteria and so it was left to the fallen Volunteers' comrades to be the arbiters of whom they considered had given their lives for Ireland's freedom. Just as the fight for freedom in Kerry was fought by local men with little outside assistance or influence, thus the patriotic dead would be remembered by locally erected memorials without any 'official' twenty-six county government input. The names of the fallen were inscribed by their comrades on monuments at Ballyseedy, Cahersiveen and Rathmore, and on memorials in numerous cemeteries and on roadsides, in fields and on the streets of Kerry. It is these men, whose names are carved in stone and who generations before us considered to have had died for 'The Cause', that are remembered in this book.

A strong sense of local identity has always been a defining feature of the Kerry persona. That bond between the person and native place was forged by centuries of battling nature and foreigner to maintain a precarious foothold on a land that was challenging but beautiful, unyielding but embracing. These young men defined themselves by the land which nurtured them. Thus they were part of a townland, part of a parish, part of a village or town. They fought and died with comrades from their own areas and so guided by this, they are listed not by rank or chronology, but in the battalions to which they were attached. Each battalion was formed from companies which generally represented parishes and from 1919 onwards these battalions evolved and divided, were named and renamed, designated to brigades and re-designated. As such, assigning fallen soldiers into precise military units is inherently flawed but does serve a useful purpose in the pursuit of local remembrance. Other Kerrymen died outside the county. There are several Volunteers from other counties who died in Kerry and others who were buried in Kerry soil having fallen elsewhere in the fight for freedom. All had a story and all died for 'The Cause' and so are included in these pages. Finally there are some who died, not in the line of fire, but whose surviving comrades thought their contribution or sacrifice sufficient to inscribe their names in stone on monuments so that these men too would be remembered.

With his last breath Con Looney wished his people to know that he was dying for 'The Cause'. This book is not a history of Kerry's contribution in the fight for Irish freedom in the twentieth century. Rather, it was written as a memorial to those men who gave their lives in that struggle, so that all those who died for 'The Cause' would be remembered with pride by their people.

Tim Horgan
2015

Introduction

On a winter's evening in November 1583 in Glanageenty, Ballymacelligott, another war of independence ended. The Earl of Desmond was finally captured and beheaded by Irishmen in the service of the English crown. All that remained of his army after four years of warfare was a small guerrilla band, and with his death, Queen Elizabeth I's rule over County Kerry was no longer disputed. Banished to the mountains and bogs, the people brought only their faith, their stories and a deep sense of grievance. When the rebellion of 1641 erupted in Ulster this emboldened the dispossessed in Kerry and, led by the remnants of the old Gaelic nobility, the county was quickly in the hands of the people who had become rebels in their own land. But that brief interlude lasted only until Cromwell's armies crushed the hopes of Gaelic Ireland. When General John Ludlow captured Ross Castle in 1653, the rebellion was over and English rule was made more secure as the lands of Kerry were planted with Cromwellian officers as part of the division of the spoils of war.

For two centuries the county would remain in a peaceful but unjust equilibrium, victor and vanquished, landed and landless, prosperous and impoverished, English and Irish. The ideals of the American and French Revolutions would inspire the great rebellion of 1798, but only elsewhere in the country, as Kerry remained almost untouched by the events of that summer of freedom. The agrarian unrest of the Whiteboys in the early decades of the nineteenth century did nothing to change the equilibrium between conquerors and conquered. Daniel O'Connell's great promises of a new order with Catholic Emancipation and Repeal would fail to upset the unjust balance between landed and landless as he left Ireland firmly part of Britain's now mighty Empire. Hundreds of thousands of lives spent eking out miserable existences on mountainsides and bogs would be quenched in the Great Famine of the 1840s. While corn still grew and fish still swam in rivers, the crown forces guarded food exports and starvation and disease took a third of the population of Kerry to unmarked and mass graves. Yet that unjust equilibrium between master and slave endured.

A broken people found refuge on America's shores and there Ireland's exiles gained a new confidence and the flames of freedom began to ignite once again.

Just as people went west across the ocean, the seeds of revolution in the form of the Fenian Brotherhood came east across the Atlantic. In the 1860s the Fenian message found fertile ground in the towns of Kerry and murmurings of rebellion again swept the countryside. But hampered by indecision and infiltrated by Irishmen whose loyalty lay with the crown rather than their own people, the rebellion foundered before it could start. In February 1867 Colonel J. J. O'Connor, a Valentia-born American Civil War veteran, led the Fenians of Cahersiveen in open rebellion, but within days the 'gold sun of freedom' had once again set. The might of Britain quickly crushed his heroic band that would be recalled in song as the 'Boys of Foilmore'. But still their cause endured, undeterred by the power of the Empire or the condemnation of its clerical allies.

In the 1880s the power of the landed gentry to extract rents from an impoverished people began to be resisted. The confrontation between the landlords and those whose battle cry was 'The land to the People' was most acute in Kerry. As the constitutional Land League was unable to match the power of the landlords, the police and the legal system that stood behind them, groups of young men banded together to defend their people using guerrilla tactics. These Moonlighters were especially active in the Castleisland, Ballymacelligott and Firies areas, which were described in contemporary police reports as 'the most disturbed districts in Ireland'. By the early 1890s the sway of the landlords within the county was broken.

But the people of Ireland would still not sit comfortably within Britain's Empire. The colonial government had been largely successful in suppressing Ireland's identity, with our native language and culture pushed towards extinction as the Irish became increasingly anglicised. Then, in 1884, the Gaelic Athletic Association was formed to promote native games and in 1893 the Gaelic League was established to promote the revival of what remained of the Irish language and culture. Soon the national spirit was regaining its confidence. Politicians promised Home Rule for Ireland but failed to deliver as Britain was determined to keep its first colony within its imperial clutches. However, the separatist tradition amongst the Irish people could not all be enticed by political promises. On 25 November 1913 the Irish Volunteers were formed in Dublin's Rotunda and their founding manifesto stated the organisation's aim 'to secure and maintain the rights and liberties common to all Irish People'. Though initially unstated, Republicans saw the Volunteers as a vehicle for securing Ireland's independence, even if that entailed an armed uprising, while moderate nationalists saw the rapidly growing organisation as a force that would pressurise the British government into implementing Home Rule. Within a week Volunteer companies were formed in Killarney and Tralee. It was an idea whose time had come and soon every parish in Kerry had a group of young men drilling with rudimentary weapons and awaiting a time to strike. Britain's difficulty should have been Ireland's opportunity, but with the advent of the Great War in August 1914, John Redmond caused a split in the Irish Volunteers as he called on Ireland's young men to support Britain's war with Germany. Throughout the land the vast majority heeded Redmond's call and became the National Volunteers. He had gambled Ireland's youth in the hope of having Home Rule, now on the statute books, implemented at the end of the war, but as a result Ireland's young men died in their tens of thousands on the battlefields of Europe. In Kerry, however, the Irish Volunteers remained largely intact, with only a minority joining the National Volunteers. Shorn of moderate nationalist influence the Irish Volunteers, increasingly controlled by the Irish Republican Brotherhood (IRB), laid plans for an armed uprising while Britain was distracted by the war.

In Kerry Austin Stack, a renowned Gaelic footballer and administrator, was the commander of the Irish Volunteers. It was to him that the Military Council of the IRB entrusted the task of unloading and distributing the vast arsenal of weapons that Germany was to send on board the arms ship *Aud* at Easter 1916. The *Aud* was expected in Tralee Bay on Easter Saturday and Stack's closely guarded arrangements were based on this exact date. However, the German High Command had been given a three-day window to get its arms shipment to Fenit. So when Captain Spindler sailed into Tralee Bay on Thursday 20 April, he was not expected and neither were Roger Casement and his two companions who came ashore from a submarine at Banna Strand on Good Friday. Meanwhile, at Ballykissane, also on Good Friday, three Volunteers died during an attempt to acquire radio equipment to be used to contact the *Aud* – they were to be the first casualties of the Rising. Con Keating, Charlie Monaghan and Donal (Dan) Sheehan were also the first of about 150 Republican Volunteers to die in Kerry in an attempt to establish an Irish Republic.

When the *Aud* was scuttled and Casement detained, the plans for a rising in Kerry fell into chaos and this deteriorated into a paralysis when a lapse in judgement by Stack led to his incarceration by the RIC. Robert Monteith, who had come from Germany with Casement, was given command of the mustered Volunteers at Tralee on Easter Sunday. However, he judged it more prudent to dismiss them and prepare for another fight on another day.

The military defeat of the Rising and its subsequent executions and imprisonments did not cower the people of Ireland as it had done in other generations. Within a year the Irish Volunteers had reorganised and gained in confidence as sympathy towards the national cause replaced the apathy or antagonism a year previously. In Kerry, two Volunteers had died in April 1918 in an attack on the Gortatlea RIC Barracks and in retaliation two of the constables involved were shot in Tralee in broad daylight while attending the resulting inquest. The general election of November 1918 confirmed the popular support for the Republican cause and with the formation of Dáil Éireann in January 1919 a new era had begun. The Irish Volunteers armed themselves with weapons procured locally or captured from the enemy. Within months the paramilitary RIC had retreated from the countryside and fortified their barracks in the larger towns as they came under increasing attack from a guerrilla force that was rapidly gaining in confidence and sophistication. By the summer of 1920 vast areas of County Kerry had no police presence and the county became ungovernable. The civic administration of the British crown also collapsed in rural Ireland. With the RIC unable to cope with the deteriorating situation, they were reinforced by hastily recruited temporary constables. These Black and Tans would work in tandem with the RIC as they attempted to quell the rebellion with brutality. But their terrorist methods only provoked those they sought to control and in late 1920 a further force was sent to assist the RIC. The former British officers who made up the Auxiliary Division of the RIC were efficient and seasoned fighters. 'H' Company of the Auxiliary Division was based in Kerry under the command of the notorious and fearless Major McKinnon. But as the forces of the crown increased in strength so too did the resolve of those resisting British rule. Each battalion within the county had an active service unit by the spring of 1921 and the intensity of the conflict remorselessly grew until 11 July 1921, when, unable to quell the Republican forces, the British entered into a truce with Republicans.

Treaty negotiations went on until December until, under threat of 'terrible war', the Irish plenipotentiaries agreed to terms. Ireland was to be partitioned and those who governed the twenty-six counties were to be given limited power in exchange for an oath of allegiance to the crown. Ireland was to remain part of the Empire. The country's opinion divided, as was to be expected. Most of the men who had done the fighting objected that their sacrifices were to be sold for far less than a thirty-two county Republic free from Britain. Those under the age of twenty-five, which was the majority of active Volunteers, did not even have a vote; nor did women under the age of thirty. But Michael Collins and his pro-Treaty faction in Dáil Éireann won the day. The Anglo-Irish Treaty was ratified and from now on Irishmen would be used to do what Britain could not; quell the Republican rebellion.

The inevitable Civil War began on 28 June 1922 when Free State forces shelled the Republican headquarters in Dublin's Four Courts. Within a week the Republican forces in Dublin had been defeated, but a quick and decisive Free State victory was not to be as the men of Munster stood firm in defence of the Republic that they had fought for during the previous three years. A defensive line was formed between Limerick and Waterford, and Republican columns from Kerry, Cork, Limerick and Tipperary prevented Free State forces from entering the Republican heartland in the south. But soon this defensive strategy began to crumble in the face of better-equipped and numerically superior pro-Treaty forces. In the first fortnight of August, Free State Army units invaded by sea in Fenit, Tarbert, Kenmare, Passage West and Union Hall and quickly captured the virtually undefended towns of Munster. The Republican forces were again forced to retreat to the countryside and revert to the guerrilla warfare that had been successful against the British. Nowhere was this phase of the conflict more bloodily fought than in Kerry, as the IRA units continued to resist even as the hope of victory grew dimmer.

The Dublin Guard and 1st Western Division of the Free State Army became an occupying army in Kerry. Guerrilla warfare by the Republicans was met with mass arrests of Republican men and women, executions, the mass killings of prisoners and a brutality that the British had been reticent to use on the native population. On 10 April 1923, IRA Chief of Staff Liam Lynch was killed in action and his replacement Frank Aiken declared a ceasefire on 30 April, followed by an order for Republican forces to dump their arms on

24 May. The defence of the Republic had ended. Apart from the many dead, hundreds were imprisoned and these men and women would have to endure appalling conditions and a long hunger strike in November 1923 before most were released in December. It would be the summer of the next year when the last prisoners were finally freed. There was no attempt at any reconciliation as the new state stamped its authority on the twenty-six counties it controlled.

The Irish Free State was an unwelcome place for the defeated Republicans and hundreds left to begin their lives anew in the United States, free from the harassment, unemployment and disillusionment that was their lot following their release from prison. The Republican movement fragmented, with most following de Valera into the constitutional politics of a partitioned country. A minority remained true to the original ideals of 1916 and a much weakened IRA and Sinn Féin continued to survive. When de Valera and his Fianna Fáil party was elected to power in 1932, there were high expectations that partition might be unravelled, but this was not the case as the party diluted its Republican values and promoted populist economic policies. Figures from the revolutionary period such as John Joe Rice and John Joe Sheehy continued to carry the Republican torch in Kerry.

In 1938 the IRA launched a campaign of bombing in Britain, mirroring a similar tactic used in the 1880s by the Fenian Dynamitards. Several Kerry IRA Volunteers were amongst those who operated in English cities, but by 1940 the campaign instigated by 1916 veteran Seán Russell had petered out.

The Second World War was regarded as another opportunity to pressurise Britain into withdrawing from Ireland. While a campaign was planned in 1942 to attack British targets in the six counties, it failed to materialise as the Fianna Fáil government turned on their erstwhile allies. Hundreds of Republicans were interned, including many from Kerry. Those executed for Republican activities by the de Valera regime included two from County Kerry: Maurice O'Neill and Charlie Kerins.

While another military campaign along the border began in 1956, it too was short-lived. IRA activists from Kerry were involved and several received prison sentences. A swell of popular support for the Republican cause saw Tan War veteran John Joe Rice elected as a Sinn Féin TD for South Kerry. But by 1962 the IRA leadership accepted defeat and declared a ceasefire.

Introduction

In 1969, precipitated by demands for civil rights, Irish Republicans embarked on another struggle for independence in the six counties. A long and bloody campaign would see some Kerry IRA Volunteers on active service in Northern Ireland and in Britain. The Kerry command played an important role as the latest Troubles went on for three decades. Many from the county suffered long terms of imprisonment, hunger strikes and years on the run until a negotiated settlement allowed for an uneasy peace. A degree of self-rule for the six counties, a continuation of partition and the promise of stepping-stones to ultimate Irish freedom silenced the guns. Whether these stepping stones will go the way of those of Michael Collins and later those of Éamon de Valera, only time will tell.

An American general once memorably reminded his people 'Freedom is not for free, somebody has paid the price'. And so it is in Ireland. In the pages that follow are the stories of these men of Kerry who paid the ultimate price for our freedom.

The sacrifices of these men are as great, and often greater, than those patriots whose memory is preserved in the national narrative. Each of these fallen soldiers was an individual with his own unique story and this book tries to portray each man as such. Some fell in action with their comrades and others shared their last moments with other Volunteers, dying together in captivity. As a result there is, of necessity, a degree of repetition in many of the brief stories of these men's lives and deaths.

Those who died for 'The Cause' in Kerry are sometimes remembered by written words and more often by ever-fading oral narratives. Most are also remembered by more permanent memorials, whether a headstone or a monument at the site where they fell. On such stone testaments the dead are often recalled by the names being inscribed in their native language. This is often in the old Gaelic script and in the text of this book these Gaelic spellings are also recorded under the more anglicised form of their names. Thus it is hoped that future generations will be able to link the inscriptions on such monuments and gravestones to the stories which are preserved in this book.

Ná déan dearmad and bí bróduil astu, agus 'Beidh Éire fós ag Cáit Ní Dhuibhir'.

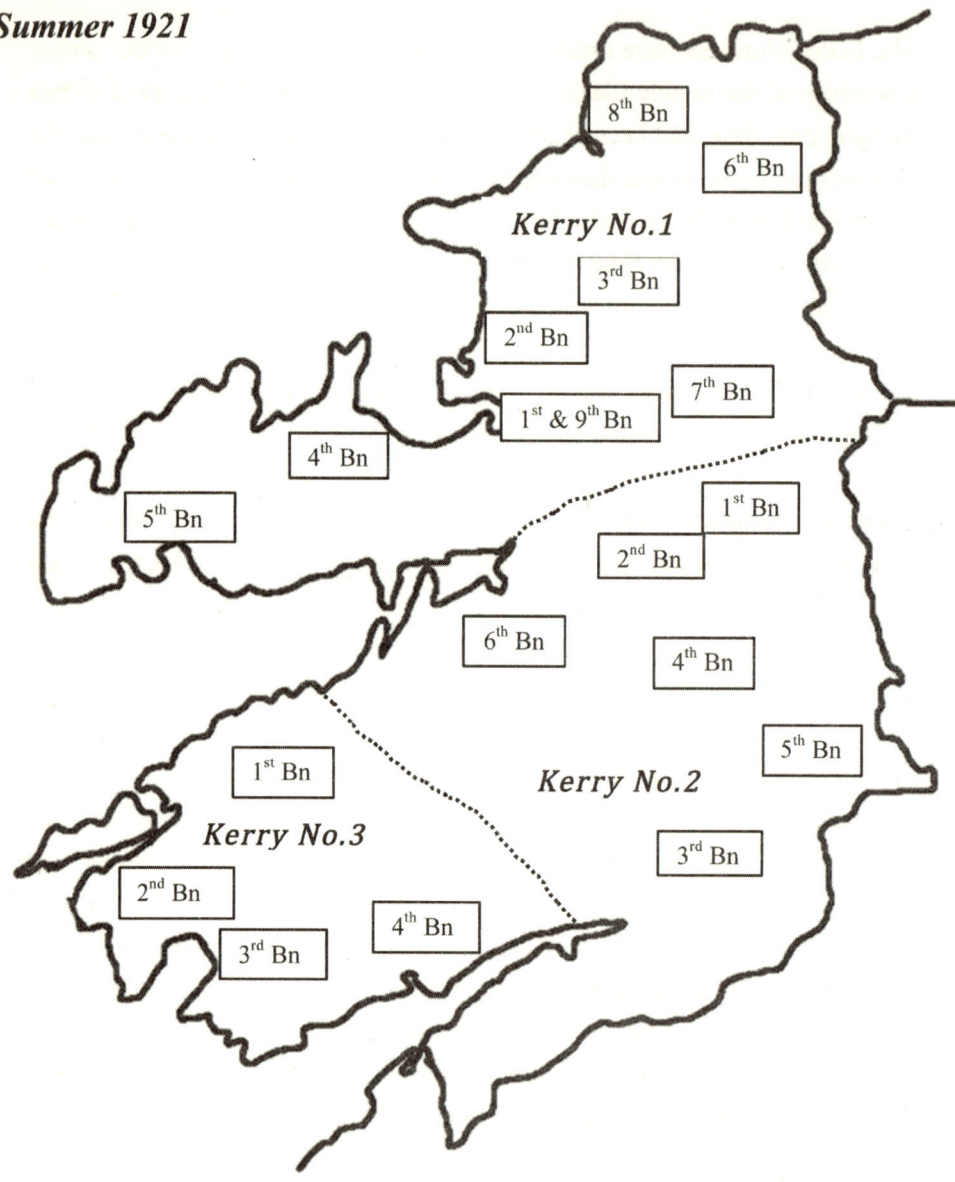

1st and 9th (Tralee) Battalions, Kerry No. 1 Brigade

The Irish Volunteers were established in Tralee on 10 December 1913 during a meeting of the weekly Gaelic League class. Matthew McMahon of Urban Terrace, Boherbue, had been at the inaugural meeting of the Volunteers at the Rotunda in Dublin fifteen days previously and at his instigation a company was formed in Tralee. Tralee had a been a centre of IRB activity in the preceding years and within a short time the Brotherhood had gained prominent positions within the fledgling Volunteer movement. Austin Stack, the head of the IRB, was appointed O/C of the Tralee Volunteers and Alf Cotton, a civil servant and fellow IRB member, was his deputy. In March 1916, weeks before the Rising, Cotton was expelled from Kerry by the authorities and Paddy Cahill became the second in command. Though well organised and drilled before the Rising, the unexpected arrival of Casement at Banna, the premature arrival and subsequent capture and scuttling of the arms ship *Aud*, and the arrest of Stack on Good Friday threw plans for a rising in Kerry into chaos. Within days, all senior members of the Irish Volunteers were under arrest and it would not be until 1917 that the movement would attempt to resurrect itself in Tralee.

During 1917 the Tralee Volunteers began reorganising, arms were collected and recruitment and drilling continued. Austin Stack remained O/C of the battalion and also the leader of the Irish Volunteers in the county. Paddy Cahill was V/C and Dan Sullivan, the chairman of the Tralee Urban Council, was the battalion adjutant. Billy Mullins served as the quartermaster. The election of 1918 resulted in Austin Stack being appointed Minister for Home Affairs in the first Dáil and following his departure to Dublin in January 1919, Cahill became the battalion O/C and Joe Melinn his deputy.

In the spring of 1919 the single Kerry Irish Volunteer command was divided into three brigades. Paddy Cahill, who had been O/C of the original Kerry Brigade and also of the Tralee (1st) Battalion, now became O/C of Kerry No. 1 Brigade, which consisted of the Tralee, North and West Kerry Battalions. The Tralee Battalion was composed of companies from Boherbue, Rock Street, Strand Street, Farmer's Bridge, Ballyroe, Oakpark, Blennerville and Curraheen.

Several of Cahill's staff from Tralee joined him in the new brigade staff and as a result a new leadership was appointed to the 1st Battalion. Dan Healy was appointed battalion O/C with Michael Doyle as his deputy. Michael Fleming of Gas Terrace was the battalion adjutant and Paddy Barry of Rock Street was the new quartermaster, with Thomas Foley being appointed the intelligence officer.

On the orders of GHQ, following the death of Terence MacSwiney on hunger strike, the IRA was to engage the crown forces wherever they could be encountered during the last week of October 1920. The killing of several RIC men in North Kerry brought about a dramatic escalation of the conflict that forced Paddy Cahill and other active IRA men in his Tralee command to go into hiding. They set up a brigade headquarters at Fybough, near Keel, seventeen miles by road from Tralee. In this remote location Cahill also located his brigade active service unit, which was mainly composed of Tralee IRA Volunteers who could not return to the town. The exodus of so many fighting men hampered the activity of what remained of the 1st Battalion in Tralee. However, in March 1921 Brigade Adjutant Paddy Garvey was detailed to set up a battalion active service unit within the town. This was commanded by the 'A' Company officer, Captain John Joe Sheehy, and was composed of IRA Volunteers still living in Tralee. This battalion unit was soon taking the fight to the local RIC and Auxiliaries. Their most notable successes were the killings of Auxiliary commander Major John McKinnon on 15 April and Head Constable Francis Benson on 14 May 1921. By this time Paddy Cahill had been relieved of his command by GHQ, who had judged him to be ineffectual as a military leader.

While Cahill's military leadership of the brigade could certainly be questioned, there was no doubt that he was a popular figure with many of the fighting men. He had a loyal following within the brigade staff and especially within the Strand Street area of Tralee in which 'B' Company was based, the district of Tralee where Cahill was from. His second in command, Tadhg Brosnan, refused to become the Kerry No. 1 Brigade O/C such was his loyalty to Cahill, with the result that GHQ was obliged to appoint Andy Cooney, an organiser who had been operating in South Kerry, as brigade commander. While Cahill withdrew from his position, his staff were defiant and refused to cooperate with Cooney in an attempt to isolate the new brigade O/C. Cooney's orders were ignored, especially by 'B' Company. However, within the town John Joe Sheehy's active service unit was now waging the fight against the crown forces and this unit remained aloof from the Cahill controversy. Dan Healy's command as O/C of the Tralee-based 1st Battalion was transferred to Sheehy, though Cahill loyalists within the town refused to accept his leadership and they remained outside the battalion structure.

This situation whereby a significant section of the town's IRA Volunteers refused to accept the command of the local 1st Battalion was to remain a source of contention for nearly fourteen months. Eventually IRA Chief of Staff Liam Lynch brokered a deal in the summer of 1922 whereby the Cahill loyalists would form a separate battalion in the Tralee district and this was to be termed the 9th Battalion. This new battalion was composed of companies from Strand Street, Blennerville, Ballyroe, Churchill and Curraheen. Its O/C was Paddy Paul Fitzgerald and in theory it was not to be under the direct command of the brigade O/C, who by that time was Humphrey Murphy. However, although the outbreak of Civil War saw both the 1st and 9th Battalions united in their opposition to the Treaty, the personality differences that arose from GHQ's ill-considered removal of Paddy Cahill remained simmering under the surface until well after the war ended.

Following the withdrawal of the British Army in January 1922, the 1st Battalion used its barracks in Ballymullen as their new headquarters. The outbreak of the Civil War saw many of the town's experienced fighters in action in the Limerick and Tipperary area, but the Free State's seaborne invasion at Fenit on 2 August 1922 caught the battalion unaware, as most of the active Volunteers were engaged in the faltering defence of the Limerick to Waterford line. After some bloody fighting, General Paddy Daly and his Dublin Guard captured Tralee on that summer's day and went on to establish garrisons in the towns of Kerry. However, the rural areas remained in Republican hands and within days Sheehy's battalion was waging a guerrilla war against the Free State Army, which had its headquarters in Ballymullen Barracks. The next nine months of fighting would see the deaths of many of the 1st and 9th Battalion's Volunteers, some of whom would be summarily executed following capture. Others would die in captivity due to poor prison conditions, while hundreds were interned in prison camps in the Curragh, Newbridge and Gormanston, and in Mountjoy and Limerick Gaols and women's prisons at the South Dublin Union and Kilmainham Gaol. The suffering of the bereaved, imprisoned, exiled and brutalised unfortunately cannot be measured, but the following pages contain the stories of those of the Tralee battalions who paid the ultimate price in the search for an independent Irish Republic.

John Conway

Seán Ó Conbuide

John 'Sonny' Conway was born in Abbey Street, Tralee, in 1894 into a large family. His younger brother, Dan Joe, gained fame as an All-Ireland-winning Kerry footballer. John, like his father, worked as a general labourer. He was married and lived at 61 Caherina, Strand Street, Tralee. As a young man he had emigrated to the United States and had enlisted in the American Army under the name John Rundle.[1] During the Great War he served with the American forces in Europe. On demobilisation following the end of the war he returned to Tralee. On doing so, he joined the Irish Volunteers in the town. Conway was attached to 'A' Company, 1st Battalion, Kerry No. 1 Brigade and later was part of the 9th Battalion formed in 1922.

Courtesy of the Martin Moore collection.

In February 1923 he was in custody in what was called the Workhouse Barracks in Tralee. This was the town's workhouse, which had been occupied by the Free State Army to be used as a barracks to supplement their main garrison in Ballymullen and is now the County Council offices. Free State Army reports at the time of the inquest into John Conway's death indicate that he was a civilian prisoner when he was killed. However, the IRA lists him amongst those Volunteers killed during the Civil War. While his status as a prisoner may be in doubt, the circumstances of his death are not.

On 24 February 1923 Captain Patrick Byrne shot John Conway dead while a prisoner in the barracks.[2] Byrne was an officer in the Dublin Guard and was from Gardiner Street in Dublin. Conway was brought by the officer to a

1 Information from Martin Moore, Tralee.
2 *The Freeman's Journal*, 6 April 1923.

place on the main road opposite the town's Rath Cemetery. There he was shot. Initially the Free State officer claimed that he had shot the prisoner as he was attempting to escape, but later confessed that he had summarily executed him for no apparent reason.

A coroner's court investigated the death in custody of John Conway and the medical evidence revealed that he had been shot six times and died as a result of shock and haemorrhage. General Paddy Daly gave evidence at the inquest and said that Byrne had confessed to him that he had shot the prisoner and that he could give no explanation for the killing. Daly said that he had known Byrne for fifteen years and that the officer had fought in the Tan War. Daly went on to say that Captain Byrne had been captured and badly beaten by the IRA some months previously. He gave evidence that his mind had become 'unhinged' as a result and that he had attempted suicide. Despite his unstable character Byrne was left on active duty in the barracks. The court held that Captain Patrick Byrne was responsible for the killing, but General Daly's evidence ensured that he was not held accountable.

John Conway was buried in the family grave in Rath Cemetery, Tralee and his name is inscribed on the Republican monument there.

DANIEL DALY

Domnall Ó Dálaig[1]

Dan Daly was thirty-seven when he was shot dead by Free State forces near Tralee's railway station. He was a native of Killorglin and was employed by the Great Southern and Western Railway in Tralee. He joined the company as an engine fireman and when single he lived in Rock Street in Tralee, close to the station. He was promoted to the position of engine driver and drove trains on the rail network in the Tralee area, which was then far more extensive than now. By 1923 he was married to Julia O'Connor, whose family had a business in Upper Bridge Street in Killorglin. The couple had five children and were expecting a sixth child when he was killed.[2]

While in Tralee Dan enlisted in the 1st Battalion of the Irish Volunteers and played an active part in the conflict with the crown forces in his adopted town. In July 1920 he used his train to carry a detachment of his fellow Tralee Volunteers for a surprise attack on the British Army post in the Tralee railway station. Daly and his engine fireman, named Mulchinock, stopped their train at Ballyroe as it was coming to Tralee from Fenit. There they allowed a large contingent of IRA Volunteers to board. The train then arrived shortly afterwards on the lightly guarded platform at Tralee. The Volunteers got off and quickly disarmed the surprised British Army picket who had a post at the station. The military offered no resistance and the IRA unit disarmed the soldiers and escaped with a valuable haul of Lee Enfield rifles.

During the Civil War, on the evening of 23 January 1923, several armed men left the Free State barracks which was situated in Tralee's workhouse. Arriving near the house in Railway Terrace where Dan was living, they waited on the street outside. Dan Lynch of Cork, a colleague of Dan Daly's at the nearby railway station, arrived at the house as he and Dan Daly were to go together to the local Dominican church for the devotions which were held nightly at 7.30 p.m. Lynch told Daly of the five men in trench coats who

---

1 There is no known photograph of Dan Daly.
2 Information from Margaret (Daly) Cagney, the only grandchild of Dan Daly.

were loitering outside the house but Daly was not worried by their presence. When the two railway workers left together to go to the church, the men in the trench coats had already departed from outside Daly's house. Daly and Lynch proceeded down to the top of Edward Street, passing the station as they walked. Further down this street, Lynch saw a group of men whom he presumed were the same men who had been lingering outside Daly's home a few minutes earlier. He advised Daly to proceed to the Dominican church through Nelson Street, which is now Ashe Street, thus avoiding the men who had been acting suspiciously. However, Daly was curious and opted to continue down Edward Street where the men were now standing. As Daly and Lynch walked along the path, a man came running down the street and crossed over to where Daly and Lynch were. He stopped and asked Daly to identify himself and when he revealed his name the stranger pulled a gun from his coat and shot Daly at point blank range. The wounded Daly slumped on his companion, whereupon the attacker fired five or six more shots, wounding Lynch in the process. The shooter then ran up Edward Street towards the railway station and into the night.

Lynch managed to carry his seriously wounded friend up to the railway station where some Free State soldiers placed him in a waiting room and called the military doctor. Dr George O'Riordan arrived while Daly was still conscious and asked him if he had recognised his attacker. Daly said that he had not seen him before and then drifted into unconsciousness, dying from his wounds minutes later.

A few days before this incident the IRA had issued a proclamation warning against the use of the railways in support of the Free State war effort. It was assumed by the public that it was the IRA that shot the men for a breach of this instruction. However, an inquest was held two days later, on 25 January, at which the Free State O/C Paddy Daly made an unexpected appearance. He testified that shortly after midnight on the day before the shooting four Republicans had been arrested and they had two documents in their possession. General Daly stated that these papers implicated Dan Daly in a plot to disable railway engines, to kidnap a Free State officer and to participate in an attack on soldiers at the station. General Daly made no apology for the summary execution of Dan Daly and the wounding of Dan Lynch near Tralee's railway station on 23 January 1923.[3] The inquest jury brought in a verdict of the wilful killing of Dan Daly by persons unknown.

Thirty-seven-year-old Dan Daly was buried in the family grave at Dromavalla Cemetery in his native Killorglin and was survived by his wife, Julia, and five young children. Mrs Daly subsequently lost the child that she was pregnant with following her husband's murder. Dan Daly's widow and family lived in the railway houses on School Road in Killorglin.

3   *Irish Independent* and *The Freeman's Journal*, 27 January 1923.

Thomas Drummond

Tomás Ó Droma[1]

The Drummond family were millers and had come to Tralee to work in the large O'Donovan's Mills in the town. Thomas was born in Tipperary before his family moved to Charleville and eventually to Tralee. The family originally lived in Church Lane and by 1920 Thomas Drummond was living at 32 Rae Street, in the Strand Street area of Tralee. He and his wife, Mary (Mae), had four children.[2] He was a member of 'D' Company, 1st Battalion and had joined the Irish Volunteers in 1916.[3]

Following the capture of Tralee by Free State forces on 2 August 1922, IRA Volunteer Thomas Drummond was arrested as he was a known Republican. With many other prisoners, he was being held in the Free State Army's headquarters in Ballymullen Barracks on the outskirts of Tralee. The barracks was a large fortified complex surrounded by a high wall and had been the headquarters of the Royal Munster Fusiliers before February 1922.

At 4 a.m. on 22 August, IRA Volunteers lay waiting near the gate of the army barracks in the expectation that a Free State detachment would leave on an early morning patrol. The attack force consisted of a large number of men, including Johnny O'Connor, who manned his machine gun set up in the large Castlemorris House which was adjacent to the barracks. Con Casey and William 'Duffer' Tangney were also part of the IRA force. When the sounds of men mobilising were heard just inside the gate, the Republican Volunteers outside assumed that this was the enemy patrol about to emerge. Grenades were lobbed over the wall and this was followed by sustained gunfire.[4] According to Free State reports the movements near the gate were in fact soldiers gathering Republican prisoners for the short march to Ballymullen Gaol, a few hundred

1   Surviving images of Thomas Drummond were not of sufficient quality to reproduce.
2   Information from Patrick (Paddy) Drummond, Upper Rock Street, Tralee, recorded by Martin Moore.
3   Notes of Coiste Chuimhneacháin Bhaile Uí Shíoda on Kerry No. 1 Brigade casualties (private collection).
4   Information from Con Casey recorded by Martin Moore.

yards away. However, Republicans claimed that the Free State patrol had hostages with them and they were unaware of this when they commenced their attack. Shrapnel from the exploding grenades fatally injured Thomas Drummond and he died in hospital two days later. A Free State soldier, Private Galworthy of County Galway, died on the same day as a result of the injuries he sustained in the attack. Several other prisoners were also wounded but all survived. Failing to press home the element of surprise following the initial explosions, the IRA force retreated intact to the Farmer's Bridge area, two miles outside the town.

Thomas Drummond is buried in the family grave in Rath Cemetery, Tralee, where his name is inscribed on the Republican Plot memorial. His widow, Mae, with whom he is buried, died in 1977.

Eugene Fitzgerald

Eogan Mac Gearailt

Courtesy of the Martin Moore collection.

The Fitzgerald family originally lived in Castle Street, Tralee, but later moved to Rock Street. Eugene and his older brother Anthony were initially members of Na Fianna Éireann, but later joined 'D' Company of the Irish Volunteers in the town's 1st Battalion, Kerry No. 1 Brigade. Na Fianna, a Republican youth organisation, provided valuable support for the active service units of the IRA. Chief among their duties was the gathering of intelligence and the monitoring of enemy movements.

At the outset of the Civil War, Eugene was in the IRA force that captured the town of Listowel from its Free State garrison. His unit then advanced to Limerick. He was involved in actions in Kilmallock and Bruree. Following the defeat of Republican forces there, he returned to Kerry.[1] Anthony was arrested when the Free State Army captured Tralee on 2 August 1922. Eugene continued on active service and because his home was raided on several occasions he went 'on the run'. He frequently stayed with his aunt at Carrahane, near Banna, two miles from Ardfert.

On 16 January 1923, late in the night, a Free State search party swooped on his aunt's house at Carrahane and arrested Eugene Fitzgerald. That day they had reportedly discovered several unoccupied dugouts in the Ardfert area and suspected that there was an IRA column in the vicinity. Fitzgerald was taken in a military lorry to the nearby beach and there he was tortured in order to make him divulge information on local IRA active service units. His captors broke his left arm. Having failed to provide any information, the prisoner was

---

1   Notes of Coiste Chuimhneacháin Bhaile Uí Shíoda on Kerry No. 1 Brigade casualties (private collection).

taken from the strand and put back into the lorry. A mile further along the road from Carrahane townland, while travelling towards Ardfert village, the Free State lorry stopped. Whether by coincidence or design, they halted beside McKenna's Fort, a large ring fort where Roger Casement was captured on Good Friday 1916. Fitzgerald was thrown on the roadside and, still refusing to give information, he was shot and severely wounded. The soldiers argued amongst themselves as to what to do with their gravely wounded prisoner. Rather than shoot him again, he was put back in the lorry and brought to Ballymullen Barracks.[2]

Initially Eugene Fitzgerald's parents were refused admission to see their dying son, but eventually his mother was allowed a short visit on 20 January. At this time he had spent four days in captivity in the barracks hospital. At that brief meeting her son related to his mother the details of his capture and torture. Two days later he succumbed to his wounds as Mrs Fitzgerald waited in vain at the barracks gate, having been denied permission to visit him a second time.

Eugene Fitzgerald, aged twenty, was buried in a family grave in Rath Cemetery, Tralee. His name is inscribed on the Republican monument in the graveyard. A traditional white roadside cross marks the spot where he was fatally wounded by Free State soldiers at the entrance to McKenna's Fort near Ardfert village.

2   Dorothy Macardle, *Tragedies of Kerry* (1924), p. 17.

Jackie Fleming

Seán Pleamonn

Courtesy of Mercier Archive.

John Joseph (Jackie) Fleming was born in Gas Terrace, Tralee on 16 May 1893. His father, John Fleming, had a painting business in the town. The Fleming family were steeped in the Republican tradition. On Easter Saturday 1916, as Roger Casement was being taken up Nelson Street by several RIC men to the railway station to be transferred to captivity in London, John Fleming played Republican tunes on his whistle as he sat on the roof of one of Nelson Street's shops.[1] It was no surprise that his sons were active Volunteers in the IRA. Jackie's older brother, Michael (Mick), was an officer in the Rock Street ('D') Company of the 1st Battalion, Kerry No. 1 Brigade. Jackie himself was also active in the Tan War, having joined Na Fianna in 1914. He was a piper in the Volunteer Pipe Band and was trained as the first aid officer of the battalion.

His brother Mick, though sympathetic to the Republican cause, did not take an active part in the Civil War, but his sister May, an active member of Cumann na mBan, was imprisoned in Kilmainham Gaol, having been brought there from Kerry by boat in November 1922. The exact position that Jackie took in the conflict was not evident to the Free State Army in Tralee, although he was a member of the Tralee-based 9th Battalion and was later recorded as a Volunteer in the battalion's active service unit.[2] Much of what is known about Jackie Fleming's final days comes from a revealing interview that fellow Tralee man Bill Bailey, who was a soldier in the Free State Army, gave to Ernie O'Malley in the late 1940s.[3]

1   Information from Dervil (Fleming) Townsend, his niece.
2   Notes of Coiste Chuimhneacháin Bhaile Uí Shíoda on Kerry No. 1 Brigade casualties (private collection).
3   Ernie O'Malley, *The Men Will Talk to Me – Kerry Interviews* (2012), interview with Bill Bailey.

Bailey records that Jackie Fleming's role in the IRA was that of a 'Red Cross man' and that he was not a fighter on active service. In March 1923 Fleming was unsure whether he was wanted by the Free State Army and so presented himself to David Neligan, the intelligence chief of the Dublin Guard. Neligan accused him of having been observed carrying a weapon and also said that he had information that Fleming acted as a Republican sentry on a bridge near Tralee, possibly Blennerville Bridge. Neligan ordered him to retrieve the weapon and to present it to him in Ballymullen Barracks a few days later. After a week, Jackie Fleming asked Bill Bailey to accompany him to the barracks again. However, shortly beforehand he decided that he would not present himself as ordered, fearing what might happen if he were to appear without the rifle that he was supposed to have had. As the Civil War progressed, Ballymullen Barracks, and David Neligan in particular, gained reputations for the excessive brutality exacted on the prisoners there. Earlier in the month of March, Neligan and other senior officers had been complicit in the Ballyseedy massacre. As Fleming had failed to appear as arranged, Neligan sent Bailey out with a search party to arrest him. However, Bailey and his patrol didn't manage to locate him. Later that evening, 28 March 1923, Jackie Fleming was arrested by two other Free State soldiers and brought to the guardroom of Ballymullen Barracks.

Bailey had been with another detachment of Free State soldiers and had just returned to the other army barracks which was situated in the town's workhouse, a mile away. This is now the Kerry County Council Building at Manor. From there Bailey recalled that he heard shots in the distance. A short time later an officer came in and said that a man had been shot on the Workhouse (now Killerisk) Road, which led southwards to Ballymullen Barracks a mile away. Apparently at a point midway between the two Free State barracks, Jackie Fleming was shot in the head as an officer named McAuliffe was bringing him to the Workhouse Barracks. Today a roadside memorial marks the site of the shooting.

Fleming was put in a makeshift coffin and the journey to the Workhouse Barracks was continued. However, the sentry there would not admit the soldiers and their prisoner, who was apparently lifeless. As a result, the Free State detachment had to return to Ballymullen Barracks, bringing Fleming's body with them. There Paddy Daly, the Free State O/C, signed a warrant ordering the coffin to be admitted to the Workhouse Barracks. Bailey grimly reported that his fellow soldiers were alarmed as Fleming was still alive despite his gunshot wounds. However, he died later that night and was buried in the workhouse cemetery. His remains were reinterred in the Republican Plot of Rath Cemetery following the Civil War, on 29 April 1924.

Michael Flynn

Míċeál Ó Floinn

Michael Flynn, who was known as Mickey Joe Flynn, was born in Spa Road, Tralee, on 10 September 1893. His family had a long Republican tradition as his grandfather was the head centre of the Fenian movement in the town during the 1860s. Mickey Flynn fought in the ranks of 'B' Company, 1st Battalion, Kerry No. 1 Brigade during the Tan War, having joined the Irish Volunteers on their foundation in the town in 1913.[1] When Brigade O/C Paddy Cahill was relieved of this command by GHQ in March 1921, many of the Volunteers in Tralee refused to accept the authority of his replacement. As a compromise, in July 1922, a new 9th Battalion was formed under the leadership of Paddy Paul Fitzgerald, Cahill's ally. This battalion drew its men from the Strand Street area of the town and from the Fenit and Spa districts to the north and out to Derrymore in the west. During the Civil War Mickey Flynn was a Volunteer in this 9th Battalion.

Courtesy of the Martin Moore collection.

Following the capture of Tralee by Free State forces in August 1922, the active Volunteers of the 9th Battalion formed a column which was based in the area to the west of the town in the foothills of the Sliabh Mish Mountains. Deep within the high mountains lies the long and narrow Derrymore Glen and in the safety of this cliff-lined valley the Republican unit had their base, which they called 'the hut'. From there they harassed the Free State forces that garrisoned Tralee. This mountainous area was well known to the men who had fought with Cahill in the Tan War, as it was on the southern side of Sliabh Mish that Cahill had his brigade command headquarters.

1   Notes of Coiste Chuimhneacháin Bhaile Uí Shíoda on Kerry No. 1 Brigade casualties (private collection).

On 17 November 1922 a large contingent of Free State forces carried out a sweep of the Derrymore area in the hope of capturing the 9th Battalion column. Spotting some IRA Volunteers near the entrance of Derrymore Glen, the troops gave chase. Tim Quirke, a local Volunteer and a sheep farmer who was with Flynn, escaped by following the rock-strewn river on the valley floor, knowing that its twists and high banks would give him cover from the bullets as he retreated to the safety of higher ground. Flynn, a native of the town, opted to try to reach the shelter of the glen by taking the shortest route, which involved crossing open moorland. This was a fatal error, as Flynn was taken prisoner as he attempted to cross the exposed barren mountainside. Tim Quirke made good his escape into the mountains he knew so well.[2]

Mickey Joe Flynn was brought down to near where the Derrymore river is crossed by the main Dingle road. There Jack Flavin, a Tralee-born Free State officer and a member of what was termed 'The Dandy Six', shot him dead in cold blood. 'The Dandy Six' were a group of former IRA Volunteers who had accepted the Treaty and, departing from Tralee at the outset of the Civil War, joined the Free State Army. They were attached to the 1st Western Division. The members' notoriety arose from the fact that they could identify their former comrades, something the officers of the Dublin Guard and 1st Western Division of the Free State Army could not do. It would seem probable that Flynn refused to give information about the whereabouts of his comrades and this sealed his fate.

Michael Flynn's body was brought to a nearby house owned by another Quirke family and a wake was held there. The next day two women, who came to the scene in an attempt to contact the IRA column, were fired upon by Free State soldiers who were still searching the area for other members of the Republican column.[3]

Mickey Joe Flynn's remains were refused entry to the parish church and his family were denied permission to bury him in the family plot in the town's cemetery. The local clergy were forbidden by Bishop Charles O'Sullivan to offer prayers for the repose of the dead man. However in 1923, after the ceasefire,

2   Information from John Quirke, Derrymore, son of Volunteer Tim Quirke.
3   Information from George Rice whose mother, Nora Ahern, was one of those Cumann na mBan women.

his coffin and that of Billy Myles were disinterred and brought to St John's church. There the funeral mass was celebrated and the remains of both men were subsequently reinterred in the Republican Plot in Rath Cemetery, Tralee. Today his sacrifice is recalled by a housing estate in his native Spa Road, Tralee, named in his honour. A monument now stands at Derrymore Bridge on which are inscribed the names of Michael Flynn and the other fallen Volunteers from the 1st and 9th Battalions. This monument was unveiled in March 1933 by John Joe Rice, O/C of Kerry No. 2 Brigade, and today is cared for by the Quirke family whose father was with Michael Flynn on that fateful day in 1922. Volunteer Michael Flynn's name is also inscribed on a similar memorial at Churchill near Fenit.

Tom Flynn

Tomás Ó Floinn

Courtesy of Julie McEvoy McCarthy.

Thomas Flynn was a native of Kilfenora, a townland between The Spa and Fenit. He was born on 9 January 1897, the son of John Flynn and Helen Moriarty. His father, a labourer, died while Tom was still a young boy.

Tom enlisted in the Irish Volunteers and held the rank of adjutant in the Churchill or 'D' Company of the 2nd Battalion, Kerry No. 1 Brigade. His captain was Jim Walsh of nearby Lisodigue, who also lost his life in the Civil War. In the summer of 1921 this company was transferred to the 9th Battalion of the brigade and Tom Flynn retained his rank until his death in action.

On 2 August 1922 the Dublin Guard of the Free State Army arrived unexpectedly in Fenit Harbour on board the *Lady Wicklow* and hurriedly disembarked. The Republican contingency plan was to explode mines attached to the long wooden pier in the event of such a landing. However, the wires to the explosives had been cut by local men without the knowledge of the small IRA garrison whose task it was to defend the port from a Free State invasion. As a result, the landing of 450 Free State soldiers, their armoured car and field artillery was almost unopposed. The greatly outnumbered Republican forces retreated, some northwards towards Barrow, and the remainder, including Tom Flynn, along the road to Tralee, fighting a rearguard action as they went. A section of IRA Volunteers came from Tralee and attempted to halt the rapid advance by establishing a firing position on the summit of the large limestone hillock named Sammy's Rock, which holds a commanding view of the road from Fenit as it passes near Kilfenora. Under intense gunfire, and in danger of being outflanked, these IRA men were quickly forced to abandon the hilltop, leaving Volunteer John O'Sullivan dead on the rocky slope. The Republicans retreated in disarray to the small village of The Spa, a mile away.

Paddy Paul Fitzgerald was O/C of the 9th Battalion of the Kerry No. 1 Brigade, and he and Tom Flynn went into Dan Lyons' bar in The Spa and then out the back door in an attempt to escape from the rapidly advancing Free State forces. Their aim was to get to the beach that lay behind the pub and from there travel to Tralee along the shore. This was a more direct route than the now dangerous road. Unknown to the two men, Free State soldiers had entered Kent Lodge, a large house further to the west which had a commanding view of the sandy shore. Another detachment of soldiers was in the village and they could also see the men on the beach. Shots were aimed at the two fleeing Volunteers, who replied with rifle fire. However, in their exposed position on the shore, Tom Flynn was shot dead and Paddy Paul Fitzgerald was quickly captured.[1]

Lieutenant Tom Flynn was buried in the family plot in Churchill Cemetery near to his home. Today he is commemorated by a well-tended white roadside cross at The Spa, adjacent to the shoreline at Seafield where he was killed. His memory is also recalled on the battalion monument at nearby Churchill, which was unveiled on 5 March 1933, and on the monument at Derrymore.

1   Niall Harrington, *Kerry Landing* (1992), p. 107.

Daniel Foley

Domhnall Ó Foghludha[1]

Daniel and Johanna Foley lived in the townland of Ahane in Glencar, where they farmed the mountain soil to support their family. As there were many families with the surname in the area, Dan Foley's family were known as the Bán Foleys. They had four children, Bridget (Delia), John (1902), Timothy (1904) and Daniel (1905). Johanna Foley died of a vascular complication while pregnant with a fifth child and subsequently her husband was unable to maintain the farm and may have gone to work in a bakery in nearby Killorglin. John, Tim and Dan were sent to live in an orphanage in Killarney and their sister was sent to a different institution where she had an aunt who was a nun. Later, when a little older, the three boys were transferred to the care of the Christian Brothers at Balloonagh, Tralee, where they lived in the order's orphanage and learned a trade in the St Joseph's Industrial School.[2]

The Irish nationalist ethos of the Christian Brothers was probably very influential on the three boys, as all became involved in the Republican movement. Dan was recorded as having joined Na Fianna in 1918. His brothers John and Tim, being older, were members of the IRA during the Tan War.

Dan Foley's Republican activities came to the attention of the Free State forces occupying Tralee in 1922. He was arrested on 29 November 1922 and subsequently interned, though the circumstances relating to his capture and imprisonment are not recorded. He was living in 24 Nelson Street, now Ashe Street, in Tralee.[3] This area of Upper Ashe Street was noted for the number of active members of Na Fianna who lived there, including Percy Hannafin who was killed in action and Patrick 'Belty' Williams.

As with other Kerry Republican prisoners, he would have initially been brought to Ballymullen Barracks and held in a barbed wire compound in the large former British Army barracks. Subsequently, most of these captives were

1   There is no known photograph of Dan Foley.
2   Information from Liam Canny, United States, historian and grandnephew of Dan Foley.
3   Prisoner records, Military Archive, Cathal Brugha Barracks, Dublin.

transferred to the Curragh Camp in Kildare, where they joined thousands of other internees and sentenced prisoners. The conditions of captivity were harsh and the medical facilities offered by the Free State Army to their prisoners were rudimentary. Young Dan Foley's health began to fail as a result of the conditions of his incarceration. He was admitted to the military hospital suffering from tuberculosis and died from complications of the disease on 25 January 1923. When a list of the IRA casualties of Kerry No. 1 Brigade was compiled in 1958 for inclusion on the Ballyseedy memorial, it was noted that the remains of Dan Foley were still buried in his place of detention in the Curragh. And so the grave of this young Kerry orphan remained unmarked and unremembered far from his native county. However, in October 2014 his exact burial place was finally discovered. Following his death Foley's remains had been brought from the Curragh Military Hospital to the nearby town of Newbridge. There, on 30 January 1923, he was buried in what was termed a 'free plot' or pauper's grave in St Conleth's Cemetery. His death certificate describes him as political prisoner.[4]

Dan's brother Tim returned to the Glencar area when he left St Joseph's Industrial School in Tralee. He was a Volunteer in the Glencar Company of the 6th Battalion and was wounded in action. Tim Foley was captured during the Civil War and like Dan, he was incarcerated in the Curragh, but survived the ordeal to join the thousands of Republican fighters forced into exile in the United States in the post-Civil War period.[5]

As Volunteer Dan Foley had died for the cause of Ireland's freedom, his comrades in the Kerry No. 1 Brigade inscribed his name on their roll of honour on the brigade's memorial at Ballyseedy. His name, in Irish, is also on the monument at the Republican Plot in Tralee's Rath Cemetery, where it notes that he was buried elsewhere. As Dan Foley was a native of Glencar, the committee who organised the erection of the Republican monument in Cahersiveen also included his name amongst the dead of the Iveragh Peninsula and the Kerry No. 3 Brigade area. Following the recent identification of his grave, it is planned to erect a fitting memorial at the site.

4   Notes of Coiste Chuimhneacháin Bhaile Uí Shíoda on Kerry No. 1 Brigade casualties (private collection).
5   Information from Liam Canny, grandson of Tim Foley.

PATRICK (PERCY) HANNAFIN

Pádruig Ó hAinifín

Courtesy of the Martin Moore collection.

Patrick Hannafin was born in Nelson Street, now Ashe Street, Tralee, in 1902. His father was a commercial agent for a sugar company and Percy, as he was nicknamed, was the second eldest in a large family. He was an active Republican from an early age and served as the Kerry No. 1 Brigade adjutant of Na Fianna in the Tan War. He was noted by his comrades as having a flare for organising.

At 5 p.m. on Friday 20 January 1922, during the Truce, Percy Hannafin and two comrades, Pat 'Belty' Williams and Mick Mullaly, attempted to seize a military vehicle which contained provisions. They intended to drive this to the IRA training camp which was located in Ardfert. Such an undertaking was in violation of the Truce that had been in force since 11 July 1921, but the unplanned opportunity presented itself when the three Volunteers saw a military lorry parked in Edward Street, Tralee. The vehicle was stopped at Benner's Garage, which was situated across the street from the town's post office. The driver had remained in the vehicle while his companions had gone into the garage. The Volunteers planned to take the driver hostage and force him at gunpoint to drive the lorry out of town where they would free him. However, the hastily conceived plan went awry. The surprised driver was ordered out of the vehicle but his predicament was observed by his two fellow Black and Tans from within the garage. They opened fire on the three Volunteers. Percy Hannafin was hit in the head and left arm. Mick Mullaly was fortunate to be only lightly wounded when a ricochet bullet went up his nose and into his mouth. The driver was severely wounded in the legs by the gunfire of his comrades.

The IRA Volunteers managed to escape, taking the seriously injured Hannafin with them. He was brought to the Bon Secours Hospital in Strand

Street. The Tans took their wounded comrade away in his vehicle. For three hours that evening the crown forces went on the rampage in the town. Gun battles were fought on the streets between mobilised IRA units and the Tans seeking vengeance. With the arrival of the regular British Army on the streets, the confrontation was defused. The Republican authorities apologised for the breach in the Truce but refused a demand to surrender Hannafin, Mullay and Williams.[1]

The next morning the gravely ill Percy Hannafin, his brothers, Michael and Jerry, and Pat 'Belty' Williams were brought by brigade transport officer, Tim Leahy, to the Mercy Hospital in Cork city. However, Percy Hannafin failed to recover from his injuries and he died on 27 January 1922 with his brothers and Williams at his bedside.

His remains were brought back to Tralee, the journey taking seven hours due to flooding and ceaseless rain. After requiem mass on Sunday 29 January, Percy Hannafin was buried in the family plot in Rath Cemetery. The remains were followed to the town's graveyard by a very large cortège in which an estimated 800 IRA Volunteers participated. A firing party of his comrades in Na Fianna fired three volleys of shots over the grave.[2] Today he is remembered by a memorial plaque on the wall of the laneway which is named Percy Hannafin Way in his honour. This small lane joins Edward Street, where he was fatally wounded, to Ashe Street, where he lived during his short life.

1   *Memoirs of Pat Williams* (unpublished, private collection).
2   *The Freeman's Journal*, 1 February 1922.

WILLIAM HARRINGTON

Liam Ó hArractáin[1]

Friday 8 December 1922 will always be remembered as the day the Free State government executed four senior Republican leaders in Mountjoy Gaol: Liam Mellows, Dick Barrett, Joe McKelvey and Rory O'Connor. They were shot in that Dublin prison yard without recourse to any semblance of justice. On the same day in Tralee, unarmed Republican William Harrington was also shot dead by Free State forces.

The Feast of the Immaculate Conception traditionally marks the beginning of the Christmas period and in the parish of Tralee, then as now, a bazaar was held to raise funds for the local Catholic church. In 1922 this gathering was held in The Rink, a large hall on Basin Road which has now been demolished and replaced by housing. Today the site of the building, which had been used as a skating rink, is marked by a plaque, as it was there that the Volunteers mustered at Easter 1916.

The parish bazaar, an important event in the parish calendar, was attended by hundreds of people. It may have been that some of the money raised would have gone towards supporting the dependants of the many political prisoners from the parish. A five-man party of Free State soldiers went to The Rink that evening and these included some 'red caps' or military policemen. On entering the hall, the Free State soldiers drew their pistols and fired over the heads of the large attendance, apparently without provocation. This caused panic amongst the crowd. William Harrington, an IRA Volunteer from nearby Strand Street, was in attendance and he remonstrated with their officer, Lieutenant Joseph Parsons. He protested about the recklessness and provocative behaviour of the soldiers, whereupon Parsons shot Harrington dead in front of hundreds of witnesses.[2]

The callousness of the murder was such that an inquiry was held and although Parsons denied discharging his pistol, the evidence of the witnesses

1 Surviving images of William Harrington were not of sufficient quality to reproduce.
2 *The Cork Examiner*, 29 January 1923, report of inquest.

caused the presiding judge to conclude that the killing was malicious. However, no action was taken against Lieutenant Parsons or the soldiers he commanded that evening.

William Harrington was twenty-three years old when he was killed and had worked as a builder's labourer. He was the only child of a widow.

Though not killed on active service, William Harrington's name is inscribed on the Republican memorial in Rath Cemetery, Tralee. He is buried in the family plot in the graveyard. He was a member of 'D' Company, 1st Battalion, and had been in the Irish Volunteers since 1916.

TOMMY HAWLEY

Tomás Ó hAllaíde

Courtesy of the Martin Moore collection.

Thomas Hawley was born in McCowen's Lane, off Edward Street, Tralee, in 1897. His father, William Hawley, later moved his family to the nearby Pound Lane, off what is now Ashe Street. Young Tommy enrolled in Na Fianna shortly after its formation in the town and later joined the Irish Volunteers, where he held the rank of section leader in 'A' Company of the 1st Battalion, Kerry No. 1 Brigade.[1]

Following the death of Terence MacSwiney on hunger strike on 25 October 1920, a general order came from GHQ stating that the crown forces were to be engaged wherever they were encountered. Throughout the Kerry No. 1 Brigade area the following weekend and during the first week in November, there were numerous attacks on RIC targets resulting in several fatalities, including the capture and killing of two RIC constables in Tralee town. This provoked swift retaliation by the crown forces and resulted in most of the active Volunteers in the town leaving their homes to seek shelter in the townland of Fybough on the south side of the Dingle Peninsula. There Tralee man Paddy Cahill, the brigade O/C, established an elaborate headquarters hidden behind a large rock on the mountain slopes. The twenty or so men who were billeted there became the flying column of the Kerry No. 1 Brigade and among its members was Tommy Hawley.

During the spring of 1921 this column became increasingly active and Paddy Cahill decided to attack a British patrol at Lispole on Sunday 20 March. A military convoy passed through the small village each Sunday at 2 p.m., coming

---

1   Notes of Coiste Chuimhneacháin Bhaile Uí Shíoda on Kerry No. 1 Brigade casualties (private collection).

from Dingle, five miles away. Cahill and his column, supported by the local IRA companies, took up position at midday on that Sunday, unaware that the convoy was not due to travel to Lispole. It had been re-deployed and went to Ballydavid to the west of Dingle to supply a detachment of marines stationed there. The following day the ambush party returned to Lispole but to no avail. On Tuesday 22 March they returned again to their positions, awaiting the arrival of the British. At 1 p.m. the enemy was sighted about a mile from the village, where they stopped their vehicles and dismounted. Cahill mistakenly assumed that they had come to raid some local houses, though it is likely that the British were aware of the proposed ambush which had been prepared for them further along the road.[2]

Leaving their vehicles, the soldiers advanced towards Lispole through the fields on either side of the road, thus outflanking the ambush party of approximately sixty men. Belatedly, Cahill ordered his men to retreat, but as the Volunteers were divided over five separate locations, the command did not reach some of his men and the first that they knew of the impending danger was when machine-gun fire raked their positions from the fields behind.

Tommy Hawley received a head injury during the initial engagement as he and the men in his position were captured by soldiers who had come unexpectedly from their rear. As the injured Hawley was being carried across an open field by his fellow prisoners, the accompanying soldiers panicked when they came under attack from one of the IRA parties that had been trapped in a small cleft following the departure of the main body of Volunteers. The soldiers fled, leaving Hawley and the other prisoners behind.

Fighting continued along the roadway for a considerable duration and another Volunteer, local man Tom Ashe, was severely wounded in the engagement. Such was the intensity of the fire from the IRA men, who were pinned down in the small gully, that the British forces assumed that they themselves had now been outflanked. The soldiers disengaged and retreated towards their transport vehicles, which were half a mile to the west.

Both wounded Volunteers, Tommy Hawley and Tom Ashe, were brought to

---

2   Bureau of Military History (BMH) Witness Statements (WS) of James Fitzgerald (999), Patrick Houlihan (959), Michael O'Leary (1167), Dan Mulvihill (938) and Robert Knightly (951).

a nearby farmhouse. At this stage the main body of Cahill's force had left the area and a small group, which included Gregory Ashe and James Fitzgerald, accompanied the two wounded men on a horse-drawn cart to the home of the O'Sullivan family at Acres, a secluded townland in the hills south of Annascaul.[3] There Nurse Nancy Scully dressed their wounds, but Thomas Ashe died later that night.

Tommy Hawley's wound was treated by Dr Kane of Annascaul and the next day he was moved six miles to the east across back roads, again on a horse-drawn cart. The journey over rough roads exacerbated the pain of his injuries as he was being brought to the Herlihy house in Ballinahunt, three miles to the east of the village. There the bullet wound to his head was operated on by Dr Ferris, who had come across the mountains from Castlegregory, and this stabilised Hawley's condition. Ferris made the journey on foot as he had given his car to the local IRA to transport some landmines and they had not returned it in time to allow him to drive to Ballinahunt. Also in this house was Jim Daly from near Castlegregory, who had been wounded during the ambush as well, although his injuries were less serious.

Hawley and Daly were subsequently brought across the mountains to the home of the Cahillane family in Glenlough on the north side of the peninsula. There they were cared for by Nurse O'Mahony while they sheltered for nearly six weeks. The wounded men were subsequently transferred to the secluded valley of Glanteenasig, where they stayed in the home of Tom O'Donnell. However, while Daly's condition improved, that of Tommy Hawley deteriorated. He died of complications from his head wound on 2 May 1921.

Twenty-three-year-old Tommy Hawley's remains were removed to Tralee and he is buried in the Republican Plot at Rath Cemetery. He is remembered in his home town, where a housing estate is named in his honour. His name is also inscribed on the monuments at Lispole and on The Mall in Dingle.

---

3   Ernie O'Malley, *The Men Will Talk to Me – Kerry Interviews* (2012), interview with Greg Ashe.

Con Healy

Concubar Ó hÉalaiġte

Con Healy was born in Walpole Lane in the Boherbue district of Tralee on 10 April 1897. As a young man he and his brother became renowned as excellent marksmen when shooting game, which supplemented the family's income.[1] Con Healy enlisted in the British Army during the Great War and on demobilisation in 1919 he returned to Tralee. He subsequently joined the IRA and was attached to the Boherbue Company of the 1st Battalion, Kerry No. 1 Brigade.[2] His brother James was also a Volunteer and was fortunate to survive being shot during the Civil War when his comrade Seán Moriarty was killed at Caherslee.

Courtesy of Mercier Archive.

Con Healy's name will always be associated with that of Major John McKinnon, O/C of the Auxiliaries' 'H' Company, which was based in the Technical School in Moyderwell, Tralee. McKinnon, a decorated officer in the British Army during the Great War, was from Kilmarnock in Scotland. His detachment arrived in Tralee in November 1920 and McKinnon soon gained a reputation for brutality and fearlessness. On Christmas Eve 1920 he shot dead two captured IRA Volunteers, John Leen and Mossy Reidy, at the house of John Byrne in Ballymacelligott. Several attempts were made to kill him, but his reputation only grew as, despite these attacks, he continued to be the scourge of the local Republicans, treating their attempts to assassinate him with characteristic contempt. He travelled fearlessly throughout the district, often on foot, and could arrive unexpectedly anywhere.

1   Information from Jimmy O'Mahony, Tralee.
2   Notes of Coiste Chuimhneacháin Bhaile Uí Shíoda on Kerry No. 1 Brigade casualties (private collection).

In November 1920 the leading IRA figures had left the town to set up a flying column under the command of Paddy Cahill, brigade O/C, and this was based near Keel on the south side of the Dingle Peninsula. The brigade adjutant, Paddy Garvey, subsequently established a smaller active service unit of those Volunteers who remained in Tralee. This was under the command of John Joe Sheehy. Sheehy made it his priority to kill the feared McKinnon and so set up a special squad to undertake the task. It comprised Con Healy, Denis Donoghue, Paddy Kelly, Patrick O'Connor and John O'Riordan. It was known that McKinnon regularly played golf at Tralee's golf course, which was then situated in Oakpark on the northern outskirts of the town. The major's movements were monitored and soon enough information had been gathered to allow a plan to kill him to be finalised. The small unit waited several days for McKinnon to play the course and on the evening of 15 April 1920 scouts finally signalled that the major and his party had arrived. The ambush site chosen was in a tree-lined ditch which overlooked the third hole. Fearing that their target was wearing a steel vest, Con Healy, the marksman, took the only rifle available to his group, while the others were armed with shotguns and revolvers. On the third green, Healy's shot struck McKinnon in the head and his second shot also found its target immediately before the major fell. Con Healy and his companions made good their escape as McKinnon's golfing companions ran for cover.[3]

Con Healy was suffering from tuberculosis and he died on 22 February 1922 at the age of twenty-four.[4] Although he was not killed on active service or in captivity, such was the respect he earned from his comrades in the Tan War that he was buried with his fellow Volunteers in the Republican Plot of Rath Cemetery, Tralee.

---

3   John O'Riordan, BMH WS 1117.
4   Kerry No. 1 Brigade casualties, Con Casey Papers, Kerry County Library.

Frank Hoffman

Pɼionɼiaɼ hoɼɼman

Frank Hoffman was born in 1899 in Lisardboola in the Farmer's Bridge district about three miles east of Tralee. His antecedents had come from the Palatine district of Germany in the 1700s, escaping religious persecution in their homeland. While most settled in the Rathkeale district of County Limerick, others, including the Hoffman family, came to live in Ballyseedy where they became tenants of the local landlords, the Blennerhassett family.

Frank Hoffman was a Volunteer in the Farmer's Bridge 'F' Company of the 1st Battalion, Kerry No. 1 Brigade, where his rank was that of lieutenant. During the Black and Tan War this company was particularly active and consisted of over fifty men.

Courtesy of Kitty Galvin, Tralee.

In March 1920 it was decided to destroy the files in Tralee's government offices, including all the tax documents, in order to impede the civic administration of the town. These offices were located fifty yards from the town's RIC barracks and each of the battalion's companies were asked for two volunteers to implement the plan. Frank Hoffman and Johnny O'Connor were the Farmer's Bridge men who participated in the attack, which achieved its aim.[1] Hoffman was also involved in several other incidents in the Tralee area.

On 9 November 1920 a unit of IRA Volunteers from Ballymacelligott, led by Tom McEllistrim and John Cronin, shot two Black and Tans who were returning by train from Killarney to Farranfore. The attack happened at Ballybrack, a small, now disused, railway station midway between Farranfore and Killarney.

The following day, 10 November 1920, a convoy of Auxiliaries, military and

---

1   John O'Connor, BMH WS 1181.

RIC left Tralee and travelled to the Ballybrack area where they burned several houses in reprisal. Learning of their journey and the destruction that they had wreaked on Ballybrack, Tom McEllistrim and the Ballymacelligott active service unit set up an ambush at Ballyseedy, anticipating that the Tans would return from Ballybrack through Firies and on into Tralee by the small road that runs to the south of the main Tralee to Farranfore road along the foothills of the Sliabh Mish Mountains. They were then expected to turn right along the Ballyseedy road to join the main road, where an ambush had been set up just at the site where the monument now stands.

However, instead of turning right at the junction to go along by Ballyseedy church, the five-vehicle convoy continued along the smaller road, which went through the townland of Farmer's Bridge. There, at 3.30 p.m., they encountered Frank Hoffman and Patrick O'Connor of Dromavalla, who were travelling towards Ballyseedy along the narrow country road in a pony and car. The first vehicle in the crown force convoy stopped and the police dismounted and ordered Hoffman and O'Connor off their car. O'Connor then received a blow to his head which knocked him to the ground and into a drain on the far side of the road. Hoffman was then asked his name and it was reported that he was told, 'You're the man we want.' He was placed standing against the ditch on the roadside where the memorial cross now stands. Then a single shot was fired from the third vehicle in the convoy. Frank Hoffman was hit in the left side of his chest and was mortally wounded. The convoy then moved on, leaving Hoffman dying on the roadside. After the third vehicle had travelled 150 yards, it returned and three soldiers and some police dismounted. They then put the wounded man in the horse-drawn car and O'Connor brought him to Hoffman's home 200 yards away. Frank Hoffman died a few minutes later. The convoy then moved off, completing its journey to Tralee.[2]

The killing of Frank Hoffman was investigated by the RIC in Tralee, probably because the callousness of the shooting troubled some members of the military there. Constable Edward Johnston was charged and brought before a field general court martial in Victoria Military Barracks in Cork on 2 February 1921. The accused policeman did not deny that he fired the

2   *The Freeman's Journal*, 4 February 1921.

fatal shot, but claimed that it occurred accidentally as the vehicle in which he was standing stopped suddenly at the scene. He claimed that the convoy was expecting an ambush and his weapon was loaded and ready to fire when it was discharged, even though the evidence of Patrick O'Connor would contradict this. Constable Johnston was acquitted and freed.[3]

Frank Hoffman is buried in the Church of Ireland graveyard at Ballyseedy church, a short distance from his home. A limestone Celtic cross at Farmer's Bridge marks the place where he was killed at the age of twenty-three. This was unveiled on 12 July 1931. Hoffman's Terrace on Basin Road, Tralee, near where The Rink was sited, is named in his honour.

3   *The Kerryman*, 12 February 1921.

Seán Moriarty

Seán Ó Muirceartaig[1]

John (Seán) Moriarty lived with his mother and brother, William, in the family home in Francis Street, better known as Walpole Lane. This small, narrow street is situated off Upper Castle Street in Tralee and was where he was born on 15 March 1892, the eldest son in a large family. As a young man he was apprenticed to a tailor and would later ply his trade in the town. Seán Moriarty was a member of the British Army during the Great War and on returning home he joined the Irish Volunteers in Tralee and was attached to the Boherbue based 'A' Company of the 1st Battalion.

The Free State intelligence department based in Ballymullen Barracks suspected him of being involved in attacks on Free State forces in the town in the three weeks since they had captured Tralee in August 1922. Several days before his killing, local IRA units had attacked Free State soldiers at the barracks and apparently there was information linking Seán Moriarty and another Volunteer, James Healy, to this attack and also to an attempt to bomb the town's post office.

Shortly before 3 a.m. on 27 August 1922, a four-man detachment of Free State soldiers left Ballymullen Barracks to walk the half-mile to Upper Castle Street. They initially went to McCowen's Lane, where Republican James Healy lived with his uncle. Like Moriarty, Healy had been in the British Army during the Great War and had joined the IRA on returning home. His brother Con was the marksman who had shot the commander of the Auxiliaries, Major John McKinnon. Having detained James Healy, the Free State soldiers went to nearby Walpole Lane, where they knocked on the door of the Moriarty house.

Mrs Margaret Moriarty answered the knock on her door shortly after 3 a.m. The men outside demanded to see her son Seán. They were masked and their leader had a pistol in his hand and a rifle slung over his shoulder. They claimed to be from the IRA and alleged that Moriarty had gone to Ballymullen

---

1   There is no known photograph of Seán Moriarty.

Barracks the previous day to give information to the Free State forces there. They claimed that he was a soldier but Mrs Moriarty denied this and said that it was the British Army that he had been in and not the Free State Army. She told the men to go to Neddy (Éamonn) Horan, a senior Tralee officer at Ballymullen, and he would confirm that her son had not been at the barracks. At this stage they demanded her 'Republican son' and promptly arrested Seán after he had dressed. The men, who wore handkerchiefs over their faces and civilian caps, were dressed in army great coats and leggings. With Seán Moriarty and James Healy as captives, the detachment went down the lane but turned right instead of going left towards Ballymullen.

The prisoners were marched through the town in the darkness to Caherslee, which was then on the outskirts of Tralee. There the men were ordered into what was known as Hilliard's Field on the other side of the road, where the prisoners were separated by their captors. James Healy was questioned about his part in recent IRA attacks and in particular about the attempt to bomb the post office. The officer asked him if he was a Catholic and when he replied that he was, he was told he had five minutes to say his prayers. Healy fell to his knees and began to pray and was interrupted to be told that he had two minutes left. Having finished he stood up and the officer fired at point blank range. Healy was hit in the abdomen and fell to the ground. He was then shot several more times before his would-be executioner left the scene, confident that Healy was dead.

James Healy regained consciousness and crawled to a nearby house. As he did so he heard firing close by and these were the shots that dispatched his friend Seán Moriarty. Healy was brought to the infirmary by the family who owned the house he managed to crawl to and subsequently survived to give an account of what had happened at Hilliard's Field in Caherslee that night. Seán Moriarty's body was found the next morning. A post-mortem revealed that he had multiple bullet wounds, including one to his head.[2]

A single man, Seán Moriarty was thirty years old when he was killed. His remains were interred in the Republican Plot in Rath Cemetery, Tralee. His was to be the first of many summary executions of Republican prisoners to be carried out in Kerry over the next nine months.

2   *The Cork Examiner*, 18 December 1922. Report of inquest into the death of Seán Moriarty.

Billy Myles

Liam Ó Maolmuire

Courtesy of the Martin Moore collection.

William (Billy) Myles was born into a strongly nationalist family in the Moyderwell area of Tralee in 1902. In 1916 he enrolled in Na Fianna at the age of fourteen. On the reorganisation of Na Fianna in Tralee in 1918, Myles was appointed quartermaster of the Na Fianna section of the Kerry No. 1 Brigade.

On 1 November 1920, following the killing of two Black and Tans in Tralee, any active Volunteers who could be identified by the RIC left the town. They set up a headquarters in Fybough, near Keel, and there, under the command of the brigade O/C, Paddy Cahill, they formed an active service unit or flying column. Billy Myles and his brother Jerry were part of this unit. The Myles brothers were involved in the many engagements of the column, most notably the Lispole ambush on 22 March 1921. During this engagement, Billy Myles was taken prisoner by the British Army, but a subsequent counter-attack by the IRA forced the soldiers to flee, leaving their prisoners, including Billy, behind them. On 1 June 1921 Billy and Jerry were part of the column that attacked an RIC patrol at Ballymacandy, Castlemaine, resulting in five crown force fatalities. Jerry Myles was seriously injured in that incident, having been shot in the lung, and he spent many months recuperating in safe houses in Glencar.

During the Civil War, Billy resumed active service with the IRA. He was a member of the Republican column that fought in the Kilmallock area under the command of Tadhg Brosnan. Following the defeat of the Republican forces in south County Limerick and the landing of the Free State Army in Fenit, he returned to Tralee. He was appointed commanding officer of Na Fianna as the guerrilla war against the Free State grew in intensity in and around Tralee. Myles and his unit had a dugout at Curraheen, three miles from Tralee on the road to the west. There, from the foothills of the Sliabh Mish Mountains, they harried Free State forces as they travelled to Castlegregory and Dingle. From there also Myles coordinated the scouting activities of Na Fianna in nearby Tralee.

On Friday 20 October 1922 a large force of Free State troops arrived to search the districts of Curraheen and Annagh, where Myles and his comrades had their base. While the other Republicans escaped into the mountains behind, Myles remained and held the advancing troops at bay with his rifle. In the exchange of fire he was fatally wounded and died where he fought. He was twenty-one when he was killed in action.[1]

His remains were removed to Tralee but were refused entry to the parish church, and a funeral mass and burial in the family plot were denied. In 1923, as tensions eased following the cessation of fighting, his remains were disinterred and brought to St John's church and a proper funeral was accorded to the young soldier. He was subsequently buried in the Republican plot in Rath Cemetery. A white cross now stands on the roadside at Annagh on the Dingle Road, adjacent to the spot where his young life was taken as he fought for the Irish Republic.

1   Information from the late Babs Myles McInerney, sister of Billy Myles.

George Nagle

Seoirse de Nógla

Courtesy of Mercier Archive.

George Nagle was born in Ballygamboon, Castlemaine, in 1897. He lived in Church Street, Tralee, and was a Volunteer in 'D' Company of the 1st Battalion, Kerry No. 1 Brigade, where he held the rank of section commander. His Republican activities led to his arrest and imprisonment in Cork Gaol during the Black and Tan War. Following his release he rejoined his unit in Tralee and took the Republican side in the Civil War. In the initial phase of this conflict he was a member of one of the four IRA columns from Kerry that were involved in an attempt to hold a defensive line from Limerick to Waterford. He fought in Limerick city in early July and then, following the fall of the city to Free State forces, he saw active service in Kilmallock and Bruree as a member of a unit led by Tadhg Brosnan of Castlegregory.[1] The landing at Fenit by a large Free State force on 2 August 1922 forced the IRA to once again adopt guerrilla tactics. Nagle was subsequently involved in attacks on Free State targets around Tralee and in the unsuccessful attempt to capture Killorglin in late September 1922.

By 1923 the active service unit of the Tralee's 9th Battalion, which operated in the Derrymore area and of which Nagle was a member, had been reduced to only a small number of fighting men. These Volunteers then joined with the 6th Battalion column, which was operating in the foothills of the McGillycuddy Reeks to the south of Killorglin.[2] In April 1923 the column was billeted in

---

1 Notes of Coiste Chuimhneacháin Bhaile Uí Shíoda on Kerry No. 1 Brigade casualties (private collection).
2 *Memoirs of Pat Williams* (unpublished, private collection).

Derrynafeena and it is with this remote glen that Lieutenant George Nagle's name will always be linked.

Derrynafeena, the oak wood of the Fenians, lies at the foot of Carrantuohill, Ireland's highest mountain. It extends southwards into the heart of the Iveragh Peninsula, being flanked on each side by high mountains, and its northern entrance is partially guarded by the scenic Lough Acoose. It was to such places that the harried columns of the Republican Army retreated in the spring of 1923. Though these desolate mountain glens provided security from the large-scale Free State round-ups, they provided no shelter from the elements and so it was to the hospitality of the people who lived at the foothills of the mountains that the Volunteers entrusted themselves.

An IRA column under the command of Bertie Scully of Glencar, O/C of the 6th Battalion, Kerry No. 2 Brigade, was billeted in the cottages at the entrance of the glen. The column was composed mainly of men from Tralee and the mid-Kerry region. On the morning of 6 April 1923 the night sentries, Bill Landers and Dan O'Shea, saw Free State forces advancing and their shots alerted the scattered column. George Nagle and several other Volunteers were staying in a cottage owned by Tim and Molly O'Brien. As the cottage was occupied by the O'Briens and their children, the Volunteers inside decided to head further up the valley, rather than try to halt the Free State advance from the little house. Bill Landers from Tralee covered their escape with his machine gun, but while running from the house, George Nagle was shot in the leg. Nagle was reported to be ill that day and this may have hampered his escape.[3] His comrades returned and attempted to carry him, but were unable to bring their wounded comrade with them due to the pain he was suffering. So they took his rifle and retreated to a safe position deeper in the glen. Molly O'Brien witnessed the events and Nagle shouted to her to fetch him some water. She ran back to the house to get this, but was stopped by the Free State soldiers when she reached her home. She then heard several shots and when she was finally allowed out of her house again, she saw that George Nagle had been shot dead by his captors.[4]

It was later reported by Free State forces that Nagle had been involved in

3   Con Casey papers, Kerry County Library Archives.
4   Dorothy Macardle, *Tragedies of Kerry* (1924), p. 61.

an action at The Spa, near Tralee, on 18 August 1922, when a Free State officer had been killed. Sergeant Jack Lydon, a Tralee native serving in the Dublin Guard, had died of bullet wounds following an IRA attack on the Free State outpost at Lyons' pub in the small village.[5] While this may or may not have been the case, the summary execution of a wounded prisoner needed no pretext on that day at Derrynafeena, as Volunteer William Conway O'Connor was also shot following his capture there.

While history has forgotten the names of their killers, Lieutenant George Nagle and Volunteer William Conway O'Connor are remembered by a Celtic cross at picturesque Lough Acoose, near to where they fell.

Lieutenant George Nagle was buried in St Cartach's Graveyard in Kiltallagh near Castlemaine and close to his home in Ballygamboon. In this cemetery also lie the remains of General Charlie Daly and Dan Keating, who was the last surviving veteran of the Tan and Civil Wars in Ireland.

---

5   Niall Harrington, *Kerry Landing* (1992), p. 132.

James O'Connor

Séamus Ó Concubair

James Joseph O'Connor was a member of 'D' Company of the 1st Battalion, Kerry No. 1 Brigade, which was based in the Rock Street area of Tralee. He had joined Na Fianna at the age of fourteen and later became an active Volunteer during the Tan War. Early in that conflict he was arrested and imprisoned in Cork Gaol. However, while there he began a hunger strike and was released ten days later. Following his release he went back on active service and was among those who captured a haul of twenty rifles from British forces at Tralee railway station in July 1920.[1] On 2 August 1922, during the early stages of the Civil War, he was one of the IRA Volunteers who fought a rearguard action in the attempt to prevent Free State forces capturing Tralee following their landing at Fenit.

Courtesy of the Martin Moore collection.

In the winter months of 1922–23, O'Connor and several other men from Tralee operated in the Barrow area near Ardfert and Churchill. This small unit contained Michael Sinnott of The Spa, Tim (Taidhgín) Drummond, James O'Connor, a Volunteer from Tralee named Clifford and a young local man named Greer. This local man had enlisted in the Free State Army but was persuaded by his friends in the area to desert to the IRA. However his commitment to the Republican cause was suspect and it is probable that he betrayed his companions to the Free State Army in Tralee.

On 13 February 1923 Captain Wilson of the Free State Army came to the Carrahane and Barrow districts in search of the small IRA unit. Wilson's troops managed to capture Clifford, Drummond and Greer. The prisoners were brought to the Free State Army's intelligence section in Ballymullen Barracks. That evening the Free State soldiers returned in two lorries, firstly going to the

---

1 Notes of Coiste Chuimhneacháin Bhaile Uí Shíoda on Kerry No. 1 Brigade casualties (private collection).

Ryle house where the three captured men had sheltered before their capture. Then, after dark, they proceeded to the Lyons' farm nearby, at Carrahane, near Banna Strand. James O'Connor and Michael Sinnott had constructed a dugout in the hay shed of the Lyons family. With their accurate information, the Free State soldiers went to the hay shed where O'Connor and Sinnott were sleeping in their elaborate dugout. Both men were shot dead by machine-gun fire where they lay. Though greatly outnumbered and with no chance of escape, it would appear that no opportunity to surrender was offered to the two men. The Lyons family were held captive in their house while these events were taking place in their farmyard. Following the shooting the soldiers departed immediately, leaving the bodies of their victims behind.[2]

James O'Connor was nineteen years old when he was killed at Carrahane, Ardfert. He is buried in the Republican Plot in Rath Cemetery, Tralee. He and his comrade, Michael Sinnott, are remembered by traditional white crosses at Carrahane, near Banna Strand. Their sacrifice is also recalled on the battalion monuments at Churchill and Derrymore.

2   Dorothy Macardle, *Tragedies of Kerry* (1924), p. 20.

Jerry O'Sullivan

Diarmuid Ó Súilleabháin[1]

Little survives today in the written or oral records about the short life of Jeremiah (Jerry) O'Sullivan. He was born in 1906 and his family lived in Pembroke Street, Tralee, where his father was a pig buyer. As a young man he joined the Tralee Na Fianna. His role is not recorded and it is likely that he was a member during the Civil War period.

At a Republican commemoration in Rath Cemetery at Easter 1925, former Brigade O/C Paddy Cahill recalled the name of Jerry O'Sullivan as he listed the dead of Na Fianna in Tralee. The six men he named in his address were Percy Hannafin, Michael Ryle, Billy Myles, Paddy Reidy, Jerry O'Sullivan and Dan Foley.[2]

Nothing now is remembered of young Jerry O'Sullivan's contribution to the fight for freedom, but what he had done was sufficient for him to be recalled amongst the Republican dead by Cahill as early as 1925 and to be recalled on the brigade roll of honour at the Ballyseedy monument.

In 1949 Johnny O'Connor of Farmer's Bridge gave an account to Ernie O'Malley of his significant role in the Republican defence of Tralee on the day the Free State Army captured the town on 2 August 1922. O'Connor was a noted Lewis gunner and had earned the nickname Machine Gun Connor. The Lewis gunner would usually require a companion to carry the pans of ammunition for the weapon and during the action on that day O'Connor was accompanied by a young Volunteer whose name O'Malley transcribed as 'Scully'. The census reviews and other records reveal that there was no young man of that name or age in Tralee at the time and it is the editor's opinion that 'Scully' was in fact 'Sully', a common colloquial diminutive for O'Sullivan. It is possible that Jerry O'Sullivan was the Na Fianna member who fought heroically with Johnny O'Connor on that day and this would have earned him

---

1 There is no known photograph of Jerry O'Sullivan.
2 *The Kerryman*, 18 April 1925.

a place in the Republican lore of the town in his day.³

Jerry O'Sullivan is buried in the Republican Plot in Tralee's Rath Cemetery.

---

3   Ernie O'Malley, *The Men Will Talk to Me: Kerry Interviews* (2012), interview with Johnny O'Connor.

John O'Sullivan

Seán Ó Súilleabáin

John O'Sullivan, born in 1894, was a native of Aughacasla, which lies between the villages of Camp and Castlegregory on the southern shore of Tralee Bay. He was employed in Tralee and was sworn in as a member of the IRB in Tralee in 1918. On the reorganisation of the Irish Volunteers in the town he was attached to 'D' Company of the 1st Battalion, in which he held the rank of first lieutenant. During the Tan War he had a contact in the crown forces who supplied him with high quality ammunition, something that was in short supply for the limited number of service weapons that the town's battalion possessed. In November 1920 he joined the active service unit which was formed by Paddy Cahill, the brigade O/C.[1]

Courtesy of the Martin Moore collection.

On 2 August 1922 approximately 450 Free State troops disembarked at Fenit Pier taking the small Republican garrison there by surprise. Mines that had been placed on the pier failed to explode, as their detonating cords had been cut some days previously by local men who feared the destruction of the pier, which provided much of the village's employment. As a result, the invading force was able to land their soldiers, artillery and armoured car in an orderly fashion. The few IRA Volunteers who garrisoned the port quickly retreated along the Tralee road and regrouped in a large ring fort that still lies in a field about a mile from Fenit. There they divided into two groups, one heading inland towards Barrow and the other section under Tommy Sheehy retreating to Sammy's Rock in the direction of Tralee. This is a large limestone hillock which holds a commanding view of the road to Tralee as it follows the coastline to the hamlet of The Spa.

1   Notes of Coiste Chuimhneacháin Bhaile Uí Shíoda on Kerry No. 1 Brigade casualties (private collection).

Meanwhile, alerted by a phone call from Fenit and later by another communication from The Spa, the Republican brigade headquarters in Tralee's Ballymullen Barracks prepared to send reinforcements to Fenit to halt the Free State advance. Paddy Paul Fitzgerald, O/C of the 9th Battalion, staff officer Paddy Garvey and a group of IRA Volunteers went by car out towards Fenit to assess the situation. They were followed ten minutes later by experienced IRA Volunteer Mick McGlynn, who had initially rushed to the area to confirm the enemy landing and had then returned to Tralee to bring out reinforcements. The Volunteers in McGlynn's Crossley tender were mainly from the 9th Battalion and included John O'Sullivan. McGlynn left his men at Oysterhall, near where the Fenit road runs along the shore and behind Sammy's Rock, and returned to Tralee for a further detachment of Republicans.

Some of the men retreating from Fenit were already positioned on the summit of Sammy's Rock and were firing at the Free State column on the roadway below. The large Free State column divided its troops, with one detachment proceeding to the left around the north side of the steep rock-faced hill. Meanwhile, the troops on the road to the west used the machine gun on their armoured car, 'the Ex-Mutineer', to augment their intense gunfire towards the Republicans firing at them from the summit. McGlynn's men attempted to climb up the limestone hill to reach their beleaguered colleagues who were temporarily holding the Free State column at bay. It was while climbing up the side of the hill that John O'Sullivan was hit by Free State bullets; he died at the scene. Outmanoeuvred and outgunned, the Republicans on Sammy's Rock were forced to surrender, while their comrades retreated into Tralee. By the evening of that August day the town would be under the control of General Paddy Daly of the Free State Army's Dublin Guard.[2]

Lieutenant John O'Sullivan of Aughacasla was killed on 2 August 1922, the first Republican to be killed in Kerry during the Civil War. His remains were buried in Killiney Cemetery, in his native parish of Castlegregory, where his headstone records his death on active service. Today a white roadside cross stands at the foot of Sammy's Rock on the slopes of which he died in defence of the Irish Republic.

2   Niall Harrington, *Kerry Landing* (1992), p. 104.

Paddy Reidy

Pádruig Ó Riada[1]

Patrick Reidy was born in Tralee and lived in Oakview on the northern side of the town. His father was a tailor. Paddy Reidy joined Na Fianna, the youth section of the Republican movement and was attached to the Tralee 1st Battalion's 'D' Company, which drew its members from the Rock Street area of the town. During the initial stages of the Civil War he was on active service in County Limerick, where he was one of almost thirty men in a column of IRA Volunteers commanded by Tadhg Brosnan of Castlegregory, of which six were members of Na Fianna from Tralee.[2] The nature of Paddy Reidy's early death is not recorded, but when speaking at the Republican commemoration in Rath Cemetery in April 1925, Paddy Cahill, the former O/C of Kerry No. 1 Brigade, paid tribute to the dead of Na Fianna from Tralee. He lists them as Percy Hannafin, Michael Ryle, Billy Myles, Paddy Reidy, Dan Foley and Jerry O'Sullivan.[3]

Paddy Reidy is buried in the Republican Plot in Tralee's Rath Cemetery.

---

1 There is no known photograph of Paddy Reidy.
2 Niall Harrington, *Kerry Landing* (1992), p. 90.
3 *The Kerryman*, 18 April 1925.

MICHAEL RYLE

Míceál Ó Raġaill[1]

Michael Joseph Ryle was born in 1905 in Tralee's Pembroke Street, where his father was both a publican and a grocer. At the age of fourteen he joined the very active Na Fianna unit in Tralee which was commanded by Mike O'Leary. It was while he was on active service as a scout at Ballycarty, near Tralee, on 5 August 1922, that Michael Ryle was killed in action.

Following their capture of Tralee on 2 August 1922, the Free State forces consolidated their presence in the town over the next two days. On Saturday 5 August they were confident enough to organise a push inland to gain possession of the town of Castleisland from Republican forces, who at this time were in disarray. The Free State officers were unsure of what resistance they might meet as they travelled eastwards along the main road from Tralee. However, the Republican forces in the county had not yet reorganised following the surprise seaborne invasion by the Free State Army and most of the experienced Republican fighters were still in the Limerick, Tipperary and north Cork areas attempting to hold a defensive line there.

At Ballycarty, four miles east of Tralee, where the roads to Castleisland and Killarney diverge, there stood a large old house belonging to the Quill family. Modern road realignments, the present-day Earl of Desmond Hotel and recently planted trees have now obscured the hillock on which the house stood. The meadow in front of the old Georgian house commanded a view of the road and the strategic junction. It was there that Michael Ryle was posted to observe Free State troop movements. However, as members of the Free State convoy were cautiously advancing towards Castleisland, they were expecting an attack and spotted the young Republican as he tracked their movements. He had been hiding in the tall August grass in the meadow overlooking the road, but this did not afford him adequate cover when he was spotted by the soldiers. Fire was opened on his position by an armoured car

---

1   There is no known photograph of Michael Ryle.

and he was shot in the head. He died instantly at the scene.[2]

He was buried in the family plot in Rath Cemetery and is remembered by the traditional white roadside cross at Ballycarty adjacent to where he gave his young life in the service of the Republic.

---

2   Notes of Coiste Chuimhneacháin Bhaile Uí Shíoda on Kerry No. 1 Brigade casualties (private collection).

Michael Sinnott

Míceál Sionóir

Michael Sinnott was the son of a labourer who had come to Kerry working with the Great Southern and Western Railway Company. His mother was Sarah Brosnan from Kilmorna, near Listowel. The family had settled in Knockanish, The Spa, two miles from Tralee on the road to Fenit. Michael, the eldest boy in a family of nine children, was born in 1904 in Waterford into a family that had originally come there from Wexford and would eventually settle in Kerry. His grandfather was a Fenian and had spent several years in prison in Britain for his Republican activities.

Courtesy of the Martin Moore collection.

Initially Michael Sinnott was a member of Na Fianna in Tralee, but he later became a Volunteer attached to the 9th Battalion, Kerry No. 1 Brigade. This battalion covered part of the town of Tralee and out along the coast to Fenit village. During the Civil War he was part of the battalion's active service unit.[1]

During the winter of 1923 Sinnott was a member of a small Republican unit that was operating in the area near Churchill and Ardfert. They had a dugout in the outhouse of the Lyons family at Carrahane, a large, flat, sandy tidal area a few hundred yards from where Roger Casement was captured at McKenna's Fort. The unit consisted of five Volunteers: Sinnott, James O'Connor and three others, Drummond, Clifford and Greer.

On 13 February 1923 a Free State Army sweep of the area captured Drummond, Clifford and Greer and they were brought to Ballymullen Barracks where Drummond and Clifford were badly beaten. Apparently, Greer gave

---

1   Notes of Coiste Chuimhneacháin Bhaile Uí Shíoda on Kerry No. 1 Brigade casualties (private collection).

information as to the whereabouts of his comrades Sinnott and O'Connor, who had evaded capture that morning. Greer, though a local man, had initially joined the Free State Army but was persuaded to desert and join the Republican forces operating in his native area. There was some suspicion among local people about his commitment to the Republican cause. Whether the information given by him in Ballymullen Barracks with regard to the whereabouts of Sinnott and O'Connor was given willingly or under duress is uncertain.

Following the capture of their comrades, Sinnott and O'Connor had returned under the cover of darkness to the dugout in the Lyons' farmyard. They were asleep there when the Free State troops arrived in two lorries with Greer as their guide. The Free State party was led by Captain William John Wilson, a Dublin Guard officer who was implicated in other similar incidents during the Civil War. Some soldiers entered the house and held the Lyons family captive, while others went directly to where the sleeping Volunteers lay. Mrs Lyons reported that there were a large number of shots and then the soldiers left to return to their barracks. When she went out to her yard to investigate the fate of O'Connor and Sinnott, both were lying in pools of blood where they had slept, having been shot numerous times.[2]

Initially Sinnott's remains were refused entry to the parish church in Tralee because of the Catholic Church's official excommunication of Republicans, but when his mother persisted, the parish priest relented and a funeral mass was permitted.[3]

Michael Sinnott was eighteen years old when he was killed on 13 February 1923. His sister Annie heard of her brother's killing in the South Dublin Union where she was imprisoned for her activities on behalf of the Republican cause. Michael Sinnott's remains are buried in the Republican Plot in Rath Cemetery, Tralee. A white roadside cross stands at Carrahane near the site where he and James O'Connor were killed.

---

2 Dorothy Macardle, *Tragedies of Kerry* (1924), p. 22.
3 Information from Mary Cashman, niece of Michael Sinnott, to Martin Moore in 1998.

Jim Walsh

Séamus Breatnac

Courtesy of Martin O'Dwyer, Cashel.

James Walsh was born in Lisodigue, between the small village of The Spa and nearby Churchill, approximately six miles from Tralee, on 3 May 1890. He was a member of 'D' Company, 2nd Battalion, Kerry No. 1 Brigade, having joined the Volunteers in 1914. This detachment was based in the Churchill district. On Easter Sunday 1916 he was one of those who gathered at the Irish Volunteer headquarters at The Rink in Tralee in preparation for the Easter Rising. He was an active Volunteer in the Tan War and held the rank of captain in the Churchill Company. Highly respected within his community, he was appointed a 'justice' at the Republican parish court at Churchill. In May 1920 he was elected a local councillor for Sinn Féin in the Tralee Rural District Council. Later during that war he was arrested and imprisoned. He remained an IRA Volunteer after the Treaty and during the Civil War he was on active service with the battalion column. During the Truce, the Churchill Company had been transferred to the newly formed 9th Battalion of Kerry No. 1 Brigade and Jim Walsh remained its leader.

Following the evacuation of Tralee by Republican forces in August, many of the Volunteers of the 1st and 9th Battalions retreated to the foothills of the Sliabh Mish Mountains to the west of the town. From there they carried on a guerrilla campaign in the Tralee area. Walsh was a member of the IRA unit that attacked the Free State Army post in the village of The Spa near to his home and four miles from Tralee. This incident resulted in the death of a Tralee-born Free State soldier, Jack Lydon of James's Street, a sergeant in the Dublin Guard.[1]

1   Niall Harrington, *Kerry Landing* (1992), p. 132.

The 9th Battalion had a base near Derrymore during the Civil War. This was across the bay from Walsh's home in The Spa. On 1 February 1923 Walsh and another Volunteer had arranged to cross the bay on a currach which was to collect them at Derrymore beach. The boat did not arrive and the two men walked back to the house of Republican sympathisers, the Quirke family, on the main road at Derrymore. A Free State lorry happened to break down as it was passing and the troops went to this house to seek assistance. There they found Walsh and he was placed under arrest.[2] He was subsequently badly beaten in Ballymullen Barracks by his captors in an attempt to extract information from him.[3] During the interrogation his left wrist was broken in two places and this injury prevented him from being transferred with other Kerry Republican prisoners to the Curragh internment camp later that month. As a result he was one of the prisoners that Colonel David Neligan, chief of intelligence for the Kerry Command of the Free State Army, selected to be massacred at Ballyseedy Cross on 7 March 1923. It is likely that, as with the other prisoners chosen, he was selected because he was active in an area of Republican resistance, which in Jim Walsh's case was Derrymore. The nine prisoners selected were tied around a mine and it was detonated, killing eight of them, including Walsh.

The remains of the Ballyseedy victims were released to their families later on the day of the atrocity. Jim Walsh's coffin was interred in Annagh Graveyard, two miles from Tralee on the Dingle road, in the Walsh family tomb in the ancient cemetery. His name is inscribed on the 1st and 9th Battalion memorial at Churchill, close to his home in Lisodigue. He is also remembered on the monument in Derrymore near where he was captured, as well as on the Ballyseedy monument.

2 Information from Dan King, Tralee.
3 Notes of Coiste Chuimhneacháin Bhaile Uí Shíoda on Kerry No. 1 Brigade casualties (private collection).

2nd (Ardfert) and 3rd (Lixnaw) Battalions, Kerry No. 1 Brigade

The ancient barony of Clanmaurice is flat and fertile with its rich farmland dotted with a series of villages. It was far from ideal countryside for a guerrilla force to operate in. It was on its shore at Banna Strand that the Rising of 1916 was dealt a mortal blow with the capture of Roger Casement and the failure to land the arms to be used to establish the Republic that Patrick Pearse was to declare on Easter Monday. Here also, the Republic made its last heroic stand, at the windswept Clashmealcon Caves in April 1923.

When the Irish Volunteers were reorganised in 1919, the area north of Tralee and south of the River Feale was divided into two battalions. That centred on the village of Ardfert was initially called the 5th Battalion, Kerry No. 1 Brigade, but was later designated the 2nd Battalion. The Lixnaw Battalion was originally the 7th Battalion, but was later renamed the 3rd Battalion of the brigade.

From the outset the 2nd Battalion was commanded by Tom Clifford, a native of Cahersiveen who had a business in Tralee. Clifford's command contained the following companies: Churchill (which later moved to the 9th Battalion), Ardfert, Kilmoyley, Causeway, Ballyheigue, Kerry Head, Abbeydorney and Kilflynn.

The O/C of the Kerry No. 1 Brigade, Paddy Cahill, was considered a cautious man and slow to bring the men under his command into direct conflict with the crown forces. This was reflected in the relative lack of activity by many of the North Kerry battalions in the first year of the Tan War. And so it was with the 2nd Battalion. However, by the summer of 1920 the RIC had withdrawn from all their barracks in the battalion area, with the exception of Abbeydorney and Causeway, following attacks on such buildings elsewhere in the county.

As the control of the brigade commander loosened, the men on the ground became more active. In February 1920 an RIC patrol near Ballyheigue was disarmed and this was followed two months later by another attack in the same locality. In May of that year the coastguard station at Ballyheigue was captured and destroyed. A month later Causeway RIC Barracks was attacked for the first time and the evacuated Ardfert Barracks was burned. By October 1920 there were sufficient men 'on the run' in the battalion area to form a flying column under the command of Michael Pierce of Ballyheigue. In a large attack by the column at Abbeydorney on 31 October, two Black and Tans were shot dead, and in January 1921 another was killed by a sniper in Causeway. On 5 March Michael Pierce's column led a prolonged attack on Causeway's RIC Barracks. At Abbeydorney's Shannow Bridge, a large force of local Volunteers engaged a patrol of Auxiliaries, reportedly killing one. Throughout the remainder of the conflict, the men of the battalion continued to harry the enemy wherever they could be engaged in the villages and byroads of this area of North Kerry.

Following the Truce, the brigade headquarters was transferred to Ardfert and a training camp for the North Kerry battalions was established there. The subsequent divisions over the Treaty in the spring of 1922 saw the loss of very few men and officers from the 2nd Battalion to the Free State Army.

The invasion of the county by the Free State Army, which was superior in numbers and arms, forced the IRA to return to guerrilla tactics and so it was with the 2nd Battalion. Though operating in countryside not conducive to such warfare, the battalion had several columns in the field, which attacked the Free State forces as they operated out of their garrisons in Tralee and Abbeydorney. A flying column led by Michael Pierce and another led by Tom O'Driscoll of Kilmoyley attacked the railway and road network, preventing easy movement of enemy forces. Ambushes, such as that at Ballyrobert in October 1922, harried the Free State Army as it attempted to claim the upper hand in a land that was largely hostile to it. Sweeping through the countryside with substantial numbers of troops, large numbers of Republican prisoners were captured by pro-Treaty forces and some were summarily executed.

The Free State eventually gained the upper hand as it gradually wore down Republican resistance. On 20 October Causeway Company Captain Paddy O'Connor was captured and a month later twenty-five Republicans were captured in a round-up near Abbeydorney. In February 1923 Michael Pierce and his column of sixteen men surrendered and a week later Tom O'Driscoll did likewise with his thirteen-man unit. Later that week George O'Shea and the men of his small column were captured at Kilflynn. Only Aero Lyons and his column, operating along the coast area near Causeway, remained on the field of battle. Soon, these men too would be defeated as they made a last stand at the Clashmealcon Caves. Thus, what Kerry No. 1 Brigade O/C Andy Cooney would later call 'a splendid resistance' was at an end.

Listowel is the major town in North Kerry and it was there that the original battalion in this area was centred. The Listowel Battalion, originally called the 4th Battalion, Kerry No. 1 Brigade, proved to be too large and in September 1920, while under the command of James Sugrue, it was divided. The companies to the south and west of the town were designated as the Lixnaw Battalion. Initially, this was called the 7th Battalion, but was soon afterwards given the designation of 3rd Battalion. The remainder of the original Listowel unit became the 6th Battalion.

The 3rd (Lixnaw) Battalion consisted of the following companies: Lixnaw, Ballyduff, Leam, Ballydonoghue, Ballybunion, Ardoughter and Rathea. On formation of the battalion Stephen Grady was appointed its commanding officer. He was replaced by Tom Kennelly of Moneen in November 1920. In January 1921 the North Kerry flying column was formed and Kennelly was appointed commanding officer of this thirty-man unit. Ned Joe Walsh of Tullamore took over as O/C of the 3rd Battalion.

During the Tan War the men of the 3rd Battalion were very active, both within their own districts and as part of the flying columns that were established in 1921. On 13 March 1920 a large force entered Ballybunion and launched a fierce attack on the town's RIC barracks. A month later the men of Ballydonoghue Company ambushed an RIC patrol at Gale Bridge. In the same month the RIC garrison at Lixnaw was attacked, causing the post to be abandoned. On 16 July 1920 Lixnaw was the scene of another attack on an RIC patrol from nearby Ahabeg. On 1 September the Cashen coastguard station was captured and destroyed. The 3rd Battalion was part of the Kerry No. 1 Brigade's offensive on 31 October when it killed two RIC constables in Ballyduff. In January 1921 the most active fighters in the battalion were assigned to the North Kerry flying column and this unit, under the command of Thomas Kennelly, saw action throughout the area over the next two months. In March 1921 this column was divided into two, one of which was the 3rd Battalion column under Tom Kennelly and the other was the 6th Battalion column commanded by Denis Quille. There was some crossover of fighters between these units from time to time. The 3rd Battalion column continued effective action against the crown forces during the spring of that year, including attacks on the RIC barracks in Ballyduff and Ballybunion and ambushes at Lixnaw station and at Mountcoal.

Unlike other areas of the county, there was a significant division of opinion regarding the Treaty amongst the officers and men of the 3rd Battalion. Approximately half of the men in the active service unit followed Tom Kennelly into the Free State Army, whose only garrison in Kerry before the Civil War was in Listowel. The capture of Listowel on 29 June 1922 by Republican forces saw Kennelly surrender to Kerry No. 1 Brigade O/C Humphrey Murphy. However, six weeks later the 1st Western Division of the Free State Army was in control of the towns and villages of North Kerry, having landed with superior numbers, arms and equipment at Tarbert. The IRA's reversion to guerrilla tactics during the autumn and winter of that year was greatly hampered by large-scale arrests of active Republicans in sweeps based on information supplied by their former comrades, but the remnants of the battalion still managed to harry the Free State forces with frequent ambushes and sniping. However, they lacked the organisation for any large-scale engagements. The Ballyduff and Ardoughter companies were particularly active and remained in the field of battle until the siege at the Clashmealcon Caves, which effectively marked the end of the Civil War in North Kerry.

THOMAS ARCHER

Tomás Airtéir[1]

Thomas Archer was born in 1904 at Cloonnafinneela, near Kilflynn village, where his father had a small farm. Thomas Archer worked as a farm labourer, and in November 1920 he was working on the farm of the Casey family at Foxfort, a mile to the north of Causeway village.[2] He was a Volunteer in the 2nd Battalion of the Kerry No. 1 Brigade, as were his brothers Edmond, Florence, John, William and Richard. The 2nd Battalion area stretched from Archer's native Kilflynn in the east to Kerry Head in the west.

By November 1920 the crown forces had abandoned all their posts in the 2nd Battalion's district, with the exceptions of the Causeway and Abbeydorney RIC Barracks. These garrisons became the focus of attention of the battalion's increasingly active Volunteers during the winter of 1920.

Michael Pierce was the captain of the Ballyheigue Company of 2nd Battalion. In October 1920 there were so many Volunteers in the district who were 'on the run' that it was decided to form a battalion flying column and Pierce was appointed its commanding officer. On the evening of 4 November the column arrived in Causeway with the intention of attacking any RIC member who might venture from their fortified barracks in the centre of the village. Their specific target was Sergeant McGrath, who had been responsible for the burning of the home of Paddy O'Connor, the captain of the Causeway Company. Pierce's column was supported by Volunteers from the local company, including Thomas Archer, and these men acted as scouts during the operation. However, the RIC became aware of the presence of the IRA unit and remained in their barracks that night. Eventually the column withdrew to Ballyheigue.[3]

In the early hours of 6 November they returned. Pierce and his men occupied several houses adjacent to the barracks at 4.30 a.m. and waited for

---

1 There is no known photograph of Thomas Archer.
2 Information from Imelda Murphy, niece of Thomas Archer.
3 Michael Pierce of Ballyheigue, BMH WS 1190.

the RIC to appear. Several hours later a regular RIC constable and three Black and Tans left the barracks and proceeded along the street. However, McGrath, the primary target, was not with them so the attackers held their fire. Soon McGrath appeared at the barracks door, but the nearby presence of civilians deterred Pierce from opening fire. At 9.30 a.m. a retired RIC man named Roche passed the house where Pierce and Paddy O'Connor were positioned and he noted the two men acting suspiciously. Roche went into a public house and from there entered the barracks from the rear to warn the garrison of the impending attack. Subsequently the RIC and Tans who had already left the barracks returned and the garrison prepared for an attack. Somewhat unusually at the time, the barracks had a communications radio and its defenders were able to contact the British Army garrison in Tralee, which sent reinforcements to Causeway. As the military vehicles rushed to the village, Pierce was informed by his scouts that there were crown force reinforcements approaching at speed from Tralee, Listowel and Abbeydorney. He hastily gathered the column together and as they were leaving the village through the fields, the military vehicles were arriving. The reinforcements went directly to the O'Driscoll house where O'Connor and Pierce had been located, but found it empty except for a dog, which they shot.

The enemy then split their forces in two and headed off in pursuit of the escaping column. They managed to cut off their retreat and heavy machine-gun fire meant that the column had to remain under cover. Eventually, one of the Volunteers, John Joe O'Sullivan, a Royal Navy veteran, managed to shoot the machine gunner and the subsequent lull in the firing allowed the column to make good its escape. However, while acting as a scout some distance from his comrades, Thomas Archer was alarmed by the sudden arrival of the military. His attempt to run for cover was detected by the troops, but he managed to run through one field and into another which was part of the farm of Neilus Flynn, a noted Kerry hurler. There he was hit by the gunfire of the pursuing soldiers and died at the scene. His remains were taken to nearby farm buildings.[4]

His family was informed and his father travelled from Kilflynn to Causeway to collect the remains. Thomas Archer was buried in the family plot in the old

---

4   Information from Seán Seosamh Ó Conchubhair, local historian.

graveyard that lies in the centre of Kilflynn. His headstone on his well-tended grave just behind the Republican Plot notes the circumstances of his death.

The former RIC sergeant, Patrick Roche, was later shot dead on 4 March 1921 on the instructions of the brigade O/C, as he was judged to be an informer for the crown forces arising from the failed attack in Causeway on 6 November 1920.

Today Thomas Archer is remembered by a roadside memorial at the entrance to Causeway village and his name is inscribed on the brigade monument at Ballyseedy.

James Barry

Séamus de Barra[1]

James Barry was a Volunteer with the Causeway Company of the 2nd Battalion, Kerry No. 1 Brigade. His father, Thomas Barry, and his mother, Margaret Carroll, reared their family on a farm on the outskirts of the village. James was the eldest boy and was born on 1 June 1897. It was as a result of an incident in Causeway during the Black and Tan War that he was to die in the service of the Irish Republic.

In March 1921 a supporter of the crown forces had been captured by the IRA unit based in the Causeway area. While it was unusual for such prisoners to be harmed, it was decided locally in this case that, because of his actions, the captive would be shot. He was brought to the Fair Field in Causeway, an open area in the centre of the village, but out of sight of the street. The local IRA unit had planned to execute their prisoner there. One of the execution party was Ned O'Connor, the brother of Company Captain Paddy O'Connor. Volunteer James Barry was also in the group that brought the prisoner to the Fair Field. As O'Connor was preparing his weapon, the prisoner produced a hidden pistol from his pocket and shot Ned O'Connor in the thigh. He fell injured and the prisoner escaped in the commotion. The Volunteers had not been masked and so the escaped prisoner would have had no difficulty in identifying them. Having tended to their wounded comrade, the party fled the village shortly afterwards, before they could be apprehended by searching RIC and soldiers.

James Barry headed to Tullamore, a townland four miles to the north of Listowel. On the long journey, which he travelled on foot, it rained incessantly. Many hours later he arrived into the shelter of a safe house, but was wet and cold by the time he reached his destination. Away from his home, he had no change of clothing and within days he developed pneumonia. As his condition worsened he was brought to the hospital in Tralee and admitted under a false

---

1 There is no known photograph of James Barry.

name. In those pre-antibiotic days, his health continued to decline and he died some days later.[2]

The circumstances of his flight from Causeway militated against burying his remains following a traditional funeral, as this may have brought unwanted attention down on the family from the local RIC. It is thought most probable that Barry is buried in the family tomb in Killury Cemetery less than a mile from his home in Causeway. He is remembered on the Ballyseedy monument, where his name is inscribed with his dead comrades of the 2nd Battalion, Kerry No. 1 Brigade. The official IRA report on his death compiled in 1925 states that James Barry died as a result of illness arising from active service in March 1921.[3]

---

2   Information given by local source, name with author.
3   Con Casey papers, Kerry County Library Archives.

John Cantillon

Seán de Cantalún

John Cantillon was the second eldest of the six children of Patrick and Nora Cantillon of West Commons, Ardfert. He was born on 2 August 1896 and worked, as his father did, as a farm labourer. A sportsman, he was a member of the Tubrid hurling team which represented the Ardfert area and which won the County Championship in 1917.[1]

John Cantillon was a Volunteer in the Ardfert Company of the 2nd Battalion, Kerry No. 1 Brigade. In late October 1920 an order was issued from GHQ in Dublin stating that there was to be an intensification of the war against the crown forces following the death of Terence MacSwiney on hunger strike in Brixton Prison on 25 October 1920. On 5 November Tom Clifford, the 2nd Battalion O/C, gathered a large party of Volunteers in Ardfert village in preparation for an attack on a patrol of Black and Tans who were expected to travel through the nearby village of The Spa. However, at least five lorries of Tans arrived unexpectedly in Ardfert village as the assembled Volunteers were about to leave the village to travel the four miles to The Spa. The Tans began firing as they dismounted from their vehicles. Most of the Volunteers who had gathered in the village managed to escape, and it is thought that while John Cantillon received a slight wound in the gunfire, he too managed to evade arrest.

Three days later he returned to Ardfert to have his wound dressed by the local doctor. As he walked through the village he was detained by several RIC men and Black and Tans, who were part of a group that had arrived in lorries and unexpectedly entered Ardfert from two directions. John Cantillon

Courtesy of Tommy O'Connor.

---

1 Tommy O'Connor, *Ardfert in Times Past* (1999), p. 52.

was taken prisoner, as were Michael Brosnan and Maurice McElligott. The men were put on the military vehicles and were used as hostages as the Tans travelled the nearby countryside. Eventually, on a road to the west of the village, the three men were taken to a field and told to run. This large field was near the village's old school and today is the site of Hazel Grove housing estate.[2] Cantillon and Brosnan began to run as they were ordered and both were shot dead after they had gotten about fifty yards from their captors. On the advice of one of the RIC men, Mossy McElligott stood his ground. It was reported that the bodies of Johnny Cantillon and Michael Brosnan were 'riddled with bullets', while Mossy McElligott was badly beaten with a gun but survived his ordeal.[3]

The Black and Tans then walked through the field and, crossing over a stile, they went into O'Sullivan's public house, now named Kate Browne's, entering by the rear door. There they demanded free drink, which the publican was forced to give them.

Volunteer John Cantillon is buried in Ardfert Cemetery. His name is recorded on the Republican monument which stands opposite the village's church and near the field where he met his death. This monument was unveiled on 12 August 1934 by Seán Ryan in front of a crowd of 4,000 people.[4]

2 Information from Tommy O'Connor, local historian and County Librarian.
3 Patrick Sheehan, BMH WS 1088.
4 *The Kerryman*, 18 August 1934.

Edward Greaney

Éamonn Ó Gruanna[1]

Edward (Ned) Greaney was raised in Ballinbranhig, near Causeway. His mother emigrated to New Zealand while Ned was still young and he was left in the care of the Quinlan family who were related to his mother and lived nearby. Ned, as he was called, joined the Irish Volunteers in 1918.[2] As the conflict intensified in the summer and autumn of 1920, Ned Greaney was forced to go 'on the run'. In October 1920 Michael Pierce, the captain of the Ballyheigue Company of the 2nd Battalion, formed an active service unit consisting of some twenty Volunteers in the Causeway and Ballyheigue districts whose activities meant that it was no longer safe for them to live in their own homes. Greaney was a member of this flying column. Pierce's column was to take part in many attacks on the crown forces, including assaults on Causeway RIC Barracks and the capture and destruction of Ballyheigue coastguard station and castle.[3]

Following the Treaty Greaney remained in the Republican Army, as did Michael Pierce and the rest of the unit. Greaney is recorded as having been a member of one of the Republican columns that marched to Limerick city following the capture of Listowel from Free State forces in the first week of the Civil War.[4] With the defeat of the IRA defensive operations in County Limerick in August 1922 and the invasion of his native county by Free State forces, Greaney returned to the Causeway area. There he was a member of Michael Pierce's IRA column, which was active in the Causeway district, while the 2nd Battalion's other column fought under the command of Tom O'Driscoll, operating in the Ardfert and Abbeydorney districts.

In early February 1923 Liam Deasy, the second in command of the IRA, was captured in Tipperary. He was sentenced to death but was reprieved when he agreed to sign a document calling on Republican forces to unconditionally lay

---

1   Surviving images of Edward Greaney were not of sufficient quality to reproduce.
2   Information from Cecilia Lynch and Tom Harrington.
3   Michael Pierce, BMH WS 1190.
4   Notes of Coiste Chuimhneacháin Bhaile Uí Shíoda on Kerry No. 1 Brigade casualties (private collection).

down their weapons. This document was widely circulated and had the desired effect of causing widespread demoralisation within the IRA. Undoubtedly influenced by this event, Pierce reached an agreement with the Free State's Kerry Command and surrendered his unit's weapons on 22 February 1923. As part of this agreement with the Free State's Kerry commander, General Paddy Daly, Pierce and his men undertook to take no further part in the hostilities. Daly granted Pierce and his men a conditional amnesty. Other Volunteers of Pierce's unit who had previously been captured by the Free State forces were also granted a pardon and subsequently released from custody in Ballymullen Barracks, including Greaney. These prisoners included men captured at James Hanlon's house in Dromkeen in October 1922, when several members of the column were surprised as they billeted there. However, inspired by loyalty to their cause and to their fellow column member, James Hanlon, who had been executed by the Free State Army in January 1923, Greaney and some of his comrades took up arms again following their release. The battalion column was now commanded by Timothy 'Aero' Lyons and they remained in the field until they were eventually taken captive after a siege at the Clashmealcon Caves.

Following his surrender at Clashmealcon on 18 April 1923, Greaney was brought to Ballymullen Barracks with the other survivors of the siege. Later that evening they faced a military tribunal, charged with taking part in an attack on Free State Army troops. The inevitable death sentence was handed down by General Paddy Daly but this had to be confirmed by the Free State's GHQ. This General Richard Mulcahy did on the back of a brown envelope. Edward Greaney was executed by a firing squad composed of former British Army soldiers at Ballymullen Gaol on 25 April 1923.[5] His remains were denied to his family and were interred at the barracks.

On Tuesday 28 October 1924, eighteen months after the end of the Civil War, the remains of the men shot by firing squad at Ballymullen Gaol were returned to their families. The coffins were disinterred from the barracks grounds, placed in fresh outer coffins and given to the relatives, who were part of a very large crowd led by local Republican John Joe Sheehy that waited at the barracks gate. An attempt was made to arrest Sheehy, who was still a

5   Ernie O'Malley, *The Men Will Talk to Me – Kerry Interviews* (2012), interview with Bill Bailey.

wanted man, but following a stand-off between IRA Volunteers and Free State soldiers, the procession was allowed to proceed to the nearby St John's church mortuary.[6]

The next day the funerals of Ned Greaney, Jim McEnery, Reg Hathaway and James Hanlon proceeded to Rathela Cemetery at Ballyduff, where all four men were interred in the Republican Plot.

Today Ned Greaney is remembered on the monuments at Clashmealcon, Ballyduff, Ballymullen Gaol and on the brigade memorial at Ballyseedy.

6   *The Kerryman*, 1 November 1924.

James Hanlon

Séamuʀ Ó hAnalám[1]

James Hanlon was born in 1895 at Dromkeen West, Causeway, where his father was a cooper. From 1918 until his death he was a Volunteer in the Causeway Company of the 2nd Battalion, Kerry No. 1 Brigade. During the Tan War he served under Paddy O'Connor, the captain of the Causeway Company. He was not a member of the battalion active service unit at this stage, but was involved in the numerous attacks on the crown forces that took place in the Causeway and Ballyheigue areas. During the Civil War James Hanlon became a full-time member of one of the battalion columns. He was on active service in Limerick city and county during the initial period of that conflict, as the Republican forces attempted to hold a defensive line between Limerick and Waterford cities.

Following the Republican retreat from Limerick and the Free State landings in Kerry, James Hanlon and his comrades returned to their native area and engaged in a campaign of guerrilla warfare in North Kerry. His unit was commanded by Michael Pierce of Ballyheigue. Several of the men on active service with this unit, including Hanlon and Reg Hathaway, were captured at the Hanlon home in Dromkeen on 20 October 1922. As James Hanlon and his comrades were captured under arms, they could expect the death penalty following their arrest. It is probable that Hanlon and the other IRA Volunteers captured with him in Dromkeen were betrayed, as in his last letter Hanlon forgives the man whose action he believed would result in his execution in Ballymullen Barracks.[2]

In December 1922 four IRA Volunteers were sentenced to death by W. R. E. Murphy, the former British officer who commanded the Free State forces in Kerry. A proclamation issued by Humphrey Murphy, O/C of Kerry No. 1 Brigade, threatening reprisals amongst Free State supporters in Tralee resulted in a reprieve for the condemned prisoners. However, in January 1923

1   There is no known photograph of James Hanlon.
2   James Hanlon's final letter to his family courtesy of Tom Harrington, Clashmealcon.

Paddy Daly succeeded W. R. E. Murphy as the senior officer of the Free State Army in Kerry. Daly had a reputation for ruthlessness and had been a member of Michael Collins' 'Squad' in Dublin during the Tan War. He was anxious to establish his authority following Murphy's departure from the county. As a consequence of an increase in attacks on Free State forces throughout the county in January 1923, Daly selected four men from different parts of Kerry to be executed on Saturday 20 January in Ballymullen Gaol, Tralee. Though captured with several other Volunteers who were also under arms, it was James Hanlon who was chosen to face the firing squad. This may have been because it was in Hanlon's father's house that the Republicans had been captured. The execution of Hanlon was to have consequences later in the Civil War, when Reg Hathaway, who was released under a local amnesty several weeks later, went back on active service citing a duty to the memory of his comrade Hanlon.[3] In April 1923 Hathaway faced a firing squad following his capture at Clashmealcon Caves.

In his last letter James Hanlon states, 'I am meeting my death for the Republic' and that he 'was proud to be one of those chosen to die for such a noble cause'. He was shot with James Daly, Michael Brosnan and John (Jack) Clifford by a Free State firing squad in Ballymullen Barracks, Tralee. The firing squad was commanded by Captain Ed Flood.[4] The Hanlon family were not made aware of his execution until a notice was posted on the prison gates stating that the executions of the four named men had been carried out earlier that morning.

Initially the remains of James Hanlon were buried within the barracks grounds at Ballymullen, but in 1924, on the intervention of a priest, General Daly was persuaded to release the coffins of the executed men. James Hanlon is buried in the Republican Plot in Rathela Cemetery, Ballyduff. He is recalled on the monument in Ballyduff village and on a roadside memorial at Causeway. His name is also inscribed on the memorial at Ballymullen Gaol recalling the seven men executed there by Free State forces during 1923.

3 Ernie O'Malley, *The Men Will Talk to Me – Kerry Interviews* (2012), interview with Dan Flavin.
4 *Ibid.*, interview with Bill Bailey.

Reginald Hathaway

Raġnall de hAtaburde[1]

Reginald Hathaway, or 'Rudge' as he was affectionately known by his comrades, was born in Slough, England. His actual name was Walter Stennings or Stenning, but he also used the name Walter Stephens. He was a private in the British Army and was attached to the East Lancashire Regiment which was billeted in Tralee during the Tan War. A fellow prisoner of his during the Civil War, Dan Flavin, states that Hathaway came to Ireland in 1918 with his regiment. He deserted the British Army in May 1921 and made his way to Ballyheigue. There he contacted the local IRA company, whose captain was Michael Pierce, and offered his services as a soldier. Initially he was regarded with suspicion, but eventually the local Volunteers accepted his bona fides. He apparently returned to Ballymullen Barracks in Tralee in order to secure some weapons, then joined Pierce's 2nd Battalion flying column, which operated in the Ballyheigue and Causeway district. He was particularly friendly with Aero Lyons and Ned Greaney. In August 1922 he enlisted in the Free State Army at Ballymullen Barracks in Tralee, but soon deserted to rejoin his former comrades in the 2nd Battalion.

On 20 October 1922 he was captured with several other members of Michael Pierce's IRA column at Hanlon's house in Dromkeen, Causeway. These men were captured in possession of arms, an offence which carried the death penalty. This was duly passed by General Paddy Daly in January 1923 when the Volunteers arrested at Dromkeen appeared before the Free State military court in Ballymullen Barracks. However, only James Hanlon, in whose father's house these men were captured, was executed. Hanlon and three other Volunteers were shot by a Free State firing squad on 20 January 1923. Following the executions, morale in the gaol amongst Republican prisoners was low and Dan Flavin, a fellow prisoner, reports in his account of the period that it was Hathaway who kept their spirits alive.[2]

---

1   There is no known photograph of Reginald Hathaway (Walter Stenning).
2   Ernie O'Malley, *The Men Will Talk to Me – Kerry Interviews* (2012), interview with Dan Flavin.

On 22 February 1923 Michael Pierce came to an agreement with the Free State command in Tralee that he and his men who remained in the field would surrender their arms if they were granted an amnesty. Under this arrangement, those men who had been part of Pierce's column and who were already being held prisoner would also be released, if they too agreed to be bound by the agreement. As a result, Hathaway was freed from Ballymullen Gaol. However, Hathaway felt bad about the execution of his comrade Hanlon and considered himself honour-bound to return to active service. He rejoined the IRA column that remained active in the Causeway district which was now under the command of Aero Lyons. Eventually Lyons and this group, including Hathaway, were forced to surrender after a three-day siege at the Clashmealcon Caves.

Following Lyons' surrender and death there on 18 April 1923, Hathaway and his three remaining comrades, Ned Greaney, Jim McEnery and Jim McGrath, were brought to the top of the cliff, where their hands were bound and they were then marched to Harrington's house a short distance away. At 7 p.m. that evening a car carrying Colonel James Hancock arrived and he then brought Hathaway back down to the cliff's edge. There Hathaway was brutally beaten. James Hancock had been a soldier in the Australian Army in the Great War and later had a commission in the Free State Army's Dublin Guard.[3] There is some evidence that Hancock may have remained in the service of the British crown even after his demobilisation at the end of the Great War. He, along with many of the Free State soldiers who had served in the imperial forces prior to joining the Free State Army, would have regarded Hathaway with particular odium, as they would have judged him as a deserter not only from the Free State Army but also from the British Army.

After a military court condemned three of the remaining survivors of the Clashmealcon Caves to death, Reg Hathaway, Jim McEnery and Edward Greaney were executed by a firing squad composed of former British soldiers in Ballymullen Gaol at 8 a.m. on Wednesday 25 April 1923. Permission to take their bodies was refused to their relatives and the remains were buried in Ballymullen Barracks. On 28 October 1924 Reg Hathaway and his two

3   Cecilia Lynch, *From the GPO to Clashmealcon Caves* (2003), p. 20.

comrades, along with James Hanlon, were reinterred with full Republican honours in Rathela Cemetery, Ballyduff.[4] For several years afterwards, Hathaway's family would visit the district, encouraged by the high esteem in which their son was held by the local community.[5]

Today Reginald Hathaway's name is inscribed on the Republican memorials at Ballyduff and Clashmealcon, as well as on the small monument that marks his place of execution at the gaol wall.

4   *The Kerryman*, 1 November 1924.
5   Information from Tom Harrington, Clashmealcon.

Seán Houlihan

Seán Ó hUallacáin

John (Seán) Houlihan was born in the village of Ballyduff on 8 January 1887. He lived with his family in the village where he and his brothers, Willie and James, were members of the Ballyduff Company of the 3rd Battalion, Kerry No. 1 Brigade.

In late October 1920, following the death on hunger strike of Terence MacSwiney and the order from GHQ to engage the crown forces wherever the opportunity presented itself, an attack on an RIC patrol in Ballyduff was planned. Men of the Ballyduff and Lixnaw companies of the 3rd Battalion were involved and the ambush took place on the evening of 31 October 1920. It resulted in the death of Constable George Morgan and the wounding of another RIC constable.

Courtesy of the Martin Moore collection.

Reports of the attack were conveyed to the RIC at Listowel and several lorries of regular RIC supported by Black and Tans arrived in Ballyduff village at around 4 a.m. One detachment of police stopped outside the Houlihan house, which was situated at the edge of Ballyduff village. The other group set about burning buildings, including the creamery, in reprisal for the earlier killing of Constable Morgan. Fearing such a reprisal, James and Willie Houlihan had not stayed at the family home that night, but Seán felt secure enough to remain at his parents' house. A group of Tans entered the Houlihan house and proceeded to drag Seán down the stairs and out onto the road. One of the Tans stabbed him in the chest with a bayonet as they forced Mrs Houlihan to watch. Another shot him three times, then he was finally killed by a blow from a rifle to the head. Having killed Seán Houlihan, the raiding party then burned the family hayshed. Leaving Seán dead on the roadside with his distraught mother beside him, the RIC and Tans then proceeded along the village's main street and looted several shops, firing as they went.[1]

On the day of the funeral, the RIC returned in force to prevent any military display at the burial and to apprehend any Volunteers who might attend. However, the funeral passed off without incident.

Seán Houlihan was thirty-three years of age went he was killed outside his home. He was buried in the Republican Plot in Rathela Cemetery, just outside his native Ballyduff. As one enters the village today there is a roadside monument to mark the site of his killing and he is also remembered at the Republican memorial near the village's church.

---

1   James Houlihan of Ballyduff, BMH WS 1118.

Jack Lawlor

Seán Ó Leaċloḃair

John (Jack) Lawlor, from Glendahalan, Ballyheigue, was born on 4 September 1900. He was a Volunteer in the Ballyheigue Company of the 2nd Battalion, Kerry No. 1 Brigade from 1918 and was active throughout the Tan War. Following the Treaty Lawlor remained on active duty with the 2nd Battalion. He served in his native area where he was attached to Michael Pierce's active service unit.

During the Civil War the Free State Army was garrisoned in Tralee and Abbeydorney and did not have a presence in Ballyheigue. However, the use of armoured cars and other military vehicles supplied by the departing British made their forces highly mobile. The rural areas remained in Republican hands and when they ventured from the towns the Free State troops moved in large numbers to prevent IRA attacks.

Courtesy of the Michael Moore Collection.

On the evening of 30 October 1922, one such large force of Free State soldiers attached to the 1st Western Division raided the Ballyheigue area. The local Volunteer units managed to evade capture and escaped the encircling Free State cordon. However, as they had left their arms behind in a dump, some men volunteered to return and retrieve the valuable rifles. Jack Lawlor was one of those who returned. While on this mission he and two of his comrades were captured by the searching troops. Some time later the three Volunteers managed to disarm one of their captors and escaped with his rifle. Lawlor became separated from his comrades in the darkness and had the misfortune to encounter another Free State patrol. He was fired on and wounded. He was taken to Ballyheigue village and held until the next morning. What happened next is not recorded, but local lore says that he was brought to the local St James' Cemetery just outside the village. Sensing that he was to be shot, he grabbed the cemetery gate as he was being brought into the graveyard, but his grip was lost as his fingers were broken by rifle butts.[1] He was summarily executed by his Free State captors and his body left on the graveyard path.

Free State reports of his capture published in the pro-Treaty *Cork Examiner* are somewhat different. They report that Jack Lawlor was captured after a firefight at a local farm from which he covered his comrades' retreat from the advancing troops. However, local accounts of his capture and killing are more likely to be correct and neither version disputes his summary execution on 31 October 1922. He was twenty-three years old when he was laid to rest in St James' Cemetery, Ballyheigue.

The spot where his bullet-riddled body was found at the entrance to the cemetery is marked by a large Celtic cross.

---

1   Information from Seán Seosamh Ó Concubhair, local historian.

Timothy 'Aero' Lyons

Tadg Ó Liatáin

Timothy Lyons, the oldest of six siblings, was born in Garrynagore, between Lixnaw and Abbeydorney, on 7 December 1895. Before his involvement with the struggle for freedom he worked as a labourer. During the Tan War he and his and neighbour, Timmy Egan, were dedicated and active Volunteers in parishes to the north of Tralee. His exploits earned him the nickname 'Aeroplane' or 'Aero' as he had a reputation of being able to appear suddenly anywhere and to escape with ease from the tightest of situations. His home was frequently raided by the Tans and he would leave it to the last moment to escape, so much so that his father is reputed to have eventually asked him to leave as the house would be burned by the crown forces if they caught sight of him fleeing from it. Such was his bravery and perhaps recklessness that in his short life 'on the run' he achieved almost legendary status among the people of North Kerry.[1]

Courtesy of Mercier Archive.

A noted marksman, Lyons was present at the Shannow Bridge ambush in June 1921 when a column under Captain George O'Shea attempted to ambush a party of Auxiliaries and Tans. The crown forces were expected to come from Tralee to investigate the destruction by the IRA of the Shannow Bridge, which was on the main road a mile north-east of Abbeydorney. The column's plans were foiled by the unexpected early arrival of the crown forces and it was soon in danger of being encircled. However, the tide of the engagement changed when Lyons shot the Auxiliary officer who was in command, forcing the British to retreat.

On the outbreak of the Civil War, Lyons participated in the IRA capture of Listowel and later was present at the battle for Limerick, which saw Free

---

1   Information from James 'Sonny' Egan of Garrynagore.

State forces take the city after several days of fierce fighting. In the autumn he was captured near Athea and imprisoned in Limerick Gaol. He gained his freedom in November 1922, probably by taking another man's identity and walking out of the prison. Lyons then went on foot to Kerry, arriving in Knocknagoshel the next day. There he stayed for several days and was given a rifle by Séamus O'Connor before he set off to walk to Garrynagore.[2] He then returned to active service in his own native area. A natural leader of men, he commanded the column from the 2nd Battalion which was eventually trapped at the Clashmealcon Caves on 16 April. After a three-day siege he agreed to surrender his unit; he expected no mercy for himself but he hoped that his fellow fighters would not be executed. However, such was the hatred that the Free State forces had for him that he was killed following his capture. As he was being brought up the cliff face at Clashmealcon on a rope lowered by the soldiers at the ledge, it was cut as he was almost at the top and he fell to the rocky shore below.[3] If he did not die immediately from the fall, the Free State soldiers were determined to show no mercy and his body was riddled with bullets fired by the troops who lined the cliff edge. This was despite the pleading of Father Cahill of Causeway, who had attempted to negotiate an end to the siege.[4]

Lyons' lifeless body was swept out to sea on 18 April 1923. A week later, his comrades from the Clashmealcon siege, Reg Hathaway, Jim McEnery and Ned Greaney, were executed in Ballymullen Gaol. Two other Volunteers drowned as they attempted to escape from the caves and the sea was never to yield up the remains of Patrick O'Shea or Tom McGrath.

On 5 May 1923 the remains of Aero Lyons were washed ashore. They were badly decomposed and had only one leg, having been immersed in the water for three weeks. The body was identified by his boot – his cobbler from Kilflynn, Tomeen Kenny, confirmed that it was one that he had made for Lyons. The remains were removed to his home in Garrynagore and subsequently were buried in the Republican Plot in Kilflynn Cemetery. He lies there with George

2   Séamus O'Connor, *Tomorrow Was Another Day* (1970).
3   Information from local sources, who tell how the soldiers boasted of the fact that they had cut the rope. The names of the soldiers responsible are known.
4   Cecilia Lynch, *From the GPO to Clashmealcon Caves* (2003).

O'Shea and Tim Tuomey, and over their grave a large cross was erected in 1924. Today Tim 'Aero' Lyons is also remembered on monuments in Ballyduff, Clashmealcon and Ballyseedy, and by a plaque on the house where he was born at Garrynagore.

WILLIAM MCCARTHY

Liam Mac Carταιg

Courtesy of Mercier Archive.

William 'Sonny' McCarthy was a native of Lixnaw. He worked with the Kerry Farmers' Union and in this role travelled widely throughout North Kerry. He was educated at St Michael's School and later in St Kieran's College in Kilkenny. In 1918 he joined the Irish Volunteers and served as an intelligence officer with the 3rd Battalion, Kerry No. 1 Brigade, which was centred around his native village.

On Easter Saturday 1921 he came from Lixnaw to Tralee, where he delivered some intelligence dispatches. Tadhg Kennedy, who was the intelligence officer for Kerry No. 1 Brigade, recalls in his memoir that he received information from an RIC man named Costello that McCarthy would be shot if he was captured. Kennedy located McCarthy at Lawlor's Railway Hotel and alerted him to the danger. With this in mind, rather than returning to Lixnaw by train as he had planned, he decided to journey by horse and trap to relatives in Ardfert instead. However, he stayed to go to confession in the town's Dominican church and when he returned to the hotel he was apprehended by the RIC. He was brought to Tralee RIC Barracks for interrogation. Local lore suggests that he was initially brought to a nearby public house where an attempt was made to entice him to divulge information, but failing in this his captors then brought him back to the barracks where he was beaten. He was then to be transferred to the gaol at Ballymullen. His captors brought him down past the Dominican church and into what is now the town park, which at that time was enclosed by high walls. There he was shot dead by his RIC escort and his bullet-riddled body was left on the spot where his memorial cross now stands. It would appear that the shooting of McCarthy by the RIC occurred at 9.30 p.m., as a patrol of Auxiliaries on nearby Denny Street thought they were under fire when they heard the shots that killed him. As a result they sent up flares and began shooting randomly, some of the shots hitting the roof of the nearby St John's church where an Easter religious ceremony was taking place.[1]

Willie McCarthy's body was found where he had been killed the following day. His coffin was draped in the Tricolour and an IRA Volunteer named John O'Sullivan accompanied it to the railway station where it was placed on a train to Lixnaw. The RIC demanded that O'Sullivan remove the flag, but this he refused to do and was subsequently arrested. O'Sullivan was brought to the Auxiliaries' barracks where he was questioned but then released. His interrogator, the notorious Major John McKinnon, asked O'Sullivan to tell his fellow Republicans that it was not the Auxiliaries who had murdered Willie McCarthy.[2]

William 'Sonny' McCarthy was buried in Kiltomey Cemetery, Lixnaw. At the time of his death, on 24 March 1921, he was two days short of his twenty-sixth birthday. In Tralee's town park a memorial cross now stands to his memory. It was unveiled by General Tom Barry in 1949.[3]

1   Tadhg Kennedy, BMH WS 1413.
2   Patrick Garvey, BMH WS 1011.
3   *The Kerryman*, 7 May 1949.

Jim McEnery

Séamus Mac Inneirí

Courtesy of the Martin Moore collection.

Captain James (Jim) McEnery commanded the Clashmealcon Company of the 3rd Battalion, Kerry No. 1 Brigade. He was a native of Slieveadara where he had a farm and was married with an infant son, Henry. McEnery was on active service during the Tan War and took the Republican side in the Civil War. Following the surrender of Michael Pierce's column in February 1923 and the local amnesty given to men under his command, McEnery remained in arms in his native area and continued to fight for the Republic against hopeless odds in the Causeway and Ballyduff districts.

On Sunday 15 April 1923 a Free State raiding party was attacked by Aero Lyons' column in the area of Meenoghane, on the cliff-lined coast to the north of Causeway village. Having secured reinforcements, later that day Free State troops arrived in force at Slieveadara and arrested Jim McEnery at his home on suspicion of involvement in the fighting at nearby Meenoghane. However, a short time later, McEnery escaped from his captors and made his way to Clashmealcon, where he met up with Aero Lyons and his column who had retired there after the day's fighting further to the north. They had planned to seek shelter for the night in Dunworth's Cave, the largest of the Clashmealcon Caves, as they expected Free State forces to saturate the area that evening and to carry out reprisals. Before Jim McEnery, Aero Lyons and the other members of the column went to the cave, they were met by Catherine McEnery, Jim's sister. Expecting only an overnight stay in the cave, the men took no provisions with them.

After a three-day siege at Clashmealcon, the surviving men surrendered. As their leader, Aero Lyons, was being hauled up the cliff face, the rope he was holding was cut and he fell to his death below. His body was riddled with bullets as it lay on the rocky shore. Initially the remaining four men trapped in the cave refused to come out. However, Fr John Cahill, the Causeway parish priest, was on the cliff top and he prevented further killings of the men who had agreed to surrender. As a result, Jim McEnery was next to be brought up using a rope. He and his three remaining comrades were then marched to the Harrington house which still stands approximately 200 yards from the shore. There McEnery met his wife and son for the last time before being brought to Ballymullen Barracks by Colonel James Hancock.

Captain Jim McEnery, Reg Hathaway and Ned Greaney, three of the survivors of the siege, were brought before a military tribunal on 18 April and charged with various offences, including being 'in armed opposition to the government'. The Free State Army made a claim that these men were forced to join Lyons' column by Humphrey Murphy, O/C of Kerry No. 1 Brigade, having been threatened that they would be shot by the IRA if they did not do so. However, General Paddy Daly provided no evidence to support this assertion. This was seen as an attempt by Daly to discredit the Volunteers of the IRA who remained defiant despite the hopelessness of their military situation. The three men were sentenced to death by firing squad.[1]

The decision to execute the three men was seen as being very harsh. As three Republican soldiers had already died at Clashmealcon, further deaths did not seem warranted. Additionally, at this stage the Civil War was almost over and there was no effective organised resistance remaining in North Kerry. In the case of Jim McEnery, he was a married man with a young child. His brother Thomas, who was a priest in Bradford, England, rushed home in an attempt to intercede with General Daly. However, Daly refused to meet him and told him that if he did not desist he too would be arrested and charged with being an accomplice.

James McEnery, Reg Hathaway and Ned Greaney were executed at 8 a.m. on 25 April 1923 by a firing squad composed of former British soldiers who were serving in the Free State Army. Adopting the practice of the British in the Tan War, the bodies of the executed men were not released to their relatives

---

1   Cecilia Lynch, *From the GPO to Clashmealcon Caves* (2003), p. 15.

but were buried at Ballymullen Barracks. Several months after the conflict had ended the McEnery family requested that the remains be transferred to them so that McEnery could be given a dignified burial in consecrated ground. The Free State government refused.

However, following the intervention of a local cleric, the remains of Captain Jim McEnery and the six other men executed in Ballymullen were disinterred on 28 October 1924 and released to their families. McEnery, Ned Greaney, Reg Hathaway and James Hanlon were buried in the Republican plot in Rathela Cemetery, Ballyduff, four days later. A monument was erected over the grave and was unveiled by Seán MacBride on 13 September 1931. They are also commemorated on the memorials in Ballyduff village, at Ballymullen Gaol and at Ballyseedy.

Tom McGrath

Tomás Mac Craith[1]

Thomas McGrath was born in Clashmealcon, near Causeway, in 1904, where his father had a farm. As a Volunteer he was attached to the 3rd Battalion of the Kerry No. 1 Brigade, as was his older brother Jim. Both men remained loyal to the Republican cause to the bitter last days of the Civil War. Their small column operated under the command of Aero Lyons in the Causeway and Ballyduff districts. From their base in Ballymullen Barracks in Tralee large columns of Free State soldiers scoured the countryside in search of these diehard Republican Volunteers.

On Sunday 15 April 1923 a detachment of Free State soldiers were engaged in a gun battle lasting several hours at Meenoghane, a townland on the coast three miles north of Causeway village. The Republican column, which consisted of nine men, evaded capture and forced the Free State Army to send to Tralee for reinforcements. A detachment of soldiers under the command of Michael Hogan returned to Tralee, taking with them Jim McGrath, whom they had arrested on his way to mass in Causeway. Hogan had a brutal reputation and had killed Jack Galvin, a prisoner with a broken arm, at Ballyseedy the previous September. Jim McGrath was taken to Ballymullen Barracks where he was tortured for information about Aero Lyons' column. Local lore says that he was made to dig his own grave at Ardfert where Hogan's column stopped on their journey back to Tralee. As a result of this maltreatment, McGrath told his interrogators that the IRA used the caves at Clashmealcon as a refuge, totally unaware that on that particular night, Lyons and his men had decided to sleep in Dunworth's Cave, named for a Fenian who had hidden there in a previous fight for freedom. Three of the column, Seán Fuller, Paddy Healy and Michael O'Shea, risked making their way to a dance in Ballybunion that evening rather than spend the night in the expected safety of the Clashmealcon Caves with the other six men of the small column.[2] Little did Jim McGrath realise that his

---

1 There is no known photograph of Tom McGrath.
2 Information from Ann Deenihan, daughter of Michael O'Shea and niece of Pat O'Shea.

own brother and his comrades in Lyons' column would meet their doom as a result of the information that was extracted from him.

On Monday morning, 16 April 1923, a large force of Free State troops arrived at Clashmealcon along with their battered captive, Jim McGrath. With McGrath, some Free State soldiers descended the cliff face and found the IRA Volunteers in the cave, whereupon a gunfight developed. Two Free State soldiers were fatally wounded attempting to dislodge the Republican fighters from the rocks which guarded the entrance of the deep cavern. As the soldiers retreated, Jim McGrath was left behind and joined his comrades inside the cave.

The night of 17 April was dark and windy. The Free State searchlights on the cliff edge above were shot out by the marksmanship of Aero Lyons. This allowed the column to move along the cliff base under the cover of darkness to another cave. Tom McGrath and Patrick O'Shea volunteered to go further along the rocky shore where there was no pathway, only sheer cliff face, in an attempt to find an escape route. However, in the stormy conditions, as both men attempted to swim around the rocky headland at the northern end of the cliff-lined inlet, they were swept out to sea and drowned. Their bodies were never recovered. Tom McGrath and Patrick O'Shea were first cousins.[3]

While Reg Hathaway, Ned Greaney and Jim McEnery were executed at Ballymullen Barracks, Jim McGrath was not charged with a capital offence before the same military tribunal. He survived a brief incarceration but was never to recover psychologically from his horrific torture in Ballymullen Barracks. He returned to live on his small farm in Clashmealcon, just a quarter of a mile from where his brother lost his life. Although he lived until 1972, he never walked down the little roadway to the cliff's edge where his comrades met their fate.[4] In recent years a plaque was erected by local Republicans on the old McGrath home at Clashmealcon to commemorate Tom and Jim McGrath.

3   Cecilia Lynch, *From the GPO to Clashmealcon Caves* (2003), p. 23.
4   Information from Tom Harrington, Clashmealcon.

Michael McGuire

Mıċeál Mac Uıḋıɼ

Following an attack on Fenit Barracks in June 1920, the RIC abandoned their base in Ardfert village. The family of the local sergeant continued to live in the building but the 2nd Battalion O/C, Tom Clifford, ordered that the building be burned. The local company, under their captain Patrick Sheehan, undertook the task. They obtained the fuel to set fire to the large building from Michael McGuire, a Volunteer who had a shop in the village.[1]

Courtesy of the Martin Moore collection.

Following the death of Terence MacSwiney on hunger strike, a general order was issued by the IRA's GHQ to attack the crown forces wherever they could be engaged. While the order was poorly implemented in much of the country, in Kerry the IRA went on the offensive. As a result the number of attacks on the RIC in the county increased considerably in the first two weeks of November and the police suffered a large number of casualties. As part of this offensive, Tom Clifford planned an attack on an RIC patrol which was due to travel its regular route between the villages of Fenit and The Spa. The Ardfert Company was ordered to gather in the village and from there to march to The Spa. About forty Volunteers from the 2nd Battalion, including Clifford, had assembled in Ardfert, where it was thought the destruction of the RIC station would have ensured the relative safety of the gathering attack party.

However, as the Ardfert Company captain, Patrick Sheehan, later recalled, fourteen lorries of Tans arrived suddenly in the village that morning and the Tans quickly began shooting. The Volunteers who had been gathering for

---

1 The name is also spelled Maguire.

the attack hastily retreated through the fields, though one, Tom Healy, was wounded. A fifteen-year-old girl named Sarah O'Connell, who was holding a child in her arms, was shot dead by the marauding Tans, some of whom were drunk. As the Tans entered the village Michael McGuire ran to take shelter in the Church of Ireland church, but was pursued and brought back to his shop.[2] McGuire, James McCrohan, Philip Healy and six others were arrested that day. McGuire was separated from the others and brought to Causeway RIC Barracks, some eight miles away.[3]

However, McGuire had not actually been part of the group that was gathering to attack the RIC patrol in Ardfert. Earlier that day, 5 November, Michael Pierce, the battalion active service unit commander, and Causeway Company Captain Paddy O'Connor had planned an attack on the Causeway Barracks. Michael McGuire was part of Pierce's unit in Causeway that day. The plan failed when the IRA was observed by a former RIC sergeant who had noticed suspicious activity in a house where Pierce and O'Connor lay in wait and reported this to the local RIC. With military reinforcements arriving, the Volunteers at Causeway were forced into a hasty retreat under British gunfire. Pierce recalls that only one of his Volunteers, Michael McGuire, was captured and this happened in Ardfert when he had returned home from the earlier attack in Causeway.[4] McGuire was then brought as a prisoner from Ardfert to the RIC barracks in Causeway where he was interrogated about his activities.

The McGuire family had a shop in the centre of Ardfert village – it was there that Michael McGuire was born in 1876. This shop was the only place in Ardfert where petrol could be bought and it is probable that the RIC suspected him of supplying the fuel used in the burning of Ardfert RIC Barracks the previous June. Later that evening McGuire was shot dead while in custody. His body was found the next day in the Fair Field which lies behind what was formerly the RIC barracks in Causeway. He had died of multiple gunshot wounds and he also had injuries caused by bayonets. Forty-five-year-old Michael McGuire was buried the family plot that lies in the grounds of Ardfert's parish church. He was survived by his wife and six young children.

2 *Irish Independent*, 11 November 1920.
3 Patrick Sheehan, BMH WS 1088.
4 Michael Pierce, BMH WS 1190.

Michael Nolan

Mícéál Ó Nualláin[1]

Michael Nolan was born on 2 August 1895 in Kilmoyley, between the villages of Ardfert and Causeway. His father was a farmer and Michael was a Volunteer in the local company where he held the rank of first lieutenant. His company was attached to the 2nd Battalion, Kerry No. 1 Brigade. He was a prominent hurler and was secretary of the local Kilmoyley Hurling Club.

On Tuesday 11 May 1920 Dan Donnelly, who had a public house in Causeway village, was summonsed to appear before the petty magistrates court in that village for an offence relating to the licensing laws. Donnelly was a Republican sympathiser and it would seem that his premises was frequently used by the local IRA Volunteers as a meeting place. As a result they were concerned that the court case would result in Donnelly losing his licence. The presiding magistrate in the court case was E. M. P. Wynne, who travelled from Tralee with his driver in a horse-drawn trap. Edward Melville Philip Wynne, a sixty-two-year-old Englishman, had been an officer in the British Army and had served in the Boer War twenty years previously. He had also been a district inspector of the RIC before being appointed a resident magistrate in Kerry.

Mike Nolan and his comrades had planned to surprise Wynne on his journey from Tralee in an attempt to influence the outcome of the Donnelly case at the Causeway court session later that morning. According to other men involved, they had not planned to kill the magistrate, but it is probable that their aim was either to abduct him or intimidate him into giving a favourable decision. That morning Mike Nolan and about six other Volunteers waited for the approach of Wynne inside the ditch at McGrath's of Knockbrack on the Ardfert to Causeway road. On the arrival of Wynne and his driver, Dan Breen, Mike Nolan, armed with a shotgun, jumped onto the road. This forced the horse-drawn sidecar to a halt and the remaining masked Volunteers jumped over the fence and onto the road. This probably distracted Nolan and seizing

---

1   There is no known photograph of Michael Nolan.

this opportunity, Wynne produced his pistol and shot Nolan dead. Several other shots were fired, but there were no further injuries and Wynne and his driver escaped to Causeway. Mike Nolan's comrades, including his brother Maurice, took his lifeless body from the road and across the fields. Within about ten minutes an RIC vehicle passed the scene of the shooting but the attackers had left the area. The police had been in the district to inform the Brick family of Lerrig that their son, William Brick, a constable in Timoleague, West Cork, had been shot dead the previous day. Having reached the courthouse in Causeway, Wynne, shaken but uninjured, quickly concluded the court business and returned to Tralee in the RIC vehicle.[2]

A coffin was made by a local carpenter, Tadhg Meehan, and the remains of Mike Nolan were temporarily buried in a shallow grave in a newly ploughed field in the townland of Togherbane. Within a few days, his comrades returned under the cover of darkness to bring the remains to the old cemetery at Ballyheigue and there they placed it in a tomb, wrongly believing it to be the family tomb of Mike Nolan's mother, Hanoria McCormick. Realising their error, they returned several nights later and placed his coffin in its final resting place with the McCormick family.[3]

At the next sitting of the petty courts at Tralee, Mr Wynne declared that he was truly sorry for the death that had occurred on his way to Causeway and expressed his condolences to the dead man's relatives and friends. However, fearing for his safety, the magistrate left the county shortly afterwards. Never again would a British court enforce the rules of the crown in Causeway village, the last session having been held on Tuesday 11 May 1920, the morning of Lieutenant Mike Nolan's death.

2   Seán Seosamh Ó Conchubhair, *Kilmoyley to the Rescue* (2000), p. 31.
3   Information from Seán Seosamh Ó Conchubhair.

Daniel O'Driscoll

Domhnall Ó hEidirsceoil[1]

Daniel O'Driscoll was the son of a stonemason and lived in East Commons, Ardfert. On the evening of Saturday 9 April 1921 he was in the company of other young men at the small bridge at Liscahane, a mile and a half from Ardfert on the Tralee road. The police later claimed that the youths were 'digging trenches and blowing up bridges at Liscahane' though local sources contradict this report. In any event, three military vehicles containing Auxiliaries approached unexpectedly from the direction of Tralee. The youths ran from the scene, fearing what would happen if they were apprehended, as at this stage of the conflict the Auxiliary Division of the RIC had gained a notorious reputation. Sixteen-year-old Daniel O'Driscoll was shot in the abdomen and grievously wounded. He was placed in a lorry and brought to the Ardfert dispensary where he was treated by Dr Lawlor. However, he died of his wounds within a short time. His friend, John O'Sullivan, who was a year younger, was also injured in the gunfire. O'Sullivan received three bullet wounds to his right arm and two in his side, but managed to escape through the fields. While the Auxiliaries later reported that they had been fired on and that one of their men was injured in the incident, there was no evidence to support this version as there were no armed Volunteers in the vicinity at the time.[2]

Daniel O'Driscoll, despite his young age, was noted to be an IRA Volunteer and his name is inscribed on the Kerry No. 1 Brigade roll of honour at the Ballyseedy monument. The IRA report into his death, which was compiled in 1925, states that he was killed 'while scouting'.[3] A white roadside cross marks the spot where he died at Liscahane.

On Sunday 12 August 1934 a memorial was unveiled in Ardfert village by IRA veteran Seán Ryan. It was erected to the memory of Daniel O'Driscoll

1   There is no known photograph of Daniel O'Driscoll.
2   *The Kerryman*, 16 April 1921.
3   Con Casey papers, Kerry County Library Archives.

and the other Volunteers from the Ardfert district who fell in the cause of Irish freedom.

George O'Shea

Seoirse Ó Seaġḋa[1]

George O'Shea was born in 1897 and was a native of Fahavane, Kilflynn, six miles north of Tralee. He was appointed captain of the Kilflynn Company, 2nd Battalion, Kerry No. 1 Brigade, during the reorganisation of the Irish Volunteers that took place in 1917. He retained this position throughout the Tan and Civil Wars. His lieutenant was Stephen Fuller, who six years later accompanied him as a fellow prisoner on the fateful journey from Ballymullen Barracks to Ballyseedy Cross on 7 March 1923.

O'Shea's unit were very active during the Tan War. On 31 October 1920 he led the Kilflynn Company during an attack on the RIC in Abbeydorney in which two constables were shot dead. Probably the most notable engagement he took part in was at Shannow Bridge in June 1921, where men under his command ambushed an Auxiliary detachment. The Auxies had come from Tralee to investigate the destruction of the bridge, which was a mile outside Abbeydorney, by the members of the Abbeydorney and Kilflynn companies. The Volunteers were almost outflanked by the sudden arrival of the enemy but following a fierce gun battle along the little Shannow river, O'Shea managed to drive the Auxiliaries from the scene, leaving one of their officers gravely wounded. As well as his military role, George O'Shea also played a role in the civil administration of the county, having been elected to the Rural District Council for the Kilflynn area in June 1920.

George O'Shea and his men remained loyal to the Republican cause during the Civil War. While Michael Pierce and Tom O'Driscoll surrendered their large columns to General Paddy Daly in February 1923, George O'Shea and his small force continued actively resisting the enemy despite the overwhelming odds which they faced.

However, O'Shea, Stephen Fuller, John Shanahan and Tim Tuomey were captured in a dugout near Kilflynn in the last week of February 1923. This

---

1 The surviving image of George O'Shea was not of sufficient quality to reproduce.

well-constructed shelter was built under a ditch at Loughnane's quarry and was large enough to accommodate the four men who were all over six feet tall. They were initially brought to Lixnaw and from there to Ballymullen Barracks. Fuller later described how they were tortured by David Neligan's intelligence section at Ballymullen. Subsequently the prisoners were brought to the other Free State barracks in Tralee, at the workhouse, now the County Council offices at Manor. There, all four Kilflynn men were brought before a military tribunal and found guilty of bearing arms against the Free State. Though they were not informed of their sentence, being convicted of this crime carried a sentence of execution by firing squad.

However, Colonel David Neligan, the Free State's intelligence chief in Tralee, ensured that three of the men would not face their death in Tralee Gaol, but on the roadside at Ballyseedy. O'Shea, Fuller and Tuomey were among the nine men who were tied around a mine constructed by Captains Ed Flood and Jim Clarke, senior members of the Dublin Guard. Stephen Fuller, the sole survivor of the massacre, recalled George O'Shea's last words as 'Goodbye lads', as the soldiers backed away from the mine to a site at a safe distance, from where Captain Ned Breslin detonated the shrapnel-filled landmine. However, the explosion alone did not kill the prisoners and as smoke enveloped the scene, machine-gun fire was directed at the wounded and dying until all were dead except for Stephen Fuller, who miraculously escaped the fate of this comrades.

Later that day, General Paddy Daly released the coffins of those his troops had killed. Captain George O'Shea's family brought his remains to Kilflynn, where they are interred in the Republican Plot in the village's old churchyard together with those of Tim Tuomey. Later that spring the remains of another veteran of the fight at Shannow Bridge, Aero Lyons, would also be laid to rest in Kilflynn's Republican Plot and nearby is the grave of Volunteer Thomas Archer, who was killed in the Tan War.

PATRICK O'SHEA

Pádraig Ó Séaġda[1]

Patrick O'Shea was the son of a farmer and was born in the townland of Ballinbranhig near Causeway in 1902. Both he and his younger brother Michael were members of the 2nd Battalion, Kerry No. 1 Brigade. By the end of February 1923 the two battalion columns under the commands of Michael Pierce and Tom O'Driscoll had surrendered as Republican resistance was slowly ground down by the Free State Army. Only one column remained in the field against overwhelming odds and this was led by Timothy 'Aero' Lyons. Both Patrick and Michael O'Shea were members of this unit, as was their first cousin Tom McGrath.

On Sunday 15 April 1923 a detachment of the Free State Army's 1st Western Division based in Tralee was searching for Aero Lyons' column, which was known to be active in the Ballyheigue and Causeway areas. At Meenoghane a prolonged engagement ensued as the Republican column attacked their pursuers. As evening fell the Free State forces returned to Tralee taking one prisoner with them. This man was Jim McGrath of Clashmealcon and he was apprehended as he made his way to mass that morning. In Ballymullen Barracks, McGrath was subjected to a brutal interrogation and revealed to his torturers that the IRA unit in his area had a billet in the large cave at Clashmealcon.

Meanwhile, with the enemy having left the Meenoghane area, Lyons led his nine-man column from the scene. Three men – Michael O'Shea, Seán Fuller and Paddy Healy – decided to go Ballybunion to attend a dance that night, though Lyons warned them of the danger of capture. The trio headed north, crossed the Cashen river by boat and spent the evening in Ballybunion. While Mike O'Shea travelled northwards, his older brother Pat went with Lyons and the other four members of the column to spend the night in the relative safety of Dunworth's Cave.[2] The very large cave was at the base of high cliffs and was

---

1   There is no known photograph of Patrick O'Shea.
2   Information from Margaret O'Shea Deenihan, daughter of Michael O'Shea and niece of Pat O'Shea.

accessed by a narrow pathway which has now eroded. While safe from sudden attack, the cave was uncomfortable and the rats that inhabited the shoreline ensured a sentry would be needed to ward off the rodents. Expecting to spend only a night in the secluded cave, the men brought no provisions with them as they descended the steep rocky path into the cliff-lined inlet.[3]

The arrival of a large force of Free State soldiers at Clashmealcon took the men by surprise. Four inexperienced soldiers and their captive, Jim McGrath, descended down the cliff face to the mouth of Dunworth's Cave. The opening of the cave had a natural wall of rock that the sea had broken from the roof and as the troops advanced towards this natural barricade, a fierce firefight developed. Private James O'Neill was killed instantly and Lieutenant Henry Pierson was seriously injured. Jim McGrath took cover amidst the boulders and the two remaining Free State soldiers escaped. In time, all three surviving soldiers were hauled up the 100-foot high cliff on ropes. Lieutenant Pierson died of his wounds in Tralee despite medical treatment. Under the cover of darkness, Jim McGrath made his way into the cave to join his brother and the five other IRA Volunteers. O'Neill's body was recovered by his comrades under the cover of a Red Cross flag.

For the remainder of that day, Monday 16 April, the soldiers above attempted to dislodge the Republicans from the cave. They lowered burning bales of hay in an attempt to smoke the men out, but to no avail and the constant gunfire was also ineffective. As evening fell large lights were beamed onto the mouth of the cave, but Aero Lyons, a noted marksman, shot them out with his Lee Enfield rifle. Towards midnight the tide ebbed and in the darkness the Republicans made their way along the base of the cliff to another cave. Though the sea was rough, Pat O'Shea and Tom McGrath volunteered to swim out around the eastern edge of the U-shaped sea inlet. If they could manage to swim around the rocks that guarded the left flank of the little bay, they would be free to escape by foot along the bottom of the cliff face unseen by the enemy above. Tired from the two days of constant gunfire and without food to eat or water to drink all the previous day, the pair set out to swim in what was a rough sea. The swell of the tide and the fierce currents on the rocky shore proved too

---

3   Information from Tom Harrington, Clashmealcon.

much and both Pat O'Shea and Tom McGrath drowned in their vain attempt to swim to freedom in the early hours of Tuesday morning. There would be no escape for their comrades who remained behind and who would surrender some thirty hours later, thus ending the siege of the Clashmealcon Caves.

The bodies of Patrick O'Shea and Tom McGrath were never yielded up by the unforgiving seas that batter the North Kerry coast. Today they are remembered on the monuments that stand on the cliffs at Clashmealcon and at Ballyduff village. Pat O'Shea's brother Michael survived because he went to Ballybunion that Sunday night. To this day his Lee Enfield rifle survives, engraved with the initials of the men who fought in Clashmealcon in what was to be the last stand of the Irish Republic in Kerry.

Tim Tuomey

Tadg Ó Tuama

Courtesy of Mercier Archive.

Tim Tuomey was born in Kilflynn in the townland of Gortclohy in 1902.[1] He was a Volunteer with the Kilflynn Company of the 2nd Battalion, Kerry No. 1 Brigade. On 21 February 1923 he, together with Captain George O'Shea, Stephen Fuller and John Shanahan, were captured in a dugout near Kilflynn. All four were armed when taken into custody and were initially taken to the Free State Army post in Lixnaw. From there the four Kilflynn men were brought to the Workhouse Barracks, located on the site of what is now Tralee's County Council building. There they were brutally interrogated regarding IRA activities in the North Kerry area. The intelligence section of the Kerry Command of the Free State Army under the leadership of David Neligan respected no boundaries when extracting information from their captives. Shanahan was so badly beaten that he received a serious injury to his back and was unable to stand as a result. While in the barracks, they faced a military tribunal for being caught with arms and were found guilty. Niall Harrington, who later wrote a thoroughly researched account of his Civil War experience in Kerry, was an officer in the court martial. Tim Tuomey was sentenced to be detained for the duration of the conflict.

On 6 March 1923 Harrington was walking into the Workhouse Barracks in Tralee when he noticed Tuomey in the guardroom adjacent to the main door, though why he and other prisoners were waiting there only became obvious later. Tim Tuomey was recognisable due to his distinctive hair. Later that day these prisoners were brought to Ballymullen Barracks.[2]

Tim Tuomey, George O'Shea and Stephen Fuller were chosen by Colonel

1 The surname is now more commonly spelled Twomey.
2 Information given by Niall Harrington to Dan King, Tralee.

Neligan to be among nine prisoners to be taken to Ballyseedy Cross on the night of 6 March 1923. Local lore suggests that John Shanahan was to have been the tenth prisoner to be brought by Captain Breslin to Ballyseedy Cross but his injuries prevented him from being put on board the lorry that day. Tim Tuomey, George O'Shea and Stephen Fuller were taken with six others from Ballymullen Barracks to be tied to the mine in the early hours of 7 March.

When Captain Breslin brought the bodies back to Ballymullen from Ballyseedy, Niall Harrington was surprised to see Tuomey among the victims. That afternoon the Free State Army released the remains of Tuomey and his comrades in hastily constructed coffins to their relatives at the gates of Ballymullen Barracks. As the procession of coffins left the barracks the army band was playing ragtime music in a mockery of the grief of those waiting outside. The relatives opened the flimsy coffins and placed the victims in proper caskets, throwing the discarded wood in the marshy land where the Ballymullen roundabout now stands.[3]

The remains of Tim Tuomey were brought to Kilflynn Churchyard, where he is buried alongside his comrades George O'Shea and 'Aero' Lyons, who was to die at the Clashmealcon Caves the next month. A year later a large Celtic cross was erected over the grave of the three men. This was damaged by a storm in 1995 but was repaired by local people committed to remembering the sacrifice of Tim Tuomey and his comrades.

---

3   Ernie O'Malley, *The Men will Talk to Me – Kerry Interviews* (2012), interview with Bill Bailey, a Free State soldier at Ballymullen Barracks.

4TH (CASTLEGREGORY) AND 5TH (DINGLE) BATTALIONS, KERRY NO. 1 BRIGADE

Following the reorganisation of the Irish Volunteers that took place in January 1919, the Volunteer units in the Dingle Peninsula were assigned to two battalions. The 3rd Battalion was based around the only centre of population on the northern side of the peninsula, Castlegregory, and it was commanded by Tadhg Brosnan. The 2nd Battalion area extended from Dún Chaoin in the west along the south of the peninsula to Inch and included Dingle town, Ballyferriter, Lispole and Annascaul. The Dingle Battalion was initially commanded by the Irish language enthusiast and Gaelic scholar Pádraig Ó Siochfrada. Following a further reorganisation of the Kerry No. 1 Brigade's battalions during the Tan War, the Castlegregory Battalion was re-designated the 4th Battalion and the Dingle Battalion was called the 5th Battalion.

The 4th (Castlegregory) Battalion was composed of six companies. These were from Cloghane, Ballyduff, Aughacasla, Maharees, Camp and Castlegregory. It was commanded by Tadhg Brosnan, a blacksmith from Castlegregory.

The staff of the 5th Battalion was led by O/C Pádraig Ó Siochfrada, who was known by his nom de plume, An Seabhac. He was later replaced by Michael Moriarty. The battalion V/C was Jim Fitzgerald and its quartermaster was Maurice Keane. The 5th Battalion was composed of companies from Inch, Annascaul, Ballyferriter, Dingle, Milltown, Cuas, Ballydavid, Ventry and Lispole.

During the Black and Tan War, the fortunes of these two battalions varied considerably. Castlegregory became perhaps the most active battalion in the brigade, while the Dingle Battalion was perceived as being poorly led and relatively ineffectual. Dingle town had a significant garrison of RIC and Royal Marines and it proved difficult to attack this force in the prosperous town where there was a degree of hostility towards the Irish Volunteers. While an attempt was made to engage the RIC in Dingle in late October 1920, the Dingle, Milltown, Ventry and Ballyferriter companies were otherwise relatively inactive. The Lispole and Annascaul Volunteers on the other hand played significant roles in attacks in their native districts, where they acted in conjunction with Brosnan's unit.

In the Castlegregory Battalion district, the Volunteers managed to clear their area of crown forces early in the conflict. The RIC had barracks in Castlegregory, Cloghane and Camp. Camp Barracks was subjected to a sustained attack on 19 February 1920 and within three months the other two barracks were also abandoned. The coastguards had a presence in the district at the start of the conflict, but these were also withdrawn following an attack by Brosnan's unit. By the end of the Tan War the sole enemy garrison on the peninsula was in the town of Dingle.

Once cleared of enemy forces, the 4th Battalion became a centre of activity. A munitions factory for the brigade was established. The Kerry No. 1 Brigade staff regularly held meetings in the area with the North Kerry Battalion officers being brought in by boat from Fenit. The active men in the district took part in ambushes outside their area, including engagements at Annascaul (August 1920), Lispole (March 1921), Glenbeigh (April 1921) and Ballymacandy, Castlemaine (June 1921).

Following the divisions resulting from the signing of the Anglo-Irish Treaty, the 4th and 5th Battalions remained intact, with few defections to the newly formed Free State Army. Volunteers from West Kerry were involved in the Republican capture of Listowel in the early days of the Civil War and played a role in the fighting along the defensive line from Limerick to Waterford during July 1922. Following the defeat of Republican forces in Limerick and Tipperary, and with the landing of Free State troops in Fenit on 2 August 1922, the men under Brosnan's command returned to West Kerry and once again adopted the tactics of guerrilla fighters that had served them well during the fight with the British.

The Civil War in West Kerry was not marked by any major engagements as the scattered IRA units could only harry the numerically superior and better armed Free State forces. In March 1923 Tadhg Brosnan, Michael Duhig and Dan Rohan were captured near Castlegregory and so the backbone of resistance in the peninsula was broken. However, despite the hopelessness of their situation, a few scattered IRA units continued to be active until the end of the conflict in May 1923.

Following the cessation of hostilities, the large number of Republican captives would still have to endure the hardships of imprisonment and later a hunger strike. Prisoners began to be freed in December 1923, but it would be over six months later that the last Republicans would be released. Tadhg Brosnan and the men who stood by his side in the field of battle would not be welcome in the new Free State. Having driven the British from their native parishes in West Kerry, these Republican soldiers were forced to emigrate to foreign lands. By the end of 1924 many had followed Tadhg Brosnan to the cities of the United States, from where they would continue to support the Republican cause in their native land.

Thomas M. Ashe

Tomás M. Agás

Thomas M. Ashe was born in 1897 in Kinard East near Lispole, into a farming family with strong nationalist convictions. His namesake and first cousin would play a prominent role in the 1916 Rising when he defeated the crown forces in Ashbourne, County Meath, and would later die on hunger strike in 1917. However, Thomas M. Ashe, who was killed at the Lispole ambush, also played a significant role in the national struggle, but in his native parish.

Tom Ashe was appointed lieutenant in the Lispole Company of the Irish Volunteers which was attached to the 5th Battalion of the Kerry No. 1 Brigade. The Lispole Company had an active service unit composed of fifteen men who were constantly available at short notice. It was this Lispole unit that was present with Paddy Cahill's brigade flying column at the Lispole ambush.

Courtesy of the Martin Moore Collection.

The ambush party had been in position for three days before the British arrived outside Lispole village on 22 March 1921. A section of the Volunteers lay hidden behind a ditch on a small road which overlooks the main road. This small side road lies behind where the modern monument now stands. Another section occupied a now demolished schoolhouse along this small road, while others lay in wait at Keane's house on the south side of the road. A fourth section composed of riflemen was assigned to the now disused railway viaduct on the north of the main Tralee to Dingle road. Aware that an ambush had been prepared, the British convoy eventually arrived on the third day but stopped half a mile from the village on the Dingle side. The soldiers got out of their vehicles and spread out to the north and south of the ambush party. As they waited in their positions, Cahill's men were unaware that they were being outflanked. In the intense fighting that took place as the Volunteers tried to extract themselves, Tom Ashe was wounded in the abdomen. He was brought to the relative safety of a small gully adjacent to where the memorial now stands. However, the British soldiers continued to advance and soon the small party in the gully were trapped, the main section of the attack party having retreated to the east. The men who were now surrounded included Ashe's first cousin, Greg Ashe, and also Tadhg Brosnan, James Fitzgerald, Alf Fullerton, Michael Harrington, Tom Bawn Kennedy and Jack Griffin. Though this IRA party was now almost encircled in the small gulley, Brosnan shouted at the soldiers to surrender. Fearing that they themselves had been surrounded, the troops retreated, unaware of the hopeless position of the trapped men. Leaving their prisoners and some weapons behind, the soldiers quickly withdrew in the direction of their vehicles.[1]

Tom Ashe, with his abdominal wound, and Tommy Hawley, who had a gunshot injury to his head, were taken by their comrades to a nearby farmer's house and then transferred on a cart to the home of the O'Sullivan family at Acres, two miles to the south-west of Annascaul. There the men's wounds were attended to by the local doctor, Dr Kane, and Fr Lyne of Annascaul administered the last rites. The wounded men were left in the care of Cumann na mBan nurse Nancy Scully. At 1 a.m. the next morning, as those in the house were saying the rosary, Tom Ashe died of his wound. Hawley was to succumb to his head injury several weeks later.[2]

Lieutenant Tom Ashe's remains were secretly buried in Ballinacourty Graveyard near Annascaul. Nine months later, on 1 January 1922, they were reinterred in the Ashe family plot in Kinard Cemetery. Today a stone cross marks the scene at Lispole where Tom Ashe was fatally wounded on 22 March 1921.

1   BMH WS of James Fitzgerald, Dan Mulvihill, Patrick O'Neill, James Cronin, Thomas O'Connor and Michael O'Leary.
2   Ernie O'Malley, *The Men Will Talk to Me – Kerry Interviews* (2012), interview with Greg Ashe.

John Casey

Seán Ó Catharaigh

At the end of the nineteenth century, Castlegregory and its hinterland were not regarded as centres of discontent. The Land Wars of the 1880s and early 1890s convulsed the areas to the east and north of Tralee as young local men organised into groups known as Moonlighters and sought to right the wrongs inflicted by the landlord class on their people. These Moonlighters were driven by local grievances and a revolutionary spirit ignited by the Fenian movement of the previous decade. However in the Dingle Peninsula, especially in the areas of Castlegregory and Annascaul, the landlords were relatively benign and the crown forces in the guise of the RIC and Royal Navy found a receptive recruiting ground.

Courtesy of Mattias Ó Dubhda (enhanced by Stephen Kellaghan).

And so it was that John Casey of Castlegregory, and men like him, were to plough an unpopular furrow as they strove to keep the national spirit alive in Castlegregory at the beginning of the twentieth century. John Casey was born in 1864 and followed in his father's profession as a cooper in the village. On the formation of the Irish Volunteers in Castlegregory he enlisted, despite the fact that he was now a man in his late forties. During the division in the Volunteer movement in 1914, when John Redmond encouraged young Irishmen to fight in the British Army during the Great War, John Casey remained with Tadhg Brosnan and his small band of Irish Volunteers, as the planning towards the 1916 Rising secretly progressed.

In an act of defiance, on the Sunday following the defeat of the Easter Rising in Dublin, Tadhg Brosnan marched his Castlegregory Company of Volunteers through the village after mass although they were ordered to disperse by the RIC. This led to the arrest of Brosnan and six of his officers. Though hampered by their leader's imprisonment, the Castlegregory Company continued to gather in strength and by 1919 the men of what was now the 4th Battalion, Kerry No. 1 Brigade, were ready to bring the fight to the enemy. A younger generation of men now came to the fore, but John Casey, then in his mid-fifties, remained a Volunteer, though not on active service. His primary role within the Republican movement was that of secretary of the Castlegregory Sinn Féin Cumann.

Casey took the anti-Treaty side in the Civil War and he would pay for his Republican principles with his life. He was shot dead by Free State soldiers while standing at the half door of his home in Castlegregory on 17 November 1922.[1] He was buried in Killiney Cemetery near his native Castlegregory, where his gravestone notes that John Casey 'died for Ireland'.

When the monument to the Republican dead of the 4th Battalion was erected in 1934, his comrades inscribed on it the name of Volunteer John Casey, who had carried the flame of freedom in Castlegregory throughout his fifty-eight years.

1   Information from Mattias Ó Dubhda, Baile na Leacan, An Clochán.

James Cronin

Séamus Ó Cróinín[1]

Jimmy Cronin was born in 1900, one of sixteen children born to John and Margaret Cronin of Illaumcaum, a townland near Castlegregory where the Cronin family lived on a small farm. Jimmy worked on the family farm and, with his brothers Michael and Denis, was a Volunteer in the Aughacasla-based 'C' Company of the 4th Battalion, Kerry No. 1 Brigade.[2]

In February 1921 an elaborate ambush was planned by Tadhg Brosnan, O/C of the Castlegregory-based 4th Battalion. At this stage in the Tan War the crown forces held only one post in the Dingle Peninsula and that was in Dingle town. This was heavily fortified and the regular garrison was reinforced by Royal Marines. As a result, an assault on the town was not considered viable and so it was planned to lure the enemy into the mountainous terrain that surrounded the town.

A letter was written by a local woman to the O/C of the crown forces in Dingle, Captain Hamilton, informing him that a Sinn Féin court was to be held in Ballyduff, a townland to the north of the Conor Pass that links Dingle with the Castlegregory area. Acting on this information, on Saturday 19 February 1921 a large contingent of RIC men on bicycles headed through the pass, but finding no such illegal court was being held, they ventured further into the Castlegregory area. Brosnan and his men watched their quarry pass through the narrow defile, but waited for their return later during the short winter's evening to launch their attack. So as the RIC patrol was returning through the pass, the men of the 4th Battalion began a fierce assault. The RIC were forced from the road and had to scramble into the steep valley below. Suffering only minor wounds, the police eventually reached Dingle across rough mountain paths.[3]

The next day, Sunday, a large number of soldiers and RIC left Dingle in

---

1 There is no known photograph of James Cronin.
2 Information from Noreen Finn, Caher, Castlegregory, niece of James Cronin.
3 *Irish Independent*, 1 March 1921.

lorries to search the Castlegregory area, aware that it was in this district that the attackers were based. However, many of the roads were blocked to prevent their vehicles moving with speed. To the east of the village, they came across a freshly dug trench and saw several men escaping from the nearby strand. One of these men was Jimmy Cronin, and he and two other Volunteers, one named Denis Sugrue, were launching a currach from the beach in which to escape. While his comrades managed to get the boat afloat, Jimmy Cronin was shot dead as he stood on a large rock at the shore's edge.[4]

Volunteer Jimmy Cronin was twenty years old when he was killed and his remains were interred in the family grave in Killiney Cemetery just outside Castlegregory. The site of his death at the shore near Aughacasla is marked with a concrete cross which stands at the sandhills adjacent to the beach where he was shot. Today his sacrifice is also recalled on the Republican monument at Castlegregory and on the memorial to the Republican dead of West Kerry on The Mall in Dingle.

4   Information from Noreen Finn, Caher, Castlegregory, niece of James Cronin.

Maurice Fitzgerald

Muiris Mac Gearailt

Maurice Fitzgerald, a native of Minard West, Lispole, was born in 1894. His family had a small farm there on which Maurice worked. He was a Volunteer in the Lispole Company of the 5th (Dingle) Battalion of the Kerry No. 1 Brigade. This company was commanded by James Fitzgerald of Lispole, who was also V/C of the battalion. In February 1920 Fitzgerald organised a seventeen-man group who would be available at short notice and these men served as the Lispole active service unit. Maurice Fitzgerald was one of these Volunteers.

Courtesy of Breandán Ó Cíobháin.

On 20 March 1921 the flying column of the Kerry No. 1 Brigade, under the command of Paddy Cahill, moved into the small village of Lispole. Their objective was to attack a crown force convoy that would pass through the village on its way from Dingle to Tralee. While the brigade column contained about twenty men, it was supplemented by Volunteers of the local 5th Battalion companies from Lispole and Annascaul.[1] Maurice Fitzgerald was a Volunteer in the one of these local IRA units who played their part in the Lispole attack. The men attached to the column would have been armed with rifles, while the local Volunteers were often armed with inferior weapons.

The ambush site is today marked by a Celtic cross which stands on the roadside near the church. In a small sloping field behind this memorial stood an old schoolhouse that has long since been demolished. With a good view of the main road, this building was on the side of a smaller road that ran above and parallel to the main road. The IRA attack force was divided into several

---

1   Ernie O'Malley, *The Men Will Talk to Me – Kerry Interviews* (2012), interview with Greg Ashe.

sections. One section occupied the schoolhouse, while the main body of men lined the ditch on the side road looking down on the main road along which the military convoy was expected to travel. A third group of riflemen were sited in a house on the opposite side of the road, while another section was located at the railway viaduct and finally another section was located at the eastern approach to Lispole. The ambush party took their positions at 10 a.m. on Sunday 20 March 1921 but, as there was no sign of the military patrol, they retired at 6 p.m. to stay in local houses for the night. They waited in their ambush positions on the second day but again the enemy failed to travel along the road. The ambush party again retired to local houses with plans to return to their positions the next morning.[2]

Maurice Fitzgerald was one of a group that went to billet in the townland of Foheraghmore, which lay a short distance to the south-west of the ambush site. Some of these men were armed with shotguns which they had taken from local fowlers. They were unfamiliar with the weapons and there was an accidental discharge of one of the guns. The bullet struck and seriously injured Fitzgerald. He was nursed in the Brosnan family home in Foheraghmore but succumbed to his injuries the next day. His remains were removed from the Brosnan house under cover of darkness and brought over the hill to the old Aglish Graveyard, within sight of his family home. There his comrades placed his coffin in the Fitzgerald tomb in a ceremony that was of necessity held in secret.[3]

Today his name is recalled on the monument in Lispole which marks the site of the ambush and which was unveiled in 1962. His name is also inscribed on the West Kerry memorial on The Mall in Dingle.

2   James Fitzgerald, BMH WS 999; Michael O'Leary, BMH WS 1167 and Patrick O'Neill, BMH WS 1049.
3   Information from Breandán Ó Cíobháin, nephew of Maurice Fitzgerald.

Thomas Greaney

Tomás Ó Gráinne[1]

Thomas Greaney (or Greany) was born in Deelis near Camp on 23 May 1899. His parents, John Greaney and Johanna Donoghue, moved with their family to Fahamore, north of Castlegregory, shortly afterwards. It was from this townland that John Greaney's mother's family came and it was there that his father worked as an agricultural labourer to support his large family.

Young Thomas Greaney joined the Irish Volunteers of Tadhg Brosnan's 4th Battalion. He was attached to 'D' Company, which encompassed the Maharees area on the peninsula north of Castlegregory and where the company captain was his neighbour Patrick Lynch.

Thomas Greaney was an active Volunteer and was noted to have taken part in the attack on Camp RIC station on 19 February 1920. Following the outbreak of the Civil War he remained on active service with the Republican Army until his capture. In the first week of December 1922 he was taken prisoner with three other IRA Volunteers near Castlegregory.[2] He was interned for the remainder of the conflict but in the crowded prison conditions his health deteriorated and he failed to recover following his release.

He died in 1924 and his comrades judged that his early death at the age of twenty-five was a consequence of his active service with the IRA and his related incarceration.[3] As a consequence they elected to have his name inscribed on the Republican monuments in Castlegregory and Dingle as well as on the Kerry No. 1 Brigade memorial at Ballyseedy. It is thought that he is buried in Killiney Graveyard near Castlegregory, but his grave is unmarked.

---

1 There is no known photograph of Thomas Greaney.
2 *The Cork Examiner*, 8 December 1922.
3 Irish Military Archives, pension lists for Kerry No. 1 Brigade, RO 92.

Paddy Kennedy

Pádraig Ó Cinnéide

Courtesy of the Martin Moore collection.

Patrick Kennedy was born near the West Kerry village of Annascaul in 1891. His father was a Fenian and had served a jail sentence in Clonmel for his activities during the Land Wars. He later returned to Annascaul and opened a shop. Young Paddy Kennedy and his brother Tadhg were members of the Irish Volunteers from their inception. While Tadhg went to London to work in the civil service and later returned to Tralee as an accountant with Kerry County Council, Paddy remained in Annascaul. There he worked as a farmer, having earlier been a monitor in the local school. Tadhg became the intelligence officer for the Kerry No. 1 Brigade, while Paddy was an active Volunteer with the Annascaul Company of the 5th Battalion of the same brigade.[1]

The most significant action in Annascaul during the Tan War occurred on Wednesday 18 August 1920. Under the leadership of Tadhg Brosnan, O/C of the Castlegregory-based 4th Battalion, a large force of men from the 4th and 5th Battalions arrived in the village on the evening of 17 August. They had with them a landmine taken from Cloghane RIC Barracks, which had been evacuated in July. About half a mile to the west of the village the ambush party placed the mine on the roadside and waited for a British Army lorry to pass along its regular route. When it did so, the mine was detonated and the lorry was thrown into the air. After a brief firefight, the soldiers surrendered to Brosnan's men. Their wounded were cared for locally and the uninjured soldiers were sent by car to Dingle. Tadhg Brosnan kept his men in the Annascaul area that evening fearing that the British would arrive in force to carry out reprisals.

---

1   Tadhg Kennedy, BMH WS 135.

While they did come late that night, no revenge attacks occurred and so the IRA units withdrew.[2]

However, two days later, on Friday 20 August, the British returned in force from their Tralee barracks. Patrick Kennedy, who had taken part in the 'ambush, was making hay in a field with another man. They were made aware of the fact that the British were about to arrive in numbers to the village and so they went to Gurteen to work in the fields in order avoid being taken prisoner. There they were joined by two other men who were returning from a local funeral. When the soldiers arrived in Annascaul, they looted the shops and mistreated some of the villagers. The troops then divided, with one party going to Gurteen. A soldier saw the four local men as they walked past a gap in the hedge around the field where they had been working and which was about ten yards from where he stood. The soldier opened fire on the four men – a bullet struck Paddy Kennedy in the head and he was killed instantly. The other three men were taken into custody. A local boy, Jimmy Mannix, who was with the men, asked to be allowed to get a priest for Paddy Kennedy and was told to do so, but on walking a short distance, he was fired upon by an armoured car and had to return.[3]

Paddy Kennedy's remains were removed to the local church the next day and on Sunday a crowd of over 2,000 followed the Tricolour-draped coffin to Ballinacourty Cemetery. There a party of Irish Volunteers fired a volley of shots over the grave. Kennedy was thirty years old when he was killed.

Volunteer Paddy Kennedy is remembered on the monument that stands on The Mall in Dingle, and Annascaul GAA club named their Gaelic football field in the village in his honour.

2   Ernie O'Malley, *The Men Will Talk to Me – Kerry Interviews* (2012), interview with Greg Ashe; Patrick O'Neill, BMH WS 1049, Patrick Walsh BMH WS 960, Robert Knightly BMH WS 951 and Patrick Houlihan BMH WS 959.
3   Patrick Walsh, BMH WS 960.

Daniel 'Bob' McCarthy

Domhnall Mac Carthaig

Courtesy of the Martin Moore collection.

Daniel (Bob) McCarthy was born on 7 July 1899 in Monaree, a townland between Dingle town and Ventry. He was more commonly known by his nickname 'Bob'. Dorothy Macardle records that he fought against the forces of the British crown in Dublin and during the Civil War he was a Volunteer in the 5th Battalion, Kerry No. 1 Brigade.[1]

Bob McCarthy was apprehended at Dún Síon, two miles to the west of Dingle, on March 1923. At the time of his capture he was reported to have had in his possession a copy of a photograph of himself in uniform (reproduced here). He was taken prisoner by a Free State officer named Denis Griffin, who was a native of the area. A fellow Volunteer in the 5th Battalion, Greg Ashe, the brother of Thomas Ashe, later recorded that McCarthy was given an 'awful death'.[2] Griffin, Colonel James Hancock of the Dublin Guard and another unnamed officer spent three days torturing him before he died. He was initially brought to the workhouse in Dingle, where he was reportedly placed in a corner of a field and stoned by some of the soldiers. The next day a Free State escort brought him to Tralee. Ashe reports that at Gleann na nGealt, near Camp, McCarthy was tied to a lorry and pulled along the road for over a mile. When the convoy reached Ballymullen Barracks on the evening of 25 March McCarthy was thought to be dead and placed in a coffin. However, a witness brought it to the attention of an officer that there appeared to be some life still in McCarthy's body, whereupon the Free State officer fired several shots into

---

1   Dorothy Macardle, *Tragedies of Kerry* (1924), p. 67.
2   Ernie O'Malley, *The Men Will Talk to Me – Kerry Interviews* (2012), interview with Greg Ashe.

the coffin. The Free State version of his death is that McCarthy was killed when the escort bringing him from Dingle was fired upon by Republicans, although Republicans denied that there were any attacks in the vicinity on that day.

The remains were buried in the cemetery at Tralee workhouse, which was then in use as a Free State Army barracks. The body was interred within the barracks grounds as it was policy not to return the remains of men who died in custody to their relatives.

On 31 May 1924, over a year after the ceasefire that ended the Civil War, the coffin was exhumed and brought to Dingle. The hearse was met by a large crowd a mile from Dingle town and the funeral procession was led by the local fife and drum band. The remains of Bob McCarthy reposed in the parish church overnight. The next day a very large crowd was present at Kildrum Cemetery, an old graveyard on the road from Dingle to Ballyferriter. Seán a' Chóta Kavanagh, a recently released prominent local Republican, gave the funeral oration.[3]

Today Volunteer Daniel 'Bob' McCarthy is remembered on the West Kerry Republican memorial which was unveiled in 1963 on The Mall, Dingle. He is also commemorated by a white roadside cross at Annagh, three miles west of Tralee on the Dingle road, the site where it is thought that he was mortally wounded by his captors on 25 March 1923.

3   *The Kerryman*, 7 June 1924.

Michael McKenna

Mícheál Mac Cionnaith[1]

The short life of Michael McKenna is typical of many men who gave their lives in the fight for the freedom of their native land. He died, not as the result of an English bullet or inside a prison wall, but in a bed, his body wasted as the result of the hardships of several years on active service. His comrades of that fight declared that he had died as a soldier of the Republic and inscribed his name in stone on the 4th Battalion memorial in Castlegregory and the Kerry No. 1 Brigade monument at Ballyseedy.[2]

Michael McKenna was born in Magherabeg, to the north of Castlegregory village, on Christmas Day 1895. The McKenna family were farmers on this narrow neck of land which separates Tralee Bay from Brandon Bay. As a young man he joined the Irish Volunteers in 1914 and remained loyal to the movement when a majority left on John Redmond's advice to form the National Volunteers. By early 1916 the Castlegregory Company, under the command of Tadhg Brosnan, was reasonably well armed with shotguns which they had purchased. On the Sunday after the Rising had been defeated in Dublin, Brosnan, in an act of defiance, marched with his men through Castlegregory. By doing so they were openly defying orders from the RIC that no parade should be held. The next day Brosnan and six others – Michael McKenna, James Kennedy, Abel O'Mahony, Seán Brosnan, Michael Duhig and Dan O'Shea – were arrested. They were brought to Tralee Gaol and then transferred to Richmond Barracks in Dublin.[3]

The seven Castlegregory men were brought before a military court martial in Richmond Barracks. The charges laid before Tadhg Brosnan were judged as proven and he was sentenced to twenty years' penal servitude. However, his comrades from Castlegregory, including Michael McKenna, were acquitted and released. The six men returned to Kerry and within months they had set

1   There is no known photograph of Michael McKenna.
2   Information from Mattias Ó Dubhda, An Clochán and John Duhig, Castlegregory.
3   Patrick O'Shea, BMH WS 1003 and Patrick McKenna, BMH WS 1205.

about reorganising the Irish Volunteers in Castlegregory. Their efforts were boosted when Tadhg Brosnan was released in 1917 as part of a general release of those imprisoned after the Rising.

Michael McKenna was attached to 'D' Company of the 4th Battalion. He was prominent in the early engagements of his unit. He took part in the large-scale attack on Camp RIC Barracks on 19 February 1920. He was also involved in the attack and capture of Brandon coastguard station in July 1920.

However, from the summer of 1920 his health began to deteriorate and he was no longer able to go on active service. On 22 October 1921, having seen his efforts in ridding his native place of British occupation come to fruition, Michael McKenna died of pneumonia in Castlegregory. He was buried in the family grave in Killiney Cemetery.

Thomas Moriarty

Tomás Ó Muircheartaig[1]

Thomas Moriarty was a member of Na Fianna Éireann and his unit was attached to the 4th Battalion, Kerry No. 1 Brigade. His parents were Maurice Moriarty of Ballyferriter and Maggie Callaghan of Cloghane and they lived at Faha, to the west of Cloghane village. Thomas was their eldest child and was born in 1903.

The death of this young Republican on the evening of 5 September 1920 was the result of an unfortunate accident. The district around Castlegregory was noted as an area that had supplied the RIC with numerous recruits since the inception of that paramilitary force. However, following the events of 1916 and the growth of the Irish Volunteers, such men who served the crown were now regarded with hostility as the guerrilla war increased in intensity. Two RIC constables from the Cloghane area who were posted elsewhere in the country were warned by the Volunteers of the 4th Battalion that they should not return to their West Kerry homes while they served in the crown forces. Disregarding the threat, the two policemen came to spend their holidays near Cloghane and this set in train a series of events that led to the death of Thomas Moriarty.

The Moriarty farm was two miles from Cloghane village. Late one evening a horse on the farm became seriously ill. In the village there lived a man named O'Connor who had a knowledge of animals and their ailments, and in an era when veterinary care was unavailable, such men were called on to assist local farmers with distressed livestock. Young Thomas was sent by his father to Cloghane to seek the assistance of this animal healer. When he eventually arrived home again, it was dusk and he was late for a Volunteer gathering he was to attend at Cloghane. He set off again on foot for the two-mile journey, heading east to the meeting point. To shorten the journey he ran through the fields in the dim light, hoping to make up for lost time.

Unknown to Tom, men of the local IRA company had prepared an ambush

---

1 There is no known photograph of Thomas Moriarty.

for the two RIC constables who had defied the order not to enter the parish. As the local Volunteers lay in wait at a spot near Cloghane, they saw a figure running in the field a short distance away and assumed that it was one of the RIC men. Shots were fired by the ambush party and unfortunately one found its mark and Thomas Moriarty was fatally wounded. A priest was summoned from Dingle who happened to be a cousin of the young victim. The funeral rites were hastily and secretly performed. The remains of Tom Moriarty were buried before dawn by his distraught comrades in the Moriarty family tomb in Cloghane Graveyard before the sun arose the next day.[2]

Tom Moriarty is commemorated on the memorial cross erected to the memory of the dead of Tadhg Brosnan's 4th Battalion, Kerry No. 1 Brigade. The monument was unveiled in April 1934 and stands opposite the church in Castlegregory. The Republican memorial on The Mall in Dingle also bears his name.

2   Information from Mattias Ó Dubhda, Baile na Leacan, An Clochán.

Tom O'Sullivan

Tomás Ó Súilleabháin

Courtesy of the Martin Moore collection.

The son of a farmer, Tom O'Sullivan was born in Ballineanig, Ballyferriter, on 8 December 1900. His parents were John O'Sullivan and Ellen Devine. He was a member of the Irish Volunteers and during the Tan War he was the second lieutenant in the Ballyferriter Company of the IRA which was attached to the 5th Battalion, Kerry No. 1 Brigade. During that conflict there was little activity in the area west of Dingle, as the battalion leadership in Dingle was relatively ineffective militarily.

During the Civil War O'Sullivan was an officer in the 5th Battalion and was probably O/C of the remnants of the battalion when he was killed on Sunday 18 February 1923. He had narrowly escaped capture a few days earlier when a Free State raiding party arrived at his mother's house at Ballineanig, Ballyferriter. At this time his brother Dan, who was a Volunteer in the Ballyferriter Company, was interned in the Curragh and their mother, Ellen, fearing for Tom's safety, asked him to surrender his rifle. However, he replied that this was something he could not do as he was determined to fight on despite overwhelming odds.[1]

On the evening of Sunday 18 February 1923 O'Sullivan and his comrade Thomas O'Dowd were attending what was called a 'ball night', a local colloquialism for a party. This was being held either in the house of Mike Ferriter in Cathair Chaoin or the nearby home of Eibhlín a'Tae Feirtéar at Béal Bán. The local information concerning that fateful night states that somebody left the party that evening and travelled into Dingle to alert the Free State

1   Dorothy Macardle, *Tragedies of Kerry* (1924), p. 65.

Army that O'Sullivan, a wanted man, was at the gathering. By the time the military patrol reached the area, O'Sullivan and O'Dowd had left the party and were travelling across a field, unaware of their betrayal.[2]

Tom O'Sullivan and his comrade were captured in a field close to the O'Sullivan house at Ballineanig. Free State forces reported that they were captured after a gun fight in which O'Dowd was wounded, and that O'Sullivan was killed when he attempted to disarm his guard. However, it would appear that the men were surprised when their voices were heard in the darkness by a Free State raiding party which was nearby. A local Free State officer from Dingle, Denis Griffin, recognised O'Sullivan and opened fire, seriously wounding him. Lying on the ground he was shot again and died at the scene. O'Dowd was taken prisoner and sentenced to fifteen years in prison for his part in the alleged gun battle with Griffin's men.

Tom O'Sullivan was buried in Kildrum Graveyard which lies on the road between his native Ballyferriter and Dingle town. There he rests with Volunteer Daniel 'Bob' McCarthy of nearby Monaree, who was killed by Free State forces a month later.

An iron cross used to stand at the entrance to Ballyferriter village in memory of the sacrifice of Commandant Tom O'Sullivan, but with the passage of time this rusted and was eventually removed. It was not replaced with a more permanent structure. Tom O'Sullivan is remembered with the Republican dead of West Kerry on the monument that stands on The Mall in Dingle.

Lieutenant Denis Griffin was attached to the intelligence section of the Free State Army and was under the command of David Neligan. Being a native of West Kerry, he was a valuable asset to Neligan's Special Services Section, as it was officially called. Ruthless in the pursuit of his former comrades, he showed no mercy to his captives.[3] Following the Civil War Griffin was *persona non grata* in his native county and went to live in Donegal. There his murky past was discovered by local Republicans in the late 1920s. Word was sent to Kerry as to his whereabouts because it was thought that the IRA were anxious to exact retribution for his part in the killing of their Volunteers. However, with

2   Information from Fr Tom Hickey, *sagart paróiste*, Ballyferriter.
3   Ernie O'Malley, *The Men Will Talk to Me – Kerry Interviews* (2012), interviews with Greg Ashe and Bill Bailey.

the drift towards constitutional nationalism by some senior Kerry IRA officers, it was decided not to kill Lieutenant Griffin.[4] He later emigrated to the United States.

4   Information from local source (name with author).

TIMOTHY SPILLANE

Tadg Ó Spealáin[1]

Timothy Spillane was born on 26 April 1893 in Carrigaha, a townland between the villages of Camp and Castlegregory. There his parents, Maurice and Nora Spillane, raised a large family on their farm. Tim remained on in national school to become a monitor but later left and by 1920, when he was incarcerated, he was describing himself as a labourer. Both he and his younger brother Michael were Volunteers in the Aughacasla-based 'C' Company of the 4th Battalion, Kerry No. 1 Brigade.

Ten miles from Tralee, at Deelis near the village of Camp, the RIC had a barracks and it was from there on 24 June 1919 that Sergeant Barney Oates and Constable J. O'Connell travelled westwards on their bicycles to the small village of Aughacasla. As they returned from their patrol they were ambushed at Meenascarthy. A number of attackers emerged from a gateway and surprised the RIC men. Constable O'Connell's rifle was taken from him, but a struggle developed as he and his sergeant refused to surrender. In the fracas Oates was shot and seriously wounded and O'Connell then stopped struggling. The Volunteers made good their escape.[2]

However, on 3 July Timothy Spillane, Michael Griffin, Michael Maunsell and Michael Flynn were arrested. Michael Spillane was already in custody and soon all five were charged with the attempted murder of Sergeant Oates.[3] The five Volunteers refused to recognise the court, claiming that it had no right to try them as they were 'soldiers of the Irish Republic'. They were remanded in custody and were eventually brought before the Cork Assizes in December 1919 and convicted of the charges. Timothy Spillane was sentenced to three years' penal servitude, with the judge commenting that 'he had murder in his heart'. Michael Spillane and Michael Flynn were each sentenced to eighteen months' penal servitude, Michael Maunsell to fifteen months and young

---

1   There is no known photograph of Timothy Spillane.
2   Patrick O'Shea, Castlegregory, BMH WS 1003.
3   *Irish Independent*, 4 July 1919.

Michael Griffin got nine months' hard labour.[4]

The men were transferred to Maryborough Gaol in what is now Portlaoise to serve their sentences, but on arrival Timothy Spillane immediately went on hunger strike to protest at the conditions under which he was being imprisoned. Within days his health began to deteriorate, whereupon he was visited by his father who carried instructions from the Republican leadership that he was to come off his fast. The prison doctor declared that he should be released due to his deteriorating health but the governor refused and had him examined by a prison doctor from Mountjoy Gaol who recommended his continued incarceration.[5]

In April 1920 twenty-year-old Michael Flynn embarked on a hunger strike for political status and in June 1920 Tim Spillane commenced another hunger strike with Cork prisoner Michael Condon. They too were demanding political status. However, at this stage the attitude of the prison authorities to hunger striking had significantly changed and the men were told that if they persisted, then they would be allowed to die. Having served his sentence, Spillane was released and returned home.

He resumed his role with local Volunteers and was involved in drilling and training in the Castlegregory area. While engaged in such activities, he was reported to have developed pneumonia as a result of being out in all types of weather. This may have the Spanish Influenza which was endemic at the time or may have been due to his health being damaged by his incarceration and hunger strike. He died prematurely and was buried in the family plot in Killiney Graveyard near Castlegregory. His name is recorded among the dead of the 4th Battalion on the brigade memorial at Ballyseedy.

4   *The Kerryman*, 20 December 1919.
5   *Evening Telegraph*, 24 December 1919.

6TH (LISTOWEL) AND 8TH (BALLYLONGFORD) BATTALIONS, KERRY NO. 1 BRIGADE

The Irish Volunteers were formed in Listowel in early 1914. However, when the split occurred later that year the Irish Volunteers in the town became inactive. In 1915 they were reorganised and a local blacksmith, Paddy Landers, was appointed O/C. James Sugrue, a shop assistant originally from Reenard, was his deputy in the Listowel Company. This company played no part in the Easter Rising and, having decommissioned the few weapons that he had, Landers surrendered the guns to the RIC the following week.

In 1917 the Volunteers in the town and surrounding districts began to grow in strength again. When the Kerry No. 1 Brigade was formed in 1919, the Listowel Battalion was initially called the 4th Battalion. With a further reorganisation in 1921, the battalion was renamed the 6th Battalion and the original 6th Battalion in the Killorglin area was transferred to Kerry No. 2 Brigade. The rural districts to the south and west were designated the 3rd Battalion and this was centred on the Lixnaw and Ballyduff areas. During the Truce an 8th Battalion was formed from the companies to the north and west of the town, and was centred on the village of Ballylongford.

During the reorganisation in 1917 James Sugrue was appointed the battalion's commanding officer. A fellow South Kerry man, Tomás O'Donoghue, was his V/C. Following an unsuccessful attack in Ballybunion in 1920, Sugrue resigned his command in favour of Michael Bob McElligott, who led the battalion until he was killed in February 1921. He in turn was replaced by his brother Paddy Joe, who remained O/C until the divisions that arose due to the Treaty.

The battalion area was initially very widespread, covering nearly 400 square miles. There were companies in Listowel town, Tarbert, Newtownsandes (Moyvane), Asdee, Ballylongford, Bedford, Behins, Duagh, Knockanure, Beale and Finuge. Originally the Listowel Battalion also included the Lixnaw, Ballyduff and Ballybunion Companies. However, in the summer of 1920 the 3rd Battalion was formed to include the area to the south and west of Listowel and these companies were transferred to the new battalion.

From 1917 Listowel town was a hotbed of Republican activity and in 1919 a detachment of British troops was sent there to reinforce the town's police. In June 1920 the increasingly aggressive and brutal behaviour of the local RIC caused several members to resign rather than implement a shoot to kill policy. This incident became known as the Listowel Mutiny. In 1920 Black and Tans were sent to aid the RIC. Under increased pressure from the crown forces, the focus of IRA activity moved to the surrounding countryside. The Volunteer companies in Moyvane and Ballydonoghue became particularly active as the war intensified in the rural districts. In January 1921 a flying column was formed in the North Kerry area and this was commanded by Tom Kennelly. The column went into action immediately and changed the nature of the conflict in the Listowel area. In two months it grew to include over thirty full-time fighters and so was divided into two smaller units. Kennelly continued to command what was now the 3rd Battalion column and Denis Quille became O/C of the 6th Battalion column. Quille's unit would wage a successful guerrilla campaign in the district around Listowel, but in the process would lose several active Volunteers, most notably at Gortaglanna.

During the period of the Truce, several Republicans from the 6th Battalion volunteered for duty in the six counties where there was a shortage of experienced fighters to continue the war against the British presence. Dan Enright and Tim O'Sullivan were executed in Donegal in 1923 and the remainder were imprisoned following their capture there.

The divisions over the Treaty resulted in dissension in the 6th Battalion that was not mirrored elsewhere in the county. Numerically about half of the active Volunteers followed the pro-Treaty stance of Tom Kennelly and the other half opposed the settlement and remained in the IRA, with a few remaining uncommitted. The result was that Listowel town had both a Free State Army garrison and a Republican garrison. In the spring of 1922 tensions in the town were high as a stand-off between erstwhile comrades persisted until the outbreak of the Civil War. Following the attack on the Four Courts, IRA columns from Kerry No. 1 and Kerry No. 2 Brigades captured the town after some intensive fighting. The defeated Free State forces were disarmed and allowed to leave the town.

On 4 August 1922 Free State forces of the 1st Western Division landing at Tarbert would recapture the town with little resistance, as IRA Volunteers retreated to the surrounding rural areas to wage a guerrilla war in defence of the Republic. Slowly resistance grew weaker throughout the autumn and winter due to mass arrests of Republicans by Free State forces that included many former IRA Volunteers. The killing of John Linnane in April 1923 was to mark the effective end to the sad conflict in the Listowel district, though it would be over a year later that the last Republican prisoners returned to their North Kerry homes.

In July 1921, when Humphrey Murphy became O/C of Kerry No. 1 Brigade, there was a reorganisation of some of the battalions in the brigade. This was necessitated by Murphy's own battalion in Castleisland becoming part of the Kerry No. 1 Brigade and the overall increase of active Volunteers in the command. To improve the effectiveness of the companies in the Ballylongford area, a new battalion was formed which would allow a greater independence of action when confronting the crown forces, should the Truce collapse. The companies that formed this new 8th Battalion were Ballybunion, Ballylongford, Tarbert, Asdee and Beale. Con Dee, who was the only survivor of the Gortaglanna incident when his three comrades were killed in custody, was appointed the 8th Battalion's O/C.

Eddie Carmody

Éamonn Ó Cearmada

Courtesy of the Martin Moore collection.

Edmund Carmody was born in 1894 and lived in Ballylongford, ten miles north of Listowel. Eddie enrolled as a member of the Irish Volunteers on their foundation in his local parish in 1914. The split in the Irish Volunteers caused by John Redmond's call on the members to join the British war effort caused the Ballylongford Volunteer Company to become inactive, but it was reorganised again in the early months of 1916, prior to the Rising. The Ballylongford Company waited in vain for orders to arrive on that fateful weekend and when they did not, it took no part in the events of Easter Week. However, in 1917 the Ballylongford Volunteers became active again and Eddie Carmody was appointed second lieutenant.[1] During the Tan War, this company was to the forefront of the campaign against the RIC in North Kerry.

On 21 November 1920 a force of Black and Tans and regular RIC arrived in Ballylongford in an attempt to apprehend local IRA Volunteers. They engaged in indiscriminate shooting and destruction of civilian property, and local public houses were looted. Three IRA Volunteers – Brian Dillane, Edmund Hayes and Eddie Carmody – were in Brian O'Grady's house when the police arrived in the village. The O'Grady house was on the Ballyline road on the outskirts of Ballylongford. The three IRA Volunteers made their way out the back of the house and they went to the village sports field. There, Hayes volunteered to get three weapons from an IRA arms dump so that some shots could be fired at the police. The three men then agreed to meet at Rusheen, near the local doctor's house and to the west of the village. Hayes could acquire only

---

1   Thomas Carmody of Ballylongford, BMH WS 966.

one rifle and then went searching for two other weapons. Meanwhile Carmody and Dillane were joined by another Volunteer, Peter Deegan, who had also fled from the centre of the village. After a while Carmody heard footsteps along the road and, thinking it was Eddie Hayes returning, he ventured out onto the roadway. However, it was a group of RIC and so Carmody turned and hastily retreated. The RIC saw him as he attempted to flee and they opened fire on him. Eddie Carmody was shot in the back but still managed to jump the wall of the doctor's house, behind which he hid. The police, assuming that he had hidden inside the doctor's house, searched this but found nothing. However, it being a moonlit, frosty night, one of them spotted Carmody lying beneath the roadside wall of the garden. He was dragged onto the road and summarily executed. The RIC then returned to the village, about a half mile away, and burned the local creamery, saw mills and several shops. They brought with them Eddie Carmody's lifeless body and returning to the local RIC barracks, they put it in a shed at the rear of the building. It was from there that his father removed the remains the next day.[2]

Eddie Carmody was buried in Murhur Cemetery, near Moyvane. He is remembered today by a roadside cross which was erected at the spot where he was killed just outside Ballylongford village.

The killing of Eddie Carmody had a sequel during the Truce. On 12 December 1921, in violation of the terms of the ceasefire of the previous July, four armed men approached Sergeant John Maher from Carlow and Constable Gallagher as they walked through The Green in Ballybunion. Sergeant Maher died in a hail of bullets, while his companion was slightly injured. The dead RIC officer was the man responsible for the shooting of Eddie Carmody over a year before.

2   *Ibid.* and Brian O'Grady, BMH WS 1390.

Paddy Dalton

Pádraig Daltún

Courtesy of the Martin Moore collection.

Patrick Dalton was born in the townland of Upper Athea, a mile from Athea, a village with a strong nationalist tradition seven miles from Listowel just over the County Limerick border. As a young man he went to work as an assistant in John Faley's hardware shop in Listowel and there he became a member of the Irish Volunteers. An active soldier, he volunteered for service with the 6th Battalion flying column that was established in January 1921 under the command of Tom Kennelly. In late February he was wounded in the leg when the column attacked a police raiding party who had just boarded a train at Lisselton station as it was returning to Ballybunion. When this large North Kerry column was divided into 3rd and 6th Battalion active service units, Dalton continued on active service with the Listowel area unit commanded by Denis Quille.

This unit took part in actions in Kilmorna, Tarbert and Ballylongford. An outbreak of scabies caused the column to temporarily cease its actions and disperse for a fortnight in early May 1921. Dalton returned to Listowel but when he received information from a local source that the crown forces were about to raid the parish mission in his native Athea in an attempt to capture the West Limerick column, he went to Athea to warn them. He made the journey with Con Dee, a comrade from the 6th Battalion active service unit. Dalton and Dee remained in Athea for three days and on their last day were joined by Paddy Walsh of Gunsboro, another column member.[1]

When returning to Listowel by foot, Paddy Dalton, Con Dee and Paddy

---

1   Patrick Joseph McElligott, BMH WS 1013.

Walsh met Mick Scannell, another IRA Volunteer, on the road. Scannell, a local farmer, was checking on grazing for his cattle when he encountered the three men as they walked along the road from Athea near Gortaglanna. He accompanied them and at the McMahon house at a crossroads half a mile from Gortaglanna, they halted. Mick Scannell, a brother-in-law of the McMahons, and Con Dee went a few yards further on and stopped to chat on the roadside near the house. Walsh and Dalton went to the McMahon house where they were given some milk as they chatted to the lady of the house. Their thirst satisfied, Walsh and Dalton went through the farmyard and back onto the main road where they rejoined Dee and Scannell. At this point Jerry Lyons of Duagh, another member of the column, came cycling towards them from Knockanure. Then, without warning, a convoy of Black and Tans sped towards the men from the direction of Knockanure. The open-topped car and two lorries were upon the men before they had a chance to seek shelter. It may have been that the noise of the vehicles was mistaken for that of a passing train on the nearby railway or perhaps the men had just let their guard down and did not appreciate the noise of the vehicles until they were too close.

Scannell turned and headed back towards the McMahon house while Dee, Walsh, Dalton and Lyons jumped over a ditch into a field and proceeded to run. After a warning shot was fired at the men in the open field, all four raised their hands in surrender. The prisoners were put in the vehicles and meanwhile a section of Tans went to McMahons' where Mick Scannell was also arrested and told that he was to be shot. The house was ransacked and Scannell dragged from the building. The commanding officer was Scottish and Bridget McMahon pleaded with him, saying that she had nursed soldiers from Scotland when she worked in London during the Great War. This struck a chord with the officer and Scannell was freed.[2]

However, the other four men were not released and, having left McMahons' house, the convoy headed towards Athea. Further down the road, they turned and went back in the direction of Listowel. At about a mile further on from where the four prisoners had been captured, the three-vehicle convoy stopped. The prisoners were taken out of the vehicles and ordered to run, but they

---

2   J. Anthony Gaughan, *Listowel and its Vicinity* (1973); *Irish Independent*, 18 May 1921.

refused to do so, fearing what would happen. Then the four men were brought into a field in which there was a ring fort and lined up. The Tans stood in front of them and formed an impromptu firing squad. While the man in front of Con Dee hesitated momentarily, allowing him to make good an escape, his three comrades died in a volley of gunfire.³

The bodies of Paddy Dalton, Paddy Walsh and Jerry Lyons were brought initially to Tralee and then returned to St Mary's church in Listowel. There they reposed overnight. The next day the three funerals went to the men's local parishes. As they departed the town, the shops closed and the houses pulled their curtains as a mark of respect, but the military demanded that the houses keep their doors open on pain of reprisal.⁴ The official military inquiry found that Dalton, Lyons and Walsh had died when the crown forces returned fire on a large party who had ambushed them and that their bodies were left behind when the attackers fled.⁵

The remains of twenty-eight-year-old Paddy Dalton were buried in Templeathea Cemetery in his native Athea. In that village he is remembered by a plaque on the main street. A fine monument, unveiled in 1950, stands in the field where the men died, but it is probably in the song 'The Valley of Knockanure' that the memory of those who died at Gortaglanna is best recalled.

3   *Shannonside Annual 1958*, article by Con Dee, survivor of Gortaglanna killings.
4   *Irish Independent*, 18 May 1921.
5   *Ibid.*, 25 June 1921.

Patrick Foran

Pádraig Ó Fuaráin

Patrick Foran was a native of Tullamore, a townland between Listowel and Ballylongford in North Kerry. He was born on the 5 April 1896, the son of a small farmer. His mother died when he was still a young child. As a young man he joined the Ballydonoghue Company, which was initially in the 3rd Battalion, but was later part of the 8th Battalion, Kerry No. 1 Brigade. He was on active service during the Tan War in the North Kerry area. Before the conflict he had worked as a labourer, often in the neighbouring county of Limerick, but returned home in 1920.

Courtesy of Noreen McAuliffe, Duagh.

Following the bombardment of the Four Courts in Dublin which began the Civil War on 28 June 1922, Republican forces quickly mobilised in Kerry. Within a day a large force of fighting men from the north and south of the county gathered in Tralee and marched on Listowel, the only town in Kerry with a Free State garrison. After a few hours of fighting the Free State commander in the town, Tom Kennelly, surrendered. His men were disarmed and those who did not join the Republican forces were free to leave the county. The Republican columns under Humphrey Murphy and John Joe Rice then marched eastwards into County Limerick. The Free State forces in Abbeyfeale, Newcastle West and the other towns on the road to Limerick quickly capitulated. When they reached the city an uneasy truce had been negotiated by the IRA Chief of Staff Liam Lynch and the Free State commander in the city, Michael Brennan.[1] Lynch commanded over 400 well-armed, seasoned Republican fighters, while Brennan's force numbered 400 men armed with 150 rifles. However, Lynch, a reluctant participant in the Civil War, hoped the ceasefire would allow a

---

1   Ernie O'Malley, *The Men Will Talk to Me – Kerry Interviews* (2012), interviews with John Joe Rice and Johnny O'Connor.

negotiated settlement that might halt the fighting. Brennan, on the other hand, used the truce to reinforce his units with soldiers from Dublin and the west, many of whom were from Irish regiments in the British Army that were being disbanded at the time. Crucially, the ceasefire also allowed Brennan to obtain the field artillery which would play an important role in his capture of the city.[2]

Having reached Limerick, the senior IRA officers were ordered by Lynch to return to their own areas and make preparations locally for the conflict that was spreading throughout the country as Free State forces attempted to subdue Republican resistance to the new twenty-six county government. However, the bulk of the IRA fighters remained in the city and Patrick Foran was one such Volunteer. On Tuesday 11 July Free State forces, now greatly strengthened in numbers and equipment, attacked Republican positions throughout the city. The IRA was quickly forced to adopt defensive positions as Brennan's greater firepower became evident. In the fierce street fighting that ensued, Patrick Foran was wounded by machine-gun fire in a laneway as his comrades prepared to retreat from their positions. The Republican forces evacuated their remaining positions in the city on 21 July and retreated south to make another stand around the County Limerick town of Kilmallock.

Twenty-five-year-old Patrick Foran died of his wounds on 23 July 1922. His remains were interred in Gale Cemetery, near to his home. He was to be the first of many Kerry Republican casualties in the Civil War. In the years following his death there was a commemorative march from Coolard Creamery to Paddy Foran's grave. The commemoration in 1931 was addressed by Seán MacBride and that evening MacBride and leading Republicans from the area were arrested, with several men being charged with illegal drilling.[3] A monument was unveiled over the grave of Paddy Foran and five other Volunteers from the area in April 1932.

---

2   Pádraig Óg Ó Ruairc, *The Battle for Limerick City* (2010), p. 119.
3   *The Kerryman*, 25 July 1931 and 23 July 1932.

Michael Galvin

Mícéál Ó Gealbáin

Michael Galvin was born on 1 November 1894 at Drombeg, four miles north of Listowel. Like his brothers, Jack and Murt, he was an active member of the Ballydonoghue Company of the 6th Battalion, Kerry No. 1 Brigade, which he joined in 1917. He volunteered for service with the North Kerry active service unit which was formed in January 1921 under the command of Tom Kennelly.

In late April the large column was divided into a 3rd Battalion column and 6th Battalion column. Galvin was attached to the 3rd Battalion flying column but in the first week in April he was operating with the 6th Battalion column. On 6 April one section of the 6th Battalion went to Ballyduff to attack the barracks there. The

The body of Michael Galvin, taken at Listowel RIC Barracks. Courtesy of the Martin Moore collection.

remainder, including Mick Galvin, went to Tarbert but their planned attack on the police was abandoned due to the presence of Royal Marines in the village. Galvin and his comrades returned to the Moyvane area. The next day they were informed by Timmie Carroll, a Volunteer from nearby Knockanure, that a column of British soldiers had left Listowel. They had travelled to the home of Sir Arthur Vicars at Kilmorna House and there they were being entertained. It was planned to attack these soldiers as they returned to Listowel later that evening, at a place on the road called Kilmeany Wood.

The Kilmorna ambush party consisted of Con Brosnan, Mick Purtill, Jack Carroll, Timmy Egan, Mick Galvin, Donailín O'Grady and Paddy Reidy. The Volunteers took up positions on the roadside at Kilmeany between two bends on what is a winding road. To their rear were open fields with ditches that would allow shelter for a retreat. Michael Galvin's firing position was behind a gate pier and towards the front of the ambush party. The main body of military, who were from the Oxfordshire Regiment, were preceded by two soldiers who cycled some distance ahead. When these two outriders rounded the bend, fire was opened on them and they fell seriously wounded. Timmy Egan bravely left his cover and ran onto the road to take the service rifle of one of these soldiers. The main body of British military were also fired upon when they came into range. These soldiers quickly discarded their bicycles and took up firing positions. The firefight was intense, with several soldiers being slightly wounded. Their O/C, Captain J. B. Watson, was injured by a bullet which struck his head. Galvin apparently believed the captain had been killed outright and left his position of cover. However, Watson had received only a superficial wound and, quickly recovering, he shot Galvin. With ammunition running low, the Volunteers were obliged to retire across the fields, with the injured Galvin covering their retreat. Losing blood, he stumbled as he attempted to escape across a stream and died where he fell.[1] The remainder of the ambush party managed to escape.[2]

The body of Michael Galvin was initially taken to the RIC barracks in Listowel and while there the body was photographed. Subsequently, the remains were taken to the mortuary at Listowel workhouse. The body was still unidentified and, having left it in the mortuary, the Tans departed, taking the key of the building with them. The hospital administrator got another key and admitted two Republicans from nearby Market Street, who identified the remains but decided that it would be safer not to take the body as this would bring retribution on the staff of the workhouse hospital. The Tans returned with Michael Galvin's mother, but she found the strength to deny that the dead man was her son, again for fear of reprisals on her home or family. The Tans then buried the body in nearby Teampaillín Bán Cemetery, in a pauper's grave.

Three weeks later Captain Paddy Walsh, who was later killed at Gortaglanna, gave the order to transfer the coffin from Teampaillín Bán to Gale Cemetery. Danny Brown and John Barrett undertook the task, assisted by Listowel Volunteers Thomas Pelican, Thomas Quirke, Edward Quirke, Jack

1   Patrick Joseph McElligott, BMH WS 1013, James Costello, BMH WS 1091 and Matthew Finucane, BMH WS 975.
2   *The Kerryman*, 23 April 1932.

Neligan and Tim Neligan. The coffin was carried to Barrett's home in Curraghatoosane. There the seven were joined nearly two hours later by Paddy Walsh and Tom Collins of Ballydonoghue. The nine men then shouldered the coffin almost three miles along the Ballybunion road. On the way they were met by John Linnane and Paddy John Walsh, who had brought a sidecar. The men refused their offer to put the coffin on the car, saying that they would soon depart from their comrade forever at Gale Cemetery, but would carry him until then.[3]

Michael Galvin lies in what is now the Republican Plot in Gale Cemetery, together with other dead Volunteers of the 3rd, 6th and 8th Battalions. A monument was unveiled over the graves of Lieutenant Galvin and his comrades, including Captain Paddy Walsh, in 1932.[4] A roadside memorial stands at Kilmeany on the Kilmorna to Listowel road to mark the spot where Michael Galvin lost his life for the cause of Ireland's freedom.

3   *The Kerryman*, 13 April 1935, an article by John Barrett.
4   *The Kerryman*, 23 April 1932.

Pat Hartnett

Pádraig Ó hAirtnéada

Courtesy of the Martin Moore collection.

Patrick Hartnett, the eldest child of a farmer, was born on 6 February 1898 at Gortnaminch, about two miles to the west of Listowel town. His family had a small farm there and Patrick, the eldest of six children, worked with his father on the land. He was a Volunteer in the 6th Battalion, Kerry No. 1 Brigade. He had joined the Irish Volunteers in 1917 when they were reorganised in the Listowel area under the command of local blacksmith and former Kerry footballer, Paddy Landers. During the Black and Tan War he was on active service with the 6th Battalion and was first lieutenant of the Finuge Company. As his activities became known to the RIC he was forced to go 'on the run' during that conflict. His brother, Moss, was also a Volunteer in that company and his sister, Mary Ann, was a member of Cumann na mBan.[1]

Following the split that occurred as a result of the Treaty, the Finuge Company lost nearly half of its strength. In January 1922 Pat Hartnett was promoted to the rank of company captain when he replaced Richard McCarthy of Ballycuneen. During the Civil War he led the men from Finuge in defence of the Irish Republic and fought in the area to the west and south of Listowel.

The fact that many of his former comrades now regarded those who continued to fight for the Republic as enemies meant that using the dugouts and safe houses that sheltered such men as Pat Hartnett during the Tan War was no longer as safe as it had been. And so it was that Captain Pat Hartnett was captured in a safe house near Finuge Bridge not far from his home. His location was betrayed by a local person to Free State forces in Listowel. Hartnett was subsequently transferred as a prisoner to Ballymullen Barracks in Tralee.

1   Information from Seán Harnett, Listowel, nephew of Pat Hartnett.

While a prisoner in Ballymullen, for reasons that are not clear, David Neligan, the chief of the Free State's intelligence section, selected Hartnett to be one of the men who were to die at Ballyseedy Cross. The atrocity that occurred at Ballyseedy was all the more horrendous as Neligan had the prisoners who were to be killed tortured the evening before the massacre. The prisoners told their families and other prisoners of being beaten with a hammer as they were being interrogated for the last time.

The nine men were placed on a lorry and the military convoy travelled to Ballyseedy Cross in the early hours of 7 March 1923. Having had his captives tied together and placed around the landmine which his colleagues had constructed, Captain Ned Breslin had it detonated remotely. The explosion probably killed some of the men outright, but several survived the blast and these wounded men, with the exception of Stephen Fuller who escaped, were shot dead by machine-gun fire.

When the smoke had cleared, Breslin's troops collected the mangled bodies and brought them back to Ballymullen Barracks. The remains of the eight victims were placed in nine coffins, as Breslin had not realised that Fuller had survived the blast and had by this time reached a safe house. Word quickly spread of the massacre and a large crowd gathered at the gates of the barracks awaiting news of who had died. That evening the coffins were released to the families who were among those gathered outside. A Free State soldier, Bill Bailey, described how, as the coffins were passing through the barracks gate, General Paddy Daly had the army band assembled and they were playing ragtime music as they taunted the angry crowd on the street. A procession of crudely made coffins was given to the men's waiting families. It was apparent that the remains had not been properly identified and so the relatives had to open the coffins and to place their dead sons in caskets that had been brought by the waiting crowd.[2] Mrs Hartnett had travelled to Tralee from Gortnaminch by horse and car having heard that her son had been one of the victims. She had the coffin opened and was able to identify Pat by his black curly hair. Across the road from the barracks gate were four tenement houses. From there the women got water to wash their sons' remains and the bodies were prepared

2 Ernie O'Malley, *The Men Will Talk to Me – Kerry Interviews* (2012), interview with Bill Bailey.

for burial with the help of the local women.[3] Mrs Hartnett then left Tralee and brought the coffin back to Lixnaw, where it remained overnight.[4]

The following day the remains of Captain Pat Hartnett were brought to the small graveyard at Dysert in the parish of Lixnaw. An enormous crowd witnessed his burial in the family plot. His headstone bears testament to his rank and date of death. Pat Hartnett is recalled on the monument at Ballyseedy as one of the victims of the massacre and also as a fallen member of the 6th Battalion of Kerry No. 1 Brigade.

3   Information from Jerry O'Sullivan, Tralee, whose mother, Sheila O'Sullivan, was one of those who assisted.
4   Information from Seán Harnett, Listowel, nephew of Pat Hartnett.

John Lawlor

Seán Ó Leaclobair

John Lawlor was born on 3 May 1903. He was the son of the town's parish clerk and the Lawlor family lived in Convent Street. John Lawlor had been a member of the Irish Volunteers, but at the time of his killing was studying for the priesthood.[1]

The Great War had ended on the eleventh hour of 11 November 1918 and at that hour a year later church bells throughout Britain and Ireland tolled to remember the fallen soldiers of that conflict. In deference to those Listowel men who fell in the war, the bells of the parish church in the town's square rang out on Armistice Day 1919. However, a year later the political climate in the town had changed considerably, and when approached by the town's crown forces to ring the church's bells at the eleventh hour, David Lawlor, the parish clerk, refused the request. For this act of defiance he was threatened, and subsequently lived in fear of the town's RIC and Black and Tans.

Courtesy of the Martin Moore collection.

At Christmas 1920 David Lawlor's son John was home on holiday from his clerical studies in All Hallows College, Dublin. On New Year's Eve, as he was going to the church for confession, he was accosted by a group of Black and Tans on William Street and brutally assaulted. This unprovoked attack was in response to his father's refusal to comply with the request to commemorate Armistice Day the previous month. John Lawlor died of his injuries the next day and was buried in Listowel Cemetery. He is remembered on the Kerry No. 1 Brigade monument at Ballyseedy, where he is listed as a Volunteer in the Listowel Battalion.

1   *The Kerryman*, 8 January 1921.

The intimidation of the Lawlor family did not cease with this murder. On 23 February 1921 David Lawlor was bringing the family's cow to 'The Cow's Lawn', an area of grazing ground within the town, when he was accosted by the RIC. Without provocation, the cow was riddled with bullets, though David himself was not hit by the gunfire.[2]

---

2   J. Anthony Gaughan, *Listowel and its Vicinity* (1973).

John Linnane

Seán Ó Luinneáin

John (Jack) Linnane was born on 1897 in Glouria in the parish of Ballydonoghue. His family were farmers and John became a draper's assistant in The Arcade in nearby Listowel. He is recorded as having a strong interest in the Irish language and culture and was a member of the Irish Volunteers in the town from their reorganisation in Listowel in 1917. He was attached to the Listowel Company of the 6th Battalion, Kerry No. 1 Brigade.

On the formation of the North Kerry flying column in January 1921, he volunteered for active service with the unit. At this time he was adjutant of the 6th Battalion.[1] When this large column was divided into separate columns for the 3rd and 6th Battalions, he served in Denis Quille's active service unit based around Listowel. This group was very active during the later stages of the Tan War. On the eve of the Truce Linnane was in command of a group of Volunteers from the column that entered Tarbert and ambushed a party of Black and Tans who were known to frequent a public house there. In this, the final attack of the Tan War in the North Kerry area, Linnane's men wounded two of the Tans.[2]

Courtesy of the Martin Moore collection.

Linnane remained in the Republican Army during the Civil War and he was adjutant of the 6th Battalion, with James Sugrue as his commandant. In this role Linnane commanded a detachment of Republican soldiers stationed at Gurrane Bridge near Bruree as they attempted to hold a defensive line south of Limerick city in July 1922. With the capture of James Sugrue, Linnane became the battalion O/C until his death.

1 Patrick Joseph McElligott, BMH WS 1013.
2 *Ibid.*

Linnane managed to evade capture until the final days of the conflict. In April 1923, along with Dick Bunyan and Jack Mullaly of Listowel, he took shelter in a dugout hidden in a hayshed in Jim Costello's farm in Trieneragh, a townland beside the River Feale between Listowel and Duagh. This elaborate hideout, which contained mattresses for the three men, had a bale of hay camouflaging its entrance. At 7.30 a.m. on Friday 13 April the three men were awoken by a nine-man Free State raiding party led by Sergeant Ned Hannafin. Initially they searched the farmhouse and then went to the farm's hayshed, where they became suspicious of how the hay was arranged. The bale of hay at the entrance was removed and the three men were ordered out of the dugout which lay beneath. The men were unarmed and agreed to surrender. As he was coming out through the narrow opening, John Linnane was shot in the head by Ned Hannafin and died immediately. Dick Bunyan, who was behind him, was injured in the chest by what turned out to be bone fragments from his commander's shattered skull. The initial reports stated that Linnane was a 'much wanted officer' and that he was killed when Free State soldiers threw a grenade into the dugout, but later they admitted that he was shot by the officer in charge.[3]

Dick Bunyan's wounds were dressed in Costello's house and he and Jack Mullaly were taken to the military barracks in Listowel. John Linnane's remains were brought by the patrol to the workhouse hospital at Listowel, where they were identified by his mother.[4] His Tricolour-draped coffin was brought to Gale Cemetery, which lies midway between Listowel and Lisselton. There he was buried in the Republican Plot and later, under the cover of darkness, his comrades fired a volley of shots in salute.

According to Denis Quille, a senior Republican in the Listowel area during the period and leader of the battalion column, the soldier who shot Linnane claimed he did so in error. The Free State Army officer Ned Hannafin, who was from Ballymacelligott, later approached Quille to express his remorse, saying that he had inadvertently fired the shot that had killed John Linnane as he surrendered.[5]

3 *The Freeman's Journal*, 14 April 1923, 1 May 1923, 16 May 1923; *Irish Independent*, 1 May 1923, 15 May 1923.
4 Information from Fr James Linnane, Listowel.
5 Unpublished memoir of Denis Quille, a senior IRA officer in the 6th Battalion, Kerry No. 1 Brigade, quoted by J. Anthony Gaughan in *Listowel and its Vicinity* (1973), p. 413.

John Linnane

John Linnane was the sixth member of the original 6th Battalion column of about eighteen men who would die during the Tan and Civil Wars. At Easter 1932 a memorial was unveiled over his grave and that of his five IRA comrades who lie in the cemetery on the banks of the River Gale, four miles from Listowel.

Jerry Lyons

Diarmuid Ó Liatáin

Courtesy of the Martin Moore collection.

Jeremiah (Jerry) Lyons was born in the village of Duagh on 3 March 1897. His father had a shop and a farm near the village which lies midway between Listowel and Abbeyfeale. Lyons was a Volunteer in the Duagh Company which was attached to the 6th Battalion, Kerry No. 1 Brigade. In December 1920 a flying column or active service unit was formed in the North Kerry area. The brigade O/C, Paddy Cahill, had already formed such a unit, which he commanded, composed of men mainly drawn from battalions from Tralee, mid Kerry and West Kerry. The new column for the northern section of the brigade area was composed of men from the 3rd and 6th Battalion areas and was commanded by Tom Kennelly, an ex-RIC man from Moneen who was O/C of the 3rd Battalion. The column was composed of some thirty men and Jerry Lyons was one of the Duagh Volunteers who was on active service in its ranks.

In late March it was decided that the column was too large and so the unit was divided into a 3rd Battalion column and a 6th Battalion column. Christy Broderick, or Broder as he was better known, and Jerry Lyons were the Duagh men on the 6th Battalion column, which was commanded by Denis Quille. The other members of the column were Con Dee, Brian O'Grady, Mick McNamara and Tom Carmody, all of Ballylongford; Jack Sheehan, Con Brosnan, Dan O'Grady and Jack Ahern, all from Moyvane; Paddy Dalton, an Athea native who was working in Listowel; John Linnane and the Quille brothers, Martin and Denis, all from Listowel; and Patrick Murphy of Ennismore. Later James Sugrue, who had earlier been the battalion O/C but had resigned this position in 1920, was taken into the column, as were Listowel men Tim O'Sullivan and Dan Enright, and Donal Bill O'Sullivan of Derry, near Listowel.

Following an outbreak amongst the column of the infectious skin disease scabies, the medical officer of the brigade, Dr Roger O'Connor, advised that the unit break up for some time. The men, who were 'on the run', split into smaller groups. On Wednesday 11 May Lyons and Broderick attended a meeting of the battalion at Coolard, near Listowel, and stayed there that night. Next morning, 12 May, they planned to travel by bicycle to their native Duagh before rejoining the column, which was to reform a day or so later. They cycled to Knockanure and then planned to go to Kilmorna and on to Duagh. On the way, early that morning, Broderick stopped to visit friends at Gortdromagowna, but Lyons cycled on to the home of Tim Carroll, the captain of the Knockanure Company. He then departed from Carroll's house and left a message for Broderick to follow him. Lyons then cycled towards Gortaglanna. It was there on the roadside that he met Paddy Walsh, Paddy Dalton, Con Dee and Mick Scannell. Whether this was a chance meeting or whether he was carrying a dispatch is not known, but the route he took from Coolard, which lies three miles from Listowel on the Ballybunion road, to his destination in Duagh was certainly circuitous.

Earlier that morning, at 9.30 a.m., Dalton, Walsh and Dee had left Athea by foot and headed towards Listowel. They were joined along the road by Mick Scannell, a local IRA Volunteer from Gortaglanna who had been over near Athea checking on grazing for his cattle. The townland of Gortaglanna lies in the valley of Knockanure, halfway between Listowel and Athea. As the four men journeyed on foot along this road they stopped at the McMahon farm which lies half a mile to the east of Gortaglanna crossroads, where the Moyvane road joins that going to Listowel. Walsh and Dalton went inside where Mrs McMahon gave them some milk, while the other two remained outside talking on the roadside. Walsh and Dalton left the house and went through the yard to the road where Scannell and Dee were chatting and all four then walked down the road towards Listowel. A little further on is a bridge and the four men stopped there when Jerry Lyons arrived on his bicycle having travelled from the Moyvane area.

The expected crown forces activity in the area that followed the IRA's killing of Sir Arthur Vicars at nearby Kilmorna House a few days earlier should have placed the men on their guard. However, it may have been that they were on a particular mission. It is known that Liam Lynch, O/C of the 1st Southern Division, was in Kerry that day and had met senior staff in Brackhill, Castlemaine, on or about that day, 12 May. Dan Mulvihill, a Kerry No. 2 officer in whose house Lynch met his Kerry staff, remarked that all roads in Kerry were manned at regular intervals with Volunteers to prevent an enemy raid, as Lynch was the most wanted man in Munster at the time. It is reasonable to surmise that the men in Gortaglanna were part of this operation or that Lynch was to pass through this area along the Kerry–Limerick border on his way home. Local information suggests that they were waiting for a dispatch, though it is not known what this was and it may have been that the men did not know what it contained. For whatever reason, the five men were waiting and talking on the road when the noise of engines was heard in the distance. Local lore suggests that the men dismissed the noise as coming from a train on the railway which was not too distant. However, the din of engines was that of two military lorries and a car which came upon the men suddenly, having turned onto this road from Gortaglanna Cross. The five men scattered. Mick Scannell, a brother-in-law of the McMahons, ran back towards their house. The other four jumped over a ditch and ran into an open field. After some initial shots from the Tans, the men raised their hands and surrendered. The four prisoners were placed in the vehicles and then the Tans turned their attention to McMahons' house. There they captured Mick Scannell and told him that he was to be shot. Mrs Bridget McMahon grabbed her brother-in-law and pleaded with the officer in charge, recognising him as Scottish, explaining that she had worked as a nurse for a Scottish family in London where she cared for wounded servicemen who had returned from the Great War. As a result of her pleading, Scannell was released and the Tans returned to their vehicles.[1]

After twenty minutes the convoy moved off in the direction of Athea with the four prisoners. Jerry Lyons was in the third vehicle, Walsh and Dalton in the second and Con Dee in the first. About a half a mile from the McMahon house the convoy stopped, turned and headed back towards Listowel. Passing McMahons' again and two small bridges, they halted a mile further up the road. On the right was a field with a large ring fort and it was into this field

---

1 Information from Mick Scannell, a nephew of Mick Scannell.

that the four men were brought. They were ordered to run but refused and then were marched forty yards into the field, to the edge of the ring fort. There they were lined up and a firing squad formed. As the men stood, Con Dee was on the right side, Jerry Lyons beside him, then Paddy Dalton and finally Paddy Walsh. Four Tans were selected to be the executioners and the remainder stood behind them. Jerry Lyons was shot first and then Walsh and Dalton were killed. The Tan in front of Con Dee hesitated and as Dee saw Lyons fall, he began to run, but having gotten about twelve yards, he was shot in the thigh as the other Tans then directed their fire at him. The bullet failed to fell Dee, who kept running despite the intense firing. He ran beside a ditch which was parallel to the road and while some of the Tans followed him on foot, others fired from the vehicles as they drove in pursuit. Discarding his coat, collar and tie, he managed to run about three miles before he collapsed, exhausted, in a drain. There he was found and sheltered by local farmers.[2] He recovered and was able to testify as to the true nature of the events at Gortaglanna on 12 May 1921, events that the British official reports of the incident termed the 'Ambush at Kilmorna'.[3]

The bodies of Jerry Lyons and his two comrades were put into the lorries and brought to Tralee that evening. The remains were subsequently released and brought to the parish church in Listowel. From there the coffin of Jerry Lyons was brought to his native Duagh. Following a large funeral he was buried in what is now the Republican Plot in the local cemetery. There he lies with six other IRA Volunteers under a large Celtic cross which was unveiled in May 1933 by former O/C of Kerry No. 1 Brigade, Andy Cooney, and the commander of Lyons' 6th Battalion, Denis Quille of Listowel.

2   *Shannonside Annual 1952*, article by Con Dee.
3   *Irish Independent*, 25 June 1921.

Michael (Bob) McElligott

Mícheál Mac Uilleagóid

Courtesy of the Martin Moore collection.

Michael Robert (Bob) McElligott was a native of Listowel. He was born on 27 February 1898 and lived in William Street where his family had a business. His father, also named Michael, died at a young age and the family subsequently moved to Convent Street. Bob, as he was known, became involved in the Volunteer movement at an early age and in 1917 he was O/C of the reorganised Fianna in the town. With a restructuring of the Irish Volunteer company in Listowel in May 1918, Bob McElligott was appointed to the rank of second lieutenant. At this time James Sugrue, a Cahersiveen native, who was working as a shop assistant in Listowel, was O/C of the 4th Battalion, Kerry No. 1 Brigade. Following an unsuccessful attack on the RIC barracks in Ballybunion in March 1920, Sugrue resigned his command and subsequently the Kerry No. 1 Brigade O/C, Paddy Cahill, confirmed Bob McElligott as the new O/C of the Listowel-based 4th Battalion.[1] Under his leadership, the IRA in the Listowel area took part in many engagements with the forces of the British crown. In January 1921 a new intensity to the conflict resulted from the formation of an active service unit, commanded by Tom Kennelly in Bob McElligott's battalion area.[2]

From November 1920 the Brigade O/C Paddy Cahill had his headquarters at Fybough on the southern side of the Sliabh Mish Mountains. In January 1921 GHQ in Dublin sent an organiser named Joe Byrne to increase the

---

1   During this period there was another officer in the Listowel company named Michael 'Pikie' McElligott with whom Michael (Bob) McElligott may be confused. The Listowel-based 4th Battalion became the 6th Battalion in April 1921 following a brigade restructuring.
2   Patrick Joseph McElligott, BMH WS 1013, brother of Michael Robert McElligott.

effectiveness of the brigade. Byrne was one of a number of such organisers who were sent to various brigades at the time, but, unlike Andy Cooney, his counterpart in South Kerry, Joe Byrne proved to be ineffectual and commanded little respect from the Kerry No. 1 Brigade staff.[3]

On 18 February 1921 Byrne summoned all battalion commanders to a meeting at Camp, ten miles west of Tralee and across the mountains from the brigade headquarters. Bob McElligott travelled to Camp for the meeting and stayed overnight. The next day, a Saturday, at 8 a.m. he left by bicycle with Paddy Garvey, heading towards Tralee on the initial leg of his journey home. At Derrymore, six miles from Tralee, they encountered a cycling patrol of British military. Garvey and McElligott abandoned their bicycles and ran for cover, whereupon the soldiers, who were 400 yards away, opened fire. The two men were well within range of the rifle fire and, as they were not carrying anything incriminating, Garvey advised McElligott to surrender. Garvey stopped and gave himself up, but Bob McElligott kept on running and soon was wounded and fell. The Listowel man was known to be an active Republican while Garvey was not. The soldiers brought their wounded captive by ambulance to the military hospital at Ballymullen Barracks in Tralee, where he died the next morning. Garvey was questioned for a few days but was released after he convinced his interrogators that he had only met McElligott on the road that morning.[4]

The remains of twenty-two-year-old Michael Robert McElligott were released to his family and initially brought to St John's parish church in Tralee. From there they were transferred by train to Listowel. He was buried in the McElligott family plot at Listowel Cemetery after a large funeral. Bob McElligott was succeeded by his brother Patrick Joseph (P.J.) as battalion O/C. Commandant Michael Robert McElligott is remembered on the Republican Plot memorial in Listowel Cemetery which was unveiled by Seán MacBride on 20 April 1930.

---

3   Ernie O'Malley *The Men Will Talk to Me – Kerry Interviews* (2012), interview with Billy Mullins.
4   Patrick Garvey, BMH WS 1011.

Charles O'Hanlon

Cormac Ó hAnaláin[1]

Charlie O'Hanlon was born in Listowel in 1906. He was the son of a victualler and the family lived in the town's William Street. Charlie O'Hanlon was a Volunteer in the Listowel-based 6th Battalion, Kerry No. 1 Brigade. Despite his young age he was involved in the military activities in and around Listowel. It is recalled that when standing on a reek of turf retrieving some weapons, the pin from a grenade that he was holding slipped from the bomb and fell down beneath the sods of turf. He managed to stay calm and summoned his father, who searched and eventually found the pin and replaced it in the grenade.[2]

The only town in Kerry which was in possession of the Free State forces in June 1922 was O'Hanlon's home town of Listowel. At the outset of the Civil War, with the attack on Dublin's Four Courts, the Kerry IRA Brigades quickly massed their forces and on the morning of 30 June captured Listowel. The Kerry units then advanced on Limerick city, with the Free State garrisons in West County Limerick fleeing before them. When they reached the city an uneasy truce was in place between the Free State Army and Liam Lynch's Republican forces, with Lynch unwilling to spill Irish blood in pressing home his advantage. Within a week the Free State forces had been reinforced by men from the disbanded British regiment, the Connaught Rangers, and were now supported by field artillery. With inferior forces, the Republicans were forced to yield their positions in the city after a local truce collapsed and the Free State Army renewed fighting. Largely intact, the Republican units retreated to the towns south of the city and hoped to hold a line all the way to Waterford. Charlie O'Hanlon was attached to a Kerry IRA unit under the command of Thomas O'Connor of Milltown, which defended Kilmallock and its hinterland.[3]

---

1 There is no known photograph of Charlie O'Hanlon.
2 Information from Michael O'Hanlon, Listowel, a nephew of Charlie O'Hanlon.
3 Ernie O'Malley, *The Men Will Talk to Me – Kerry Interviews* (2012), interviews with Bertie Scully and Tom O'Connor.

Republican forces held the town of Kilmallock but Free State forces under the command of Frank Flood captured and garrisoned the nearby village of Bruree. On the morning of 2 August 1922, two IRA columns left Kilmallock in a counter-attack on Bruree. O'Hanlon was a member of the column led by Bertie Scully of Glencar, along with John Cronin of Ballymacelligott and several other Kerrymen. With them was Erskine Childers, the Republican director of publicity. They had surrounded a Free State post at Bruree Lodge when Con O'Leary of Kerry No. 2 Brigade, V/C of operations in the area, passed by in an armoured car. Fire was opened on the armoured car from inside the house, but then it stopped. Men got out to crank up the vehicle and shooting did not resume. It was assumed then by the Republicans that the Free State soldiers inside Bruree Lodge had thought it best to follow the example of their comrades in the other two outposts in the village and surrender. Charlie O'Hanlon was approaching the door of the house when shots were fired through the door from the inside, grievously injuring him. His comrades managed to get him into the armoured car and to safety, but he died later of his wounds, probably on 4 August 1922.

John Pinkman, a Free State soldier, recalled the incident in his published memoir, *In the Legion of the Vanguard*. He states that O'Leary's armoured car stopped within six yards of the front door and Republican soldiers jumped out and attempted to storm his position in Bruree Lodge. However, intense firing from the house drove them back leaving one man badly wounded, who was evacuated by his comrades.[4]

Charlie O'Hanlon's remains were to be returned to his family in Listowel. However, on 2 August the Free State Army landed in Fenit and later that day captured Tralee. A further seaborne landing at Tarbert allowed Free State forces to capture Listowel while the experienced Kerry Republican forces were fighting in Limerick and Tipperary. O'Hanlon's remains were transferred to the care of Commandant Jeremiah O'Leary of Scartaglin, O/C of the 7th Battalion, Kerry No. 1 Brigade, centred on Castleisland. However, Free State activity in North Kerry prevented the completion of Charlie O'Hanlon's final journey and, with regret, Jeremiah O'Leary had to inform the O'Hanlon family

4   John A. Pinkman, *In the Legion of the Vanguard* (1999), p. 157.

by letter that their son was buried in Kilbannivane Cemetery, Castleisland.[5] Today his name in Irish, Cormac Ó hAnaláin, is inscribed on the Celtic cross that stands over the Republican Plot there.

---

5   Letter from Jeremiah O'Leary, O/C 7th Battalion, Kerry No. 1 Brigade, to the O'Hanlon family.

Paddy Walsh

Pádraig Breatnac

Patrick Walsh was born at Knockenagh South, Gunsboro, in North Kerry on 29 July 1894. His father was a farmer there. His mother, Margaret Keane, died when he was young. Patrick Walsh senior was remarried in 1899, to Julia Kissane. Paddy Walsh was the fourth child in a large family.

Walsh initially joined the Irish Volunteers when they were established in North Kerry in early 1914. In 1917 they were reorganised throughout Kerry following the defeat of the rebellion a year earlier. His local Ballydonoghue Company elected Walsh to be their captain, with Mick Kissane as his lieutenant. Within a short time Walsh's company of Volunteers had eighty men and were drilling regularly under the instruction of Tom Kennelly of Moneen. Kennelly had been a member of the RIC but resigned following the 1916 Rising because of his Republican sympathies. Kennelly later became O/C of the 3rd Battalion, Kerry No. 1 Brigade. As a result of his activities, Walsh received a prison sentence for illegal drilling, which he served in Limerick Gaol.

Courtesy of the Martin Moore collection.

The first major event that the Ballydonoghue Company was involved in was the confrontation that occurred over the 'Cows' Lawn' in Listowel in 1918. This was an area within Listowel comprising about thirty acres owned by Lord Listowel that was used by some of his tenants as grazing ground for their livestock. The local Sinn Féin organisation petitioned Lord Listowel to allow local people to plant crops there to alleviate the food shortages caused by the Great War. Their request was refused and the Irish Volunteers of the Listowel district were mobilised to take control of the fields. A confrontation between the Volunteers and the military was narrowly averted when the two sitting tenants, who had sided with the landlord, conceded that the land could be ploughed to allow crops to be planted rather than have it as a grazing ground. This decision may have been made under duress, as several Sinn Féin members were jailed for two months having been convicted of their part in the confrontation. Paddy Walsh led his Ballydonoghue Company at the stand-off in Listowel on that day.

In 1919 Paddy Walsh resigned as company captain and was replaced by Edmond Walsh. At this stage Paddy Walsh was taking a more active role at battalion level in the increasingly military resistance to British rule.

On 13 March 1920 Ballybunion RIC Barracks was the target of a large-scale attack. James Sugrue was O/C of the Listowel Battalion and he was in charge of the proposed attack, with sixty men under his command, though few had useful weapons. One of the Volunteers armed with a rifle was Paddy Walsh. The home-made mines that Sugrue had hoped would cause devastating damage to the barracks failed to explode and after forty-five minutes of gunfire the attackers were forced to withdraw. There were no casualties on either side.

At about this time the Listowel Battalion was reorganised and the Ballydonoghue Company to which Paddy Walsh was attached was re-assigned to the Lixnaw-based 3rd Battalion.

On 3 May 1920 Sergeant Francis McKenna and Constables Rabbett and Colgan were cycling back to Ballylongford from the Listowel Quarterly Sessions. When they reached Gale Bridge, about three miles from Listowel, they were held up by a group of IRA men. The ambush party comprised Volunteers Paddy Walsh, John Walsh, Michael Ahern, T. P. O'Shea, Thomas O'Connor, Mick Galvin and Paddy Corridon. They called on the policemen to surrender but one drew his weapon, whereupon the attackers opened fire. Sergeant Francis McKenna of Waterford, who previously had been a detective in Tralee, was shot dead immediately. In the gunfire, Constable Colgan managed to wound O'Shea but not seriously and he himself was subsequently shot and wounded by O'Shea. After some fighting at close quarters, both RIC constables surrendered, having been severely wounded.

In August 1920 Paddy Walsh was a member of a 3rd Battalion force that went to attack the coastguard station at the Cashen. They expected stern resistance, but the coastguards quickly surrendered and the building was burned.

Paddy Walsh

On 31 October 1920 a general order went out from GHQ for a concerted series of attacks on the crown forces wherever they could be encountered. Paddy Walsh was a member of the 3rd Battalion attack force that converged on Ballybunion to attack an RIC patrol there. The ambush failed, as a premature discharge of a weapon apparently warned the crown forces of the impending attack, and, despite some sustained gunfire, the RIC could not be dislodged from their barracks.

The North Kerry flying column was formed in January 1921 and such were the number of men in the unit that in March of that year it divided into a 3rd Battalion column under Tom Kennelly and a 6th Battalion column under the command of Listowel man Denis Quille. Paddy Walsh was a member of Kennelly's unit. These men saw action all over North Kerry. However, in early May the active service unit temporarily disbanded. On 10 May P. J. McElligott, who had been appointed as O/C of the 6th Battalion after his brother Bob was killed in February, was summoned to a brigade meeting in Derrymore, west of Tralee. McElligott was accompanied by Paddy Walsh for some of the journey and at Doonferris they narrowly escaped a crown force mobile patrol. Walsh then parted company with McElligott, who went south to the Derrymore meeting. Walsh headed to Athea to meet with Paddy Dalton and Con Dee, who had already been in the West Limerick village for the previous two days of the parish mission.[1] Dee was Walsh's first cousin. Apparently Walsh had earlier received a dispatch from a Listowel Volunteer named Buckley that a named woman was passing information to the RIC and this would be used to capture West Limerick IRA men who would be attending the parish mission in Athea. Walsh sent Con Dee and Paddy Dalton, who was from Athea, to the village to warn the local Volunteers of a possible round-up during the mission.

Returning from Athea, Walsh, Dee and Dalton were met by Jerry Lyons at Gortaglanna Bridge. As the four men stood talking to local IRA Volunteer Mick Scannell, they were unaware of the approach of crown force vehicles until it was too late. As they tried to escape the men were quickly captured. Scannell was released, but the rest were put into the vehicles and driven away. They were eventually brought into a field not far from where they had been captured and

---

1 Patrick Joseph McElligott, BMH WS 1013.

were lined up near a ring fort for execution. As the four men stood before their executioners, Paddy Walsh was on the extreme right. With Dalton and Lyons he was killed on the spot where a monument now stands, while Dee managed to escape.

Walsh's remains were brought back to Tralee by the crown forces. Later they were released to his family and a funeral mass was held in Listowel parish church for the three men killed at Gortaglanna. Following this Captain Paddy Walsh was laid to rest in Gale Cemetery, near Listowel.

Daniel Scanlon

Domnall Ó Scannláin

Dan Scanlon was a native of Ballybunion and lived on Sandhill Road.[1] He was employed as a groundsman by Ballybunion Golf Club.[2] On the formation of the Irish Volunteers in his native town in 1914, Dan Scanlon enrolled as a member. In 1917, with the release of the prisoners and reorganisation of the Irish Volunteers, the Ballybunion Company was particularly active.

On 11 July 1917 a parade was held in Ballybunion to celebrate the election of Sinn Féin candidate Éamon de Valera in the County Clare by-election. The Volunteers marched up along the town's main street, past the RIC barracks and on to the village green.

Courtesy of the Martin Moore collection.

Dan Scanlon was the flag bearer for the Ballybunion Volunteer Company in the victory parade. As they marched in military formation along the main street, an onlooker, Mick Downey, threw a stone through a window of the barracks, shattering the glass. Downey was from Gortnaskehy just outside the town and was a serving British soldier, though he was not in uniform at the parade. The parade continued up the town to The Green and then returned to pass the barracks again at about midnight. As it did so, the RIC opened fire without warning from inside the building. The Volunteers and onlookers scattered but one, Dan Scanlon, was fatally wounded in the back. Following the shooting, the local Volunteers and Na Fianna attacked the barracks with stones, but the RIC did not fire any further shots and remained inside the building. Seriously wounded, Dan Scanlon was brought into a premises across the road from the barracks and, despite medical attention, died of his injuries five hours later.[3]

1 The surname is also spelled Scanlan.
2 Information from Michael Scanlon, Ballybunion, nephew of Dan Scanlon.
3 William McCabe, BMH WS 1212.

An inquest subsequently judged that Constable Lyons had fired the fatal shot. The coroner recommended that this RIC man and Sergeant Mulcahy, the commanding officer in the barracks, should be charged with murder as the police had recklessly fired on the unarmed crowd.[4] The two RIC men were charged before the Cork Assizes, where a witness, Mary Mason, identified Lyons as the shooter of the fatal shot. Disregarding the evidence, the case was quickly dismissed and Lyons and Mulcahy were not convicted. The RIC claimed in defence that those on the street had fired on the barracks, though overwhelming evidence contradicted this.

At a special court held in Tralee on 7 August 1917, six local men – J. Sullivan, M. Beasley, P. Mulvihill, J. Houlihan, J. Stack and J. Breen – were all charged with offences arising out of the incident that night.[5]

Volunteer Dan Scanlon was buried with full military honours in Ballybunion's Killahenny Cemetery, where an impressive memorial stands over his grave. Today he is remembered by a plaque on the wall of the premises where he died of his injuries.

---

4   *The Kerryman*, 21 July 1917.
5   *Ibid.*, 15 August 1917.

Jack Sheehan

Seán Ó Séadacáin

John (Jack) Sheehan was born in 1888 in the townland of Coilbee which lies between Listowel and the village of Moyvane. In 1917 he joined the Newtownsandes (now Moyvane) Company of the Irish Volunteers which was attached to the 6th (Listowel) Battalion.

In January 1921 an order came from Paddy Cahill, the Kerry No. 1 Brigade O/C, stating that District Inspector Tobias O'Sullivan was to be shot. O'Sullivan had been the sergeant in Kilmallock RIC Barracks when it was attacked in May 1920. The stubborn resistance of the garrison prevented the barracks being captured and resulted in the death of Kerry Volunteer Liam Scully. For his leadership during the defence of the barracks, Tobias O'Sullivan was promoted to the rank of district inspector and was transferred to Listowel. It was probable that he would have been able to identify several of the Limerick Volunteers who took part in the Kilmallock attack. This would have had serious implications for any of those men who were in custody for other suspected IRA activities by January 1921. Fearing this, GHQ issued an order to Paddy Cahill, O/C of Kerry No. 1 Brigade, to have O'Sullivan killed. The 6th Battalion O/C asked for volunteers to shoot the district inspector and the Newtownsandes Company took on the job. Con Brosnan, Jack Ahern and Dan O'Grady were armed for the task, while Jack Sheehan was their scout, tracking the movements of their target. DI O'Sullivan was shot dead a short distance from the barracks in Listowel on 20 January 1921 and the four Moyvane men made good their escape.[1]

Later that month, the North Kerry flying column was formed and was

Courtesy of the Martin Moore collection.

---

1   Con Brosnan, BMH WS 1123 and Jack Ahern, BMH WS 790.

comprised of approximately thirty men from the 6th and 3rd Battalion areas. It was commanded by Tom Kennelly. Sheehan, O'Grady, Brosnan and Ahern volunteered for active service with the column. The column was involved in several engagements in the North Kerry area before it was divided into two battalion columns. Jack Sheehan and his three Moyvane comrades served in the 6th Battalion column under Denis Quille of Listowel.

On 25 May 1921 some of the column was sent to Dromerrin where, with the local company, they were to attack a crown force patrol. However, the arrival of a much larger force than had been expected led to the attack being abandoned and the Volunteers had to withdraw without firing a shot. They headed north to Asdee and then into Ballylongford village, where they fired shots at the RIC barracks. Following this, the members of the column retired to near Moyvane, where they had their billets. Being near to his home in Coilbee, Sheehan was granted permission to visit his family. He travelled the short distance and was outside his house chatting to his brother Denis when they heard the noise of military vehicles. Denis went quickly into the family home, while Jack ran to a nearby abandoned farmhouse. Aware of the inevitable consequences of capture, he then attempted to get further away by crossing the adjacent bog. At that point he was spotted by the patrol and was fired on with machine guns and rifles but, uninjured, he continued to run across the open bog. The story is related locally that the commanding officer ordered his men to cease shooting and assembled his riflemen to fire in sequence as he called on them. The first nine men missed their mark but Jack Sheehan was mortally wounded in the abdomen by the tenth man at a distance of 500 yards. He died with his pistol in his hand on Carhooearagh Bog.

His remains were initially interred in Knockanure Graveyard, but a few weeks later, during the Truce, they were reburied in the Republican Plot in Listowel Cemetery. Today a monument stands near Jack Sheehan's home at Coilbee which was erected by his fellow Volunteers from the locality. Five hundred yards away, in the Carhooearagh Bog, stands a large cross which marks the exact location where Sheehan was mortally wounded.

As a sequel to the killing of Sheehan, the policeman who claimed to have fired the fatal round was a Constable Farnlow, a Black and Tan based in Tarbert. The night before the Truce came into force, several of Sheehan's comrades from the column journeyed to the village of Tarbert in order to shoot Farnlow. He was known to be drinking in a local public house there with several other Black and Tans. A short distance outside the village, the group of IRA men halted. Three of them, Sheehan's comrades from the Moyvane Company, Jack Ahern, Con Brosnan and Dan O'Grady, went ahead on reconnaissance. Having located the Tans in a pub, Brosnan and O'Grady went back to get the main body of the column, but before they returned, Farnlow and the other Black and Tans began to leave the pub and walk up the village's main street. Ahern, then on his own, opened fire on the Tans with his revolver, slightly wounding two of them. They managed to escape to the barracks despite their injuries.

1st (Castleisland) Battalion, Kerry No. 2 Brigade

7th (Castleisland) Battalion, Kerry No. 1 Brigade

The Irish Volunteers were founded in Castleisland in April 1914. Within a short time the Volunteer movement had been established in all the neighbouring parishes. The region around the market town of Castleisland had long been a centre of militant nationalism and was described as 'the most disturbed area in Ireland' during the Land Wars of the 1880s and early 1890s. And so it was that in the following generation the Moonlighter groups had evolved into the local IRA companies that were to be at the forefront of the fight for freedom in Kerry.

On the foundation of the Volunteers in Castleisland in 1914, a local veteran of the Land Wars, Dan O'Mahony, was appointed O/C. O'Mahony had gone into exile in the United States following his involvement with the Moonlighter movement and subsequently had travelled to South Africa, where he supported the Boer cause in their fight with Britain. Having spent time as a 'big game' hunter, he returned to Castleisland and, despite his age, was regarded as the natural leader of the East Kerry section of the Kerry Brigade of the recently established Irish Volunteers. At Easter 1916 O'Mahony led his men to Camp, three miles from Castleisland, when they mobilised for the Rising. However, he was obliged to send them home again as the elaborate scheme to land arms at Fenit had unravelled and the rebellion in Kerry had failed before it could begin.

From 1917 onwards there was a significant influx of recruits into the Irish Volunteers as the Rising had woken a people from its apathy towards the cause of national independence. In 1919 the single Kerry regiment of Irish Volunteers was divided into three brigades. Castleisland's Dan O'Mahony was appointed O/C of the Kerry No. 2 Brigade and he was also the commander of the local battalion. His deputy was Humphrey 'Free' Murphy of Currow.

The area around Castleisland was designated the 1st Battalion and it remained under O'Mahony's command until a reorganisation of brigade staff in January 1921.

Andy Cooney, an organiser from GHQ in Dublin, arrived in Castleisland in early January 1921 to reorganise and reinvigorate the brigade as the war intensified. O'Mahony was willing to step aside to allow younger men to come to the fore. Humphrey Murphy became O/C of the Kerry No. 2 Brigade and Timothy O'Connor became the O/C of the 1st Battalion. Dan McCarthy was initially the battalion vice-commandant, but in a short time this role was taken by Richard (Dick) Shanahan. David Griffin was the battalion adjutant and John O'Mahony was the quartermaster. In May 1921 further changes were made for a variety of reasons. Jeremiah O'Leary of Scartaglin became O/C, a position that he held until his murder in custody following the end of the Civil War. David McCarthy of Cordal became his V/C and Dick Shanahan of Castleisland was the adjutant. John Walsh of Lyre, Currow, was the 1st Battalion's quartermaster.

The 1st Battalion was composed of companies from Castleisland and the surrounding parishes. There were Volunteer companies in Brosna, Knocknagoshel, Cordal, Castleisland, Scartaglin, Currow and Lyreacrompane. In July 1921 Humphrey Murphy replaced Andy Cooney as O/C of the Kerry No. 1 Brigade. As Murphy was from Currow and the Castleisland area was his powerbase, it was decided to transfer much of the 1st Battalion to the Kerry No. 1 Brigade. Thus this portion of the original battalion became the 7th Battalion, Kerry No. 1 Brigade. The Ballymacelligott Company was transferred to this new 7th Battalion from the 2nd (Fiaries) Battalion, Kerry No. 2 Brigade. Scartaglin remained in the Kerry No. 2 Brigade and together with companies from Rathnanane, Currow, Anabla and Knockrour it formed the reorganised 1st Battalion of Kerry No. 2 Brigade. However, in practice such units were separate only on paper, as the active Volunteers moved and fought throughout the Castleisland district as the situation demanded.

The 1st Battalion was one of the most prominent units in the Tan War. In June 1920 there was an attempt to attack the Brosna RIC Barracks. Following the failure of the initial assault, the attackers returned two weeks later and unsuccessfully laid siege to the building. Scartaglin Barracks was attacked in

March 1920 and, though not captured, this prompted the RIC to abandon the post. The topography around Castleisland favoured guerrilla tactics and the 1st Battalion waged constant warfare on the forces of the crown. With the formation of the flying column of the Kerry No. 2 Brigade in March 1921, several experienced Volunteers from the battalion saw action with this column during attacks at Headford Junction and Clonbanin Cross. The formation of a battalion active service unit in the late spring of that year resulted in further significant attacks on the crown forces, both on the streets of Castleisland and in the surrounding countryside. On the eve of the Truce, a large-scale attack on a military patrol on Castleisland's Main Street resulted in five British fatalities, but three members of Humphrey Murphy's force were also killed.

The 7th Battalion, as it now was, remained committed to the Republican cause following the division that occurred as a result of the Treaty. Castleisland was captured by Free State forces on 5 August 1922 and they established their garrison in Hartnett's Hotel at the corner of Main Street and the Limerick road. The Free State detachment stationed there soon gained a reputation for brutality as they attempted to quash resistance in an area where popular support was given to the local Republican fighters. The Free State Army suffered significant casualties in the ongoing conflict and it, in turn, responded by summarily executing several Republican prisoners who had the misfortune to fall into their hands. It is probable that the 7th Battalion area suffered more than all other areas of the county and, perhaps, in Ireland as a whole, as the Civil War dragged on to its bloody conclusion. The ceasefire of 30 April 1923 didn't halt the killing, as Commandant Jeremiah O'Leary of Scartaglin was shot dead while in custody at Hartnett's Hotel three weeks after the IRA had silenced its weapons.

Michael Brosnan

Mícheál Ó Brosnacháin[1]

Michael Brosnan was a native of Castleisland. He was born on 24 November 1900 and he followed in his father's footsteps earning his living as a cobbler. He was a member of the Castleisland Company of the 1st Battalion, Kerry No. 2 Brigade. His activities made him the focus of RIC interest and he was forced to leave his native town. He moved to Rathoneen, near Ardfert, where he lived with his aunt, Margaret Collins. This townland near Banna Strand was where Roger Casement was captured in 1916 and would be the site of several killings during the Civil War.

The first week of November 1920 saw a dramatic increase in attacks on the crown forces throughout North Kerry. This resulted in several RIC fatalities as IRA Volunteers became increasingly active in the villages north of Tralee. The intensification of the conflict provoked a harsh response from the RIC, who were now supported by Black and Tans. Hampered by the abandonment of many of their rural barracks, including that in Ardfert, the RIC were forced to patrol the hostile countryside in military vehicles and in large numbers to prevent guerrilla attacks.

On 8 November 1920 one such RIC convoy entered the village of Ardfert, arriving by two different routes. Their sudden arrival surprised the villagers, as the RIC had carried out raids in the village three days previously following an attack on Causeway Barracks. They detained Michael Brosnan at his workplace. They also arrested John Cantillon, an Ardfert IRA Volunteer who was going to the doctor in the village that morning, and another local man, Maurice (Mossy) McElligott. The three prisoners were placed on the police vehicles to be used as hostages when the convoy moved off in the direction of Rathoneen, where further raids were carried out.[2]

Returning towards Ardfert, the convoy stopped and the three men were ordered out of the Crossley tender and were brought into a field at the edge

---

1   There is no known photograph of Michael Brosnan.
2   Patrick Sheehan, BMH WS 1088.

of the village near the old school. This field is now the Hazel Grove housing estate. The Black and Tans ordered Michael Brosnan and John Cantillon to run, but the RIC officer standing in front of Mossy McElligott advised him not to move for his own safety. Brosnan and Cantillon were both shot dead after they had run about fifty yards. Their bodies were described as having been riddled with bullets. McElligott, although he received a beating from his captors, survived the ordeal. The Black and Tans then crossed the field and, going over a stile, entered O'Sullivan's public house, now Kate Browne's, by the back door. There they demanded free drink from the publican.[3]

Michael Brosnan's remains were returned to his native Castleisland and he is buried in the Republican Plot at Kilbannivane Cemetery. The Republican monument in Ardfert is adjacent to where this Castleisland man gave his life for Ireland's freedom.

---

3   Information from Tommy O'Connor, local historian.

Patrick Buckley

Pádraig Ó Buacalla

Patrick Buckley was born near Tournafulla in West Limerick. He joined the RIC in 1909 and by 1916 he was stationed in Farranfore Barracks. He had no nationalist sympathies and had a reputation as a stern constable in a district that had been a hotbed of Moonlighter resistance to British rule a generation earlier. Following the Rising in Dublin a proclamation was issued stating that persons holding firearms should surrender these to the RIC before 6 May 1916. Buckley was one of two constables from Farranfore to journey to nearby Currans to post the proclamations, while another pair travelled the two miles to Firies village to issue the order there. The latter RIC men were met by local Irish Volunteer, Jim Riordan of Longfield, as they walked along the village street. Riordan shot and seriously injured both of them with his pistol before they could react. Jim Riordan went 'on the run' and Constable Patrick Buckley was to the forefront in attempts to capture him and his brother, Paddy Riordan, the Firies Company captain. Constable Buckley went to the extreme of going undercover in the district in an attempt to apprehend the Riordan brothers, dead or alive. However, the two Firies Volunteers evaded capture, with Jim escaping initially to America and later to Australia, where he died in 1947.[1]

Courtesy of the Martin Moore collection.

Such was Buckley's antipathy to the Volunteers in the Farranfore area that he quickly became a figure of hatred and was transferred to Sixmilebridge in County Clare for his own safety. In 1917 he gave evidence against some Clare Volunteers who were tried for illegal drilling, but, following this episode, he

1   *The Kerryman*, 27 November 1948.

began to reassess his loyalty to the crown and to the RIC who were Britain's 'eyes and ears' in his native land. He made contact with the Clare Brigade of the Irish Volunteers and urged them to consider taking the Sixmilebridge Barracks where he was stationed, which could easily be achieved with his help from the inside. The brigade was initially apprehensive and wary of Buckley. However, on 5 August 1919 Volunteers under the command of Michael Brennan, aided from within by Buckley, captured the barracks and took the weapons of the RIC garrison who had quickly surrendered. Two days later, Buckley tendered his resignation from the force, which had not suspected his role in the capture of Sixmilebridge Barracks.[2]

Buckley, who was married with four children, at this stage returned to his native West Limerick. There he opened a small shop in order to support his family. With his conversion to the Republican cause now complete, he joined the local IRA unit and was one of the sixteen Limerick Volunteers under the command of Mossy Harnett who joined with units from North Kerry to attack Brosna RIC Barracks on 5 June 1920.[3] Five weeks later he fearlessly walked up the main street in Abbeyfeale with local IRA leader Jimmy Collins, both armed with rifles, as they set up an attack on the Black and Tans in that town.[4] Although active in the West Limerick IRA, there was still a lingering suspicion of the ex-RIC constable among the local Volunteers which prevented him from taking a more prominent role. However, he was appointed to the Republican Police in the Abbeyfeale district. In October 1920 one of the senior officers in the West Limerick Republican Police was detained. In his possession were incriminating documents naming Buckley as one of his staff and as a result Patrick Buckley became a wanted man and had to go 'on the run'. Unable to stay at home, his business soon closed and his wife then returned to her home near Castleisland. In January 1921 Paddy Buckley joined her in Kerry. At this stage his wife had given birth to their fifth child.

Patrick Buckley joined the 7th Battalion of the Kerry No. 2 Brigade, the O/C of which was Jeremiah O'Leary of Scartaglin. His experience with fire-

---

2   Uinseann Mac Eoin, *Survivors* (1980), statement by Patrick Buckley in the appendix, p. 536.
3   Mossie Harnett, *Victory and Woe* (2002), p. 54.
4   James Collins of Abbeyfeale, BMH WS 1272.

arms from his service with the RIC meant that Buckley was appointed as a training officer in the battalion. During the Truce he was appointed O/C of the Republican Police in the Castleisland district. A proficient machine gunner and explosives expert, Buckley was active in the Republican forces during the early Civil War when he was again forced to go 'on the run'.

Former RIC men such as Buckley were seen as valuable assets for the fledgling Free State police force if they could be enticed to join the pro-Treaty Civic Guard. In October 1922 he wrote an account of his role in the events from 1916 until the Treaty and indicated that he had no intention of joining a Free State police force that would have at its core former RIC men who had no nationalist leanings. This testimony also stated that he was no longer on active service with the IRA, though this would appear not to have been the case and it is possible that the testimony was written to protect his family in the event of his being captured.[5]

On 4 February 1923 a Free State Army unit operating from Hartnett's Hotel, their garrison in Castleisland, captured Buckley and also John Daly, who shared his fate at Ballyseedy over a month later. These men were transferred to the main detention centre in Ballymullen Barracks, Tralee. When David Neligan, the Free State intelligence chief in Kerry, was choosing the men to die at Ballyseedy on the morning of 7 March 1923, he included Patrick Buckley. It was thought that his Tan War record and the fact that he had a wife and five young children might protect him from execution, but this was not to be the case. It is most likely that Patrick Buckley's refusal to accept a position in the Free State police or army, thereby giving these forces a degree of legitimacy, sealed his fate in the eyes of a man such as Neligan. It is said that he was called a 'deserter from the RIC' by his captors and there is other evidence that men who had defected from the British Army or RIC during the Tan War were held in particular contempt by some Free State officers, many of whom served in the crown forces before joining the Free State Army.

Patrick Buckley was buried in the Republican Plot in Castleisland's Kilbannivane Cemetery. His death at Ballyseedy Cross is noted on the monument there.

5   Uinseann Mac Eoin, *Survivors* (1980), statement by Patrick Buckley in the appendix, p. 536.

John Daly

Seagán Ó Dálaig[1]

John Daly was a native of Ahaneboy, Castleisland. He was born into a family of small farmers in this townland which lies three miles to the north of Castleisland on the main road to Abbeyfeale. John Jack, as he was known, was a Volunteer in the 7th Battalion of Kerry No. 1 Brigade. He was a member of the battalion's active service unit in the Tan and Civil Wars.

The main road from Castleisland to Abbeyfeale, having climbed the hill overlooking the market town, then divides into two routes. The smaller road, known as the Meinleitrim Road, initially travels parallel to the main road as it journeys to the village of Brosna. During the Civil War the Free State Army had a post in Brosna, which was supplied by the larger garrison in Castleisland. A military convoy regularly passed along the Meinleitrim Road and in the late autumn of 1922 Humphrey Murphy, O/C of Kerry No. 1 Brigade, planned a major attack on it. The convoy was noted to pass by Meinleitrim at precisely 1 p.m. and so Murphy brought a large force drawn mainly from the 7th Battalion area to the proposed ambush site. The road was trenched to make it impassable for the military vehicles and the Republicans waited for the expected arrival of Free State troops. However, having been forewarned, the convoy did not travel that day. Murphy waited for about twenty minutes at the ambush site, but when his scouts reported that the expected vehicles were not to be seen, he withdrew his fighters. At 4 p.m. the townland of Meinleitrim was surrounded by a large Free State force from Tralee and Castleisland, but the Republicans had already left the area. It was apparent that the presence of the IRA attack party had been betrayed to the enemy by a local person and so an investigation began.[2]

Suspicion fell on Pat O'Connor, a seventy-three-year-old local farmer. John Daly and Patrick Buckley, Volunteers in the 7th Battalion, dressed up in captured Free State uniforms and went to the home of O'Connor in Ahaneboy.

1   There is no known photograph of John Daly.
2   Information from Micheál Walsh, Knocknagoshel.

Assuming that the pair had come from the Castleisland's Free State garrison, Pat O'Connor proceeded to give them further information about Republican activity in the area. Due to his advanced age, it was decided that the informer would not be shot. Instead he was fined the large sum of £100 and was threatened about any further contact with the enemy. O'Connor refused to pay the fine imposed on him. So on 16 December 1922 local IRA Volunteers entered O'Connor's house and took a quantity of money and some livestock in lieu of the fine. Incensed, Pat O'Connor's thirty-year-old son, also called Patrick and known as Patie Pats, went down to Castleisland and at the Hartnett's Hotel post he enlisted in the Free State Army. He was given the rank of lieutenant and with his accurate local knowledge of active Republicans, he proved a valuable asset. A large number of IRA Volunteers from the Knocknagoshel area who previously could have stayed in their own homes had now to go 'on the run' as Lieutenant Pat O'Connor led Free State raiding parties in search of his Republican neighbours. These included John Jack Daly.

On 4 February 1923 Daly, who like O'Connor was from Ahaneboy, was walking on the Meinleitrim Road when he was surprised by a Free State patrol and taken prisoner. He was brought initially to Castleisland and then to Ballymullen Barracks in Tralee. Patrick Buckley was detained on the same day and shared the same fate as Daly.

Such was his enthusiasm for hunting down IRA Volunteers, that a determined effort was made to kill Patie Pats O'Connor by the 7th Battalion. However, he was safe within the fortified hotel and would have to be lured out so that an attempt to kill him could be made. A letter was composed by Kathleen Walsh and Kathleen Hickey of Cumann na mBan in Knocknagoshel. Kathleen Hickey was a teacher in the local national school. This letter was written by Miss Walsh with her left hand to prevent the handwriting being identified and it detailed the location of an IRA dugout in Barranarig Wood, a mile from Knocknagoshel. The letter was then given to a sentry at Hartnett's Hotel by young Eily Hickey of Knocknagoshel. A similar but genuine letter written by a woman in Knocknagoshel and sent to Lieutenant O'Connor had previously been intercepted and so when this letter was delivered to Hartnett's Hotel, he suspected nothing. Using the false information O'Connor led a Free State detachment to the location at 2 a.m. on the morning of 6 March with the intention of capturing or killing the IRA Volunteers he believed were sleeping in the dugout. Arriving at the scene, the enthusiastic O'Connor began removing stones from the entrance to the shelter. As he was removing a large flagstone a booby-trap mine detonated and killed O'Connor and Captains Ed Stapleton and Michael Dunne of the Dublin Guard. Also killed in the explosion were Free State privates Michael Galvin and Laurence O'Connor from County Kerry.

When reports reached the Free State command in Tralee of the deaths of their comrades in the search party, retribution was swiftly planned. While the killing of Republican prisoners had begun with the shooting of Seán Moriarty in August of the previous year and was a regular occurrence throughout the Civil War, the mass killing of captives was a new departure. A mine was constructed in Ballymullen Barracks by two senior Free State officers, Captains Jim Clarke and Ed Flood.[3] Nine prisoners were brought by military convoy to Ballyseedy Cross and were tied to each other around this explosive. The mine was then detonated by Captain Ned Breslin and eight of the nine prisoners were killed by the blast and the subsequent shooting of the wounded prisoners.

One of the eight IRA Volunteers who died early on the morning of 7 March 1923 was John Jack Daly. It is probable that he was chosen because he lived not too far from the site of the Knocknagoshel attack. Having been a prisoner in Ballymullen Barracks for over a month, he could not have had any connection with the incident in Barranarig, but this did not save him when Colonel David Neligan was choosing his victims.

John Jack Daly was buried in Kilbannivane Cemetery's Republican Plot outside Castleisland. He and his comrades who were killed at Ballyseedy are commemorated there by Yann Goulet's large bronze sculpture.

---

3 Niall Harrington, an officer in the Dublin Guard, quoted by Pat Butler in the television documentary *Ballyseedy* (1997).

Tom Fleming

Tomás Fléamonn[1]

As the conflict with the crown forces gathered momentum, so too did the IRA's need to improve the weaponry that they used. In August 1920, in an attack on a mobile patrol of regular British troops just outside Annascaul, Tadhg Brosnan's 4th Battalion unit used a landmine that had been taken from the abandoned Cloghane RIC Barracks. The explosive had the desired effect of blowing up a lorry in what was the first attack of its kind in Ireland. The impact of such mines could be devastating on military vehicles and so soon the brigade engineers began to prepare their own improvised explosive devices. The metal casing was usually manufactured by blacksmiths and then loaded with either captured industrial gelignite or crude homemade explosives called 'black powder'. A detonating wire was attached to the device and it was then connected to a plunger and battery. Initially, however, such locally manufactured mines were unreliable and somewhat unstable.

Tom Fleming was a native of Currow and in his teens he had gone to Tralee, where he trained as a mechanic. While there he joined the Irish Volunteers, but in July 1920 he returned to his native parish as he became a wanted man when he participated in a raid for arms on a British military picket at Tralee's railway station. He transferred to the Currow Company of the Volunteers and in 1921 volunteered for service with the flying column of the Kerry No. 2 Brigade. He participated in the Headford Junction ambush and the other engagements of the column. His trade as a mechanic made him an obvious appointment for the position of engineer on the brigade staff. It was in this capacity that he was the instructor at an explosives training camp at Glountane near Cordal on 16 June 1921.[2]

On a summer's day, chosen men from each of the companies of the 1st Battalion gathered at the remote location for a training camp. The explosive that was being used in the construction of the mines was 'black powder', which was a mixture of saltpetre and charcoal made from the sally tree. This mixture

---

1 Surviving images of Tom Fleming were not of sufficient quality to reproduce.
2 John J. Walsh of Currow, BMH WS 1002.

was effective but varied in its constitution from parish to parish and was often unstable. The men were instructed by Fleming on the construction of mines and their detonation using batteries as a power source.

Peter Browne, a comrade of Fleming's on the column, described the scene. The class was held on a small side road so remote that guards did not have to be posted in case of the approach of the enemy. The bomb was constructed from part of a cart wheel. The metal ring was closed on one side with a circular block of wood hammered in. Then Fleming filled the cylinder with black powder and inserted the wires as the class was gathered around. The final part was to hammer in another piece of wood to tightly close the metal container. As Fleming was about to do this, an aeroplane flew overhead and the activity stopped momentarily. At this stage the device was between his knees and as he hammered the wooden cover into its place, a colleague, Tim Leahy held the container steady. There was a sudden, deafening explosion and the spectators were blown to the ground. Tom Fleming's wounds became apparent as the smoke cleared. He had deep facial, chest, limb and abdominal injuries and was bleeding profusely. Peter Browne tried to make him comfortable and a doctor and priest were sent for. However, Fleming died within ten minutes, so severe were his injuries. Tim Leahy, who was also beside the device when it exploded, was seriously wounded and several others, including David Coffey and Johnny Mahony, were injured by flying shrapnel. However, the injured Volunteers recovered, though one of them lost an eye and several fingers.[3]

The remains of Tom Fleming were brought from Glountane, the site of the explosion, and then on to Milleen, near Scartaglin. There the remains reposed for the night before continuing on to Kilsarcon Cemetery for burial the next day. The funeral was accompanied by a sizeable crowd and, despite the obvious danger, a large contingent of his Volunteer comrades marched in the funeral procession. In February 1922, during the Truce, the coffin was reinterred in the Republican Plot at Kilbannivane Cemetery near Castleisland.

Today a monument stands at Glountane near Cordal, which was unveiled in July 1950. It marks the site where Tom Fleming lost his life in the service of the Irish Republic on 16 June 1921.[4]

3   Peter Browne, BMH WS 1110 and Denis Prendiville, BMH WS 1106.
4   *The Kerryman*, 8 July 1950.

Patrick Kenny

Pádraig Ó Ceannaic[1]

Patrick Gerald Kenny, who was known by the nickname Eric, was born in Ballymacadam, a short distance to the east of Castleisland on 6 July 1903. He was a Volunteer in the Castleisland Company of the 7th Battalion, Kerry No. 1 Brigade.[2]

On 2 August 1922 Free State forces landed in Fenit and before the day was out they were in control of the town of Tralee. For the next two days they consolidated their hold on the county capital and three days later, having been reinforced by Free State units from County Clare, they pushed inland towards Castleisland. The large force that advanced towards Castleisland was backed by an armoured car and the meagre Republican forces that were based in the Castleisland area were not in a position to resist. The progress of the Dublin Guards as they advanced through Ballymacelligott to Castleisland was monitored by IRA scouts. One of these was Patrick Kenny of Ballymacadam. As they approached the town, the IRA retreated to the surrounding hills, but young Patrick Kenny was captured as he observed enemy troop movements.

Kenny was brought to Ballymullen in Tralee, where he joined the large number of Republican prisoners taken in the first week of August as the Free State forces strengthened their grip on the towns of County Kerry. In September 1922 over 300 of these men were transferred by boat to Dublin and subsequently interned in various prison camps. Patrick Kenny was incarcerated in Gormanston Camp, which took in its first prisoners on 9 September 1922. Within a short time the County Meath detention centre held over 1,000 prisoners in cramped conditions. Although the Civil War ended in May 1923, the Free State government held thousands of prisoners well after the cessation of hostilities, ostensibly to ensure that Republican resistance to the Treaty would not re-ignite.

1   There is no known photograph of Patrick Kenny.
2   Notes of Coiste Chuimhneacháin Bhaile Uí Shíoda on Kerry No. 1 Brigade casualties (private collection).

On 14 October 1923 the attempt to treat these 14,000 Republican captives as common convicts forced the prisoners in Mountjoy and Kilmainham Gaols to go on hunger strike. Within five days the strike had spread to the prison camps at the Curragh and Gormanston. Patrick Kenny endured fourteen days without food.

The unsanitary, crowded conditions, compounded by the effects of the hunger strike, broke the health of many erstwhile healthy young men. Tuberculosis became the scourge of the prisoners as infection passed easily amongst the physically weakened prisoners. Patrick Kenny contracted the disease while he was interned in Gormanston. It infected his knee joint initially and then spread to infect the rest of his body. As his condition deteriorated he was transferred to the Meath Hospital in Dublin. Unusually for the time, he was given a blood transfusion and it was stated that there were 'many willing volunteers to donate the required blood'. However, he died on 15 May 1924, as a result of what was described as 'creeping paralysis', which was probably a neurological complication of the disease. The next day his remains were transferred by train to Castleisland for his funeral.[3]

Patrick Kenny was twenty years old when he died as a result of his imprisonment. He was buried in the Republican Plot in Castleisland's Kilbannivane Cemetery.

3   *Irish Independent*, 19 May 1924.

BERTIE MURPHY

Pártalán Ó Murcáda[1]

Bartholomew (Bertie) Murphy was born in Castleisland in 1905. His grandmother was a dressmaker in the town's Main Street, where Bertie's mother, a widow, worked as a seamstress in the family business.

Bertie Murphy was a member of Na Fianna in the town and was attached to the 7th Battalion of Kerry No. 1 Brigade during the Tan War. Although it is unlikely that he was on active service due to his young age, as a member of Na Fianna he would have been involved in scouting and other support services for the local IRA company. During the early stages of the Civil War he was on active service with the Kerry IRA columns during the fighting in Limerick.

The local officer in Na Fianna was Cornelius Hickey. In May 1922 Hickey joined the Free State Army and Bertie Murphy replaced him as captain of the Castleisland Fianna Slua, as the junior wing of the Republican Army was called.

Having captured Tralee from Republican forces on 2 August 1922, the Free State Army took control of Castleisland three days later. There they established a garrison at Hartnett's Hotel on the town's Main Street at the junction with the Limerick road.

Early in September 1922 Murphy was captured at Dysert, about three miles from the town on the Farranfore road. He was carrying a rifle when he encountered a Free State patrol and was brought to the Hartnett's Hotel Barracks in Castleisland. As he was being marched up Main Street his mother saw him pass her premises with his military guard as she stood at her shop door. It was reported by Dorothy Macardle that he was bruised and battered from the treatment that he had received from his captors.[2]

Murphy was held for several days in Hartnett's Hotel, where one of his guards was his former commanding officer in Na Fianna, Con Hickey. The night of his capture he was brought as a hostage to Ballymacelligott by a Free

1 There is no known photograph of Bertie Murphy.
2 Dorothy Macardle, *Tragedies of Kerry* (1924), p. 13.

State patrol. On another occasion he was brought to Scartaglin to remove a suspicious barricade that blocked the road. On Wednesday 19 September he was transferred to the Free State barracks at the Great Southern Hotel in Killarney. There, again, he was used as a hostage on Free State convoys as they moved through the hostile Republican-held countryside.

On 27 September a unit of the Kerry No. 2 Brigade ambushed a three-vehicle patrol of Dublin Guards as they travelled through Brennan's Glen, a narrow defile six miles from Killarney on the main road to Tralee. Two Free State soldiers were killed and several wounded. That evening the ambushed convoy returned to their barracks in Killarney's Great Southern Hotel with their dead and wounded. On arrival the troops were met by senior officers of the Dublin Guard, including Colonel David Neligan. He asked the survivors of the ambush to give an account of the incident and then enquired if they had captured any Republican prisoners during the ambush. The only Republican prisoner that they had was the hostage they carried with them on that day, young Bertie Murphy.

Murphy was taken through the hotel's main door to just inside the foyer and there was beaten by a soldier. He was then brought out to the main entrance of the hotel where he was thrown down the eight steps by Colonel Neligan, who then proceeded to shoot the helpless young prisoner several times in the head as he lay on the ground.[3] Neither Neligan nor those Free State officers present knew the identity of the man they had killed.

Some of the rooms on the top floor of the hotel were being used as cells for captured Republican prisoners. On the day of the incident, four senior Kerry No. 2 Brigade officers – Tom Daly, Dan Mulvihill, Con O'Leary and Will Patrick Fleming – were detained in these cells; they had been there since their capture on 22 August after a siege in Kilcummin. O'Leary was from Glenflesk and was the brigade quartermaster. He was brought down by his guards to identify Neligan's victim. When he returned to his fellow prisoners, he told them that such was the extent of the injuries to the face, he could not recognise the young man who had been shot in the head.[4]

An inquest was held two days later and although General Paddy Daly

3   Daniel Mulvihill, BMH WS 938.
4   Information from Denis Fleming, Milleen, Kilcummin, son of Will Patrick Fleming.

sympathised with Julia Murphy, the boy's mother, he went on to blame his death on Republicans. No blame was attached to the actual perpetrator of the killing though there were many witnesses to the shooting. A month earlier, on 22 August, Neligan had attempted to kill the four IRA officers – Mulvihill, O'Leary, Fleming and Daly – who were captured at Kilcummin. On that occasion General Daly, who would later earn a notorious reputation, had prevented the killing of his captives. To protect them, Daly had extra guards posted outside the prisoners' cells on the upper floor of the hotel that evening, with orders to shoot anybody who attempted to harm the captives.[5]

Bertie Murphy was buried in the Republican Plot in Castleisland's Kilbannivane Cemetery. Today he is remembered by a plaque erected on the wall of the railway station almost opposite the steps of the Great Southern Hotel where David Neligan took his seventeen-year-old life on 27 September 1922.

David Neligan, who was from Templeglantine, Abbeyfeale, and whose father was from near Listowel, was the instigator of the massacres that occurred in Kerry in March 1923. He later became head of the CID division of the Garda Síochána in Dublin's Oriel House, where he added to his notorious reputation. He died in 1983 in receipt of five pensions, including one from the British secret service. Unlike his young victim, Bertie Murphy, Neligan has no memorial stone in Kerry and is remembered in that county only because of his many victims.

Con Hickey emigrated to America following the Civil War. When he returned to Ireland he was forbidden to enter the town of Castleisland and could only do so heavily disguised, such was the level of bitterness towards him arising from the death of Bertie Murphy.[6]

---

5   Ernie O'Malley, *The Men Will Talk to Me – Kerry Interviews* (2012), interview with May Dálaigh.
6   Information from Luke Keane, local historian.

Dan Murphy

Domhnall Ó Murchada

Courtesy of Micheál Walsh of Knockangoshel, nephew of Dan Murphy.

Daniel Murphy was born in Knocknagoshel on 27 February 1892. Both Dan and his brother John, who was nicknamed 'Coffey', were blacksmiths in the North Kerry village. The brothers were also Volunteers in the Knocknagoshel Company of the 7th Battalion, Kerry No. 1 Brigade. They had fought in the Tan War and also used their skills as smiths to manufacture casings for landmines used in the war with the British. Both men remained on active service with the Republican Army during the Civil War.

At 2 a.m. on the morning of 6 March 1923, a large Free State force came to Barranarig, just outside the village, having been enticed to the site by information that Humphrey Murphy and other senior Republicans were sheltering in a dugout there. As the local IRA unit had suspected, the soldiers went straight to where the hideout was. As one of them removed a flagstone at the entrance of the dugout, a mine exploded, killing five of the Free State soldiers and injuring others. The next day the Knocknagoshel area witnessed extensive searches by Free States forces in an attempt to capture the IRA unit that had launched the attack. All the local Volunteers had left the area, but several Cumann na mBan women had their heads shaved, including the nurse who had tended to the wounded Free State soldiers following the explosion.

Determined to capture the Volunteers of the Knocknagoshel Company, a large Free State search party arrived in the Knocknagoshel area at 6 a.m. on 23 March 1923. Dan Murphy was sleeping at home that morning when he was arrested. He had arrived back in Knocknagoshel the previous evening, having spent some time 'on the run', and was due to return the next morning to his sister Bridget's remote house in Maugha, about seven miles away, where he would be safe. He stayed in the family home on the night of 22 March, though there had been a warning sent to his mother that his life was in danger. An officer in the Free State Army, Captain Con Brosnan of Moyvane, sent the message to Dave Leahy, a pro-Treaty supporter in Knocknagoshel, advising the Murphy brothers that the Dublin Guard had determined to kill them and that they should not appear in the village for fear of capture. Brosnan had an impressive record in the Tan War and he would have known from that time of the Murphy brothers' expertise in constructing mines, a fact that the Dublin Guard in Castleisland was also now aware of.

When the Free State detachment arrived in Knocknagoshel early in the morning of 23 March, they detained Dan and John Murphy and searched their forge. They found nothing, though there was a large quantity of ammunition hidden beneath horseshoes in a trough.

Lieutenant Jeremiah Gaffney then ordered John 'Coffey' Murphy to his knees. He defiantly refused to kneel and told Gaffney that he would have to shoot him where he stood. Gaffney then raised his weapon and was about to shoot the prisoner when a local Free State soldier, Toss O'Connor, grabbed the barrel of Gaffney's rifle. Gaffney then walked away and with two other Castleisland-based Free State officers, Captain Maurice Culhane of Moyvane and William McAuliffe from near Abbeydorney, took Dan Murphy up through the village. They marched him to Burke's field at Barranarig, a short distance from Knocknagoshel village. This was where the five Free State soldiers had been killed in the explosion of 6 March. They accused Dan Murphy of constructing the mine in his forge and were determined to exact revenge on at least one of the blacksmiths.[1] However, Dan Murphy did not make the metal casing of the mine as he was 'on the run' at the time. The mine was manufactured in the Murphy forge but by his brother John.

Dan Murphy was brought by his captors to the centre of the field, where Gaffney, McAuliffe and Culhane summarily executed him. The shooting was witnessed by a local schoolgirl, Bridie Lyons, who watched the incident from her home which overlooked Burke's field. She reported seeing Dan Murphy

1   Information from Micheál Walsh, the nephew of the Dan Murphy and from the RTÉ documentary *Ballyseedy* by Pat Butler.

standing erect before his killers, who then shot him several times. He fell but managed to get himself up on his elbows, whereupon he was shot again at close range. After the Free State troops left the area, Con Lyons, Bridie's father, went down to retrieve the body and he brought it to the Murphy family home. The twenty-one bullet holes in the body were plugged by his mother, Katie Murphy, as she prepared her son's remains for burial. However, the local priest, Fr Burke of Knockaderry, would not allow the church bell to be rung as was customary to mark the death of a parishioner. Such was his antipathy to the local Republicans, that he had refused the sacraments to local women he suspected of Republican sympathies. Volunteer Dan Murphy was buried in Knockane Cemetery near Knocknagoshel, where his Volunteer comrades Richard Browne and Denny O'Connor also lie.[2]

Dan Murphy is remembered in the song 'The Blacksmith Volunteer', which ends with the following lines:

> *In Knockane let Murphy lie, for he was a noble man.*
> *And if you are doomed to meet the call and die for Ireland dear.*
> *A soldier stand, a soldier fall, The Blacksmith Volunteer.*

Lieutenant Jeremiah Gaffney, one of those who had killed Dan Murphy, was an officer in the Dublin Guard billeted in Castleisland's Free State Barracks at Hartnett's Hotel. He earned a notorious reputation during the Civil War for his ill-treatment of prisoners and the killing of Dan Murphy. On 6 December 1923 he was one of a group of soldiers who shot dead Thomas Brosnan, a civilian, in Scartaglin over a non-political matter. For this crime he was hanged in Mountjoy Gaol on 13 March 1924.[3]

---

2   Information from Micheál Walsh, Knocknagoshel, nephew of Dan Murphy.
3   Information from George Rice, local historian.

Michael O'Connell

Mícéál Ó Conaill

On 30 November 1900 Michael O'Connell was born in Fahadubh, a hilly townland to the north of and overlooking Castleisland town. There his father James had a small farm and Michael worked the land with him. During the Black and Tan War he was a Volunteer in the Castleisland Company of the 1st Battalion, Kerry No. 2 Brigade.[1] His brother James (Bob) was also on active service and following the conflict he emigrated to Canada and then America.

Courtesy of the Martin Moore collection.

Following the division that occurred due to the acceptance of the Anglo-Irish Treaty, Michael O'Connell remained in the Republican Army. By the start of the Civil War the Castleisland Company had been transferred to the 7th Battalion of the Kerry No. 1 Brigade. During that conflict the fighting in the Castleisland district was especially fierce as the Dublin Guard attempted to crush Republican resistance with the brutality of an occupying army.

The month of December 1922 saw a lull in the fighting in Kerry and the Free State commanders General W. R. E. Murphy and General Paddy Daly were convinced that the Republicans were a spent force. However, the New Year saw an upsurge in IRA attacks throughout the county and it was apparent that victory was still some distance away. Four executions at Ballymullen on 20 January 1923 did not have the desired effect of demoralising the Republican units still waging a guerrilla war in the county. When five Free State soldiers, including two officers from the Dublin Guard, were killed on a military operation in Knocknagoshel in the early hours of 6 March 1923, the event was the catalyst for bringing the campaign to crush the Republican forces

---

1   Information from Jimmy O'Connell, nephew of Michael O'Connell.

to a whole new level. The executions on 20 January were of four men from separate areas of the county. The events of the second week in March saw the mass killing of prisoners in Tralee, Killarney and Cahersiveen and it may be that another such massacre was planned for Scartaglin, although this failed to materialise when prisoners at Castleisland violently resisted being brought out of the barracks to remove a supposed barricade at Scartaglin.

Michael O'Connell had been arrested in February 1923 while attending a dance at Knocknagoshel. He was unarmed and had not resisted at the time of his capture. He was not under a sentence of death during his detention in Ballymullen Barracks. Despite this, on 6 March 1923, after the soldiers' deaths at Knocknagoshel, he was selected by Colonel David Neligan, the chief of special services of the Dublin Guard, to be among those to be killed at Ballyseedy Cross. As the Knocknagoshel attack occurred in the 7th Battalion area where Michael O'Connell had been an active IRA Volunteer, he was selected to be killed, as were Patrick Buckley and John Daly who were also members of that battalion.

Michael O'Connell was twenty-two years old when he died at Ballyseedy Cross in the early hours of Wednesday 7 March 1923. His remains are buried in the Republican Plot in Kilbannivane Cemetery outside Castleisland.

Denny O'Connor

Donnaċa Ó Conċuḃair[1]

Denis O'Connor was born into a farming family at Kilmaniheen, Knocknagoshel in 1899. He was nicknamed 'Young Denny' as his father shared his name. The countryside around Castleisland was a centre of Moonlighter activity in the Land Wars of the late 1880s and early 1890s and so it was little surprise that when the Tan War erupted in 1919, the men of the 7th Battalion were to the forefront in the fight for freedom. When the Civil War was forced upon the Irish people, men such as Denny O'Connor fought for the preservation of the Republic. An oath of allegiance to Britain's king and a less than totally free Ireland was not what they had fought for. From the time that the Free State Army landed in Kerry in the first week of August 1922, O'Connor was on active service with 'E' Company of the Castleisland-based 7th Battalion, Kerry No. 1 Brigade.

The Civil War in Kerry was characterised by the Free State Army maintaining garrisons in the towns and villages that they controlled, while the guerrilla fighters of the IRA held sway in the countryside. One such Free State outpost was in the north-east Kerry village of Brosna. A unit of pro-Treaty forces, who were part of the 1st Western Division of the Free State Army, was billeted there. These soldiers were drawn from the South Galway and Clare areas and the unit was commanded by Captain Patrick Coye.

On 27 January 1923 Captain Coye left Brosna Barracks with a detachment of five soldiers. They headed west to Feale's Bridge where the Brosna road joins the main Castleisland to Abbeyfeale road. However, Humphrey Murphy, the Kerry No. 1 Brigade O/C, planned to attack the Free State patrol as it made its way from Brosna on that day. As Captain Coye and his men approached a turn in the road in the townland of Kilmaniheen East near to Feale's Bridge, they were ambushed by units of Kerry No. 1 Brigade, comprising mainly Volunteers from the local 7th Battalion who were under the command of Jer O'Leary.

---

1   There is no known photograph of Denny O'Connor.

The bridge over the River Feale had been mined by John 'Coffey' Murphy and as the attack commenced the bridge was partially destroyed as one of the two explosive devices was detonated to prevent Free State reinforcements arriving at the ambush scene from nearby Abbeyfeale. Snipers fired at Brosna Barracks and this prevented further troops leaving that Free State Army post. The ambush party was well armed and surrounded the Free State detachment, wounding Private Martin Darcy. When asked to surrender, Coye refused and reportedly told his wounded comrade to say his prayers as the Free State soldiers fought on. However, a short time later, Captain Coye was killed by a Republican bullet and a further two of his troops were wounded in the fierce gun battle. The Free State soldiers were forced to surrender and the Republican Volunteers, under Brigade O/C Humphrey Murphy, subsequently withdrew, leaving the soldiers behind, but unarmed. Murphy brought his men southwards on the Meinleitrim road which runs parallel to the main road towards Castleisland.

Meanwhile, a Free State party from Newcastle West under Captain Joseph Fallon were travelling from Newcastle West to Listowel when they were informed of the events near Feale's Bridge. Fallon detoured southwards and collected some local Free State soldiers including Captain Con Brosnan. Arriving at Feale's Bridge, they found it impassable to their lorries and IRA riflemen were covering the remains of the partially demolished crossing. With Con Brosnan and Captains Michael Mortell and Patrick English, Fallon crossed the river undetected by means of a nearby ford. Mortell and Fallon then commandeered a horse and car. Other members of their column followed on bicycles. Though Humphrey Murphy and most of his ambush party had safely withdrawn, Fallon, Mortell and their troops did see some of the rearguard of the Republican column in the distance and they gave chase.

One of the IRA men, Mick McGlynn, was armed with a Lewis Gun and with this he managed to slow the Free State troops as he fired from high ground.

The rearguard also contained Denny O'Connor, who was fired on as he was crossing the main road at Mein, which was parallel to the road that Fallon's men were on, but the Free State bullets missed their mark. Captain Patrick English, a former British soldier, ordered the shooting to stop and he then took careful aim. English's shots fatally wounded O'Connor and injured his comrade Jerry (Jer Rua) Lyons of Knockalougha. O'Connor died at the scene while Lyons, who had been shot in the hip, was captured. O'Connor's remains and the wounded Lyons were brought back to Abbeyfeale by their Free State captors.[2] Another local Volunteer, William Den O'Connor of Gortroe, was also wounded a short distance away that day.

Jerry Lyons was denied medical aid and was brought to a room in the barracks and interrogated. Captain Patrick Coye's brother was brought to where the prisoner was and a loaded gun was placed on a table so that he could shoot the prisoner. However, the bereaved soldier refused to kill the wounded captive. Lyons survived his injury and spent the remainder of the war in captivity.

Nineteen-year-old Denny O'Connor was laid to rest in the Republican Plot at Knockane Cemetery in his native parish. Today a fine monument stands at the roadside between Castleisland and Knocknagoshel, adjacent to the site where he fell in defence of the Republic on 27 January 1923.

---

2   Information from Micheál Walsh and Luke Keane, local historians.

Jer O'Leary

Diarmuid Ó Laoġaire

Courtesy of Nora Mai Fleming, niece of Jer O'Leary.

Jeremiah O'Leary was born at Mount, a townland adjacent to Scartaglin, in 1894. He was the eldest child and only son of James O'Leary, a farmer, and Hanna Scanlon of Knockafreaghaun, Brosna. He was a bright pupil at school and an avid reader with a keen interest in scientific books. He was educated in Scartaglin National School and later worked on the family farm. He was a Volunteer in the Scartaglin Company from its foundation and his four sisters were members of Cumann na mBan.[1] The Scartaglin Company was attached to the 1st Battalion, Kerry No. 2 Brigade.

O'Leary came to prominence at an early stage in the Black and Tan War. He was one of those who participated in the attack on the barracks in his native village on 31 March 1920. Such was O'Leary's reputation as a leader of fighting men, that he was appointed to the position of O/C of the 1st Battalion in May 1921. This command included companies from Castleisland, Scartaglin, Cordal, Currow, Lyre, Knocknagoshel and Brosna. With a reorganisation in July 1921, O'Leary's battalion was transferred to Kerry No. 1 Brigade, as the O/C of that brigade was now Humphrey Murphy, whose native area of Currow was part of the Castleisland Battalion's remit. The Castleisland Battalion was redesignated the 7th Battalion, Kerry No. 1 Brigade, and Jer O'Leary was appointed Murphy's V/C on the brigade's staff. A fearless and popular soldier, he led his men in engagements at Scartaglin, Brosna, Glenlahern, The Black Banks, Feale's Bridge and on the streets of Castleisland.

Following the outbreak of the Civil War, Jer O'Leary and his 7th Battalion

---

1   Information from Alice O'Keeffe, niece of Jer O'Leary.

remained loyal to the Republican cause. As a result they suffered heavily during that conflict, with the battalion noted to have lost thirteen men either killed in action or murdered in custody from 1922 until 1924.[2] During the Civil War, Jer O'Leary had a dugout built beneath the outer stairs of the large three-storey house owned by his relatives, the Walsh family of Cordal.

On 24 May 1923 Frank Aiken, the IRA chief of staff following the death of Liam Lynch, ordered IRA units throughout the country to dump their arms. This followed the announcement of a ceasefire on 30 April. The military resistance to the Free State government had now officially halted and so ended the Civil War. Jer O'Leary and Seán Kerins, a battalion officer, met in Kilmurry House, owned by the Walsh family, in Cordal to discuss the matter on Monday 28 May. It seems that O'Leary was earlier at a nearby house owned by the O'Loughlin family, where he had gone to inspect a plough that his brother-in-law had recently purchased. Shortly after he reached Walshs', a large Free State force in vehicles passed the O'Loughlins' house, destined for where O'Leary and Kerins were meeting. The O'Loughlin home was adjacent to the main road and, having seen the military convoy, one of the family ran across the fields to Walshs' house to try to alert O'Leary of the imminent danger. However, by the time he reached Cordal House, it had been surrounded by Free State soldiers. As their position was hopeless and due to the fact that there were civilians in the house, O'Leary and Kerins surrendered.[3] They were brought to the Free State Army's headquarters in Castleisland, which was located at the fortified Hartnett's Hotel at the junction of Main Street and the Limerick road. O'Leary was detained in the guardroom of the converted building.

At 11.30 a.m. the following morning he was brought by a Captain O'Donnell to the barracks yard, which had a gate opening onto the street. The yard had been cleared of the soldiers who would usually congregate there. Having been brought into the small yard, O'Leary was ordered by an officer to close the gate which had been conspicuously left open. As he approached the gate, he was shot in the back by Lieutenant Patrick McGinn and Captain Patrick Byrne. Captain Martin Nolan, also of the Dublin Guard, fired twice

2   Irish Military Archives, pension records for the 7th Battalion, Kerry No. 1 Brigade, RO 95.
3   Information for Nora Mai Fleming, niece of Jer O'Leary.

more at the wounded man as he lay on the ground.[4] A woman on the street who happened to be passing near the gate witnessed the shooting. She rushed to the dying man's aid and held his head in her arms as his life slipped away. Local shopkeeper Con Browne also came to the scene and it was he who brought the news to the O'Leary family that their only son had been shot dead.[5] O'Leary was twenty-nine years old when he was killed on 29 May 1923.

Commandant Jeremiah O'Leary was buried in the Republican Plot in Kilbannivane Cemetery near Castleisland. His name is inscribed on the Republican memorial there amongst the men of his command. His father later bought a family grave adjacent to where his only son was buried when his wife died in 1934 and Jer O'Leary's name is inscribed on the family headstone also.[6] Today a plaque on the wall of Hartnett's Hotel, now the Castle Bar, marks the spot where Commandant Jeremiah O'Leary was killed by his Free State captors. Near his home in the village of Scartaglin stands a large Celtic cross erected to his memory. This was paid for by public subscription and unveiled in May 1946. On it is his name inscribed in his native language: Diarmuid Ó Laoġaire. On 29 May each year until her death, his sister, Kate O'Connor, took out the scarf that her brother wore when was killed and shed a tear.[7]

4   The killing was witnessed and subsequently a statement was given to the newspaper *Éire*, 7 July 1923.
5   Information from Séamus Fleming, grandnephew of Jer O'Leary.
6   *Ibid.*
7   Information from Nora Mai Fleming, niece of Jer O'Leary.

Jack Prendiville

Seaġán ꝺe Pṙenꝺiḃile

John (Jack) Prendiville was a native of Breahig, a townland between the small villages of Cordal and Scartaglin and three miles east of Castleisland. Jack was a Volunteer in the very active Cordal Company of the 1st Battalion, Kerry No. 2 Brigade. The Cordal area had a long history of resistance to British rule. During the Land Wars John Joe Twiss of Cordal was executed in Cork Gaol, while two other Moonlighters, Sylvester Poff and James Barrett, were hanged in Tralee. It was into this centre of rebellion that Jack Prendiville was born on 1 May 1899. His brother Denis (Daniel), who was a year older than Jack, was the second lieutenant in the company from its formation in 1917. Both would soldier together during the Tan War until the penultimate day of that conflict, when Jack was killed in action.

Courtesy of the Martin Moore collection.

The fight for freedom began again in Kerry in April 1918, when the men of Ballymacelligott attacked the Gortatlea RIC Barracks. Over the next year the Ballymacelligott Company and the Cordal Volunteers forged close links and formed the basis of an active service unit which operated in the Castleisland district during 1920. The Cordal men were present on 24 March 1920 when the barracks at Gortatlea was destroyed. Following this successful attack, the barracks at Scartaglin was attacked on 31 April 1920 and Jack Prendiville took part in this assault, which was to prove unsuccessful as the RIC garrison refused to surrender. On 9 June 1920 Jack Prendiville and his brother Denis were part of the attack force that laid siege to Brosna Barracks and the next day the brothers were part of the Cordal Volunteer unit which attacked a British military car at Glenlahern Cross.

With the 1st Battalion, Jack Prendiville was involved in several attempted attacks on the crown forces in Castleisland town and the surrounding countryside. On 21 February 1921 he was fortunate not to be captured when he spotted a military convoy, which had been supplied with accurate information, heading to the dugout where his brother and other Cordal Volunteers were hiding. For three days in early March, Jack Prendiville was one of the men who waited in ambush at The Bower near Rathmore for a British convoy, but it failed to arrive at the site. The ambush party, which was commanded by Seán Moylan of North Cork and was composed of units from Kerry No. 2 Brigade and Cork No. 2 Brigade, moved on to Clonbanin, where a successful ambush was carried out on General Hanway Cumming's convoy. In the spring he was part of the Kerry No. 2 Brigade flying column. Prendiville was one of the battle-hardened Volunteers from Breahig who took part in the Bog Road ambush on 4 May 1921 in which eight RIC men died.

But a fight in Castleisland on the evening of 10 July 1921 was to be his last. The Prendiville brothers were part of the thirty or so men under the command of Humphrey Murphy who entered Castleisland town to attack a large military patrol which marched up Main Street at the start of the nightly curfew. Denis was positioned in a lane at the upper end of the wide main street, where he could fire on the soldiers if they sought cover from the main ambush position near the town's library. Jack was in one of the lanes near the library and on the eastern side of the street. The five men in this area were slow to disengage following the initial attack, such was the intensity of the firing. This allowed British reinforcements to cut off their line of withdrawal through the back gardens of the houses on the street. The five IRA Volunteers were pinned down by machine-gun fire from the military as they attempted to reach the countryside to rejoin the remainder of the attack party that had earlier disengaged in good order in the direction of Cordal. Jack Prendiville and his four comrades found temporary shelter in a small quarry behind the houses of Upper Main Street. Two of the group, Mossy Galvin of Farmer's Bridge and Ned McCarthy of Breahig, managed to successfully run from the small quarry, braving the intense enemy gunfire as they fled. However, Jack Prendiville, Jack Flynn and Dick Shanahan were forced back by the overwhelming firepower of the encircling soldiers. When the fighting ended, all three were found dead in the quarry with multiple gunshot wounds. The exact circumstances of their final moments are not recorded, but it is thought that they fought until their ammunition was spent.[1]

A large stone monument stands on Upper Main Street in Castleisland, adjacent to the small quarry that lies near the street where these three Volunteers made their last stand. Jack Prendiville is buried in Kilbannivane Cemetery, Castleisland.

---

1 Denis Prendiville, BMH WS 1106 and Peter Browne, BMH WS 1110.

JOHN SAVAGE

Seaġan Ó Sabáir[1]

John (Seán) Savage was born on 16 February 1899 at Woodview, Ahaneboy, three miles to the north of Castleisland. His father, Thomas, was a farm labourer and John was his eldest child. John later lived in Carraheen, Castleisland, and was a member of the town's company of the 7th Battalion, Kerry No. 1 Brigade. He was reported as being 'a good Volunteer', but his record is unknown.[2]

On 5 August 1922 the Free State Army occupied the town of Castleisland and there they commandeered Hartnett's Hotel on Upper Main Street. Initially the seventy-five-man garrison was drawn from the 1st Western Division, which recruited its soldiers from County Clare and south County Galway. However, in the winter of 1922, probably because of an inability to crush Republican resistance in the area, the garrison was changed and the Dublin Guard occupied the town. The Dublin Guard was commanded by General Paddy Daly. Other high-ranking Kerry-based officers in the Dublin Guard, including Colonel Jim McGuinness and Jim Dempsey, had fought in Dublin against the British and had sided with Collins when he formed his Free State Army. However, many of the Dublin Guard's middle-ranking officers had played only a peripheral, if any, role in the Tan War, and the ranks were made up of demobilised Dublin Fusiliers and locally recruited privates and junior officers.

As the Civil War progressed, the Dublin Guard in Kerry displayed all the features of an army of occupation with a brutality and indiscipline that would surpass that of the crown forces. In their war to crush the Republican resistance summary executions, torture and brutality to both civilians and captured combatants was accepted and even encouraged by General Daly and the clique of officers who commanded the Guard. In this they were aided by Kerrymen such as Captain Maurice Culhane and Lieutenant Paddy O'Connor, who could identify local IRA activists.

1   There is no known photograph of John Savage.
2   Notes of Coiste Chuimhneacháin Bhaile Uí Shíoda on Kerry No. 1 Brigade casualties (private collection).

One such victim of the Dublin Guard in Castleisland was John (Seán) Savage. Aware of his involvement with the Republican forces in the Tan War and probably also in the Civil War, he was detained by Free State soldiers on a street in Castleisland. Though unarmed when arrested, he was beaten, tied to a military vehicle and dragged along Castleisland's Main Street. On arriving at the barracks he was shot by a Free State soldier.[3] He succumbed to his injuries a week later. Savage was twenty-four years old when he died on 1 March 1923, the first of several Republicans to be killed while in custody in Castleisland.

John (Seán) Savage was buried in the Republican Plot at Kilbannivane Cemetery and is remembered in the Kerry No. 1 Brigade roll of honour at the Ballyseedy monument.

3   Information from Luke Keane, local historian.

Richard Shanahan

Risteárd Ó Seánacáin

Courtesy of the Martin Moore collection.

Richard (Dick) Shanahan was born into a nationalist family at 45 Main Street, Castleisland, in 1902. His parents had a successful business in the town. He was a member of the Castleisland Company of the 1st Battalion, Kerry No. 2 Brigade. His brother, Jack, who was a chemist, was also on active service and was severely wounded by gunfire when he tried to escape from the Dalys' house at Knockaneculteen, Firies, during a military raid in May 1921. Despite his severe wounds, he survived his injuries and was later freed in return for the release of a captured British intelligence officer, Major Coombs, the only such prisoner exchange during the Tan War.[1]

Dick Shanahan was an active Volunteer from the outset of the Tan War. When Andy Cooney, the GHQ organiser assigned to the Kerry No. 2 Brigade, revamped the brigade staff and promoted the more active and younger officers, Dick Shanahan was appointed adjutant of the 1st Battalion, which was based in his native Castleisland.[2] Though the large military and police presence might have acted as a deterrent, the battalion still managed to inflict casualties on them on the streets of the town and made the neighbouring countryside a particularly hostile environment for the forces of the crown.

As the end of the war approached and with a cessation of armed action due to be implemented the next day at midday, 11 July 1921, the 1st Battalion, with the aid of units from Kerry No. 1 Brigade, organised an elaborate attack on a twenty-man British Army patrol on Castleisland's Main Street. The attack force was commanded by Humphrey Murphy and consisted of nearly thirty men.

1   Michael McEvilly, *A Splendid Resistance* (2011), p. 42.
2   John J. Walsh, BMH WS 1002.

Richard Shanahan

Originally approximately sixty men had gathered near Scartaglin for the attack in Castleisland, but an initial report from scouts indicated that the expected military patrol would not take place that evening and so some of the Volunteers left the area. The brigade staff was subsequently informed that the military would in fact conduct their routine curfew patrol along the streets before sunset.

By 7 p.m. Murphy and his staff were positioned in the ruins of the burned-out library which stood at the top of the wide Main Street and he had groups of men positioned all along both sides of the upper part of this street. As the military patrol, who marched up the street towards the library to enforce the nightly curfew, approached the ambush position, fire was opened on them from three sides. A prolonged gun battle ensued as the soldiers sought refuge in the doorways of the shops and houses. Some were caught in a hail of bullets fired by Volunteers who waited for the soldiers to retreat down the broad street. The sound of the gunfire brought reinforcements from the RIC barracks sited at the southern end of the street almost half a mile away. With the signal of a whistle, Murphy ordered his men to disengage and withdraw from the town.

Due to the intensity of fighting in the area where Dick Shanahan was posted, he and four other men delayed their retreat from the ambush site until well after the main body of men had departed the town. The Volunteers near the old cemetery further down the street also failed to evacuate promptly. At this stage, they were outflanked by reinforcements of British soldiers who converged on Upper Main Street from several sides. After a fierce firefight, Paddy Reidy and the men near the cemetery in the middle of the town managed to extricate themselves and escaped into the surrounding countryside. Shanahan's group was trapped in a small, disused quarry as they attempted to reach the Cordal Road along which the main body had retreated. Two of this group, Ned McCarthy and Mossy Galvin, managed to dash 100 yards to the safety of a fence and escape. However, the remaining three Volunteers were forced back by the intense British machine-gun fire. The exact details of their last moments are not recorded except that it appears that Shanahan, Jack Flynn and Jack Prendiville fought until their ammunition was spent and were killed in a hail of bullets.[3]

---

3   Peter Browne, BMH WS 1110.

Their bodies were returned to the families after the ceasefire which took effect the following day at 12 noon. Twenty-year-old Richard Shanahan was buried in Kilbannivane Cemetery. Today a large monument stands adjacent to the site where these three Volunteers fell in the fight for Irish freedom.

James Walsh

Seumas Breatnac

James Walsh and his twin brother John (Jack) were born at Lyre, Currow, on 10 July 1898. The village of Currow was a centre of Moonlighter activity in the late 1880s and came to prominence following the assassination of local magistrate and landlord Arthur Herbert at Lisheenbawn Cross. A generation later the successors of these men, who had brought an end to the tyranny of the landlords, were once again prepared to bring Ireland's fight for freedom to the fields and roads of the parish of Killeentierna.

Courtesy of Adrian Breathnach.

In 1917 the Currow Company of the Irish Volunteers was formed and in 1918, during the threat of conscription, a huge influx of new recruits occurred. At this time also a company of Cumann na mBan was formed in the parish and Nora Walsh, Jim's older sister, was appointed as an officer in the women's Republican organisation. In the 1919 reorganisation of the Irish Volunteers, the Currow Company was to be designated 'D' Company of the 1st Battalion, Kerry No. 2 Brigade. Jim Walsh of Lyre was the commander of the No. 2 Section of this company.

In September 1919 the men of Currow were ready to take the fight to the enemy. Jim Walsh was one of a group of armed Volunteers under the command of local IRA commander Humphrey Murphy, who lay in ambush for an RIC patrol at Dromroe, between Farranfore and Currow. However, the patrol did not travel that day and the disappointed men dispersed. From that day on the men of the Currow Company were involved in all the major actions that took place in the battalion area, including attacks on the RIC barracks at Brosna and Scartaglin.

Jim and Jack Walsh were two of six men from 'D' Company who were at The Bower between Killarney and Rathmore on 2 March 1921 where a major ambush had been planned by columns from North Cork under Seán Moylan and units from the Kerry No. 2 Brigade. The ambush failed to materialise and the IRA columns redeployed to Clonbanin Cross where, on 5 March, they successfully engaged the military convoy, killing Colonel Hanway Cumming, the most senior British officer to be killed in the Black and Tan War. Cumming was vilified during his lifetime, as it was he who had introduced the practice of military patrols carrying hostages when he was a senior officer during the Boer War in South Africa and he continued this use of hostages when he travelled in Ireland during the Tan War.

On 8 May 1921 five RIC men were raiding houses in the Dromroe district when they were confronted by Jim Walsh and five other IRA Volunteers: John Doherty, Florence Mitchel, Michael Kelliher, John Galwey and Jeremiah Walsh, all from the No. 2 Section of the Currow Company. At Killeagh they opened fire on the raiding party, which was forced to run back to Farranfore Barracks. In reprisal, three houses were burned the next day: Jim Walsh's family home at Lyre, Humphrey Murphy's at Ballybeg and Charlie Daly's at Knockaneculteen, Firies.

In early June 1921 a battalion column or active service unit was formed and six men from Currow's 'D' Company were among its members. These included Jim Walsh. Their first action was to burn the library at Castleisland on 15 June as it was to be garrisoned by a detachment of Auxiliaries the next day.

The 1st Battalion of Kerry No. 2 Brigade was transferred to the Kerry No. 1 Brigade's 7th Battalion in July 1921. The Castleisland-centred battalion remained united in its opposition to the Treaty and would suffer heavily during the Civil War. Jim Walsh was one of its Volunteers who was to make the ultimate sacrifice in the defence of the Republic.[1] He was captured at his home in Lyre, unarmed, on 22 March 1923. He was subsequently imprisoned in Castleisland's Free State barracks at Hartnett's Hotel. There he was treated with the brutality that had become the norm for Republican prisoners but, since he was not captured carrying arms, he could not be sentenced to death by firing squad. While in custody he was visited by his cousin Mary Ellen Lyons of Dromroe and on the day before his death she reported that he was unable to speak as a result of a beating that he had received.

1   John J. Walsh of Lyre, James Walsh's brother, BMH WS 1002.

Though the practice was counter to the 'rules of war', it had become standard for Free State patrols to carry Republican hostages as they ventured into the hostile Kerry countryside. Lieutenant Patrick McGinn from Clontarf, an officer in the Dublin Guard, assembled three prisoners on Tuesday 27 March 1923 to accompany his men as they went eastwards along the Cordal Road. Jim Walsh and the two other recently captured local IRA officers, Dinny Rahilly of Knockeen, Ballymacelligott, and Charlie Daly of Gortatlea, were marched along the road through Cordal and into the hills beyond.[2] At Glountane Cross, Jim Walsh was separated from the hostages and taken away by a detachment of the Free State patrol. In the townland of Mount Falvey, he was shot by his captors in a field and left to die. His body was found the next day by a farmer out working his land. The fatal wound was to Walsh's head.

The remains were brought to a nearby shed on the Crowley farm and prepared for burial. Brigade O/C Humphrey Murphy and David McCarthy, another leading IRA activist, were known to be operating in this area of Mount Falvey. The two men later married two of the Crowley sisters. It was accepted locally that James Walsh was killed in this spot as a warning to the Republicans in the area who continued to resist the Free State Army.[3]

The coffin was subsequently removed to Killeentierna church in Currow. In accordance with Bishop Charles O'Sullivan's edict, there was no priest there to receive the remains, but a cousin, Michael Walsh, defiantly rang the bell of the church. The burial took place the next day in Kilbannivane Cemetery's Republican Plot. Another cousin, Fr Maurice O'Connor of Currans, said prayers on the roadside beside the cemetery, having been forbidden from entering the graveyard by Bishop O'Sullivan.[4]

One of the Free State officers who murdered Walsh shortly afterwards went to Cork. He was pursued by local IRA Volunteers David McCarthy and Dave Ned O'Connor, but he narrowly avoided being shot by them as he escaped into a crowd. Aware that his life was in jeopardy, he left Ireland.

Jim Walsh's uncle had emigrated to New Zealand and there he raised a

2   Dorothy Macardle, *Tragedies of Kerry* (1924), p. 69. Charlie Daly was a relative of the Charlie Daly who was executed in Drumboe, Co. Donegal, on 14 March 1923.
3   Information from Con Crowley, on whose farmland the killing took place.
4   Information from Tom Walsh, nephew of James Walsh.

family, one of whom became a priest. In the late 1950s Fr Bill Walsh became acquainted with a man in a retirement home in Taranaki. In the course of the conversation he told the priest that he knew the village of Currow, Fr Walsh's ancestral home, as he had been in the Free State Army in Castleisland during the Civil War. He subsequently admitted that it was he who had shot Jim Walsh, the priest's first cousin, over thirty years previously.[5]

James (Séamus) Walsh's name is inscribed in Irish, Seumas Breathnach, at his burial plot. Today he is remembered by a well-maintained stone monument at Mount Falvey which was unveiled on the same day in 1950 as that to Lieutenant Tom Fleming at nearby Glountane. Walsh is also recalled in a popular local ballad. Section Commander Walsh was twenty-four years old when he was killed on 27 March 1923.

---

5   Information from Adrian Breathnach, grandnephew of James Walsh.

2nd (Firies) Battalion, Kerry No. 2 Brigade, and Ballymacelligott Company

The 2nd Battalion of the Kerry No. 2 Brigade was in the mid-Kerry area. It consisted of six companies when the brigade structure was reorganised in 1919. The battalion was centred on the village of Firies and it was there that the captain of the local company, Jim Riordan, fired the only shots that were to be heard in County Kerry during the 1916 Rising. Having wounded two RIC constables, Jim Riordan managed to escape the intensive search for him and eventually reached America. His brother Paddy was appointed O/C of the battalion when it was formed in 1919.

The battalion's activity was hindered by a lack of enemy targets as the area contained only two RIC barracks; one in Gortatlea that was destroyed in 1920 and the other a heavily fortified barracks in Farranfore village at the edge of the battalion area. Charlie Daly of Knockaneculteen was a full-time Volunteer organiser in the county from 1917 and would have been expected to be a natural leader in the battalion area, but he was transferred to GHQ in Dublin and later became O/C of the 2nd Northern Division, based in Tyrone and South Derry. His brother Tom was another formidable Volunteer, but he was on Humphrey Murphy's and later John Joe Rice's Kerry No. 2 Brigade staff. Allied to this was the fact that the adjacent companies in other battalions, such as the Milltown, Listry, Beaufort and Currow companies, were particularly well organised and militarily active, so those units attracted the best of the fighting men in the mid-Kerry district.

The battalion's area stretched along the valley of the River Maine and was composed of companies from Ashill, Ballymacelligott, Currans, Firies, Kiltallagh and Keel. The Ballymacelligott unit would be the backbone of the battalion during the Tan War as the remainder of the companies were relatively inactive. Most of the 2nd Battalion's casualties were from the Ballymacelligott area, reflecting that company's activity during the Tan and Civil Wars. The only other IRA casualties in the battalion's area were Mossie Casey of Ballinoe, who was killed in an accidental explosion, and Thomas McLoughlin, who died in the Civil War.

The large parish of Ballymacelligott lies within a triangle bounded by Tralee, Castleisland and Farranfore. Though without even the central focus of a village, this rural area wrote for itself several pages in the history of Ireland's fight for freedom. The district had gained a reputation for resistance to the crown as a result of the activities of the Moonlighters during the Land Wars. The bonds formed during the clandestine activities of the Land Wars set the example for the guerrilla fighters who confronted the might of the Empire from 1918 onwards.

The Irish Volunteers were formed in the parish of Ballymacelligott in December 1913 and the local company was well organised from the outset. The original captain was Thomas O'Connor of Scart, Gortatlea, and his lieutenants were John Byrne, a local creamery manager, and Tom McEllistrim. The company mobilised at Easter for the Rising and marched to Tralee. There they were ordered to return to their homes as the plans for the rebellion collapsed in the confusion of that weekend. As they marched back to Ballymacelligott, they were entrusted with the care of Captain Robert Monteith, who had landed at Banna Strand with Roger Casement and was now sought by the RIC. Monteith was successfully hidden in the parish until arrangements could be made to get him to a more secure location in County Limerick, from where he eventually escaped to America.

The arrest of the local leadership and their imprisonment in Frongoch did nothing to halt the development of the Ballymacelligott Volunteer Company. On 13 April 1918 this unit attacked Gortatlea RIC Barracks. This was the first organised attack by the Irish Volunteers on any barracks in the period after 1916 and preceded the Soloheadbeg incident, which is taken as the start of the Black and Tan War, by nine months. In June 1918 Tom McEllistrim, who was now company captain, and his lieutenant, John Cronin, shot two RIC men on the streets of Tralee. Ballymacelligott had declared war on the Empire.

Under the leadership of McEllistrim and Cronin, the company became a highly efficient guerrilla unit. They returned to Gortatlea Barracks in 1920 and destroyed it, removing the only crown force garrison in the parish. The confrontational approach of McEllistrim and his men was in contrast to the more cautious attitude of Paddy Cahill, the Kerry No. 1 Brigade commander, and so the Ballymacelligott Company was reassigned to the 2nd Battalion, Kerry No. 2 Brigade. Tom McEllistrim then became O/C of that battalion, replacing Paddy Riordan of Firies, whose ability to command had been hampered by ill-health. John Cronin subsequently became McEllistrim's replacement as captain of the Ballymacelligott Company.

In their new brigade, they found common cause with the active units from Cordal and Scartaglin, and their combined efforts resulted in an intense guerrilla war in the Castleisland area and beyond. The arrival of Andy Cooney as an organiser in the Kerry No. 2 Brigade area was followed by the appointment of a younger brigade staff and the formation of a brigade flying column. This column had a large contingent of Ballymacelligott Volunteers and Tom McEllistrim was appointed its O/C following the death of Dan Allman at Headford Junction. Having been sufficiently battle-hardened, this column was disbanded so that its members could return to their own areas and form new battalion columns. The Ballymacelligott Company active service unit was full-time in the field and saw action in ambushes at Ballymacthomas, Ballycarty, Gortatlea railway, Castleisland and Ballydwyer. The final attacks of the Tan War were at Killorglin and the large ambush in Castleisland on 10 July 1921. The Volunteers of Ballymacelligott were prominent in both locations. By the summer of 1921 Paddy Cahill had been replaced as O/C of Kerry No. 1 Brigade by Humphrey Murphy and the Ballymacelligott Company was reassigned to this brigade as part of a new 7th Battalion, which also comprised companies from the Castleisland area.

The Ballymacelligott Company remained united in its opposition to the Treaty and was mobilised to capture Listowel on 29 June 1922 from the town's Free State garrison. Later, they fought in Limerick city in July 1922. McEllistrim was the commanding officer of one of the four Kerry columns that were to hold the defensive line from Limerick to Waterford and his unit saw action in the Kilmallock area. However, the landing of Free State forces at Fenit and other coastal towns forced the Ballymacelligott men to return to their own area to fight another guerrilla war in defence of the Irish Republic. McEllistrim spurned a local ceasefire with General Paddy Daly and Colonel David Neligan when they met in Peet's House in Arabella. In spite of facing overwhelming odds in terms of weapons and men, the Ballymacelligott Company remained active on the field of battle until the ceasefire called by Frank Aiken, IRA chief of staff, that ended the Civil War on 30 April 1923. Seven years in the forefront of the battle to establish an Irish Republic exerted a heavy toll on the Volunteers of Ballymacelligott.

Jim Baily

Séamus Ó Beaglaoic

James Baily was a native of Ballymacelligott, a large parish between Tralee and Castleisland and a centre of Moonlighter activity during the Land Wars of the 1880s. He was born in Rathanny on 27 July 1892 and as a young man was a noted fiddle player. In an area steeped in resistance to British rule, he became a member of the Irish Volunteers on their formation in the parish in 1914 and was mobilised at Easter 1916. Following the arrest of Austin Stack on Good Friday, Robert Monteith, who had accompanied Roger Casement from Germany, was given command of the Kerry Irish Volunteers. Having received Eoin MacNeill's countermanding order, Monteith told the assembled Volunteers in Tralee to return to their parishes and wait for another day. For the men in Ballymacelligott, this day came much earlier than in the rest of Ireland, for in April 1918 Volunteers from this company attacked the RIC barracks at Gortatlea. Although the attack resulted in the loss of two Volunteers, it was a baptism of fire for the most active of all IRA units in Kerry.

Courtesy of the Martin Moore collection.

Within a short period the men of the Ballymacelligott Company – Tom McEllistrim, John Cronin, Jim Baily, Jack Flynn, Mossy Carmody, Maurice Reidy and their comrades – were bringing the war to the enemy both on the streets of Tralee and in the country lanes of their native parish. Following numerous attacks on the RIC, many Ballymacelligott Volunteers were forced to go 'on the run'. In January 1921 Andy Cooney, a Tipperary man, was sent by GHQ as an organiser to South Kerry. Cooney removed officers in battalions that were not active enough and replaced them with younger men and, most significantly, he set up a brigade flying column. Coonęy's arrival gave a new impetus to the efforts of the Volunteers in the field and boosted morale.

Jim Baily was one of the six from Ballymacelligott who were among the eighteen or so men who went to a training camp at the Gap of Dunloe in the first fortnight of March 1921. The column was under the leadership of Dan Allman, with Tom McEllistrim as his second in command. They moved out from their base in mid-March and set up an ambush position at Dysert on the Castleisland to Farranfore road. Shots were fired at the RIC barracks in Farranfore to try to lure any relieving party of RIC from Castleisland into the ambush site, but this attempt failed. The column then moved through Scartaglin to an area south of Rathmore. There they were informed that a party of British military had travelled from Killarney to Kenmare and would return by train, disembarking at Headford Junction, where they would await the arrival of the Mallow train to complete their return journey to Killarney. Allman led his men to the small railway station, where they took up ambush positions around the junction. Several riflemen were placed on the elevated bank on the north side of the station, including Jim Baily. Others were placed in the stationmaster's house, on the southern embankment and in the signal box. It was while Allman was on the platform finalising the ambush plans that the Kenmare train, with the Royal Fusiliers aboard, arrived prematurely. When a soldier entered the lavatory on the platform where Allman had taken shelter, he was shot dead and these shots signalled the beginning of a fierce firefight.[1]

The men on the embankment where Jim Baily was positioned had a clear line of fire on the soldiers disembarking from the train and they inflicted many casualties on the military. However, reportedly as he was about to throw a grenade, Baily was hit in the head by a British bullet and died instantly. As the firing continued, the remaining soldiers took cover under the train and were out of the line of sight of the men on the embankment. In an attempt to dislodge them, Dan Allman, who was on the platform, exposed himself to get a clear shot at these men, but he was fatally injured by a bullet to the chest and died within a few minutes. The arrival of the Mallow train, which had another detachment of soldiers aboard, caused the Volunteers to disengage.[2]

The bodies of Baily and Allman were taken by the military to Killarney

---

1   Ernie O'Malley, *The Men Will Talk to Me – Kerry Interviews* (2012), interviews with Johnny O'Connor and Thomas McEllistrim.
2   Thomas McEllistrim, BMH WS 882, James Daly, BMH WS 1111 and Daniel O'Sullivan, BMH WS 1191.

but were released to the Allman family shortly afterwards. Baily's identity was not revealed at the time of the funeral so as to prevent reprisals being carried out on his family or neighbours in Ballymacelligott. The men's requiem mass was held in the cathedral in Killarney and the huge funeral then proceeded to Aglish Cemetery in Ballyhar. Jim Baily, who was referred to as an unknown Volunteer, and Dan Allman were buried in the Allman family tomb in the ancient graveyard.[3]

In 1927 Paddy Allman, O/C of the 4th Battalion and brother of Dan Allman, died. On the occasion of his burial, the remains of Jim Baily and Dan Allman were removed from the Allman family tomb and all three IRA Volunteers were buried in a new adjacent grave. An impressive monument by the sculptor Séamus Murphy was unveiled over their resting place in 1948 by Seán Moylan, who had been O/C of Cork No. 2 Brigade. They are also commemorated by a large roadside monument at Headford, near the now defunct railway junction where on 21 March 1921 the flying column of the Kerry No. 2 Brigade lost Dan Allman, its commanding officer, and one of its most fearless fighters, Jim Baily of Ballymacelligott. On the northern railway embankment at Headford Station stands a stone cross which marks the exact spot where Jim Baily fell.

3   *The Kerryman*, 2 April 1921.

Denis Broderick

Donnacha Ó Bruadair[1]

At Ballycarty, three miles east of Tralee, the main road to Castleisland branches from the Killarney road. A few hundred metres towards Castleisland the road is crossed by a modern railway bridge. This structure replaces an older metal bridge under which the narrower old road dipped before the recent improvements. This site, as it once was, provided an excellent ambush position for the Ballymacelligott Company of the IRA in their guerrilla campaign against the crown forces.

On 24 May 1921 an ambush was prepared for a British convoy that was expected to travel from Tralee to Castleisland and so to pass under 'The Metal Bridge'. As was the pattern, several unarmed scouts preceded the main ambush party which was composed of the seasoned veterans of the Ballymacelligott Company, led by Tom McEllistrim. McEllistrim had manufactured a trap mine using a shotgun which had no stock on it. It was planned to place this device near the bridge and to detonate it as the patrol passed. McEllistrim's group of seven or eight riflemen moved towards the bridge in the dim light at 10 p.m. on that May evening. Four scouts preceded the main party to ensure that there was no enemy presence in the vicinity. Two of these scouts went by foot on the main road and the other two on byroads towards the bridge. Denis Broderick and his comrade approached the railway bridge from a side road to declare the area safe and wait for the attack party to arrive at the ambush site.[2]

Unknown to them, a party of British soldiers had travelled on the old and unused road from Ballyseedy Cross behind the modern Earl of Desmond Hotel, which crossed the Killarney road several hundred yards east of the modern roundabout which is named for Captain John Cronin, a fearless fighter in the Ballymacelligott Company. From there the soldiers could reach the railway bridge undetected and there, under cover, they waited. As Broderick and his

---

1 There is no known photograph of Denis Broderick.
2 Ernie O'Malley, *The Men Will Talk to Me – Kerry Interviews* (2012), interview with Thomas McEllistrim.

companion arrived at the bridge they had passed the enemy position without realising it.³

McEllistrim, Mossy Carmody and the others of the main party walked towards the bridge using the main road. One of the men was carrying the landmine on his back. As they drew near the railway bridge they were met by a shout to halt. Carmody replied with a shot from his rifle and then there was a hail of bullets from the hidden British soldiers. The gun battle lasted about fifteen minutes before the IRA withdrew. Broderick, who was on the bridge, was killed, but the remainder of the ambush party managed to escape.⁴

Denis Broderick of Crag in Ballymacelligott was twenty-two when he was buried in O'Brennan Cemetery in his native parish. He is remembered today by a white roadside cross which is located near where he was killed at 'The Metal Bridge' at Ballycarty. His name is also inscribed on the brigade roll of honour a mile further down the road at the Ballyseedy monument.

3   Information from Brian Caball, Tralee.
4   Thomas McEllistrim, BMH WS 882.

Michael Brosnan

Mícheál Ó Brosnacháin[1]

Michael (Mick) Brosnan was born in 1893 in Ballinfeedora, Ballymacelligott, into a farming family. Although he was the third eldest boy in the family, he was the one who worked the family farm, as his older two brothers had joined the Dublin Metropolitan Police. He joined the Volunteers in 1916 and was attached to the Ballymacelligott Company of the 2nd Battalion, Kerry No. 2 Brigade. His younger brother Jack was also a Volunteer in the company. Following a reorganisation during the summer of 1921, the Ballymacelligott Company was transferred to the 7th Battalion, Kerry No. 1 Brigade.[2]

Michael Brosnan participated in many engagements against the British forces, including attacks in Gortatlea and Scartaglin. Aside from his duty as a soldier, he was the company's finance officer, in that he collected the levy placed on the local populace to finance the purchase of arms and to support men 'on the run'. Like many experienced Kerry Republican fighters, he was on active service in Limerick with one of the Kerry IRA columns during the initial phase of the Civil War. However, following the defeat in Limerick in late July and early August 1922, these men returned to their own districts to carry on a guerrilla war in defence of the Republic.

During the autumn and winter of 1922, Mick Brosnan was on active service in his native parish and was also the quartermaster of the Ballymacelligott Company of the IRA. He had a camouflaged dugout where he sheltered with his comrade in arms, John 'Big Jack' Clifford, who was from Mount Luke near Cahersiveen. This was located in the hayshed of the Casey family at Caher, not far from the Brosnan farm. One evening in January 1923 Brosnan and Clifford had journeyed into Tralee to enjoy a few drinks in a public house. There they met a man from Keel named Griffin, who told them that he had no place to sleep. Unsuspicious, they invited him to share their dugout. Griffin

---

1   Surviving images of Michael Brosnan were not of sufficient quality to reproduce.
2   Notes of Coiste Chuimhneacháin Bhaile Uí Shíoda on Kerry No. 1 Brigade casualties (private collection).

accompanied them back to Ballymacelligott, but when they woke the next morning, he had vanished. Based on Griffin's information, Brosnan's dugout in the hayshed was accurately located that morning by a Free State raiding party. The two Volunteers, having just awoken, were unable to escape and were detained. Brosnan and Clifford were captured in possession of arms and subsequently tried before a military committee in Ballymullen Barracks. They were sentenced to death by firing squad.

On Saturday 20 January 1923 Brosnan, Clifford, James Hanlon from Causeway and James Daly from Knockeendubh, Killarney, were brought into the prison yard of Ballymullen Gaol, which lies adjacent to the military barracks.[3] The four men were forced to wait beside their coffins for nearly thirty minutes for the officer in charge of the executions to arrive. Ed Flood, whose brother Frank had been executed by the British in 1921 in Mountjoy Gaol, eventually arrived and supervised the killings.[4] A notice was placed on the prison gate announcing that the four men had been executed. No prior notice was given to the prisoners' families, though Michael Brosnan was given the opportunity to write a final letter. At this time his brother Jack was interned in the Curragh.

Michael Brosnan's remains were initially buried in Ballymullen Gaol. On 28 October 1924 the coffins of the seven men who had been executed in the gaol were exhumed and returned to the men's families. While the remains of James Daly were brought to Killarney, the coffins of Michael Brosnan and the other five men were taken to St John's church for requiem mass. The following day Volunteer Michael Brosnan was buried in the Republican Plot in O'Brennan Cemetery in Ballymacelligott, a graveyard where his family burial plot also has his name inscribed.

---

3   Information from Dan Brosnan, nephew of Michael Brosnan.
4   Ernie O'Malley, *The Men Will Talk to Me – Kerry Interviews* (2012), interview with Bill Bailey.

JOHN BROWNE

Seaġán de Brún[1]

John Browne was born into a large family at Beheenagh, Knocknagoshel, in 1893, where his father worked as a cooper. The family would later move to Ballymacelligott. There John and his brothers, Paddy and Robert, became members of the Ballymacelligott Company of the Irish Volunteers on its foundation and were mobilised in 1916. Following the Easter Rising the captain of the Ballymacelligott Company, Thomas O'Connor, and his two lieutenants, John Byrne and Tom McEllistrim, were arrested and interned in Frongoch. Within eight months they were released, as the British government was confident that the flame of freedom had been quenched in Ireland. However, in Cronin's Hall, which stood on the old main road to Castleisland, seven men met on 10 April 1918. It was there that Tom McEllistrim, Maurice Reidy, Mossy Carmody, John Cronin, John Browne, Jack Flynn and Richard Laide hatched a plan to take over the RIC barracks at Gortatlea and capture the weapons of the four-man garrison.

The little station at Gortatlea was the junction between the main railway line and the spur to Castleisland. Such was the omnipresence of the RIC in the countryside, that they had a four-man garrison stationed permanently in a building adjacent to the station. Their regular routine was that two constables went on patrol around the district each evening, leaving the other two constables to man the small barracks. On the night of 13 April 1918 Jack Flynn was posted at the station and his task was to inform the six men under the command of Tom McEllistrim when the two-man patrol left the barracks. McEllistrim and his men were concealed sixty yards away on the railway line. They were masked as all were known to the local RIC. McEllistrim was armed with a revolver, while Cronin, Carmody and John Browne had shotguns and Reidy and Laide carried batons. At 9.30 that evening, Sergeant Boyle and Constable Fallon left the barracks to go on foot patrol and they were followed by Jack Flynn, who

---

1   There is no known photograph of John Browne.

was to inform the attackers when they were about to return to their barracks. Meanwhile McEllistrim and his men advanced to the door of the barracks and were surprised to find it locked. Undeterred, McEllistrim knocked and the unsuspecting Constable Considine opened the door, whereupon McEllistrim rushed past him hoping to overpower the other RIC constable before the element of surprise was lost. John Cronin quickly subdued Considine but Constable Denning made a rush for the inner room when he saw McEllistrim coming towards him. He closed the door as McEllistrim was trying to push it open. Forcing the door open McEllistrim and Denning grappled with each other until Cronin entered and aimed his shotgun at Denning's chest, whereupon he stopped struggling immediately.

The two prisoners were placed against the wall of the kitchen with John Browne standing guard over them with his shotgun. McEllistrim and Cronin went to the guardroom where they were in the process of removing the rifles when they heard a shot in the kitchen. They rushed out and saw Browne fall to the ground having been shot in the head. The shot had come from outside, fired by one of the constables who had unexpectedly returned from their patrol. The Volunteers inside were unaware of how many of the enemy had them trapped in the barracks. At this stage, a train had entered the station nearby and McEllistrim suspected that it may have had police or military on board. In the darkness of the barracks the men decided to fight their way out. They lifted the unconscious and dying Browne and as they were approaching the front door, Mossy Carmody fired two shots as he had caught a glimpse of a policeman's cap. As they exited the door, all was quiet outside until they were lifting Browne's body over a fence at the railway, whereupon the two RIC men outside, Fallon and Boyle, fired several more shots. The fleeing Volunteers set down the body of their comrade, returned fire and fled into the darkness. A second attacker, Richard Laide, had also been wounded and was left behind. About an hour later the police left their barracks and heard the moaning of the injured Laide. Browne was brought back into the barracks and Dr Brian Coffey of Tralee was sent for. A few minutes later Browne died as a result of the bullet wound he received from Constable Fallon's gun. His remains were removed to the morgue in Tralee's workhouse where they were identified by his brother.

Apparently, Jack Flynn, the Volunteer tasked with following the RIC patrol, had been met by some local people and was obliged to walk with them some 300 yards to allay any suspicions. As a result he lost sight of the two RIC men, who had only gone as far as the railway station a very short distance away and it is likely that, glancing back, they had seen the Volunteers enter the barracks. They quickly returned and Flynn was not in a position to warn his comrades, so the RIC men were able to surprise the attacking party.[2]

Though the Browne family grave was in Knocknagoshel, the family acceded to the wishes of the Irish Volunteers that he be buried in Rath Cemetery in Tralee. John Browne's requiem mass was held in St John's parish church and a crowd of 6,000 followed the funeral procession to Rath Cemetery. Browne was buried in a grave that lies near the Republican Plot. His headstone is also inscribed with the name of his brother Robert, who was killed later in the Tan War and is buried in the Republican Plot in Knockane Graveyard at Knocknagoshel. Richard Laide, who also died from his wounds, lies on the far side of the Rath Cemetery near the Manchester Martyrs' memorial.

The sequel to the Gortatlea Barracks attack was that Sergeant Boyle and Constable Fallon were decorated for their actions and transferred from Kerry. However, they did return to Tralee on 14 June 1918 for the coroner's inquest. Tom McEllistrim and John Cronin shot them both on Tralee's main street as they walked from the courthouse at lunch hour. The war in Kerry had begun.

2   Thomas McEllistrim, BMH WS 882, and his interview with Ernie O'Malley in *The Men Will Talk to Me – Kerry Interviews* (2012).

Robert Browne

Riobard de Brún

Robert (Bob) Browne was born in 1894 at Beheenagh in the parish of Knocknagoshel. His family later owned a shop at Clogher in Ballymacelligott. He was a member of the Irish Volunteer company in Ballymacelligott which was attached to the 2nd Battalion, Kerry No. 2 Brigade, though this company transferred to Kerry No. 1 Brigade in July 1921.

In June 1918 Sergeant Boyle and Constable Fallon were attending the inquest into the deaths of the two Ballymacelligott Volunteers at Gortatlea Barracks. The proceedings, which were investigating the deaths of John Browne, Robert's brother, and Richard Laide, were being held in Tralee's courthouse. These two RIC men were gunned down in Tralee's main street in broad daylight on the day of the inquest by Ballymacelligott Volunteers Tom McEllistrim and John Cronin. A few days later, Mossy Carmody and Robert Browne were charged with the shootings, despite the fact that neither man had been in Tralee that day. After a short period the charges against Browne were dropped and Carmody's case subsequently collapsed some six weeks later.

Courtesy of the Martin Moore collection.

Robert Browne had a shop in Ballymacelligott but the business and his home were burned by crown forces in response to his suspected Republican activities. Subsequently he operated a shop at Feale's Bridge near the family home at Knocknagoshel. The shop was located at a junction where the main Castleisland to Abbeyfeale road meets the Listowel to Brosna road (it is now bypassed by the modern road). Browne was an active Volunteer and Tom McEllistrim notes his participation in a daring attempt to capture the RIC barracks at Feale's Bridge in 1920 which was abandoned at the final moment as one of the participants lost his nerve.[1]

---

1 Ernie O'Malley, *The Men Will Talk to Me – Kerry Interviews* (2012), interview with Thomas McEllistrim.

In January 1921 a flying column composed of men from the Lixnaw and Listowel Battalions was established under the command of Thomas Kennelly. Kennelly was O/C of the 3rd Battalion but had been active in the Duagh area before the flying column was established. Being familiar with the area, he based the column in the townland of Derk, a remote district in the Duagh parish. However, in early February there was a build-up of British forces in Listowel town. In a local public house a conversation was overheard suggesting that the crown forces were planning to saturate the Duagh area in an attempt to annihilate the column. On learning of this Bob McElligott, the O/C of the Listowel Battalion, sent Thomas Pelican with a warning to Kennelly, who hurriedly evacuated his column and marched them south to the safety of the Stack's Mountains. The expected sweep by the British materialised but failed to capture the column which had retreated to the south of this desolate area.[2]

On the day of the sweep of the Duagh district by the Auxiliaries, Robert Browne was taken prisoner as he walked along a road at Knockalougha, Duagh, where he had been 'on the run'. He may have been attempting to join the column, which had been billeted nearby. His final hours are not recorded but he was shot dead by the Auxiliaries on 8 February 1921 and his body was left in an area known as Willie Walsh's bog. It was later found by local people and brought on a cart by Richard 'Starry' O'Shea to the Browne family home in Beheenagh. This site in Knockalougha where the body was found was initially marked by a monument erected in July 1921 and this was replaced by another memorial in 1997.

Volunteer Robert Browne was buried in the Republican Plot in Knockane Cemetery near Knocknagoshel. His name is also on the headstone of his brother John, who was also killed by the crown forces and is buried in Rath Cemetery, Tralee.

---

2   Thomas Pelican, BMH WS 1109.

Mossie Casey

Muiris Ó Catharaigh[1]

Maurice 'Mossie' Casey was born in 1897 in Ardywanig near Ballinoe, a townland which lies between Firies and Milltown. There his family had a small hillside farm on the western edge of Firies parish. He initially enlisted in the Irish Volunteers before the 1916 Rising and was attached to the Firies 'D' Company of the 2nd Battalion, Kerry No. 2 Brigade. He was an active Volunteer from early in the Tan War and much of his activity was carried out by the side of his friend Dan Mulvihill, who was the adjutant in the 6th Battalion of Kerry No. 1 Brigade. Mulvihill, from nearby Brackhill, later became the intelligence officer for the Kerry No. 2 Brigade and he records that on two occasions he and Mossie Casey set out to shoot the notorious Major McKinnon, the commanding officer of the county's Auxiliaries, but their quarry failed to appear at the ambush site.[2] Mossie Casey held the positions of both first lieutenant and engineering officer with the Firies Company, though his military record reveals he was active in every aspect of IRA activity.[3]

The manufacture of explosives provided a challenge for the IRA. While early in the conflict commercial explosives could be obtained from quarries, this source soon dried up. Explosives then had to be manufactured locally using mixtures of easily obtained chemical ingredients. Fundamental to the process was the charcoal made from sally tree bark. However, the manufacturing process of what was called 'black powder' varied from place to place and the explosives which were locally produced were often unreliable and unstable. By the beginning of the Civil War, a standardised and safer explosive mix called 'Paxo' had become available, but before this the manufacture of explosives was a hazardous process.

During the Truce, in October 1921, Mossie Casey, Dan Mulvihill, Dinny Rahilly and four others were preparing an explosive mix in an out-house

---

1   There is no known photograph of Mossie Casey.
2   Daniel Mulvihill, BMH WS 938.
3   Con Casey papers, Kerry County Library Archives.

belonging to John Browne outside the village of Firies.[4] When the home-made explosives were being manufactured, they detonated unexpectedly. Casey was severely burned by the blast, while Rahilly was blown through the roof of the building but survived.[5] Dan Mulvihill was uninjured. His comrades brought Mossie Casey on the eleven-mile journey to the infirmary in Tralee. There he would linger in severe pain for five days until he finally succumbed to his injuries on 27 October 1921.[6]

Casey's death was one of two in Kerry ascribed to such accidental explosions, though other Volunteers were injured in several similar incidents.

Volunteer Maurice Casey was buried in the family plot in the old cemetery at Kilnanare, which lies midway between his home in Ballinoe and the village of Firies where his life was prematurely ended. The grave is unmarked.

---

4   Ernie O'Malley, *The Men Will Talk to Me – Kerry Interviews* (2012), interview with Thomas McEllistrim.
5   Information from Batt Riordan of Firies.
6   Con Casey papers, Kerry County Library Archives.

John Clifford

Seán Ó Clubáin

John Clifford was born in Mountluke, Ballycarbery, to the north of Cahersiveen town on 8 October 1901. A man of imposing stature, 'Big Jack' Clifford, as he was called, worked as a labourer at Farmer's Bridge near Tralee. There he was a member of the local 'F' Company of the 1st Battalion, Kerry No. 1 Brigade. During the Civil War he was on active service with the nearby Ballymacelligott Company of the 7th Battalion, which was in the same parish.

Courtesy of the Martin Moore collection.

It was in Caher, Ballymacelligott, in January 1923 that he was captured when the dugout where he was sheltering was betrayed to the Free State Army. Jack Clifford and his fellow Volunteer Michael Brosnan, a Ballymacelligott native, had gone into Tralee the previous day. In a pub there they befriended a man named Griffin from Keel. All three returned to the dugout in Caher that evening, but on waking the next morning they discovered that Griffin had left during the night. Acting on Griffin's accurate information, a Free State raiding party surprised and captured Clifford and Brosnan in their hideout on the farm of the Casey family. The pair were marched the five miles into Tralee. Though they had offered no armed resistance at the time of their capture, Jack Clifford and Michael Brosnan were brought before a military court and sentenced to death for the possession of arms.[1]

The previous month, December 1922, the Free State O/C, General W. R. E. Murphy had sentenced four Republicans to death by firing squad: Con Casey, Matthew Moroney, Dermot 'Unkey' O'Connor and Tom Devane. However, the

---

1 Information from Jerry Breen, local historian in Ballymacelligott, to Martin Moore.

threat of reprisals against prominent pro-Treaty supporters in Tralee issued by the IRA O/C Humphrey Murphy forced the Free State command to reprieve the condemned men. Early in January General Murphy had been replaced by Paddy Daly, who was O/C of the Free State Army's Dublin Guard. Daly had a reputation for brutality, even towards his own soldiers, and he was anxious to demonstrate that he would deal harshly with the continued Republican resistance. On Saturday 20 January 1923 four men who had been sentenced to death by firing squad were selected by Daly to be executed in Ballymullen Gaol. It would appear that geography had a part to play in his decision on which men were to die. Though captured in Ballymacelligott, Jack Clifford was from South Kerry, James Daly was from East Kerry, James Hanlon was a native of North Kerry and Michael Brosnan was from Ballymacelligott, a Republican stronghold to the east of Tralee.

Free State soldier Bill Bailey gave a gruesome account to Ernie O'Malley of the executions carried out that day. The firing squad was composed of Free State soldiers, some of whom were reluctant and crying. The officer in charge of the executions, Captain Ed Flood, was thirty minutes late coming to the prison yard, where the four men and their executioners were waiting on the cold January morning. Bailey described how the four men to be shot stood beside their own coffins and even changed the names on the coffins as they waited for Flood to arrive.[2]

Following his execution, the body of John Clifford was denied to his family and was buried in Ballymullen Gaol. Seventeen months after the end of the conflict, on 28 October 1924, the coffin was disinterred and brought to St John's church, Tralee, for requiem mass. The next day John Clifford was buried in Kilnavarnogue, Cahersiveen, close to the cemetery's Republican Plot. His name is inscribed on a memorial that stands at the wall of Ballymullen Gaol on the other side of which seven men were executed by firing squad during the Civil War. 'Big Jack' Clifford is also remembered on the monument at the Republican Plot in Tralee's Rath Cemetery and on the memorial on Cahersiveen's main street.

2   Ernie O'Malley, *The Men Will Talk to Me – Kerry Interviews* (2012), interview with Bill Bailey.

Jack Flynn

Seán Ó Floinn[1]

John (Jack) Flynn has the distinction of being one of the seven Volunteers who took part in the first armed confrontation with the crown forces at Gortatlea at the outset of the Tan War and he was to die in action on the eve of the Truce that ended that conflict in July 1921. The son of a carpenter, he was born in Gurranemore, Gortatlea, in the parish of Ballymacelligott on 12 July 1893.

Throughout the Black and Tan War Flynn was a member of the active service unit of the Ballymacelligott Company. He was described by his comrades as 'a brave and efficient officer' and at the time of his death he was a lieutenant in the Ballymacelligott Volunteers.[2] He had participated in actions at Gortatlea and Scartaglin RIC Barracks and in the numerous other incidents that made this district of Kerry such a hostile area for the forces of the crown.

On 10 July 1921, the eve of the Truce that ended the Tan War, Jack Flynn was a member of the large force that attacked a British military patrol in Castleisland town. The ambush party was mainly drawn from Volunteers from the Kerry No. 1 Brigade and these included several from Ballymacelligott. The usual routine in Castleisland was for a large party of soldiers to patrol up the town's Main Street just after the curfew came into force and then to return to the RIC station which was situated at the southern end of the town. At the centre of the northern end of the wide Main Street stood the town's library. In June 1921 this prominent building had been burned, as it had been reported to the local IRA battalion that it was to be used to house a detachment of Auxiliaries. The main body of attackers, led by Humphrey Murphy, were located in the partially destroyed library. At intervals along Main Street were small laneways and other men were placed in these to allow the military patrol to be attacked from three sides. Flynn and his group were positioned on the eastern side of the street and to the left of the library.

---

1   There is no known photograph of Jack Flynn.
2   Notes of Coiste Chuimhneacháin Bhaile Uí Shíoda on Kerry No. 1 Brigade casualties (private collection).

Following the initial intense firing as the military party entered into the ambush position, several soldiers were trapped near to where Jack Flynn and his comrades were situated. When the order came to withdraw, the Volunteers in this area were slow to disengage and this proved fatal. Following the initial assault some soldiers managed to return to the barracks and they summoned reinforcements. These advanced behind the buildings on Main Street and cut off Flynn, Richard Shanahan and Denis Prendiville from their line of retreat. These three men were trapped in a small quarry adjacent to where the monument now stands. All three were shot dead by the overwhelming military firepower. Jack Flynn and his two comrades were the last IRA Volunteers to die in the Tan War in Kerry. This was two days before his twenty-ninth birthday and a little over three years after two of his comrades were killed in the first action of the war in his native Gortatlea.[3]

Jack Flynn was buried in Tralee's Rath Cemetery. He was interred in the same plot as Richard Laide, who was killed in the Gortatlea attack in 1918.

3   Peter Browne, BMH WS 1110.

Paddy Herlihy

Pádraig Ó hIarfhlatha[1]

Paddy Herlihy was born in December 1900. The Herlihy family had a farm in Ballymacpierce, Gortatlea. As a young man Paddy enlisted in the Ballymacelligott Company of the Irish Volunteers as did his brother Jack.

Paddy Herlihy was employed at the local creamery at Ballydwyer in Ballymacelligott. On the morning of 12 November 1920 several lorry loads of Auxiliaries from Tralee suddenly descended on the area. At least four of the men at the creamery that morning were IRA Volunteers and on hearing the approach of the military vehicles, they made an attempt to escape. Fire was opened on them from a distance of 400 yards. Paddy Herlihy was hit in the arm and fell, wounded, by a fence. When the Auxiliaries approached him as he lay there, he was shot twice more and died at the scene. John McMahon, an IRA Volunteer who had a farm nearby and was delivering milk to the creamery, was shot dead in the initial volley. Jack McEllistrim and Tim Walsh were wounded as they fled but survived their injuries. Witnesses later testified that there were no shots fired at the Auxiliaries or even words exchanged before the killings, which were entirely unprovoked.[2]

Three days previously Tom McEllistrim, John Cronin and Jim Baily from Ballymacelligott were involved in the shooting of two Black and Tans at Ballybrack railway station. Constable Archibald Turner died at the scene, but Constable James Woods lived for several days and was able to give descriptions of his attackers. The following day Tom McEllistrim and the Ballymacelligott active service unit lay in wait at Ballyseedy for the RIC and Auxiliary vehicles that were returning from burning houses in Ballybrack, but their efforts were in vain. In the heightened atmosphere of that week, it was not surprising that the Auxiliaries came to Ballymacelligott in large numbers that November morning.[3]

1 There is no known photograph of Paddy Herlihy.
2 *The Freeman's Journal*, 19 October 1921.
3 Thomas McEllistrim, BMH WS 882.

Having shot the four men, the Auxiliaries then departed and approximately an hour later Tom McEllistrim and his group of twelve armed Volunteers arrived at the creamery in order to render what assistance they could. A short time later three more military lorries came unexpectedly from the direction of Castleisland. The Volunteers engaged the Auxiliaries, who dismounted from their vehicles, and a prolonged gun battle ensued.

This second Auxiliary convoy happened to be on its way to Tralee carrying a film crew from Pathé Newsreels and several newspaper reporters. They were being brought on a 'fact finding' tour of the south of Ireland by Captain Hugh Pollard, a veteran of British Army Intelligence during the Great War. During the Tan War his title was that of press officer with the Police Information Authority and he was essentially the director of British propaganda in Dublin Castle. The film crew who accompanied Pollard filmed the attack from a standing position on one of the lorries. A short time later another military vehicle approached from the Tralee direction. Thinking that this was bringing more IRA men to the scene, the Auxiliaries departed back towards Castleisland.

Pollard embellished and distorted the details of the incident at Ballydwyer when it became international news the following day.

Volunteer Paddy Herlihy was nineteen years old when he was killed. His remains are buried in O'Brennan Cemetery's Republican Plot, a short distance from where he was shot dead.

Richard Laide

Risteárd Ó Laoide[1]

Richard Laide was born on 27 November 1890 in Gortatlea, where his family had a farm. He was a member of the Ballymacelligott Company of the Irish Volunteers and was one of the seven men who met in Cronin's Hall on Wednesday 10 April 1918 to plan the attack on Gortatlea Barracks. The aim of the attack was to procure arms to supplement the meagre supply of shotguns and pistols that the Ballymacelligott Volunteers had at their disposal. This group of local Volunteers was led by Tom McEllistrim and their target was the small RIC barracks that stood near the railway station at Gortatlea, a short distance from the Laide farm.

On the evening of Saturday 13 April 1919, at 9.30 p.m., two of the four RIC men stationed in the small barracks left to go on their regular patrol. They were to have been followed by Volunteer Jack Flynn, who was to report back to McEllistrim when the patrol was about to return to their base. Shortly after the RIC men left the barracks, the six other Volunteers, with their faces masked, advanced on the small building. Expecting the front door to be unlocked, McEllistrim still managed to gain entry by brazenly asking the men inside to open the door. As Constable Considine unlocked and opened the barracks door, McEllistrim forcefully brushed him aside and moved to subdue the other policeman, Constable Denning, before he could arm himself. McEllistrim and John Cronin overpowered Denning after a struggle, while John Browne and Richard Laide held Considine prisoner in a front room. Meanwhile, Flynn had been distracted by somebody he knew and felt that he had to walk a little distance down the road with him in order not to arouse suspicion. Undetected by Flynn and suspecting something was amiss, the two constables on patrol, Boyle and Fallon, returned to the barracks. It is likely that they saw the six Volunteers entering the small barracks and they positioned themselves at a window where they could see into the building. From there they could see John

---

1   There is no known photograph of Richard Laide.

Browne and they fired on him, fatally wounding him in the head. As Laide was turning to warn his comrades he too was shot and wounded. The four uninjured Volunteers escaped outside, carrying Browne, but they were fired upon by Boyle and Fallon, so they set down the body of Browne and returned fire, then left.[2] Laide attempted to escape but was too seriously injured. The RIC found the grievously injured Laide beside the unconscious Browne about twenty yards from their barracks. Laide was brought to the nearby house of the Hogan family and by midnight Dr John Murphy of Farranfore had arrived. He telephoned from the railway station for a car to bring Laide to hospital.[3]

Richard Laide was brought to the County Infirmary in Tralee but died of peritonitis the next day, Sunday 14 April, due to the bullet wound in this abdomen. The Laide family agreed to a request from the Irish Volunteers that their son and John Browne be buried in Tralee's Rath Cemetery following a joint funeral. An estimated 6,000 people followed the funeral cortège from St John's church to the town's graveyard.[4] Richard Laide was buried near the cemetery's Manchester Martyrs' memorial in a plot he shares with his comrade from the Gortatlea attack, Jack Flynn, who was killed later in the conflict. John Browne's remains were interred elsewhere in the cemetery.

Two months later, while attending the subsequent inquest in Tralee, the RIC killers of Richard Laide and John Browne were shot by Tom McEllistrim and John Cronin on Tralee's main street in broad daylight. Less than two years later, on 25 March 1920, a large contingent of well-armed IRA men from Ballymacelligott again attacked the small barracks at Gortatlea station, destroying it and thus removing the only post that the crown forces held in the native parish of Richard Laide.

2   Ernie O'Malley, *The Men Will Talk to Me – Kerry Interviews* (2012), interview with Thomas McEllistrim.
3   *The Kerryman,* 20 April 1918.
4   *The Freeman's Journal,* 17 April 1918.

JOHN LEEN

Seán Ó Laigin[1]

John Leen was born in Knockane, Ballymacelligott, on 23 November 1893. His family were farmers and were steeped in the traditions of the Moonlighters who fought the injustices of the landlords and the British administration in general during the Land Wars, which were ending as John Leen was born. However, the end of the hated landlord system was not enough for the people of Ballymacelligott and within a generation they were to the forefront of another war – this time for complete national independence.

The Ballymacelligott Company was attached to the 2nd Battalion of Kerry No. 2 Brigade and many of its Volunteers were involved in the attacks on crown forces in the early stages of the Tan War. The result was that many men from the area were 'on the run' and these men became the active service unit of the company which was formed in June 1920 under the command of Tom McEllistrim. John Leen and his friend Mossy Reidy were two of the Volunteers in this unit.

During late December 1920 the column was billeted to the north of the parish in the hills of Lyreacrompane. On 24 December 1920 Leen and Reidy got permission to go down into Ballymacelligott and there they visited the home of John Byrne, the creamery manager who was an officer in the Ballymacelligott Company and was married to Tom McEllistrim's sister. Byrne lived in a house beside the creamery (now the post office) and he too was a wanted man.[2]

John Leen and Mossy Reidy were in the Byrne house talking to Mrs Byrne and her sister, Hanna, and being Christmas Eve they did not expect crown forces to come from Tralee raiding that evening. Shortly after they entered the house Mrs Byrne asked them if there were others accompanying them, as she had heard footsteps outside. Leen was sitting at the table and Reidy by the

---

1 There is no known photograph of John Leen.
2 Although he used the name John Byrne in his census return, he was also known as John Byrnes or Burns.

fire when three Auxiliaries entered the kitchen. They were led by Major John McKinnon, who calmly walked up to the fire where Reidy was sitting. Leen pulled his gun and attempted to shoot 'The Major' but his gun misfired. As he fired again, McKinnon shot him dead and Leen's bullet hit the ceiling as he fell. Reidy was now the Auxiliaries' captive and he asked for some time to pray. The two women were locked in a room and, after about thirty minutes or so, Reidy was also shot dead. The Auxiliaries dragged the two bodies from the house out to the adjoining yard. The two women were taken out to a car and told that they were being brought to another house for the night. Meanwhile the Auxiliaries set fire to the Byrne homestead and took the women to the nearby parochial house at Clogher.

Neighbours arrived at the scene of the burning house and found the bodies of John Leen and Mossy Reidy in the outhouse. They removed the remains and prepared the bodies for a wake. The next morning, Christmas Day, as the remains were laid out and mourners were arriving, the Auxiliaries returned. However, they did not interfere, possibly because the bodies were not yet placed in coffins. Later that evening the bodies were brought from the house where they were waked and taken to Clogher church. Again a detachment of Auxiliaries returned from Tralee and this time they removed the remains in their coffins and brought them to Tralee. Why this was done was not clear, but the bodies may have been taken to the town where the Auxiliaries could use a local informant to identify who exactly they had killed. In any case, the remains were returned to the church in time for the funeral.[3]

John Leen was buried in the family tomb in O'Brennan Cemetery.[4]

---

3   Bessie Cahill, BMH WS 1143.
4   Information from Matt Leen, Tralee.

John McMahon

Seán Mac Matúna[1]

Ballydwyer lies in the centre of the large parish of Ballymacelligott. While it is now bypassed by a modern road, it is sited on the old Tralee to Castleisland route. Though it could not be regarded as a village, it did have a creamery, a shop and a pub, and the church at Clogher was just a mile away. Being the site of one of the creameries in Ballymacelligott and so a place where many of the farmers gathered each morning, it was not surprising that it was subjected to scrutiny by the crown forces. And so it was that Major John McKinnon, commander of 'H' Company of the Auxiliaries based in Tralee seven miles away, led a large detachment of his forces to the creamery on 12 November 1920. It was reported that some twelve lorries descended on the creamery that morning in an attempt to capture any members of the Ballymacelligott active service unit who might be delivering milk there.

John McMahon was a farmer from Droum in the east of the parish of Ballymacelligott and was also a member of Ballymacelligott Company of the Irish Volunteers. On that morning in November he was one of a group of local farmers at the Ballydwyer Creamery, where he was delivering milk and a sack of corn. While he was at the creamery the convoy of Auxiliaries approached and, unprovoked, opened fire from a distance of 400 yards, killing John McMahon instantly. Another IRA Volunteer, nineteen-year-old creamery employee Paddy Herlihy, was wounded and subsequently shot dead as he lay on the ground.[2]

As it happened the main bulk of Tom McEllistrim's Ballymacelligott active service unit was about a mile away but had not engaged the Auxiliaries. The men killed were not part of the company's column.[3]

The Auxiliaries departed and McEllistrim and his men went down to the creamery where the dead and injured were. Dr Shanahan from Tralee was called for and he was attending the wounded when a three-vehicle column of

1 There is no known photograph of John McMahon.
2 *The Freeman's Journal*, 19 October 1921.
3 Thomas McEllistrim, BMH WS 882.

Auxiliaries arrived from the Castleisland direction. The Volunteers took cover but were noticed by the Auxiliaries who opened fire on them. This Auxiliary detachment was escorting a number of journalists who were making a film and were not part of the original raiding party. This party of journalists were being brought on a tour of the martial law area by Hugh Pollard, a senior figure in British Intelligence and the head of the press office at Dublin Castle. As a gun battle raged, it was filmed by a crew from Pathé News from one of the lorries.[4] Another vehicle with Black and Tans arrived at the scene from the Tralee direction. At that stage the Auxiliaries departed back to Castleisland and took seven prisoners, among them Dr Shanahan and William Herlihy, whose brother had been killed earlier. Of these prisoners, four were later charged with attacking the Auxiliary convoy: Thomas O'Connor of Scart, a man named Dowling of Ballydwyer, James Carmody and Richard McEllistrim.

John McMahon of Droum was born on 4 June 1888 and had been married two years before his death. He is buried in the family plot in Nohoval Cemetery, Ballymacelligott, where his headstone records the circumstances of this death on 12 November 1920.

---

4 Ernie O'Malley, *The Men Will Talk to Me – Kerry Interviews* (2012), interview with Thomas McEllistrim.

Thomas McLoughlin

Tomár Mac Loċlainn[1]

Little is remembered today of the short and sad life of Lieutenant Thomas McLoughlin. This may be because he was not a native of Kerry, and although a member of the Kerry IRA, he died while on active service outside the county. These facts, combined with the circumstances of his death, probably unjustly led to the memory of his service to the Irish Republic fading from local lore.

Thomas McLoughlin was a native of County Sligo and had been a soldier in the British Army. He deserted from his regiment and subsequently lived in Aubee, near Castlemaine. The date of this desertion and why he settled in Kerry are not recorded. During the Black and Tan War he enlisted in 'E' Company of the 2nd Battalion of Kerry No. 2 Brigade. This unit was based in Kiltallagh to the east of Castlemaine village. An IRA record of his service, which was dated 9 January 1925, states that 'He always did his utmost in furthering the Republican cause and was one of the best fighters and most sincere soldiers that the 2nd Battalion possessed.' He was the Kiltallagh Company's training officer and later held the rank of lieutenant in the unit. Thomas McLoughlin was a participant in the many actions in the area, including the ambush at Castlemaine on 1 June 1921 in which five RIC constables were killed.[2]

In July 1922, in the early stages of the Civil War, McLoughlin was a member of one of the Kerry IRA columns which was on active service in south County Limerick. It was while there that the stress of warfare exerted its toll on his mental health. While resting in a house with his comrades near Kilmallock on the night of 31 July, he tragically shot himself in the forehead with his own rifle, but the wound was not fatal. While being cared for by his companions, he inflicted a further wound on himself with a razor while he pretended to be going for a cigarette. This second wound was to prove fatal and he died the next day, 1 August 1922.[3] Though the condition of post-traumatic stress due to

1 There is no known photograph of Thomas McLoughlin.
2 Con Casey Papers, Kerry County Library Archives.
3 *Ibid.*

the effects of armed conflict had not been defined in 1922, it claimed the life of Lieutenant Thomas McLoughlin that summer's night in County Limerick.

The place of his burial is not recorded and no memorial stands in his honour.

Jack Reidy

Seán Ó Riada

John (Jack) Reidy was a native of Rathanny in the parish of Ballymacelligott. He was born on 30 December 1895 and worked as tailor, having been apprenticed to his uncle who was a master tailor in the neighbouring townland of Kilbane in Ballymacelligott. Jack Reidy was a member of the Ballymacelligott Company of the Irish Volunteers, though he was not in the active service unit. His brother Paddy was a lieutenant in the company.

Courtesy of the Martin Moore collection.

In January 1920 Jack Reidy was one of eleven Ballymacelligott men arrested following an attack the previous week on Serjeant at Law Alexander M. Sullivan, KC, at Clounalour, Tralee. This senior crown lawyer had been involved in a controversial legal case between Ballydwyer Creamery and a large business firm in Tralee which controlled a rival creamery in the parish. Although he had been on Roger Casement's legal defence team in his Old Bailey trial in 1916, Sullivan was opposed to the Republican movement and had actively recruited for the British Army during the Great War. However, the evidence against Jack Reidy and his co-defendants was slight and they were acquitted of the charge of the attempted murder of Sullivan.

Reidy was now considered by the RIC to be a Republican activist and this led to his death the following year. On 15 April 1921 Major John McKinnon was shot dead on Tralee Golf Course by Tralee IRA marksman Con Healy. McKinnon was the commander of 'H' Company of the Auxiliaries, which was based in the town. On Christmas Eve 1920 he had killed John Leen and Mossy Reidy at Ballydwyer, Ballymacelligott. Fearless by nature, 'The Major' was not deterred by several attempts to kill him. His Auxiliary comrades remembered him remarking that if he were to be killed, it would be John Cronin, the captain of the Ballymacelligott Company, who would probably be responsible. Thus, on the night of his assassination, several lorry loads of Auxiliaries travelled to Ballymacelligott to exact revenge on the parish for their commander's death.[1]

The Auxiliaries swooped on Ballydwyer on the evening of 15 April 1921, hours after McKinnon's death. Jack Reidy and a fellow tailor named Jim Clifford were busy at work completing an order for a suit in the house of Phil Reidy, Jack's uncle, who lived in nearby Kilbane. Phil was not in the house that evening. The cottage stood on relatively high ground, which was given the name Phil's Height, and there was only a single door. Distracted as they were, Reidy and Clifford were unaware of the presence of the enemy until they heard the vehicles approaching the cottage. Hearing the noise of the engines, the two men rushed from the house and ran into the fields. As the Auxiliaries approached in the moonlit night they saw the two men fleeing. They opened fire and Reidy was shot and died at the scene of gunshot wounds to the head and body. Clifford hid in a drain that ran along a ditch. Despite searching within feet of him and prodding the briary ditch with their bayonets, the Auxiliaries were unable to find Clifford and after an hour they returned to their vehicles. They placed the body of Jack Reidy on a lorry and brought it to his mother's house. Opening the door, they threw the remains on the floor and left. The Auxiliaries then proceeded to burn several houses in the locality, including the parochial house at nearby Clogher.[2]

Volunteer Jack Reidy was buried in the Republican Plot in O'Brennan Cemetery near his home in Ballymacelligott.

1   Ernie O'Malley, *The Men Will Talk to Me – Kerry Interviews* (2012), interview with Denis Quille.
2   Information from Dan Brosnan, Tralee, nephew of Jack Reidy.

Maurice Reidy

Muiris Ó Riada[1]

Maurice (Mossy) Reidy was born at Knockavinnane, Ballymacelligott, on 13 June 1893. His parents, James Reidy and Honora Ahern, had a farm in this townland, which lies four miles from Tralee. Described as a man of striking physique, he was a renowned sportsman and was All-Ireland champion in the fifty-six pound weight throwing, a sport that was highly regarded at the time and involved throwing the weight over various heights.[2] Today it is only played in the Scottish Highlands. At the age of twenty Maurice Reidy joined the Ballymacelligott Company of the Irish Volunteers when they were founded in the parish in December 1913. The company captain was initially Thomas O'Connor of Scart. John Byrne and Tom McEllistrim were the lieutenants in the company before the Rising.

Though three of the officers of the Ballymacelligott Company were interned after the 1916 Rising, the Volunteers managed to maintain their structure within the parish and by the spring of 1918 they were ready to strike a blow for freedom. Tom McEllistrim gathered a band of six other men together at Cronin's small dance hall near Ballydwyer on 10 April 1918 and there they planned to attack the RIC barracks at Gortatlea three days later. This small group included Mossy Reidy and the attack, on 13 April, was to be a baptism of fire as two of the Volunteers were killed in the incident which was the first attack on the crown forces in Ireland after the 1916 Rising.[3]

For the next thirty-two months, Mossy Reidy remained on active service with the Ballymacelligott Company of the Volunteers. On the evening of 24 December 1920 the battalion active service unit was billeted in Lyreacrompane, in the hills above Ballymacelligott parish. Mossy Reidy left the safety of that remote area and, with John Leen, went to visit the home of John Byrne. Byrne,

---

1 Surviving images of Maurice Reidy were not of sufficient quality to reproduce.
2 Information from Brian Caball, a relative of Mossy Reidy.
3 Ernie O'Malley, *The Men Will Talk to Me – Kerry Interviews* (2012), interview with Thomas McEllistrim.

a Volunteer officer who had been interned in Frongoch, was the creamery manager at Ballydwyer and was married to Tom McEllistrim's sister. His house was beside the creamery and it was to there that Reidy and Leen made their way on the night of Christmas Eve.

That night, probably in an attempt to arrest John Byrne, Major McKinnon and a party of Auxiliaries raided the house. Byrne was not there but Leen and Reidy had arrived in the house a short time beforehand. McKinnon and his men entered the house unannounced and found Leen and Reidy sitting in the kitchen. Leen pulled his revolver but was shot dead as he fired. Mrs Byrne and her sister, Hanna McEllistrim, pleaded for the life of Mossy Reidy, who asked for some time to pray. The women were locked in a room and Reidy was summarily executed. He received a single gunshot to the head. The bodies of the two Volunteers were brought by the Auxiliaries out to the yard of the house while they proceeded to set fire to the Byrne home. McKinnon then departed and raided several other houses before returning to a hotel in Tralee.[4]

The next morning, Christmas Day, the bodies of both men were being prepared for burial when the Auxiliaries arrived again but left soon afterwards. The remains were then brought to the church at Clogher, less than a mile away. Later that evening the Auxiliaries returned and removed the coffins from the church. It may have been that they were unsure of the identities of the men that they had killed the previous evening. The remains were subsequently returned to the church the next morning for the funeral.

Maurice Reidy is buried in the Reidy family grave in Arabella churchyard in Ballymacelligott.

---

[4] Bessie Cahill, BMH WS 1143 and Thomas McEllistrim, BMH WS 882.

3rd (Kenmare) Battalion, Kerry No. 2 Brigade

The catchment area of the 3rd Battalion, Kerry No. 2 Brigade is isolated from the remainder of the county by high mountains and is connected to more populated areas to the north by the narrow Moll's Gap and the wider Roughty Valley. However, it was to this isolated district that James Stephens and other Fenians came to find refuge in the 1860s. The Republican spirit that sheltered those IRB leaders remained dormant until the second decade of the twentieth century in this region, which was dominated by the plantation town of Kenmare. John Joe Rice was born there and he became the dominant Republican figure in South Kerry for over half a century.

Following the reorganisation of the Irish Volunteers in Kerry in 1919, the 3rd Battalion was commanded by Rice. When he joined the brigade staff as V/C, his position as battalion O/C was taken by the captain of the Kilgarvan Company, Denis Hegarty, who retained the command until the end of the Civil War. The battalion area stretched from Kilgarvan to Sneem and to the thinly populated areas of the Beara peninsula to the south of Kenmare. The companies of the 3rd Battalion at the time of the Truce in July 1921 were located in Ardea, Dawros, Lauragh, Morley's Bridge, Kilgarvan, Kenmare, Bonane, Crossroads, Tuosist, Blackwater, Templenoe and Tahilla. The Glenlough and Sneem companies later joined Kerry No. 3 Brigade in June 1922.

In April 1920 the RIC abandoned many of their smaller rural garrisons as their isolation left them vulnerable to attack. However, Kenmare remained heavily garrisoned and the Royal Fusiliers Regiment had their base in the town's workhouse. As a result the IRA's opportunities to engage the enemy were not frequent. Several of the battalion's most active fighters were subsequently assigned to the Kerry No. 2 Brigade flying column which was established in March 1921. Later in the conflict a 3rd Battalion active service unit was established but too late to see effective action in the Tan War.

With few exceptions, the 3rd Battalion remained loyal to the Republic during the Civil War. Local former IRA activist Tom O'Connor Scarteen, now a commissioned officer in the Free State Army, led a detachment of Dublin

Guards and other pro-Treaty troops when they captured Kenmare following a seaborne landing on 11 August 1922. However, on 9 September 1922, John Joe Rice successfully recaptured his native town and acquired a huge arsenal of weapons to sustain his brigade for the remainder of the conflict. While Free State forces retook the town on 6 December, the surrounding countryside remained firmly in Republican hands until the ceasefire was declared in April 1923, making it perhaps the only area in the county where the Free State writ did not run.

The battalion lost three of its Volunteers during the conflict, Denis Tuohy and Con Looney, both from the Crossroads Company, and Tim O'Shea of Rossdohan.

Con Looney

Conċuḃaır Ó Luanaıġ[1]

Cornelius (Con) Looney was born in 1901 in the townland of Rossboy, four miles to the east of Kenmare. His family had a small farm there. As a young man Looney joined the Great Southern and Western Railway Company and trained as an engine driver. He was apprenticed to the locomotive driver of the Killarney to Kenmare train and was in the process of learning his profession when the fight for freedom erupted in the hills and glens of his native Roughty Valley.[2] In 1917 he joined the Crossroads Company of the 3rd Battalion of Kerry No. 2 Brigade, which was centred on the town of Kenmare. This company was one of the most active of the battalion during the Tan War.

On 1 May 1921 Denis Tuohy of Gortalassa, Looney's neighbour and fellow member of the 3rd Battalion, was taken prisoner by the British military. Following the killing of several members of their regiment at Headford Junction six weeks previously, the Royal Fusiliers garrison at Kenmare's workhouse suspected that Tuohy was a member of the IRA column involved in that ambush. Con Looney and his comrades in the Crossroads Company resolved to attack the military at the workhouse and attempt to free Tuohy. However, their plan was vetoed by the battalion leaders as it would have resulted in too many casualties.

Following the divisions caused by the Treaty, the 3rd Battalion was almost united in its opposition to the document. The exception was Tom O'Connor Scarteen, a former active Volunteer with the Kerry No. 2 flying column, and it is with this Free State officer that the name of Con Looney became linked in the tragedy of the Civil War.

Tom O'Connor Scarteen, Scarteen being the family's native townland, was the brigade engineer of Kerry No. 2 Brigade. However, as the Tan War progressed and the degree of organisation became more formalised, GHQ in Dublin issued a decree that all such brigade engineers should have a qualification in the field of engineering. As a result, O'Connor Scarteen was removed from

1 There is no known photograph of Con Looney.
2 Information from Richard Colligan, nephew of Con Looney.

his brigade position, though he remained an active Volunteer, and Martin Wade of Killorglin was made the brigade engineer in his place. This was taken as a personal slight by O'Connor Scarteen and he held a grudge against the brigade staff. As a result, when the Free State Army was being recruited during the early months of 1922, O'Connor Scarteen eagerly took a commission and was appointed O/C of the Kerry Brigade of the Free State Army. Under his command, on 11 August Free State forces landed by sea from Limerick city and captured the undefended Kenmare. O'Connor Scarteen, from his base in his native town, tried to wrest the surrounding countryside from his erstwhile Republican comrades, who were commanded by John Joe Rice. While he may have had a degree of support in the relatively wealthy town of Kenmare, this was not the case in the countryside and his raiding parties searched the same homes in the surrounding hills where he himself had once sought shelter from the crown forces. Such actions were regarded with particular disdain and fuelled a bitter enmity towards these local Free State officers.[3]

On 9 September 1922 an advance party of IRA Volunteers entered Kenmare in preparation for an attack on the town later that day.[4] Their aim was to capture O'Connor Scarteen before an all-out attack on the town by Rice's Kerry No. 2 Brigade. Several Volunteers, including Con Looney and 'Sailor' Dan Healy, entered O'Connor Scarteen's house. He and his brother John, a Free State captain, were asleep in an upstairs bedroom having spent the night out in the surrounding hills searching for Republicans. What happened next is shrouded in controversy but the O'Connor Scarteen brothers were shot dead. It is claimed by Republicans that the Free State officers tried to get to their weapons and were shot as they attempted to do so, while Free State sources claim that they were shot while prisoners. As there was no love lost between O'Connor Scarteen and his former comrades, this may have been the case, but on the other hand, having captured the town, the IRA released their Free State prisoners, who included the brother of Kevin O'Higgins, a senior Free State government minister.

3   Information from Dan Keating, Republican Volunteer who took part in the capture of Kenmare on that day.
4   Ernie O'Malley, *The Men Will Talk to Me – Kerry Interviews* (2012), interview with John Joe Rice.

Almost three weeks later, on 27 September, the Kerry No. 2 Brigade launched a prolonged attack on the town of Killorglin. Free State forces were garrisoned in several fortified buildings in the town and repeated assaults failed to shift them. One of these Free State posts was the Carnegie Building, which was defended by troops under the command of Lieutenant Corry of the 1st Western Division. Con Looney was the leader of a section of IRA Volunteers that had laid siege to this large two-storeyed building. Due to the intense fire from the Free State troops inside the Carnegie Building, this party had to retreat and Looney covered their withdrawal.[5] While climbing over a fence during this gun battle, he was shot and mortally wounded. His final words were recorded by his comrades: 'Give my rifle to my brother, give my love to my mother and tell them I am dying for the cause.'[6]

Looney died at the scene at what is called Church Corner in Killorglin. He was twenty-two years old when he lost his life. He was buried in the Looney family grave in the old cemetery at Kenmare. His sacrifice is remembered by a large Celtic cross, which also recalls the memory of Denis Tuohy who was killed in the Tan War. This monument, which was unveiled by veteran Republican Seán Ryan on 1 May 1949, stands at a crossroads two miles east of Kenmare on the road to Kilgarvan and adjacent to the native townlands of these fallen Volunteers.

---

5   Con Casey papers, Kerry County Library Archives.
6   Information from Maureen Read, niece of Con Looney.

Timothy O'Shea

Tadg Ó Séadga[1]

Timothy (Tim) O'Shea was born on 4 July 1897 in the townland of Rossdohan, midway between Tahilla and Sneem on the northern shore of the Kenmare river. He was the middle child of the seven children of Tim and Margaret O'Shea, who had a farm on the rocky coastline.

In 1914 O'Shea joined the Irish Volunteers at the age of seventeen. Following the reorganisation that occurred in 1917, he enlisted as a member of 'A' Company of the 3rd Battalion, Kerry No. 2 Brigade. He was appointed the company's engineering officer and was also the second lieutenant in this Tahilla unit. During the Tan War he was transferred to the battalion staff, where he was the transport officer, as he was one of the few men in the area who was able to drive a car. In this capacity he was later appointed to the 2nd Brigade headquarters staff where he operated as 'driver'.

During the Civil War he returned to the Kenmare area and the 3rd Battalion, and was a member of its active service unit. This column, which was led by Mikey White, remained in the field until the end of the Civil War and it was eleven days before the declaration of a ceasefire by the IRA that Tim O'Shea lost his life.

On 19 April 1923 the IRA column was crossing the rough mountainous countryside at Brackloon, north of Tahilla, following a military operation near the village of Sneem. Their destination was the home of Michael Sheehan, which was a Republican safe house close to the Sneem to Killarney road. Sheehan's son, Paddy, was a Volunteer in the column and was guiding his comrades over the heather-covered rocky foothills of the peninsula's mountains.[2] For the members of the column this was unfamiliar terrain. Tim O'Shea's rifle was defective – the safety catch was broken and it had to be kept 'half cocked'. As they headed into the safety of the remote glens, they crossed a small hill in the townland of Brackloon. There their way was hindered by what was described

---

1   There is no known photograph of Timothy O'Shea.
2   Information from Liam Sheehan, Sneem, nephew of Volunteer Paddy Sheehan.

as 'a small cliff'. As they stood over the rock face, O'Shea lowered his rifle to gauge how great the drop was, as the vegetation below probably made it difficult to judge whether it was possible to jump down. The gun slipped from his hand and on striking the ground below it discharged. O'Shea was hit in the chest and died almost immediately.[3]

Volunteer Tim O'Shea of Rossdohan was buried in the family plot at Baile na hEaglaise Graveyard near Tahilla, but his grave there is unmarked. He was the third member of the 3rd Battalion to be killed and while Con Looney and Denis Tuohy are remembered by a monument at Crossroads, east of Kenmare, which is close to their homes, no memorial stands to Lieutenant Tim O'Shea, though he is recalled on the Republican monument in Cahersiveen.

3   Con Casey Papers, Kerry County Library Archives.

Denis Tuohy

Donnaċa Ó Tuaċaiġ

Courtesy of the Martin Moore collection.

Denis Tuohy was a native of Gortalassa, a townland to the east of Kenmare. His father, who had been a member of the local Rural District Council, had a farm there. As a young man Tuohy joined the RIC, but in 1918, when it was proposed that conscription be introduced in Ireland, he resigned in protest.[1] He initially went to England, but returned to Cork city in 1919 as his Republican activities had come to the attention of the British police.[2]

During the early stages of the Tan War Tuohy had been working in Cork city and was an active Volunteer in Cork No. 1 Brigade. By 1921 he had returned home and was appointed lieutenant and intelligence officer in the local IRA unit at Crossroads. However, he was arrested by the British Army at his father's house in Gortalassa at 4 a.m. on 1 May 1921. The army unit that garrisoned Kenmare was the 1st Battalion of the Royal Fusiliers and they had suffered many casualties at the ambush at Headford Junction on 21 March 1921. Denis Tuohy was suspected of having been involved in that attack on their men as they journeyed by train to Killarney from Kenmare.

Tuohy was brought to the Kenmare workhouse where the Royal Fusiliers had their headquarters and there he was interrogated. Apparently his brother was initially told that he would be released shortly as there were no charges against him. However, his comrades in the Crossroads Company, who included Con Looney, feared the worst and planned to rescue him, but the idea was judged foolhardy by the battalion command and the rescue plan was abandoned.[3]

1   *Irish Independent*, 12 May 1921.
2   Con Casey papers, Kerry County Library Archives.
3   Information given to Richard Colligan by Michael (Ned) O'Sullivan, a comrade of Denis Tuohy.

In the workhouse Tuohy was subjected to a brutal interrogation by the military. However, he managed to take a grenade from one of his guards and hurl it at the soldiers present. This sealed his fate. Tuohy's father tried in vain to visit him but only saw his son's battered body strapped to a chair. A priest who also tried to gain access to the prisoner to administer the last rites was refused permission to see him. Sometime during the day Tuohy died of wounds inflicted by his captors. At 6 p.m. that evening a volley of shots was heard from the workhouse and the military reported that this was a firing squad executing Tuohy. Those who saw the remains afterwards reported that it appeared he had died as a result of the torture he had been subjected to earlier in the day. The brutality of his death at the hands of the Royal Fusiliers elicited a question in the British Houses of Parliament later that month, though no satisfaction was forthcoming.

Tuohy's battered body was released to his family. His funeral mass was held in Holy Cross church in Kenmare. The Tricolour was placed on his coffin and it was reported that the funeral procession was three miles long. Aged twenty-eight when he died, his remains were buried in the Old Cemetery, Kenmare. Lieutenant Denis Tuohy and his IRA comrade Con Looney are remembered today by a roadside Celtic cross two miles from Kenmare on the Kilgarvan Road. This was unveiled on 1 May 1949 by Seán Ryan, a prominent Kerry Republican, following a parade from Kenmare town to the site at Gortalassa.[4] The monument was funded by local subscriptions and money collected in the United States by Crossroads native Patrick (Ned) O'Sullivan of New York.[5]

---

4   *Irish Press*, 3 May 1949 and *The Kerryman*, 7 May 1949.
5   *The Kerryman*, 28 August 1948.

4TH (KILLARNEY) BATTALION, KERRY NO. 2 BRIGADE

County Kerry's first unit of Irish Volunteers was founded in Killarney on 28 November 1913, just three days after the inaugural meeting at the Rotunda in Dublin. Within a fortnight, companies had been formed throughout East Kerry. Before the Easter Rising the Volunteers in East Kerry were well organised, but they failed to play any part in the rebellion as the expected arms from the *Aud* failed to arrive. Several prominent Volunteer officers were interned in Frongoch in 1916 and following their release the Volunteer movement began a period of reorganisation. In 1919 the Kerry No. 2 Brigade was formed and Killarney and the companies in its hinterland were designated the 4th Battalion. From November 1913 until April 1921 local cobbler Michael Spillane was the prominent figure in the Volunteer movement in the town, commanding the town's company and later the battalion which was centred on Killarney. The battalion was composed of the following companies: Killarney, Ballyhar, Beaufort, Listry, Black Valley, Muckross, Lissivigeen, Kilcummin and Fossa.

Spillane remained as O/C of the 4th Battalion from its formation in 1919 until his removal in April 1921, at which time the battalion was deemed to be underperforming. He was replaced by Pat Allman of Ballyhar, as the brigade leadership under Humphrey Murphy demanded a higher level of activity in the war against the crown forces. Spillane's long-standing deputy was Michael J. O'Sullivan, who was also a Killarney native. He was replaced by Edward O'Sullivan of Beaufort in the changes to the battalion staff which occurred that April. Spillane also held the post of battalion quartermaster, but he relinquished this post in favour of Michael Devane. Devane in turn was replaced by John Coffey in 1921. Spillane's adjutant was Patrick O'Shea and his position was later given to Patrick Devane.

As the Tan War progressed, the crown forces' activity forced Spillane to move his headquarters to the Gap of Dunloe. With the arrival from GHQ of Andy Cooney as the brigade organiser, an active service unit was formed and a training camp established in early March in the Gap of Dunloe. This flying column, under the command of Dan Allman and later Tom McEllistrim, was extremely effective and brought the war in South Kerry to a new level. Its membership was composed of several of the most active Volunteers of the 4th Battalion. In the early summer of 1921 this column was disbanded and local battalion columns formed. The O/C of the 4th Battalion active service unit was Jim Coffey of Beaufort.

The Killarney Volunteers operated under several disadvantages. The town's major industry was tourism and its hotels were the town's largest employers. The Kenmare Estate dominated the town and, while detested by their rural tenants, the townspeople regarded these Catholic landlords more benignly and many of their employees were former servicemen and retired RIC officers. Finally the bishop of Kerry had his seat in the local cathedral and, not unlike his vehemently anti-Republican predecessor, David Moriarty, Bishop Charles O'Sullivan was an ardent Redmondite. In contrast, the rural areas of the battalion had long suffered under the rack-rents of Lord Kenmare and in a previous generation the districts of Beaufort, Ballyhar and the Black Valley were hotbeds of Moonlighter activity during the Land War. The result was that most of the Republican activity in the Killarney area was in the surrounding countryside rather than in the town.

Killarney was heavily garrisoned with a large force of RIC in the town's large barracks in Lewis Road. The regular police were supplemented by detachments of Auxiliaries and Black and Tans. In addition, the British Army had requisitioned the large Great Southern Hotel and used it as a barracks for the 1st Royal Fusiliers Regiment. As the war progressed, the RIC abandoned their outlying barracks in Beaufort and Derrycunnihy and these were destroyed soon after by the IRA.

There was little armed activity in the district before the setting up of the Kerry No. 2 Brigade flying column, but in August 1920 the Listry Company attempted an ambush on a crown force convoy on the Killorglin road and was involved in the killing of two RIC men near Milltown in November of that year. The change in battalion leadership and the formation of a battalion active service unit in the early summer of 1921 coincided with an increase in activity. There were ambushes at the Port road, Killarney, and on the Kenmare road, and an attack on a train in Ballybrack in June 1921. Several units from the battalion participated in the large-scale attack in Killorglin on the eve of the Truce.

With the advent of the Truce in July 1921, Killarney became the headquarters of the Kerry No. 2 Brigade under John Joe Rice. Probably not surprisingly, there was a high degree of support for the Treaty within the town and those officers who had felt slighted by recent changes in the battalion staff sided with the pro-Treaty faction. While the urban company was divided in its attitude to the Treaty, by and large the rural companies remained loyal to the Republic.

The Civil War came to Killarney on 13 August 1922. Eleven days earlier the Dublin Guard of the Free State Army had landed in Fenit and within hours had captured Tralee. Their advance and capture of Killarney was unopposed as Republican forces retreated, leaving the former RIC barracks in flames, but otherwise the town was unscathed. The Great Southern Hotel became the Free State headquarters and local recruiting into their army began. However, in general Kerry-based pro-Treaty supporters were not given prominent commissions in the new army and it was the Dublin Guard that was to the fore in prosecuting the war against Republican forces in South Kerry.

John Joe Rice's Kerry No. 2 Brigade regrouped and soon the Free State forces were confined to Killarney and smaller scattered garrisons from which they ventured out to the mountainous countryside only in large numbers. The IRA's battalion columns proved very effective in a terrain which suited the guerrilla fighters, despite being outnumbered and outgunned. The autumn and winter saw both sides fight to a bloody stalemate with neither side able to deal a mortal blow to the other. March 1923 saw the violence of the conflict increase to a level that the British did not countenance during the Tan War. In a determined attempt to crush Republican resistance, captured prisoners were summarily executed in Beaufort and at the Countess Bridge in Killarney but, despite this, what remained of the 4th Battalion fought on in the mountains and glens around Killarney to the bitter end.

Dan Allman

Domhnall Ó Almán

Daniel 'Dan' Allman was born in 1893 into a nationalist family in Rockfield, a townland between the villages of Firies and Faha. The Irish Volunteers were initially organised in the parish in December 1913, but were reorganised in 1917. Dan Allman was the force behind the fledging Volunteer company in his native area in 1917. The Listry Company of the Irish Volunteers, which he commanded, was attached to the 4th Battalion, Kerry No. 2 Brigade, when the brigade was formed in 1919. This battalion included Killarney and the surrounding areas and its O/C was Michael Spillane, a cobbler from the town.

Courtesy of Mercier Archive.

The first engagement of the Listry Company was at Hillville, between Killorglin and Milltown, where Tom O'Connor and Dan Allman and their men ambushed and killed two RIC men on 31 October 1920.[1] Allman and his Listry Company remained active throughout that winter but were hampered by the lack of crown force targets in their rural area.

The arrival of Andy Cooney, an organiser from GHQ, in January 1921 was to prove the impetus the brigade needed. He placed a younger, more active staff in brigade positions and advised the setting up of a Kerry No. 2 Brigade flying column. Volunteers who were 'on the run' and those who had wished to take the war to the enemy were among the thirty or so men Cooney brought to the Gap of Dunloe for a training camp that was held during the first two weeks of March 1921. Cooney appointed Dan Allman the flying column's O/C with Tom McEllistrim of Ballymacelligott as his deputy. The column, having completed its training, prepared its first ambush at Dysert near Castleisland. However, an attack

---

1   Ernie O'Malley, *The Men Will Talk to Me – Kerry Interviews* (2012), interview with Tom O'Connor.

on Farranfore RIC station that day failed to lure the crown forces from nearby Castleisland to the ambush position on the Farranfore road. Allman abandoned the ambush position and subsequently led his men to the mountainous district south of Rathmore. It was while billeted there at Caherbarnagh that Allman was informed of a detachment of British soldiers travelling from Kenmare to Killarney on a train that would halt at Headford Junction station. These soldiers would have to alight on the platform of the small railway station to await a connecting train travelling from Mallow to Killarney. It was to Headford that Allman marched his men on the morning of 21 March 1921.

Although the train no longer stops at Headford as the Kenmare line is today defunct, much of the topography remains unchanged. There was a platform between the Killarney and Kenmare railway lines as they converged at the station. On this was a small lavatory which no longer exists. On the north side of the main railway line is a steep embankment. Allman placed some of his riflemen, including Jim Baily, along this embankment. Others were placed in the signal box overlooking the station and a further detachment on the level area to the south side of the tracks. The train from Kenmare contained a detachment of soldiers from the Royal Fusiliers Regiment and its carriages also contained several civilians.

While Allman was still arranging his men around the station in preparation for an attack, the Kenmare train arrived unexpectedly, as it was running several minutes early. Allman and two Volunteers were concealed in the platform's lavatory when the Kenmare train entered the station. When the train stopped many of the civilians alighted onto the platform, as did one soldier who went into the lavatory where the Volunteers were positioned. Jim Coffey grabbed the soldier's weapon as he entered and a struggle ensued which ended when the Fusilier was shot dead by Allman.

This shot acted as a catalyst for the engagement and the station was soon swept by the hail of gunfire. Many soldiers were shot as they tried to escape from the train. A heavy machine gun in a fortified wagon returned the Volunteers' fire. Allman exhausted his ammunition and crossed the platform to take a bandolier from a dead soldier. Rearmed, he resumed firing at the soldiers who had regrouped after the initial surprise. Several of the remaining uninjured soldiers had taken refuge beneath the train carriages and, due to the steep angle of the embankment where the main section of IRA riflemen were firing from, these sheltering troops could not be dislodged by gunfire. Allman crossed the railway to the north embankment but returned, determined to root out the soldiers under the carriages. Bending down and exposing himself to get a better angle to engage the troops under the train, he was hit by a bullet in the chest. He was pulled out of the line of fire by Jim Coffey. Asking for water, he pointed to his jacket pocket where he had a flask of holy water, which Coffey sprinkled on him. Within a few minutes, Allman had died from his wound.[2]

Tom McEllistrim took over command of the ambush party. At this juncture the train travelling on the main line from Mallow arrived at the station. Troops on that train were alerted by the gunfire and alighted before the station was reached and began to engage the Volunteers with intense gunfire. McEllistrim gave the order to retreat and the column disengaged, leaving the body of its leader, Allman, behind. The other IRA casualty was Jim Baily of Ballymacelligott. Three civilians were to die of wounds received at Headford on that day. The exact British casualty figure remains unconfirmed to this day. At least eight soldiers were killed, though this may be an under-estimation, and up to twenty Royal Fusiliers were wounded.

Allman's funeral was held next day from the cathedral in Killarney. Shops in the town closed and the cortège made its way to Aglish Cemetery, Ballyhar, near to Allman's home. There he was buried with full Republican honours in the Allman family tomb at the old graveyard. Next to him was laid Jim Baily.[3] In 1927 Dan Allman's brother, Paddy, died. He had been O/C of the 4th Battalion and his premature death was precipitated by wounds received during the Civil War. The coffins of Dan Allman and Jim Baily were removed from their tomb and buried in a new adjacent grave with Paddy Allman. An imposing monument by sculptor Séamus Murphy was unveiled in Aglish Cemetery by Seán Moylan on 21 March 1948.[4] Dan Allman, Jim Baily and the fight at Headford Junction are also commemorated by another impressive monument on the Glenflesk to Barraduff road, 200 yards from Headford Station.

2   Daniel O'Sullivan, BMH WS 1191, Thomas McEllistrim, BMH WS 882, James Daly, BMH WS 1111 and Peter Browne, BMH WS 1110.
3   *The Kerryman*, 2 April 1921.
4   *Ibid.*, 27 March 1948.

Stephen Buckley

Stiophán Ó Buacalla

Courtesy of the Martin Moore collection.

Stephen Buckley was born into a prosperous farming family at Radrinagh in the parish of Kilcummin on 26 December 1893. He was a Volunteer with the 4th Battalion of Kerry No. 2 Brigade and was active during the Tan War. He took the Republican side in the Civil War.

On Sunday 21 January 1923, following the execution of James Daly from Knockeendubh, two miles on the Tralee side of Killarney, the parish priest, Fr Brosnan, refused to pray for the soul of the dead Volunteer at the nearby Kilcummin church at Sunday mass. As the service ended, Stephen Buckley rose from the congregation to lead prayers for the repose of James Daly.[1]

On 3 March 1923 Buckley and two of his comrades, Dan O'Donoghue and Tim Murphy, were taken prisoner when they were captured at a dugout on the Buckley farm at Radrinagh. The dugout was a small but well-constructed stone structure embedded in a wall on a laneway several fields from the Buckley family home. As a Free State raiding party came into the area, Buckley's father went to the adjacent field with hay on his shoulder as if to feed his animals and warned the three men to stay where they were as there were troops everywhere. But rather than searching the area, as they would usually do, the soldiers went directly to where Stephen Buckley and this two comrades were.[2] They had accurate information from a local informer about the dugout's secluded location. The three Volunteers had two loaded rifles in their possession and this sealed their fate when they were taken before a military tribunal for sentencing. While still at the scene, the three men were

1 Information from Denis Fleming, Milleen, Kilcummin.
2 *Ibid.*

badly beaten and a young boy who was a witness was also taken into custody, though he was later released.³

Dorothy Macardle reports that Buckley defiantly shouted 'Up the Republic' as the lorry carrying the prisoners entered the gates of the Great Southern Hotel which was the Free State Army's headquarters in Killarney. She also recounts that people in the market place (now a car park), behind the courthouse and several hundred yards away, could hear the screaming of prisoners as they were being tortured.⁴

Early on the morning of Wednesday 7 March, Stephen Buckley, Dan O'Donoghue, Tim Murphy, Tadhg Coffey and Jeremiah O'Donoghue were taken from their cells. They were brought by six officers and several soldiers away from the barracks and through several fields towards the Countess Bridge. This once rural area between what was then the Great Southern Hotel (now The Malton) and the bridge at the top of the Countess Road has been developed and modern buildings obscure the path the men were brought along. When they arrived at the bridge, which was less than half a mile away, the five prisoners were ordered to remove the barricade on the road, placed there by the Free State troops shortly beforehand and consisting of rubble but with a mine concealed beneath the stones. On a signal given by an officer, the mine was remotely detonated and the prisoners were caught by the full force of the blast. The smoke and dust cast a veil over the site of carnage for enough time to allow Tadhg Coffey to escape. But the smoke could not mask the groans of the dying men and the Free State soldiers opened fire on their helpless victims, who included Stephen Buckley.⁵

Stephen Buckley's remains were interred with those of his three comrades in the Republican Plot in the New Cemetery, Killarney. A monument stands at the site where the massacre took place on the Countess Bridge, but while the dugout where they were captured still exists, it is not marked.

---

3 Information from Dan O'Donoghue, nephew of Volunteer Dan O'Donoghue, one of those taken prisoner.
4 Dorothy Macardle, *Tragedies of Kerry* (1924), p. 27.
5 Ernie O'Malley, *The Men Will Talk to Me – Kerry Interviews* (2012), interview with John Joe Rice.

Jerry Casey

Diarmuid Ó Catharaigh[1]

Jeremiah 'Jerry' Casey was born in Dunloe Upper in the parish of Beaufort in 1897. He was a farmer's son. Little is now known of his life except that he was an active Volunteer during the Tan War where he served with 'B' Company of the 4th Battalion, Kerry No. 2 Brigade. His rank was that of company engineer with the Beaufort unit and later he became the 4th Battalion engineer. He was subsequently promoted to the engineering section of Kerry No. 2 Brigade. In 1922, during the Truce, he was transferred to the 1st Western Division of the IRA along with two other Kerry Volunteers named O'Connor. They were sent to County Clare to instruct the local Volunteers in the use and manufacture of explosives.[2] When the Civil War broke out, Casey continued to run the engineering section in the 1st Western Division and was on active service there until early in 1923, when his health began to fail.[3]

In March 1923, during the height of the Civil War in Kerry, the ill Jeremiah Casey went home to his native Dunloe. On his return the local priest advised him to report to the Free State garrison at the large Beaufort House near Beaufort village and to declare that he would no longer take part in the conflict. On Tuesday 20 March 1923 he travelled the short distance to the barracks to do as he had been advised. When he arrived there the Free State officer on duty told Casey to return later that day, which he did. Again he was refused entry and was then told to return later that evening. On this occasion he was taken into the building. Jerry Casey was not seen alive again and the next morning his bullet-riddled body was found dumped in a ditch on the road between Beaufort and the Gap of Dunloe. Nothing is known of how or why he was killed by the Free State Army while he was their prisoner. However, Casey was reported to have told his companions that he suspected

1   There is no known photograph of Jerry Casey.
2   Edward O'Sullivan, Beaufort, BMH WS 1115.
3   Con Casey papers, Kerry County Library Archives.

that they might attempt to get him to divulge information concerning local Republicans while he was in the barracks.[4]

Jeremiah Casey is probably buried in the family plot at Churchtown near Beaufort, but his grave is unmarked. He is remembered by a roadside memorial at the site where his body was found in his native Dunloe outside Beaufort village. This was erected in 1953 and replaced an earlier wooden cross placed there following the Civil War.

---

4   Information from Patrick O'Sullivan, Beaufort.

PATRICK CASEY

Pádraig Ó Catharaigh[1]

When the Irish Volunteers were reorganised in 1919, foremost among their difficulties was a lack of arms. There were few arms available from GHQ and even these had to be purchased by the local battalion. Essentially, it was up to each company to arm its Volunteers with whatever weapons could be procured locally. Capturing weapons from the RIC was difficult and, as the killing of two Volunteers at Gortatlea in April 1918 sadly demonstrated, it involved a high risk for inexperienced men. However, some valuable weapons remained in civilian hands and in the large Muckross Estate in Killarney, the gamekeepers patrolled the mountains with such rifles.

Pat Casey was the captain of the Black Valley Company of the 4th Battalion, Kerry No. 2 Brigade. Derrycunnihy is a wooded and unpopulated area of what is now Killarney National Park. It is ten miles from Killarney on the road to Kenmare and was separated from Casey's home in the Black Valley by the upper of Killarney's three lakes. One of the gamekeepers on the Muckross Estate visited this remote area on his regular beat. It was there, on the evening of 19 February 1919, that Pat Casey and his comrade Jerome Griffin, a Volunteer in the 'D' (Fossa) Company of the 4th Battalion, planned to surprise the gamekeeper and relieve him of his rifle. Griffin had a shotgun but Casey was unarmed. When John Lyne, the gamekeeper, arrived at an isolated point in the road at Derrycunnihy, a few hundred yards on the Killarney side of the now abandoned small church, Casey and Griffin ambushed him. They demanded his weapon but Lyne would not surrender it, whereupon a struggle developed as Casey attempted to wrestle the loaded rifle away from him. However, Lyne managed to pull the trigger and Pat Casey was fatally wounded in the side. Meanwhile Griffin fired his shotgun and wounded the gamekeeper in the legs, but having no further ammunition, he fled, leaving his comrade dead and the gamekeeper wounded on the roadside. The gamekeeper was later removed to

1 There is no known photograph of Patrick Casey.

hospital. He lived a long life in Muckross near Killarney and always regretted the events of that day.[2]

The British military in Killarney subsequently confiscated all the firearms on the Muckross Estate fearing other such attempts by the local Volunteers to procure arms.[3]

Captain Patrick Casey was twenty-three years old when he died. He is buried in the Casey family grave in Churchtown, Beaufort and commemorated by a roadside memorial at Derrycunnihy, on the scenic Kenmare road, which marks the place where he fell.

---

2   Information from Bridget Casey of Killarney, niece-in-law of Volunteer Patrick Casey.
3   Maurice Horgan, Killarney, BMH WS 952.

JAMES DALY

Séamus Ó Dálaig

Courtesy of the Martin Moore collection.

James Daly was the son of a railway worker. He was born in the townland of Knockeendubh, two miles from Killarney on the road to Tralee, on 28 January 1898. A fitter by trade, like his father, he worked with the Great Southern and Western Railway Company. He was a Volunteer with the 4th Battalion of Kerry No. 2 Brigade, having joined the Irish Volunteers in 1915. James Daly was active in the Tan War and his rank was that of section leader. With the formation of the battalion flying column, he went on full time active service.[1]

When the Civil War erupted he was regarded as an experienced fighter and was sent to the Limerick–Tipperary area where the Republican Army was trying to hold a defensive line to prevent the Free State Army advancing into the south during July 1922. On 2 August 1922, the day of the seaborne landings at Fenit, James Daly was in Tralee, where he used his skill as a fitter in the construction of landmines. These mines were to be used in the destruction of bridges along the road from Fenit to Tralee to impede the Free State forces on their way from Fenit. However, by the time the mines were delivered to the IRA units in the field, the Free State troops were already in the town.[2] The Republican forces then resorted to guerrilla warfare and James Daly was one of the fighters of Kerry No. 2 Brigade who made the south of the county an area where Free State forces could not hold sway despite their superiority in numbers and arms.

On 21 December 1922 James Daly was staying in the McCarthys' house

---

1   Con Casey papers, Kerry County Library Archive.
2   Niall Harrington, *Kerry Landing* (1992), p. 127. The author quotes Batt Dowling, an IRA officer in the 1st Battalion, Kerry No. 1 Brigade.

in Inchycullane, Kilcummin, not too far from his home in Knockeendubh. As a Free State raiding party approached, Mrs McCarthy warned Daly of their presence. He ran with his rifle from the house but turned right instead of left and ran into the approaching troops. They were led by a former local IRA officer, who had been captain of the Anabla Company during the Tan War but had left the IRA training camp in Currow to join the Free State Army on its foundation in Beggars Bush in the spring of 1922. James Daly was taken prisoner while carrying his rifle, though he did not resist when captured. The fact that he was reported by his former comrade to have been carrying the weapon when taken prisoner was enough to seal Daly's fate.[3]

James Daly was brought before a military court in Tralee's Ballymullen Barracks and charged with possession of arms. He was sentenced to death by firing squad and was sent to the condemned cells in Ballymullen Gaol. However, after a few days he was inexplicably transferred back to the main body of prisoners in the nearby barracks and it was thought that his sentence had been commuted. At this time his brother was also a prisoner in Ballymullen.

On the evening of 19 January, while having supper with the other prisoners in the barracks, James Daly, Michael Brosnan, Jack Clifford and James Hanlon were called out and told that they were to be executed the next morning at 8 a.m. That Saturday, at dawn, the killings were carried out by firing squad. The men's families were not informed beforehand; in Daly's case, his widowed mother and his brother who was incarcerated with him.

A month earlier the Free State commanding officer in Kerry, W. R. E. Murphy, a former British officer, had planned to execute four men in Ballymullen but was forced to rescind his order when a threat of retaliation was issued by Republicans against leading pro-Treaty civilians in Tralee. However, Murphy was transferred in early January and he was replaced by the Dublin Guard O/C Paddy Daly, who had been one of Michael Collins' 'Squad' during the Tan War. Daly selected four men from different areas in the county to be executed as a deterrent against continued IRA activity throughout the county. The men faced the firing squad in Ballymullen Gaol which is adjacent to Ballymullen Barracks. A note was posted on the barracks

3   Information from Denis Fleming, Milleen, Kilcummin, the son of Will Patrick Fleming, senior IRA officer in the 4th Battalion, Kerry No. 2 Brigade.

gate and this gave the unknowing families the news of the tragic fate of the four men.[4]

The following Sunday the priest in James Daly's parish of Kilcummin, Fr Brosnan, refused to offer prayers during mass for the repose of his soul, as would be customary following the death of a parishioner. However, a member of the congregation rose and led the people in prayer for their dead neighbour. This man was Stephen Buckley, who was to die in Free State custody six weeks later at Countess Bridge.[5]

James Daly, who was described as being 'light-hearted and humorous' by his fellow prisoners in Ballymullen Barracks, was initially buried within the gaol following his execution. On 28 October 1924 his remains, and those of the men executed with him, were disinterred and released to the men's families. James Daly's coffin was give a guard of honour by members of Kerry No. 1 Brigade as far as Rath, on the outskirts of Tralee. There the remains were given to members of the 4th Battalion, Kerry No. 2 Brigade, who accompanied them to the cathedral in Killarney where they reposed overnight. The following day James Daly was buried in the Republican Plot in Killarney's New Cemetery.

Today a monument stands outside the north wall of what was Tralee Gaol and adjacent to the spot within the prison where seven men were shot by firing squads in 1923.

---

4   Information from Áine Casey, Knockaneculteen, Fries.
5   Dorothy Macardle, *Tragedies of Kerry* (1924), p. 30, and confirmed by Denis Fleming of Milleen.

John Kevins

Seán Ó Caoimín

John Kevins was from Coolmagort, near the village of Beaufort at the foot of the McGillycuddy Reeks. Behind the village lie the mountains and the Gap of Dunloe and in this district the Moonlighters of the Land Wars were particularly active. John Kevins' father, Thomas, was born in Sligo and lived in Longford for a time. Being a constable in the RIC he had been posted to several areas of Ireland during his career. He had married Julia Horgan from Kilcummin, near Killarney. On his early retirement from the force Thomas Kevins bought a small farm of about ten acres and also opened a small business in the village of Beaufort. There the couple raised nine children. The eldest of the Kevins children was John, who was born in 1892. During the Great War John Kevins joined the British Army, but while home on leave in 1918 he failed to return to his regiment. As an army deserter he was a wanted man, but despite the RIC searching for him he managed to remain in his native Beaufort.[1]

Courtesy of the Martin Moore collection.

He joined the Irish Volunteers and was an active member of the Beaufort Company of the 4th Battalion, Kerry No. 2 Brigade. In May 1921 he was a member of the battalion's active service unit. During the Truce period, in April 1922, he was appointed O/C of the Republican Police in the Kerry No. 2 Brigade area, succeeding Mick Dennehy of Rathmore who had joined the new Free State Civic Guards. His rank in the IRA was that of captain.

In July 1922, during the first month of the Civil War, Kevins fought in Counties Limerick, Waterford and Tipperary, but following the Republican

---

1   Information from Frank Kevins of Currans, nephew of John Kevins.

defeat there he returned to Beaufort. There he led an IRA unit that was active along the foothills of the McGillycuddy Reeks.[2]

The information regarding his killing comes from Volunteer Mike Coffey, who was with him on the night of his capture. Coffey later gained fame as a member of the Kerry All-Ireland winning team of 1926, but on the evening of 14 March he was with Captain John Kevins as they came by foot to Beaufort. They had been staying at the home of Tadhg Crón Sullivan in Alohert, which was considered a safe house. The pair had walked down to the village shop owned by Coffey's father, Jerry, to get provisions. While at the Coffey house they had a meal and at 11 p.m., under the cover of darkness, they left, with their rifles slung over their shoulders, to return to Sullivan's house.[3]

On their way, John Kevins and Mike Coffey had to pass Kissane's Cross, a location where any Free State patrol in the locality might be positioned. Coffey suggested an alternate route over the fields, which involved crossing a ford on the Caol river, and a discussion followed. Kevins opted to stay on the road and risk passing through the crossroads, but Coffey followed his instincts and took to the fields. As he was crossing the small river, he heard a shot and, fearing for John Kevins, he retraced his steps.

Michael 'Stanley' Bishop was an officer in the Free State Army in Beaufort Barracks. He and several of his men had donned civilian attire and attempted to infiltrate the mourners at the funeral of IRA Volunteer Séamus Taylor. Taylor had been murdered while a prisoner en route from Killorglin to Tralee and was being buried in his native Glencar on 14 March. However, fearing that their presence had been detected, Bishop and his soldiers returned to the Beaufort area. There Bishop, with ten soldiers still dressed in civilian clothes, took up position at Kissane's house which was at the crossroads. This was what was called a rambling house, where local people met socially. Bishop ordered all the local people who had gathered there to be lined up at the back of the house. He had two soldiers placed in an outhouse and gave a command that the front door of the house be kept ajar, thus illuminating a small segment of the road. As John Kevins, his rifle slung over his shoulder, passed through the lit area, he

2   Con Casey papers, Kerry County Library Archive.
3   Information from John Coffey of Killarney, as related to him by his uncle, Volunteer Mike Coffey.

was clearly visible to Bishop, who stepped suddenly from the darkness. With his gun in his hand he put Kevins against the wall of the house and asked him to identify himself. Kevins gave his name as requested and as he was asking Bishop, who was in civilian attire, who he was, the Free State officer shot him at point blank range. Kevins stumbled but then ran through the open door of Kissane's house. Bishop fired again but his shot went wide of its mark and hit a wall of the room inside and fell into the crib where a baby, Bridie Kissane, was sleeping. The injured man collapsed on the floor and Bishop was about to shoot him dead when John Kissane interceded. He pleaded with Bishop not to shoot the wounded man in his house. The Free State officer relented and sent two of the local men, Mick Flor O'Sullivan and Patrick Pats Sheahan, for a cart to remove the injured prisoner. These men set off to go to Jerry Coffey's house as he had the only cart with springs in the vicinity. On the way they met Mike Coffey and told him what had happened to his comrade. They then continued to Jerry Coffey's house. Jerry Coffey then went with his horse and cart to Kissane's house and conveyed the wounded prisoner to the Free State barracks at Beaufort House.

When Jerry Coffey reached the barracks he was detained, having been confused with his brother Johnny, who was a Republican Volunteer 'on the run'. Jerry Coffey was later released when a Free State soldier from Killorglin named O'Shea confirmed his identity. On his way home, at about 3 a.m., Jerry Coffey called to Mrs Kevins in Beaufort village to inform her that her son had been wounded and was being held in Beaufort House under armed guard. She got dressed and went up to the barracks but was not allowed to see her son. She waited outside the lodge of Beaufort House for some hours until eventually an army lorry passed. Lying on the floor was John Kevins and he raised his hand in recognition when he saw his mother. Ostensibly he was to be taken to Killarney's Free State headquarters for further medical treatment, but he was never to reach the town.

At Maulagh, Fossa, at what is known as the Gap Cross, the lorry halted. The prisoner was taken off the vehicle. Local people heard a loud shout, the sound of Kevins being bayonetted to death. His body was left at the spot where he was killed.

Later that morning of 15 March 1923, Michael Kelly was bringing the mail on his horse-drawn car to Beaufort from the post office in Killarney. The horse shied near the site where the body lay and, on dismounting, Kelly discovered the remains of Kevins. The body was brought back to the Kevins' family home, where a wake was held.

The actions of Captain Michael 'Stanley' Bishop were in marked contrast to the treatment of Colonel Jim Dempsey, who was captured by Kevins' IRA unit three months earlier in December 1922. Dempsey, who was third in command of the Dublin Guard in Kerry, was wounded and captured in an action on a mountainside at Carnahone near Beaufort. He had a serious eye injury and Kevins sent for Dr Ned Carey, the Kerry No. 2 Brigade medical officer, so that his prisoner might have his wounds attended to. As Dempsey's injury could not be adequately treated locally, he was released into the doctor's care, as were two of his companions. Dempsey survived his injuries but the humane action of Kevins in releasing a valuable but wounded prisoner counted for nothing when he himself fell into the hands of the notorious Captain Bishop.

Michael 'Stanley' Bishop, from Waterford city, was a former British soldier with the Irish Guards Regiment, who joined the Free State Army in 1922. He had been given a commission in the Dublin Guard the day before he killed John Kevins.[4]

A roadside memorial stands at the junction beyond Fossa where the road for the Gap of Dunloe branches off. This was unveiled in 1953 on the thirtieth anniversary of Captain John Kevins' murder. The unveiling ceremony was performed before a crowd of 500 by Jeremiah O'Donoghue of Lacca, Kilcummin, whose brother Dan was killed at Countess Bridge. It replaced an earlier wooden cross placed there following the Civil War.[5] This memorial stands adjacent to the site where Kevins met his death at the age of thirty. He was buried in the Republican Plot in the New Cemetery, Killarney, on St Patrick's Day 1923. The unveiling of the large Celtic cross at the grave was performed by Austin Stack on Easter Sunday 1927, before a crowd of several thousand who had marched from Killarney's cathedral.[6]

4   Irish Military Archives, military record of Michael Bishop.
5   *The Kerryman*, 21 March 1953.
6   *Ibid.*, 23 April 1927.

Patrick McCarthy

Pádraig Mac Carthaig[1]

Patrick McCarthy was born in Killarney on 1 December 1894. His father, Con, had a shop in the town's College Street and his mother, Julia Dineen, died at a relatively young age, when Patrick was just eight years old. Patrick worked in his father's substantial drapery and grocery business and lived above the shop. He was an accomplished piper and was a Volunteer in the Killarney-based 'D' Company of the Irish Volunteers, joining after its formation in November 1913.

Both Patrick and his brother Neilus were active Volunteers in 'D' Company during the Tan War. Their sister, Hannah Mary, was a leading member of Cumann na mBan in the town. In spring 1921 the McCarthy brothers came to the attention of the local RIC. Patrick and Neilus narrowly escaped capture when an RIC party from the nearby barracks unexpectedly raided their College Street home. They escaped through an upstairs window onto the roof of an adjacent building and made good their getaway. From then Patrick McCarthy had to go 'on the run' and he became a member of the 4th Battalion column which was on full-time active service.[2]

However, Patrick McCarthy's good fortune deserted him when he was part of a unit of IRA Volunteers travelling to an area known as the Black Banks, near the village of Brosna, where a large ambush was being prepared. A weapon belonging to one of his comrades was accidentally discharged as they travelled in the horse-drawn car through the townland of Lyreatough. McCarthy was seriously injured and subsequently died of his wounds on 29 June 1921.[3] His remains were initially buried by his comrades in Kilquane Cemetery near Barraduff, not far from where he was fatally injured. However, in January 1922, during the Truce, his coffin was reinterred with full Republican military honours in the family plot at the New Cemetery, Killarney. At the time of his

1 Surviving images of Patrick McCarthy were not of sufficient quality to reproduce.
2 Information from Una Kavanagh, Killarney, niece of Patrick McCarthy.
3 Information from Denis Fleming, Milleen, Kilcummin, son of Will Patrick Fleming.

death his rank was that of chief engineer, 'D' Company, 4th Battalion, Kerry No. 2 Brigade. He was twenty-five years old.

Today the bridge over the River Flesk on the Muckross Road in Killarney is named the McCarthy O'Leary Bridge in his honour and that of Seán O'Leary, a Killarney IRA Volunteer killed in Tipperary. A small monument was erected at the spot where he was fatally injured in Lyreatough.

Timothy Murphy

Tadhg Ó Murchadha

Timothy Murphy was from Kilbreanmore, a townland in the parish of Killarney and three miles to the east of the town. In this hilly countryside his family farmed. He was also known by the Irish form of his name, Tadhg, and was born on 11 October 1892, the eldest son in a family of six children. As a young man he became a Volunteer in the 4th Battalion, Kerry No. 2 Brigade, and fought in both the Tan and Civil Wars.[1]

Courtesy of Peggy Crowley, niece of Tadhg Murphy.

In the darkest days of the Civil War, IRA Volunteers such as Tim Murphy led precarious lives, constantly in danger, as they fought on in the forlorn hope of defending the Irish Republic against overwhelming odds. The comfort of sleeping at home was exchanged for the security of crudely constructed shelters or dugouts located in fields and ditches. One such dugout was concealed in a stone wall on a bothairín off the Killarney to Gneeveguilla road in the townland of Radrinagh. Being half a mile from the main road, it was considered by Murphy and his unit to be safe from any searches of the area by Free State forces.

However, early on a March morning in 1923, Murphy and his two comrades were surprised by the sudden arrival of a large force of Free State troops up the little road where the hideout was located. It appeared that their Free State captors were acting on accurate information and went directly to the dugout where the three Volunteers were captured in possession of two loaded rifles. Tim Murphy, Stephen Buckley and Dan O'Donoghue were brought to the Free State barracks in Killarney's Great Southern Hotel, together with a young local boy who happened to be in the locality during the raid. Following his

---

1 Information from Peggy Crowley, niece of Tadhg Murphy.

release shortly afterwards, this young boy testified to the brutality inflicted on the prisoners following their capture. As Murphy was not armed when arrested it was presumed that he would not be sentenced to death. O'Donoghue and Buckley expected to be condemned, as possession of weapons was deemed a capital offence and, five weeks previously, four men were executed in Tralee on such a charge.

On Wednesday 7 March Jeremiah O'Donoghue of Killarney, Tadhg Coffey of Barleymount, and Tim Murphy and his two comrades from Kilcummin were woken early. The five prisoners were marched from their cells in the Great Southern Hotel across the fields to the nearby Countess Bridge. There they were ordered to clear a rubble barricade from the roadway, unaware that the obstruction had been placed there by their captors and that the stones and debris concealed a mine. As the device that the Free State officers had placed there was detonated, Murphy, Dan O'Donoghue and Stephen Buckley took the full force of the explosion, but they apparently survived the initial blast as the survivor, Tadhg Coffey, recalled that these men were moaning as they lay wounded on the ground. Jeremiah O'Donoghue was only slightly injured by the force of the explosion. At this point, grenades were thrown to where the victims lay and this was supplemented with gunfire which took the lives of four of the men. Tadhg Coffey miraculously ran to freedom and his testimony told the true story of what happened that March morning in Killarney.

Tim Murphy's remains were buried in the Republican Plot in the New Cemetery, Killarney. Following the end of the Civil War, local Republicans, with financial assistance from the 'men and women from the Parish of Killarney' living in New York, erected a prominent Celtic cross over the grave. The memorial was unveiled by Austin Stack on Easter Sunday 1927 and still stands dominating the hillside cemetery which overlooks the town of Killarney.[2]

2 *The Kerryman*, 23 April 1927.

Daniel O'Donoghue

Domhnall Ó Donnchada

IRA Volunteer Dan O'Donoghue was born in Lacca, Kilcummin, in 1902. His parents, Jeremiah and Bridget O'Donoghue, were small farmers in this area to the north of Killarney town. Dan was the eldest son and worked on his parents' farm. He was a Volunteer in the Kilcummin Company of the 4th Battalion, Kerry No. 2 Brigade, and despite his young age he was active in his native area during the Tan and Civil Wars.

Courtesy of Dan O'Donoghue, nephew of Volunteer Dan O'Donoghue.

The local IRA unit had a dugout hidden in the stone wall which ran along a little used bothairín off a road in Radrinagh. The small shelter measured ten feet by five feet and a little over four feet high. It had a roof of camouflaged flagstones. The shelter, where the men exchanged comfort for security in those winter nights, was on the land of Stephen Buckley's farm and close to Lacca, where Dan O'Donoghue lived. However, despite all the precautions taken, the exact location of the crude shelter was betrayed to the Free State forces in Killarney and on 3 March 1923 a large raiding party surprised Dan O'Donoghue and his two comrades and neighbours, Stephen Buckley and Tim Murphy.[1] Both O'Donoghue and Buckley were armed with rifles, while Murphy was unarmed, but the Republicans did not get a chance to use their weapons. The three men were beaten by their captors at the scene. This was witnessed by a local boy and he too was detained and brought with the three captured Volunteers in a lorry to the Great Southern Hotel. There the men were subjected to further ill-treatment and local people reported hearing their screams as they were tortured.

---

1   Information from Dan O'Donoghue, nephew of Volunteer Dan O'Donoghue.

Dan O'Donoghue and his two Kilcummin comrades were woken early on the morning of 7 March 1923. They were joined by Tadhg Coffey and Jeremiah O'Donoghue and the five prisoners were brought the half mile to the Countess Bridge that crosses the railway line which at that time was on the outskirts of the town. There was a barricade of rubble on the road and the men were ordered to clear it by the Free State officers who had brought them there. When the men began to clear the rubble, they caught sight of the mine that their captors had hidden but the soldiers, who had moved off the road at that point, detonated the remotely controlled explosive. The blast injured the five men but it was the subsequent gunfire and exploding hand grenades that killed four of them, with Tadhg Coffey miraculously escaping to give testament to the grim events of that March morning.[2]

Dan O'Donoghue's remains are interred in the Republican Plot in the New Cemetery which lies two miles from Killarney, just off the Tralee road. The large Celtic cross was erected with public subscriptions from the Killarney area and from emigrants from the district in the United States. It was unveiled in 1927 by Austin Stack. Fifty-seven years later Jeremiah O'Donoghue, who, with his brother Dan, had fought with the 4th Battalion, was buried next to his brother in the Republican Plot. In 1983 the third IRA Volunteer in the family, Patrick O'Donoghue, was laid to rest in an adjacent grave in the New Cemetery.

The dugout still stands on the scenic hillside at Radrinagh. In the months after their capture a shrine was erected at the spot. Today a small black metal cross marks the scene where betrayal and brutality began a journey for three soldiers of the Irish Republic which would end with their deaths on Countess Bridge.

2   Dorothy Macardle, *Tragedies of Kerry* (1924) p. 30.

Jeremiah O'Donoghue

Diarmuid Ó Donnchada

Jeremiah O'Donoghue was born on 18 September 1899 in Lower New Street, Killarney. He was the son of Dan O'Donoghue, a labourer, and his wife, Margaret Healy. He had joined the Irish Volunteers in 1916 and was attached to the Killarney Company of the 4th Battalion, Kerry No. 2 Brigade. Jeremiah O'Donoghue worked as an attendant at Killarney's psychiatric hospital. On the outbreak of the Civil War he resigned his position and went on full-time active service with the 4th Battalion column.[1]

Courtesy of the Martin Moore collection.

O'Donoghue was a friend of Tadhg Coffey's and it was at Coffey's home in Barleymount, three miles to the north-west of Killarney, that they were captured. On 22 February 1923 a Free State raiding party under the leadership of William John (Johnny) Wilson, a Dublin Guard officer, entered the house as O'Donoghue was resting by the fire and Coffey was cleaning his gun. Dorothy Macardle, who took witness statements in 1924, states that Wilson beat his captives violently and even directed a blow at Coffey's mother as his troops destroyed the household contents. The prisoners were taken outside and placed against a wall to be shot, but they still would not reveal the whereabouts of the local IRA column or its arms dump. Such was Wilson's brutality that one of his soldiers expressed his disgust at the treatment of the two prisoners.[2]

Coffey and O'Donoghue were then taken to the Free State headquarters in Killarney, which was situated in the Great Southern Hotel. The basement contained rooms that were used as cells and it was there that they were put.

1   Con Casey papers, Kerry County Library Archives.
2   Dorothy Macardle, *Tragedies of Kerry* (1924), p. 33.

That evening Coffey was brought to a room where four officers waited. He was beaten with a poker and threatened with a loaded gun, but he still refused to answer Wilson's questions. Both Coffey and O'Donoghue were brought before a military committee the next day and, with Wilson's evidence, they were condemned to be executed for possession of a rifle. In the dark basement cellar they were visited by a priest from the nearby Franciscan friary who heard their confessions, although another priest jeered at their political principles. An officer entered the cell and sat with them and discussed the possibility of their sentence being put aside if they accepted commissions in the Free State Army, but both refused and the officer left in an angry mood.

Their only friend was the Free State Army tailor. His name was Daniel Sugrue and he was from Dominick Street in Tralee. Sugrue smuggled in a bottle of stout to the condemned men and brought them what news he could, but he advised them not to reveal his kindness to anybody as he would be shot himself.

Early on the morning of 7 March 1923, Jeremiah O'Donoghue and Tadhg Coffey were brought out of their cells with three of their comrades: Tim Murphy, Dan O'Donoghue and Stephen Buckley. They were marched by a detachment of soldiers half a mile to Countess Bridge, where Free State officers had placed a mine in the midst of a barricade of rubble that had been placed across the road.

When the mine was detonated by the soldiers Tadhg Coffey was wounded in the leg but managed to crawl away. Dan O'Donoghue, Tim Murphy and Stephen Buckley, according to Coffey, were severely injured but alive. The soldiers threw grenades at them and opened fire on the wounded and dazed men. Coffey's injury was to his knee and, while unable to stand for a time, he could crawl. Jeremiah O'Donoghue, relatively uninjured, did likewise and the two men tried to make their way to a bend in the road beside the bridge. However, O'Donoghue was fatally injured by the shooting. Coffey, having regained the use of his leg, ran and managed to climb over a nine-foot gate as bullets cut through his cap and clothes. He miraculously remained on his feet and reached a clump of trees and from there kept running as far and as fast as he could until he reached the parish of Kilcummin where he was given shelter. His four comrades lay dead on the roadside and so only Tadhg Coffey was left to recount the story of the massacre on Countess Bridge. He survived the Civil War and was one of a large number of Republicans who went on to build new lives in America.[3]

Jeremiah O'Donoghue was buried in the Republican Plot in the New Cemetery, Killarney, together with his three comrades who died on the Countess Bridge.

A sad sequel to that terrible day is the fate of the kindly tailor. The humanity of Daniel Sugrue and his acts of Christianity to the condemned men came to the attention of the Free State officers at the Great Southern Hotel. Apparently, when in Killarney town he had told some people of the horrors that were inflicted on the prisoners in the barracks. When he returned to the barracks he was shot dead in cold blood. He was a married man of thirty-eight years of age when he was killed at the Great Southern Hotel in March 1923. No plaque stands to his memory and his place of burial is unknown.

---

3   Ernie O'Malley, *The Men Will Talk to Me – Kerry Interviews* (2012), interview with John Joe Rice.

5th (Rathmore) Battalion, Kerry No. 2 Brigade

The area of the 5th Battalion, Kerry No. 2 Brigade, lies between the town of Killarney and the County Cork border. Its only centres of population are the village of Rathmore and the smaller hamlets of Barraduff and Gneeveguilla. The area is defined by its mountains and marginal farmland. The district is bisected by the main Killarney to Dublin railway and traversed by the roads from Killarney to Cork and Mallow. Popularly known in Irish as Sliabh Luachra, and long a centre of native culture, this part of East Kerry, with its close rural bonds, became a stronghold of the revolutionary movement.

The Irish Volunteers were established in Rathmore in December 1913 when officers from the newly formed movement in Killarney visited the area. The first O/C was Dan Dennehy of Clounts, Rathmore, and under his stewardship the organisation grew rapidly. Although ready to rise on Easter Week, the local Volunteer company was to remain inactive due to the failure to land the German arms shipment in Fenit and Eoin MacNeill's countermanding order. Local man Paddy O'Connor, who was a member of the London-Irish Volunteers and who visited his home in Rathmore the previous week, was one of four Volunteers from Kerry to die in action in Dublin on Easter Week.

The Rathmore Company was reorganised in 1917 and when the Kerry No. 2 Brigade was formed in 1919, this area of East Kerry was designated the 5th Battalion. The battalion O/C was Dan Dennehy and he retained his command until the arrival of Andy Cooney, a GHQ organiser, in January 1921. Cooney's arrival heralded changes throughout the brigade and battalion staffs in South Kerry, increasing the effectiveness of the IRA units. Brigade O/C Dan O'Mahony was replaced by Humphrey Murphy and in the 5th Battalion Dan Dennehy lost his command to Humphrey (Fredy) O'Sullivan. The battalion V/C was Dominic Spillane. Spillane was imprisoned in December 1920 and this led to Jerry Kennedy of Brewsterfield, Glenflesk, replacing him as battalion second in command. The adjutant was initially Mick Dennehy, a brother of Dan Dennehy, and his post passed to Con Moynihan. Mick Dennehy remained an active Volunteer and was appointed as the brigade's Republican Police officer.

Con O'Leary of Glenflesk, who proved to be one of the county's foremost soldiers, was quartermaster until he was promoted to the brigade staff in January 1921 and Michael Daly of Nohoval then became quartermaster. In the spring of 1921 the battalion flying column was established and its commander was Manus Moynihan of Nohoval Daly.

The 5th Battalion was composed of six companies. These were designated as follows: 'A' Company – Anabla, 'B' Company – Barraduff, 'C' Company – Bealnadeaga, 'D' Company – Glenflesk, 'E' Company – Rathmore and 'F' Company – Toureenamult (Gneeveguilla). In October 1921, during the Truce, the Anabla Company was transferred to the Brigade's 1st Battalion.

The crown forces had a strongly fortified RIC barracks in Rathmore and the regular RIC were supplemented by Black and Tans. It was during an attack on this barracks that the first Black and Tan to be killed in the conflict died. There was also a small garrison at the railway junction at Headford but this was abandoned early in the Tan War.

The 5th Battalion was one of the most active in the county during the Tan and Civil Wars. The railway and its transport of military material became a regular target for the battalion. The RIC abandoned their small garrison at Headford and it was soon destroyed. In July 1920 there was a prolonged attack on the Rathmore RIC Barracks, but it failed to dislodge the defenders. With the formation of the Kerry No. 2 Brigade column in March 1921, several of the battalion's most active Volunteers transferred to this unit. On 21 March 1921 the column, under Dan Allman and with support from local 5th Battalion units, inflicted heavy casualties on the British Army at Headford Junction. Two weeks before this a large ambush at The Bower near Barraduff failed to engage the expected military vehicles, but the same force did successfully attack a British convoy at Clonbanin Cross in County Cork. On 5 May 1921 eight RIC men were killed at an ambush on the Bog Road, near Rathmore. Such was the activity of the battalion that the British Army arrived in the district during late June and unsuccessfully attempted to trap the IRA units in a cordon in what became known as 'the large round-up'.

The 5th Battalion remained almost united in its opposition to the Treaty, though some of the original officers in the battalion staff who were sidelined by the January 1921 changes gave their allegiance to the Free State Army. In

July 1922, during the initial weeks of the Civil War, a column drawn from the battalion area was in active service in South Wexford and Waterford. On 2 August 1922 Free State forces landed in Fenit and quickly captured Tralee. Having taken Killarney on 13 August, the Free State Army moved quickly to establish a garrison in Rathmore. However, this force of Dublin Guards became quickly isolated, as the countryside remained in the hands of the Republican forces. The destruction of rail and road networks largely impeded the Free State's advantage in terms of armoured transport and artillery. Large-scale engagements at Carrigeens and Glenflesk halted the advances of the Free State Army in the battalion area and forced them to move about in the countryside in large columns from their Killarney stronghold. This pattern of guerrilla attacks by Republicans and the large-scale sweeps of the countryside by Free State forces defined the conflict in East Kerry. By the end of the Civil War the IRA units remained defiantly active despite overwhelming odds and they doggedly refused to submit. The price of that resistance, even after the last shots were fired, was that large numbers of Volunteers were imprisoned and others forced into exile in America, unwelcome in their native country that they had fought so hard to free.

Jeremiah Carey

Diarmuid Ó Ciardá[1]

Jeremiah Carey's name is inscribed on the Republican monument to the dead of East Kerry. The monument was unveiled in 1928 by Tom Derrig, who was a leading IRA officer during the Civil War. At the time of commissioning of this large Celtic cross, which stands prominently on Rathmore's main street, his comrades thought it fitting that the name of Jeremiah Carey be inscribed in stone for future generations to recall, such was his service to the fight for Irish freedom.

By its nature the Irish Republican Army was enmeshed in a secrecy that was born from a realisation that in generations past open resistance to the powerful forces of the British Empire was doomed to failure. Volunteers found security in anonymity and their deeds were often left unrecorded and eventually unremembered, even in local lore. And so it was with Jeremiah Carey.

Carey was born in Knocknagree village in the parish of Rathmore on 22 November 1899. His mother, Nora Sheehan, moved to Knocknageeha, Gneeveguilla, to live with her father-in-law when her husband died. Jeremiah Carey worked as a spailpín, or migrant farm labourer, in County Limerick. When he joined the Irish Volunteers is not recorded and neither is his contribution to the fight for freedom. It is recalled that he died while being brought to hospital in Cork city by horse and sidecar and the cause of his death was ascribed to a 'burst appendix'. Unmarried and with no immediate family the story of his short life was lost.[2] His grave is unknown and unmarked.

He is now remembered only on the monument in Rathmore where he is recorded as having 'died as a result of active service'. His rank is given as lieutenant.[3]

---

1   There is no known photograph of Jeremiah Carey.
2   Information from Eileen Daly, Gneeveguilla.
3   It is probable that Jeremiah Carey held this rank during the Civil War, as nobody of his name held a rank before July 1922.

WILLIAM CRONIN

Liam Ó Cróinín[1]

William (Bill) Cronin was born in Reaboy, Gneeveguilla, on 14 November 1896. As a young boy he was educated in the nearby Toureencahill National School. On completing his education there, he was employed by the Great Southern and Western Railway Company at Rathmore.

His father was a farmer and his brother Batt worked as a blacksmith and was known as 'Batty the Smith'. The townland of Reaboy is four miles to the north of Rathmore and as there were several other Cronin families in the district, Bill's people were known as the Batt Cronins. Politically the Cronins were staunch Republicans. 'Batty the Smith' Cronin was the battalion armourer and, with Den 'Gow' Murphy, they repaired and manufactured weapons for the 5th Battalion in the forge at New Quarter. With his brothers Denis, who was known as Din Batt, and Patrick, Bill joined the Irish Volunteers. With the reorganisation of the Volunteers in 1919, the Gneeveguilla Company was designated 'F' Company of the 5th Battalion, Kerry No. 2 Brigade. Bill's brother, Din Batt Cronin, was appointed captain of the company and remained so until the end of the conflict.

Captain Din Batt Cronin was an active IRA Volunteer on both sides of the Cork–Kerry border, where he often participated in engagements with Seán Moylan's battalion as well as with his own 5th Battalion. Both Din Batt and Pat Cronin were among the IRA Volunteers who took part in the Bog Road ambush near Rathmore on 4 May 1921. Din Batt Cronin was also a participant at the Toureengarrive, Headford Junction and Clonbanin ambushes.

Bill Cronin, a man of letters, played a different role in Ireland's fight for freedom. He served the 5th Battalion as an intelligence officer. His employment at the railway gave him access to all communications by rail, telephone and mail that passed through Rathmore station on their way out of the county. His valuable role remained undetected through the Black and Tan War.

1   There is no known photograph of William Cronin.

A reorganisation of the Kerry No. 2 Brigade battalions, instigated by the GHQ organiser, Andy Cooney, in January 1921, saw battalion officers who were deemed ineffective replaced by younger, more active men. In Rathmore some of these demoted officers went on to join the fledgling Free State Army and the new Civic Guard when they were formed in February 1922. Active Volunteers in the Black and Tan War were enticed with commissions in the new pro-Treaty forces, but few exchanged their Republican principles for the promise of a steady income and a secure job in the service of the Free State. Bill Cronin and his brother refused such offers to join the new Civic Guard.

However, Bill Cronin's health began to fail and he died of meningitis due to tuberculosis on 16 April 1922. He was buried in the Cronin family plot in Rathmore Cemetery. Although he did not die directly as a result of the armed conflict, his contribution to the struggle was deemed sufficient by his comrades in arms to warrant his inclusion on the 5th Battalion monument in the village. On the memorial, which was unveiled in 1928, W. J. Cronin is noted to have died 'as a result of active service' and his rank is given as captain.[2]

---

2   Information from Mrs Kate Cremins of Cullen, a niece of William Cronin.

Laurence Hickey

Labhras Ó hIceadha[1]

Laurence (Larry) Hickey lived at Shinnagh, Rathmore. There he followed his father's profession and worked as a tailor. He joined the Volunteers before 1916 and answered the call to rise at Easter Week. Hickey was one of the twenty-five men of the Rathmore Company of the Irish Volunteers who gathered on Easter Sunday morning, but no orders came from Killarney. The only instructions were Eoin MacNeill's countermanding order and so the Volunteers went home again and prepared for another day.[2]

Following the reorganisation that took place in 1917 and 1919, Hickey remained an active Volunteer in the Rathmore Company of the 5th Battalion, Kerry No. 2 Brigade. He was wounded in action in the spring of 1921 and died of his injuries on 21 June of that year. It is not known how and where he received his fatal injuries.

Larry Hickey is remembered on the 5th Battalion memorial in Rathmore village, where he is listed as having 'died of wounds received in action'. He was forty-seven years of age when he died and is buried in Rathmore Cemetery.[3]

1   There is no known photograph of Laurence Hickey.
2   Daniel Dennehy, BMH WS 116.
3   National Graves Association, *The Last Post* (1985), p. 139.

Michael McSweeney

Míceál Mac Suibne

Michael McSweeney was born in Killarney in 1906, but his family later moved to The Bower in the townland of Gortnahaneboy East near Rathmore.[1] There his father plied his trade as a cooper. Michael McSweeney's brothers, Tom ('Dundon'), John and Pat, were members of the 5th Battalion, Kerry No. 2 Brigade, which was based in the East Kerry area. Michael was just seventeen years of age when he was killed in action during the Civil War and was one of the youngest Kerry Volunteers to be killed during the period.

Courtesy of the Martin Moore collection.

The townland of Shrone lies to the south of the village of Rathmore, at the foot of the Paps Mountains, the slopes and glens of which provided a refuge to the active service unit of the 5th Battalion. In August 1922 the Free State Army established a garrison in the village of Rathmore. However, the surrounding countryside remained in Republican hands, with the topography and local support giving the guerrilla fighters a decided advantage.

On 4 February 1923 a 'gander' party was organised in the home of Maria Moynihan of Shrone, as she was to be married two days later. Some Volunteers of the local IRA unit attended the celebrations. Anxious about a possible Free State raid, they posted a guard of two sentries near the Moynihan house. These were Michael McSweeney and Jerry Reen. It is probable that the sentry duty was given to McSweeney because he was considered too young to partake of the activities inside the house.

Unfortunately, the Free State Army expected the Volunteers to be at Shrone

---

1   The surname is often shortened to Sweeney.

that evening. Led by a local former IRA officer, Dan Dennehy, who had lost his command during the Tan War when the battalion was reorganised, members of the Dublin Guard were guided along a circuitous route from Rathmore to Shrone. They arrived in the area from the foothills of the mountains to the south. Jerry Reen and Michael McSweeney went on a short sentry patrol but when they returned to near the house they were surprised by the Free State soldiers who were lying in wait for them. The two IRA Volunteers were ordered to halt and raise their hands. When McSweeney and Reen replied by asking who was there, having presumed it was a prank, a volley of shots rang out. McSweeney was wounded and Reen ran for cover. He halted, turned, fired, and then, in the darkness of the night, managed to escape. The soldiers then approached the injured McSweeney and asked his name. When he replied he was shot in the forehead, dying instantly.[2] The IRA Volunteers in the house had no chance to escape and the presence of a large crowd of civilians precluded any armed resistance to the Free State soldiers, who had at this point surrounded the Moynihan house. Six Volunteers were captured in the raid and they were brought to Rathmore Barracks.[3]

McSweeney's remains were given to his father. The family took the coffin to Rathmore church for the funeral mass, but they were refused admittance by the parish priest. The horse-drawn hearse remained in the churchyard while the requiem prayers were said over the coffin.[4] Two days after his killing the young Volunteer was buried by his comrades in the Republican Plot which lies at the corner of Kilquane Cemetery. An attempt by Free State troops from nearby Barraduff to interfere with the funeral was prevented by local IRA men, including Jeremiah Murphy, who held off an enemy patrol as it tried to leave the village to travel the two miles to the small graveyard.

Today two monuments stand at Shrone near where young Michael McSweeney was killed. The older memorial was lost during a period of road improvement and was replaced, but when it was rediscovered years later it was re-erected. McSweeney is also remembered on the Rathmore Republican monument, where he is listed as having died on active service.

2   Con Casey papers, Kerry County Library Archives.
3   Jeremiah Murphy, *When Youth was Mine – A Memoir of Kerry 1902–1925* (1998), p. 250.
4   Information from Josie Hickey, Rathmore.

Andrew Moynihan

Anoriar Ó Muimneacáin

Andrew Moynihan was a native of the East Kerry village of Gneeveguilla. He was born in 1878 and was a farmer. The local Toureenamult Company of the IRA, of which he was a member, was attached to the 5th Battalion, Kerry No. 2 Brigade.

Andrew Moynihan held a position as a judge in the local Republican or Dáil court that was formed to administer justice in place of the British judicial system. Such courts were formed at parish level by order of Austin Stack's Ministry of Home Affairs in the new Dáil and they ensured that justice would be administered free from British interference. As a consequence of his role in the local Dáil court, it would be expected that documents connected with this work would have been found at the home of Andrew Moynihan.

Courtesy of Con Moynihan.

In late December 1920 a local IRA unit stopped a train as it passed near Rathmore station and removed the mails. This was a common occurrence, as it allowed local IRA units to collect intelligence contained in the post. The closure of small rural RIC barracks due to IRA attacks had reduced the personal contact the force had with the general population, so people with no sympathy with the Republican cause often passed their information to the police by letter.

These incidents brought East Kerry to the attention of 'H' Company of the Auxiliary Division of the RIC, who were based in Tralee. On 23 December 1920 a convoy of Auxiliaries raided several houses in the Gneeveguilla area. When they arrived at his house, Andrew Moynihan was sitting by the fire suffering from a heavy cold. He was a married man with a young family. The Auxiliaries were about to set fire to his house when one of them objected, as he himself had young children and did not want to see the young Moynihan family made homeless. Instead they burned the family hayshed and its contents. The Auxiliary detachment then marched their captive, with a revolver to his back, up and down Gneeveguilla's main street as they searched other houses in the small village. Eventually Andrew Moynihan was placed in a Crossley tender to be conveyed the twenty-five miles to Tralee. It was there that the Auxiliaries had their base. However, Moynihan never reached Tralee, as on the way he was shot as 'he attempted to escape'.[1]

The remains were brought to Tralee by the Auxiliaries and, having placed them in a coffin, they were brought to the mortuary of Saint John's church. On St Stephen's Day, a Sunday, they were identified as those of Andrew Moynihan.[2]

The section commander of the Auxiliaries on that day was Charles Sutton. At the inquiry into Moynihan's death in custody, Sutton claimed that while on the journey to Tralee Moynihan asked to go to the toilet and so the tender was stopped. The exact location where this occurred is not recorded. Moynihan, guarded by Sutton, walked some way up along the road and Sutton claimed that the prisoner tried to dash over a wall as the pair walked along the road. Sutton shot him with his revolver, once in the chest and once in the head. The remains of Andrew Moynihan were put in the Crossley tender and the Auxiliaries resumed their journey to their base in Tralee. Though the wounds were certainly at variance with the evidence Sutton gave, the court of inquiry accepted that Andrew Moynihan was shot while attempting to escape. This explanation was commonly supplied by the crown forces when their captives were summarily executed.

The forty-three-year-old farmer and IRA Volunteer from Gneeveguilla, who left behind a young family, is buried in Rathmore Cemetery.

1   Information from Sr Alma Moynihan, Framington, Massachusetts, daughter of Andrew Moynihan.
2   *The Kerryman*, 1 January 1921.

PATRICK O'CONNOR

Pádraig Ó Concubair

Captain Patrick O'Connor was born in Rathmore in 1882. A brilliant student in the local national school, he sat the civil service examination and achieved a high grade. As a result he gained employment in the post office in London in 1900. While living there he became involved in the various Irish political and cultural organisations that thrived in the city in the early decades of the century. Such language and sporting groups were heavily influenced by the secretive IRB and it is likely that Patrick O'Connor became involved in the revolutionary movement in his adopted city. He was transferred to a civil service position in Dublin in 1912. He continued his involvement with the emerging separatist movement and on the formation of the Irish Volunteers in November 1913, he enrolled.[1]

Courtesy of the Martin Moore collection.

In Holy Week 1916 his brother Denis, who was also in the civil service, died and was buried in his native Rathmore. Patrick returned home for the funeral and while there he was informed of the pending Rising. He returned to Dublin on Easter Saturday and, having retrieved his rifle at his lodgings, he entered the GPO on Easter Monday evening. He was posted to the buildings in the vicinity of Clery's Department Store across the street from the GPO. Ray Bateson, an authority on the Rising, states that his unit crossed North Earl Street on Thursday and proceeded to Cathedral Place. Before dawn on the Friday of Easter Week, Captain O'Connor proceeded along Thomas Lane but was never seen alive again and the remainder of his comrades were captured. It would appear that he was either dead or mortally wounded when

---

1 *Sliabh Luachra, Journal of Cumann Luachra,* November 2012, article by Pádraig Ó Duinnín.

he was brought to the nearby Mater Hospital.[2]

His remains were removed to the St Paul's section of Glasnevin Cemetery. There they were buried in a mass grave with almost twenty other members of the Irish Volunteers and Irish Citizen Army who had lost their lives during the rebellion. Shortly after the Rising Áine Rahilly went around Dublin's cemeteries to mark the graves of the dead Volunteers and noted that O'Connor was buried in the mass grave at St Paul's. This plot was soon enclosed with a railing and later an impressive monument was unveiled at the site. Patrick O'Connor's name is inscribed on the memorial, listing him as a member of the London Volunteers.

In his native county he is remembered in Rathmore by the inscription on the town's Republican memorial which was unveiled in 1928. Patrick O'Connor was thirty-four years old when he died and was one of five Kerrymen who died in the 1916 Rising.

2   Ray Bateson, *They Died by Pearse's Side* (2010), p. 208.

Michael O'Sullivan

Mícheál Ó Súilleabáin

Michael O'Sullivan of Clohane, Headford, was better known by his comrades as 'Mick Cud'. He was born in 1898 and was a Volunteer in the Barraduff Company of the 5th Battalion, Kerry No. 2 Brigade. He and his comrades in the Barraduff area were active in the Tan War and fought bravely in the Civil War in defence of the Republic. They were affectionately described by the O/C of their brigade, John Joe Rice, as 'wild garsúns'.[1] Mick Cud was the first of this band of fighters to be killed, when he was shot dead as he lay unarmed and wounded on 2 November 1922.

Courtesy of the Martin Moore collection.

The road from Killarney to Rathmore runs almost parallel but four miles to the north of the main Killarney to Cork road. The small village of Barraduff with its church lies midway between Killarney and Rathmore and from there a county road runs southwards through Headford to Glenflesk on the Cork road. This hilly countryside was where the 5th Battalion held sway during the Civil War. On All Souls' Day, 2 November, members of the local company attended mass in Barraduff church. They included Volunteer Jeremiah Murphy, who records the episode in his memoir, *When Youth Was Mine*. To the south, near Glenflesk, a large column of men from John Joe Rice's Kerry No. 2 Brigade was on the move. Four scouts had been placed near Barraduff to secure the area while mass was being celebrated. A large column of Free State troops approached the village and two of the scouts entered the church just after communion and warned the IRA men of the approaching enemy soldiers. These men made good their escape. The two other scouts headed south to warn Rice's column. The Free State soldiers

---

1   Ernie O'Malley, *The Men Will Talk to Me – Kerry Interviews* (2012), interview with John Joe Rice.

searched the church and it was obvious to those present that they were acting on accurate information. However, their quarry had escaped minutes earlier.

Seemingly aware that the IRA men had headed south, the Free State column marched in that direction. However, their progress was hampered by rifle fire from two IRA Volunteers who maintained a sustained rearguard action. Michael O'Sullivan and his comrade Danny O'Connor held the forty-strong Free State force at bay until eventually they were surrounded. It was suspected that local information had allowed the soldiers to get to the rear of where the two Volunteers were located. O'Sullivan was severely wounded in the right arm and O'Connor had a slight wound on his cheek. O'Sullivan's injury did not allow him to escape but O'Connor managed to evade capture. Unable to fire his rifle O'Sullivan found temporary refuge in a house at Knockanes where he rendered his gun useless as he awaited capture. Minutes later he was taken prisoner and dragged from the house to the roadside. Despite his injuries and being unarmed, a witness reported that he was beaten by his captors and, as he lay on the ground, he was shot by Captain Michael 'Tiny' Lyons. Lyons, from Dublin, had a gained a notorious reputation by this stage in the Civil War. He similarly summarily executed Frank Grady on the roadside near Glenbeigh five months later. Fatally injured, Mick O'Sullivan was left to die where he was shot, as Lyons led his troops away from the scene.[2] Local women, including schoolteacher Margaret Spillane (Maggie May O'Leary), took him to the nearby house of Jer O'Leary. These events were witnessed by local schoolchildren at Knockanes National School where Mrs Spillane was teaching. The women comforted the dying man and called a local priest. However, as Jeremiah Murphy records events, one priest refused him the last rites as Mick Cud had been fighting for the Republic in defiance of the recent Catholic bishops' pastoral in support of the Free State government. However, an IRA Volunteer, Joe Favier, went for a Father Browne, who arrived and anointed the dying soldier.

A wake was held for Mick O'Sullivan in his family home in Clohane, to where his remains had been brought from nearby Knockanes. The O'Sullivan family burial ground was in Aghadoe on the far side of Killarney, but his

---

2   Jeremiah Murphy, *When Youth Was Mine* (1998), p. 224.

comrades were granted permission by his parents to bury their son in the Kilquane Graveyard four miles away near Barraduff.[3] Volunteers from the 5th Battalion removed his remains from his home and they buried him with full military honours in the Republican Plot at Kilquane Cemetery. Today he is remembered by a roadside monument at Knockanes, Headford, just beside the local school and at the spot where he was murdered on 2 November 1922 at the age of twenty-four.

---

3   Information from Maura O'Brien, Killarney, niece of Michael O'Sullivan.

Tadhg O'Sullivan

Tadg Ó Súilleabáin

Courtesy of Stephen Kelleghan.

Tadhg O'Sullivan was born on 7 January 1887 in Annagh Beg, near Rathmore, where his family had a farm. As a young man he found employment in Cork city, where he worked as what was termed a 'van man', denoting someone who delivered goods using a horse-drawn vehicle. A single man, he lived at 91 Douglas Street in the south of the city. He joined the Irish Volunteers following their foundation in the city and was active in the organisation from early on. Before the Rising he was involved in a plan to transport weapons to the Volunteers from the Curragh by train to his native Rathmore. However, this plot never materialised.

During the Black and Tan War, O'Sullivan was captain of 'C' Company which was attached to the 2nd Battalion, Cork No. 1 Brigade. He was arrested in early 1920 and imprisoned in Belfast. He went on hunger strike demanding political status and was subsequently released. Following his release he returned to his adopted city and resumed active service with his IRA company on the south side of Cork city. Though arrested in a round-up by crown forces, he was released shortly afterwards, his captors being unaware of his true identity. However, by April 1921 he was a wanted man, as he was suspected of having taken part in an attack on Barrack Street RIC Barracks a short time previously and of having killed a British soldier.

On 19 April 1921, at 7 p.m., Tadhg O'Sullivan was chatting to people on Douglas Street close to where he lived. While engaged in conversation he noted two plainclothes detectives nearby and it became obvious to him that these were part of a larger force of RIC men who were converging on the area. As he ran, he was pursued by eight RIC men who were described by witnesses as running after him in pairs and shooting their revolvers as they went. A second party of RIC men appeared and joined the chase. There was chaos on the street as civilians ran for cover in doorways.[1]

In an attempt to evade capture O'Sullivan made his way into a house which had its door unlocked, No. 82 Douglas Street. However, he was pursued by a group of eight RIC and Tans led by Sergeant Hollywood. They made no attempt to arrest him as they opened fire. Tadhg O'Sullivan ran through the house and was in the process of climbing out through a back window when he was fatally wounded by the police. He had been shot several times and died in the yard at the rear of the house.[2]

His body was brought by the RIC to Victoria Military Barracks but was subsequently released to his family and then brought to St Fin Barre's cathedral. His remains were interred in the Republican Plot in St Finbarr's Cemetery on the Glasheen Road in Cork city, where a memorial marks the place of his burial. The house at 82 Douglas Street also bears a plaque marking the site where Captain Tadhg O'Sullivan of Rathmore gave his life in the cause of Irish freedom.

Sergeant Hollywood, who was implicated in the killing of Tadhg O'Sullivan, lived in Windmill Road, a short distance from Douglas Street. Several attempts were subsequently made by O'Sullivan's comrades in the 2nd Battalion to shoot him, but he survived the conflict.[3]

---

1 *The Cork Examiner*, 20 April 1921.
2 *Cork Holly Bough*, 2004.
3 Robert C. Ahern, BMH WS 1676.

John Sharry

Seán Mac Searaigh[1]

John Sharry was born in 1892 at Direen, Liscannor, in County Clare. As a young man he found employment in Cork city but subsequently moved to Rathmore where he worked as a baker. He joined the Rathmore Company of the Irish Volunteers when it was established in the East Kerry village in 1913. His rank was that of second lieutenant and at Easter 1916, under the command of Dan Dennehy, he was one of the local Volunteers to answer the call to strike a blow for freedom. The failure of the events in Dublin on that fateful week was not to deter him and he played a significant role in the reorganisation of the Volunteers in East Kerry in the years following the Rising.

On 6 March 1918 John Redmond, the Irish Party leader and MP, died. As a result a by-election was held on 22 March in Waterford. Dr Vincent White, the Sinn Féin candidate, was defeated by 500 votes by Captain William Redmond, who was elected to his father's seat. However, the Republican vote was judged to be very significant in this Irish Party stronghold. John Sharry was one of several Republican activists from Kerry to travel to Waterford to canvass for the Sinn Féin candidate.

On 15 March 1918 an aeríocht was held in Bealnadeaga near Barraduff. This event was a community gathering where Irish culture and Gaelic sports were the focus of the activity in an open-air setting. The RIC arrived at the aeríocht but were prevented from mingling with the crowd to monitor anti-British activity by Irish Volunteers John Sharry, Con Morley and Mick Dennehy. Subsequently Sharry and Morley were charged with interfering with the actions of the police and illegal drilling when they were brought before the court in Killarney in April 1918.[2] The men refused to recognise the court and were noted to have read newspapers and books as the proceedings went on around them. Their supporters sang rebel songs in the courtroom and the magistrate ordered the public to be cleared from the building. They were

1   There is no known photograph of John Sharry.
2   Michael Spillane, BMH WS 132 and Manus Moynihan, BMH WS 1066.

sentenced to one month's imprisonment and three extra months were added in lieu of bail to each man's sentence. Following the sentencing, the crowd outside stoned the police. Sharry and Morley's supporters then left the vicinity of the courthouse led by a pipe band.³

On 12 April 1918 Joseph Dowling, a member of Casement's Irish Brigade, was put ashore from a German submarine on an island off the Galway coast. He was detained shortly afterwards by the RIC, who were convinced that they had uncovered a conspiracy between Irish Republicans and Germany. Acting on this fear, there were widespread arrests of leading Irish Volunteers throughout the country on the night of 17 May 1918. John Sharry was to serve his sentence with these men who were arrested in what was called 'The Second German Plot'. He was incarcerated in Crumlin Road Gaol in Belfast, where Austin Stack was O/C of the prisoners. In an effort to achieve political status, the Republican prisoners rioted and caused considerable destruction within the gaol. Following a hunger strike, political status was granted and subsequently Sharry was transferred to Mountjoy Gaol in Dublin and shortly afterwards released.

Within a few months Sharry was again arrested. He was taken prisoner on 23 December 1918 and was charged with possession of a revolver. He was sentenced to twenty months' penal servitude in Dublin's Mountjoy Gaol. However, on 29 March 1919 Sharry was one of twenty Republican prisoners who escaped over the wall of Mountjoy using a rope ladder. He made his way south with Ben Hickey of Tipperary. Hickey went to the Berrings district in Cork while Sharry eventually reached Rathmore.⁴

Sharry was now 'a wanted man'. Being well known in East Kerry meant that the risk of capture or betrayal was high. With the RIC determined to capture him, he led a precarious existence. His health began to fail while he was 'on the run', probably due to the Spanish Influenza endemic at the time which particularly struck young, otherwise healthy men. It was thought that he might be less liable to be captured in his native Liscannor where his Republican activities were not commonly known. So, with his health failing, he returned to County Clare.

3   *The Freeman's Journal*, 4 April 1918.
4   *Irish Independent*, 1 April 1919.

Weakened by his time in prison and 'on the run', his health continued to deteriorate. He was eventually admitted to Ennistymon Hospital under an alias, John Crawford. There this adopted son of Kerry died on 7 November 1922. He was buried in St Bridget's Well Graveyard, Liscannor.

His comrades in the 5th Battalion inscribed his name on the Republican monument in Rathmore when it was erected in 1928. Lieutenant John Sharry is noted to have died as a result of active service. On 15 August 1948 a monument to his memory was unveiled in St Bridget's Well, Liscannor, Co. Clare.

6th (Killorglin) Battalion, Kerry No. 2 Brigade

The 6th Battalion district encompassed a large area of mid Kerry. It was centred in the market town of Killorglin. The battalion initially consisted of companies from Killorglin town, Milltown, Glenbeigh, Glencar, Callinafercy and Dungeel. From its inception until April 1921, the battalion was attached to Paddy Cahill's Kerry No. 1 Brigade, as politically the area was part of the North Kerry constituency. However, geographically the 6th Battalion district was within South Kerry and so when the IRA brigades were reorganised in April 1921 the battalion was reassigned to the Kerry No. 2 Brigade. Additional companies from Kilgobnet and Caragh Lake were added in the summer of 1921.

Killorglin was the political base of Tom O'Donnell, a staunch Redmondite MP and a prominent figure in the recruitment campaign which encouraged enlistment in Britain's army during the Great War. The town benefited greatly from O'Donnell's political patronage and his hostility towards the Republican cause was reflected in Killorglin's relative apathy to the revolutionary movement. The inactivity of the region's market town was in contrast to the fighting spirit of its hinterland's Volunteer companies. These mid-Kerry IRA units were amongst the county's most active during the Tan and Civil Wars. In a countryside suited to guerrilla warfare and led by able commanders, the 6th Battalion proved to be one of the most effective in Kerry as it fought for the Republican cause from early in 1919 until the ceasefire order that ended the Civil War.

During the reorganisation of the Irish Volunteers in 1917, command of the 6th Battalion on its formation was given to Flossie Doherty. He was a veteran of the Easter Rising and was then a teacher in Killorglin. He remained as O/C of the battalion until November 1920, when he was forced to leave the district following an attack on the RIC at Hillville near Milltown. He was replaced as O/C by Tom O'Connor of Milltown and 'Bertie' Scully of Glencar was appointed V/C. O'Connor was seriously injured in fighting around Kilmallock during the Civil War in late July 1922 and Scully then commanded the battalion until the eventual ceasefire in May 1923. The battalion's adjutant was Dan Mulvihill of Brackhill, Castlemaine, and he also later served as the intelligence officer until his promotion to the Kerry No. 2 Brigade staff. When the battalion established an active service unit in the late spring of 1921, Mulvihill was appointed its commander. The initial intelligence officer was James Cronin, also of Castlemaine. Jack Cronin of the same area was the battalion area's Republican Police officer. Bertie Scully was initially the quartermaster, but when he was promoted to V/C, this role was given to Paddy Rua O'Sullivan.

While the battalion's O/C spent much time in the brigade headquarters in Fybough on the southern slopes of the Sliabh Mish Mountains, the battalion's command headquarters was near Bertie Scully's home in the remote Glencar area.

The history of this period will record that the first Irish Volunteers to die in the fight for freedom lost their lives at Ballykissane, near Killorglin, but the events of Easter Week had little impact in mid Kerry. The conflict against the forces of the British crown began there on 16 July 1920, in the remote mountainous parish of Glencar, when an RIC patrol was disarmed by an ill-armed group of Glencar Volunteers under the command of schoolteacher Bertie Scully. This set in train a series of events that did not end until the last major confrontation of the Civil War at Derrynafeena on 6 April 1923. Following the attack, the RIC abandoned their barracks in Glencar and soon the crown forces held only a strongly fortified barracks in Killorglin and a smaller post at Glenbeigh, which was reinforced by a detachment of regular British soldiers. The battalion became increasingly active, with several of its men, including Tom O'Connor and Dan Mulvihill, serving in the Kerry No. 1 Brigade's flying column. Following the killing of two RIC constables near Milltown on 31 October 1920, the conflict between the 6th Battalion and the RIC became increasingly bitter. On 13 March 1921 the RIC in Killorglin were attacked. On 22 March men from the battalion were prominent in the Lispole ambush with the Kerry No. 1 Brigade column. A month later, a daring attack on British soldiers at Glenbeigh station captured arms and ammunition that sustained the column for the remainder of the war. On 1 June 1921 five RIC men were killed in an ambush at Castlemaine as the intensity of the campaign continued to increase. The eve of the Truce, on 10 July 1921, saw a planned large-scale assault on the RIC's Killorglin Barracks being aborted due to concerns over the destruction that the use of high explosives might have on the civilian population in the town.

In April 1921 a reorganisation of the Kerry brigades took place and this coincided with the removal of Paddy Cahill as O/C of the No. 1 Brigade. The 6th Battalion was reassigned to the Kerry No. 2 Brigade. An attempt by the smaller No. 3 Brigade to have the Glencar Company assigned to its command was resisted, though in effect there was close co-operation between this company and their increasingly active neighbouring companies during the Civil War.

The 6th Battalion remained intact and was united in its opposition to the Treaty. With the outbreak of hostilities, Volunteers from the battalion were part of the Kerry No. 2 Brigade force that moved north to capture Listowel on 30 June 1922. During July 1922 an attempt was made by Liam Lynch's Republican forces to hold a defensive line between the cities of Limerick and Waterford. Four columns of Kerry active service units were sent to this line. These included a column under the leadership of battalion O/C Tom O'Connor and this force of experienced fighters was based in the Kilmallock area. In the fighting around this south Limerick town, O'Connor was grievously wounded and spent the remainder of the conflict recuperating near Keel. Bertie Scully then assumed command, but the defensive line collapsed due to superior Free State numbers, weapons and artillery, as well as the seaborne landing of pro-Treaty forces along the Cork and Kerry coasts.

In early August 1922 Scully's forces returned to their mid-Kerry heartland and adopted the guerrilla tactics that had proved successful against the crown forces. An attempt by Republican forces under John Joe Rice to capture the town of Killorglin in late September 1922 failed after two days of fighting. Soldiers of the Free State's 1st Western Division proved impossible to dislodge from their fortified positions within the town and were eventually relieved by reinforcements from Tralee. The remainder of the conflict in the battalion area was characterised by Republican control of the countryside while the Free State maintained garrisons in Killorglin, Castlemaine and Beaufort. The topography and the support of the local population ensured that the 6th

Battalion remained an effective fighting force until the end of the conflict. To counter the continued resistance, the Free State relied on large sweeps of the mountainous countryside to ensnare IRA units. Captured Republicans could expect no mercy and summary roadside executions came to define the Free State Army's conduct in this region. Still, the men of the 6th Battalion would not submit despite overwhelming odds and Scully's men remained in the field of battle in defence of the Republic until the ceasefire was declared in May 1923.

Michael Ahern

Mícheál Ó hEictigeanna

Michael 'Mike' Ahern was born in Ballycleave near Glenbeigh on 21 November 1896. His family had a small farm in this townland which lies five miles to the west of Killorglin and it was here that Mike and his sister, Molly, were reared. Mike Ahern worked as a carpenter and was engaged to be married to his sweetheart, Molly O'Sullivan, who was also from Ballycleave. He was a Volunteer in the 6th Battalion of the Kerry No. 1 Brigade. Before the Truce in 1921, a new unit in the area between Glenbeigh and Killorglin had been formed and it was designated the 'G' Company or the Caragh Lake Company of the 6th Battalion. Mike Ahern was appointed its captain, a rank that he was to hold until his death. At this time also, the 6th Battalion, which was commanded by Tom O'Connor of Milltown, was transferred to the Kerry No. 2 Brigade from the command of the Kerry No. 1 Brigade.

Courtesy of Michael O'Shea, Ballycleave, nephew of Michael Ahern.

The majority of the officers and men of the 6th Battalion remained in the IRA following the divisions that arose over the Anglo-Irish Treaty. By the autumn of 1922 the Free State Army occupied the towns of Killarney and Killorglin and had a smaller outpost in the village of Beaufort. Some members of the 6th Battalion column were operating in the area along the River Laune. On 25 October 1922 Captain Mike Ahern, Dinsy (Denis) Clifford and at least one other Volunteer were in a field just off the main Killarney to Killorglin road at Pallas. They were armed with rifles and had not been expecting any Free State Army activity in the area. Whether acting on information that they had received, or by chance, enemy soldiers approached the field where the Republicans were gathered. As they approached the unsuspecting Republicans the Free State soldiers opened fire. Ahern returned fire with his rifle but his ammunition was soon spent. Meanwhile Dinsy Clifford managed to get over a gate in the field but as he did so, he dropped his rifle. Ahern retrieved the loaded weapon and, taking cover in a clump of rushes, he resumed firing, holding the enemy at bay. Then the Free State troops brought a machine gun into play and Ahern was shot multiple times and died at the scene. The soldiers proceeded to follow Dinsy Clifford, who had reached a nearby house owned by an English woman. She hid Clifford in a wardrobe. Meanwhile, the soldiers searched the hayshed, prodding the hay with their bayonets. Quickly searching the house, they failed to find Clifford. They then went into the adjoining fields to continue to search for him, but as they did so Clifford moved to the hayshed and hid himself under the hay. The troops then returned from the fields and thoroughly searched the house again but failed to find their quarry.[1]

Local people recall that Ahern's body was thrown callously on a lorry and brought to Killarney.[2] From there it was returned to his family, but the local priest refused to conduct the funeral as the dead man was an active Republican Volunteer. Ahern was buried in Dromavalla Cemetery the next day, in a funeral attended by a very large crowd from all over Kerry. Several of the local Free State soldiers who had been on the patrol that shot Ahern also attended out of respect for their victim.

Dinsy Clifford of Dooks survived the incident, but was later captured and brought to the hotel beside the station that served as the Free State Army barracks in Killorglin. There he was tortured, and he carried on his chest until the day of his death the marks of cigarette burns.

Near Beaufort Captain Michael Ahern is remembered by a roadside monument and this was erected adjacent to the field where he was killed in action. He was also recalled by a ballad composed in his honour which is still sung in his native Ballycleave.

Molly O'Sullivan, his fiancée, emigrated to America following the death of her sweetheart and never married.

---

1 Information from Michael O'Shea, nephew of Capt. Mike Ahern.
2 Information from Thomas Clifford, the son of Denis Clifford and his wife Peggy Clifford (née O'Sullivan) the niece of Molly O'Sullivan.

William Conway O'Connor

Liam Mac Connmaiġ Ó Conċubair[1]

William Conway O'Connor was born in Rinn near Killorglin in 1902. His family subsequently lived in Sunhill on the outskirts of the town. He was a Volunteer in the Killorglin Company of the 6th Battalion, Kerry No. 2 Brigade, as was his younger brother, Charlie. During the Black and Tan War William was a scout and dispatch rider for the Killorglin-based 'B' Company.[2] During the Civil War, these two young men were on active service with the battalion flying column, which was billeted at Derrynafeena in the foothills of Carrantuohill. This active service unit, under the command of Bertie Scully of Glencar, remained an effective fighting force throughout the Civil War. The mountainous terrain and the support of the local population allowed Scully's column to continue the resistance to the Free State Army in the mid-Kerry region.

On the morning of 6 April 1923 a large Free State force arrived at Lough Acoose, which stands at the entrance to the large glen which extends into the McGillycuddy Reeks. The men of the flying column were billeted in the small cottages at the entrance to the valley on the far side of the lake. Republican sentries Bill Landers and Dan O'Shea opened fire on the advancing Free State forces as they entered the valley. Alerted by the shooting, the Volunteers hurriedly vacated their beds and rushed up the glen under fire from the pursuing soldiers.[3] William Conway O'Connor was wounded in the shoulder and was subsequently taken prisoner. Dorothy Macardle reported that he hid his weapon and thus was not captured 'under arms' when he surrendered. In this way he would not have expected to be sentenced to death by any military court he would face. The remainder of the column, with the exception of George Nagle, escaped and as the Republicans regrouped, their fire soon prevented the

---

1   There is no known photograph of William Conway O'Connor.
2   Con Casey papers, Kerry County Library Archive.
3   Unpublished memoir of Patrick 'Belty' Williams, who fought in the engagement at Derrynafeena (private collection).

pursuing Free State soldiers from advancing further into the glen. From their position on higher ground, they could see William Conway O'Connor walking towards the lake with his Free State captors. What occurred subsequently is unknown.[4]

IRA Volunteer George Nagle was also wounded when he was captured shortly afterwards. Nagle was executed by his captors having surrendered at O'Brien's cottage on the other side of the lake. A cart was brought up to remove Nagle's body and when this passed down the road it carried the bodies of two Republican soldiers, George Nagle and William Conway O'Connor. A pool of blood was left on the roadside just north of the lake and it is assumed that O'Connor was summarily executed on this spot. The exact site is where the Celtic cross stands today. William Conway O'Connor was twenty years old when he died in defence of the Republic in that remote but scenic valley at Lough Acoose, Glencar.

His brother, Charlie Conway O'Connor, who also fought in the battalion column, was one of the thousands of Republicans forced to emigrate following the Civil War. He lived the remainder of his life in Australia, far from the land which he fought to free.

A monument to Volunteer William Conway O'Connor and Lieutenant George Nagle was erected at Lough Acoose through public subscription. It was unveiled in 1949 by Bertie Scully, who was the officer commanding the Republican forces on that fateful day in Derrynafeena on 6 April 1923.

---

4 Dorothy Macardle, *Tragedies of Kerry* (1924), p. 61.

Jack Galvin

Seán Ó Gealbáin

John 'Jack' Galvin was born on 22 April 1893 in the townland of Garrahadoo on the outskirts of Killorglin. He was the son of a general labourer and, before joining the British Army in 1913, he too worked as a labourer. He enlisted in the Irish Guards and was posted to London. With the outbreak of the Great War, his regiment was deployed on the Western Front. There Jack Galvin was injured for the first time when he received bayonet wounds during the Battle of the Marne in 1914. He was wounded again in 1915 by gunfire and, having spent time in a military hospital, was declared unfit for duty and went home to Killorglin

Courtesy of the Martin Moore collection.

to recuperate. In 1916 he was recalled to Britain to work in a munitions factory. In 1917, though judged unfit to resume active service in a combat role on the Western Front, he was assigned to the Royal Engineers Regiment where he worked in the construction of military infrastructure along the Front in northern France. He was again wounded by gunfire in August 1918, though not in a combat situation. He was finally discharged in November 1918, having been awarded three service medals. He also received a medal in 1916 for saving two drowning girls in a lake near Killorglin when home on leave.[1]

After the Great War he returned home to Killorglin and there he joined the Irish Republican Army. In September 1920 he disarmed three members of the RIC who were raiding the local Sinn Féin Club and subsequently had to go 'on the run'. During the Tan War he was the officer in charge of munitions for the 6th Battalion and also the drill instructor to the battalion column.[2]

1 Stephen Thompson, *Killorglin's World War One Soldiers, Sailors & Airmen*, Killorglin Archive Society, internet publication (2013).
2 Con Casey papers, Kerry County Library Archive.

It was while on active service during the Civil War that he was captured and killed by his fellow Irishmen. On 26 September 1922 IRA units from Kerry No. 2 Brigade converged on Killorglin. Under the command of John Joe Rice, they attempted to repeat their success of earlier that month when they captured Kenmare. The Free State garrison was drawn from the 1st Western Division and located in several well-defended buildings in the town. Despite a prolonged assault on their positions, the IRA did not manage to dislodge the Free State defenders and on the arrival of a large well-armed relief force from Tralee, the Republicans withdrew.

The Free State defenders of Killorglin had a machine-gun post in the tower of the old Church of Ireland church on the Mill Road. Fire from this vantage point prevented IRA engineers from getting their explosives to the former RIC barracks which was the focus of their attack.[3] Galvin and several others were on their way up Langford Street, which runs parallel to the Mill Road, to attack this post when the relieving Free State force arrived from Tralee. With their way blocked Galvin and the other Republicans retreated down towards the town's square and entered Michael Johnston's premises. There they were trapped as Free State forces took command of the town. Following their capture, Galvin received a severe beating and his arm was broken by a blow from a rifle butt.

On 30 September the ten Republican prisoners captured at Killorglin were transferred under guard in a convoy of Free State lorries. The O/C of the 1st Western Division, Michael Hogan, was the senior officer in the convoy. Four weeks previously, on 28 August, a friend of Hogan's, Captain James Burke, had been killed as, mounted on a horse, he led a Free State column through the small village of Castlemaine. It was claimed that Jack Galvin admitted during his interrogation that he fired the shot that had killed Captain Burke.[4]

At that time the Killorglin to Tralee road passed down through Farmer's Bridge and on to Ballyseedy to meet the main Tralee to Killarney road. Three miles from Tralee, near the entrance to where Ballyseede Castle Hotel now stands, two trees blocked the road. Some few hundred yards further on towards

---

3   Memoirs of Pat Williams (unpublished, private collection).
4   Ernie O'Malley, *The Men Will Talk to Me – Kerry Interviews* (2012), interview with Tom O'Connor.

Ballyseedy Cross, a third tree had been felled by Republicans to impede Free State convoys. On reaching the barricade, the convoy stopped and the prisoners were ordered to cut through the trees which blocked the road. Galvin, because of his broken arm, remained with Hogan and some other Free State officers in the last of the lorries in the convoy. Having removed the first two trees, the prisoners were marched to where the third tree lay across the narrow road. A gentle bend in the road meant this party was no longer visible to those who remained in the military vehicles. It is reported that a Kerry Free State officer, Éamonn Horan, advised the prisoners who were cutting through the tree to keep Galvin in the middle of their group when they returned to the convoy as he feared for the wounded prisoner's safety.[5] At that point several shots were heard from the vicinity of the vehicles where Galvin, Hogan and other Free State officers were waiting while the road was being cleared.

When the prisoners were being counted after they returned to the lorries, one was missing and Brigadier Horan offered to search for the absent man. However, he was forbidden to do so and the convoy moved off to travel the three miles to Ballymullen Barracks. News was relayed by the prisoners to the local Republicans expressing fears of Galvin's fate at the hands of Michael Hogan. A search of the area revealed Jack Galvin's body, which had been thrown over a roadside hedge. It had several gunshot wounds and there were severe injuries to his head. Brigadier Éamonn Horan subsequently resigned his commission in the Free State Army as his superiors refused to enquire into the brutal slaying of Jack Galvin.[6]

A white cross now stands at the gate of Ballyseede Castle Hotel near the spot where Jack Galvin was killed. He is buried in Dromavalla Cemetery in his native Killorglin.

---

5   Dorothy Macardle, *Tragedies of Kerry* (1924), p. 15.
6   *The Kerryman*, 5 December 1936.

FRANK GRADY

##Приоnгіаг Ó Ӷrávaiɼ[1]

The killing of Frank Grady was one of the most brutal acts in a long litany of callous killings during the Civil War in Kerry. In August 1922 Seán Moriarty of Tralee had been taken to a quiet location in the early hours to be summarily executed. By March 1923 such precautions were no longer deemed necessary as Michael 'Tiny' Lyons calmly shot Captain Frank Grady dead. This cold-blooded killing was witnessed by over 100 people and perpetrated without fear of any censure by his superiors and with a disregard of the rules of conflict that armies are required to abide by.

Frank Grady was born in 1895 in Kilnabrack Lower, Glenbeigh, where his family had a farm. He joined the Irish Volunteers at an early stage and had an impressive record in the Tan War. He was appointed captain in the Glenbeigh Company of the 6th Battalion of Kerry No. 1 Brigade on its formation. In 1918 he was sentenced to a prison term for 'illegal drilling'. Such was his worth that GHQ ordered him to accept the conditions of bail which allowed him to be released so that he would be of service to the local Volunteers at the time of the conscription crisis in the spring of 1918. As an active member he was involved in many of the actions of the 6th Battalion, including the attack on a military detachment at Glenbeigh Railway Station on 26 May 1921. However, this record in the fight against the crown forces meant nothing to Dublin Free State officers such as Michael 'Tiny' Lyons.

On Sunday 11 March 1923 several prisoners were being moved from the Free State barracks at Bahaghs, near Cahersiveen, to Killorglin. These men, who included Dinny Daly, had been captured after a fight at Gurrane on 5 March 1923. Daly was a 1916 veteran and V/C of Kerry No. 3 Brigade. At Mountain Stage these prisoners were to be handed over to a detachment of Dublin Guards, who had come from Killorglin through the village of Glenbeigh where they divided into two groups, one under Captain Michael 'Tiny' Lyons and the

1   There is no known photograph of Frank Grady.

other under a Lieutenant Gerard McGuinness. Lyons' detachment travelled by the main road and McGuinness and his troops went to Mountain Stage by an inland route. On the way, McGuinness' men raided a house owned by an O'Sullivan family and there they arrested Frank Grady and Michael Cahill, who were dressed and preparing to go to mass as it was a Sunday morning. Grady told his captors that his name was O'Shea while Cahill gave his correct name. McGuinness and his detachment then continued on their way with their two captives to Mountain Stage, where they met with Lyons who had also rounded up a number of prisoners. At the meeting point at Mountain Stage they were joined by the Free State detachment bringing Dinny (Denis) Daly and the other Cahersiveen prisoners. As it was a Sunday morning there were many people on the road going to mass and several of them were also detained by the Free State soldiers. It was estimated that there were nearly 200 people at the scene, though most were not prisoners.

While Frank Grady's name was well known to the Free State officers, his identity was not and he had hoped that by giving a false name they would release him. However, being well known in the district, some of those gathered inadvertently let the Free State troops know the true identity of their prisoner. Grady was standing beside Dinny Daly when 'Tiny' Lyons walked up to him. Lyons asked, 'How are you, Frank?' and when Grady offered his hand for a handshake, Lyons hit him in the face with the butt of his pistol. McGuinness asked Lyons why he would dirty his hands in hitting Grady, whereupon Lyons turned his pistol and shot the helpless prisoner in the head. Dinny Daly described how he was splattered with Grady's brains. Lyons fired again and this was followed by some shots from Lieutenant McGuinness.

McGuinness then turned on Daly and sarcastically asked him where he was in 1916, unaware that Dinny Daly was involved in the Ballykissane tragedy and was in the GPO during Easter Week 1916. When Daly replied that he was in the GPO, McGuinness asked him 'What GPO?' When the 1916 veteran replied that there was only one GPO in Ireland, McGuinness was about to kill him when two Free State officers named Foley and George Swayne stepped in. They prevented the killing of any more of their prisoners in such a callous and public fashion.[2]

2   Ernie O'Malley, *The Men Will Talk to Me – Kerry Interviews* (2012), interview with Denis 'Dinny' Daly.

The lifeless body of Frank Grady was left on the roadside and taken by some local people to a nearby house. Lyons, having taken custody of the Cahersiveen prisoners, marched the military column and his prisoners away and returned to Killorglin.

Frank Grady was buried in Killeen Cemetery, Glenbeigh, where an impressive cross was unveiled over his grave on 16 October 1938 by 6th Battalion O/C Bertie Scully. A cross also marks the scene of Frank Grady's death. This stands on the roadside at Mountain Stage on a section now bypassed by modern road re-alignment and was unveiled in 1958 by Seán Ó Murchú of Cork. It was erected by local subscription and replaced a wooden cross placed there by his comrades in 1924.

Patrick Murphy

Pádraig Ó Murchada[1]

Patrick Murphy was born just outside Killorglin and attended the local Douglas National School. Following this he went on to work as a barman in what was Mangan's Public House in Killorglin, which stood on Iveragh Road, across the street from where the town's library now stands. It was on this street he met his death, as a battle raged during the Civil War for possession of the mid-Kerry town.[2]

During the Tan War Murphy was initially the intelligence officer in the Killorglin Company of the 6th Battalion, Kerry No. 2 Brigade. Later he became its first lieutenant and in 1922 he was appointed the company captain.

On the morning of Wednesday 27 September 1922, at 6 a.m., Republican forces commenced a coordinated attack on Killorglin. The town had a Free State garrison of about seventy men who came mostly from the 1st Western Division and were recruited in County Clare. They were commanded by Captain Dan Lehane and he had fortified several positions in the town. These were the RIC barracks in Bridge Street, now the town's garda barracks, the Carnegie Building and the nearby Morris' Hotel, which was at the corner of Lower Bridge Street and Market Street. Lehane also had men posted in the tower of the Protestant church and in a pub in Langford Street. The Republican forces were drawn from the Kerry No. 2 and No. 3 Brigades. The attack lasted thirty hours and the IRA failed to dislodge the Free State defenders.[3]

During the fighting Fr Nolan, a local priest, cycled to Tralee from Killorglin to seek reinforcements from the Free State forces in Ballymullen Barracks. These arrived in Killorglin the next day, having met resistance along the seventeen-mile route. However, most of the Republican Volunteers had safely evacuated when the superiorly equipped Free State relieving force arrived in the town.

---

1   There is no known photograph of Paddy Murphy.
2   Information from Peggy Murphy, niece of Patrick Murphy.
3   Tom Doyle, *The Civil War in Kerry* (2008), p. 181.

During the fighting two IRA Volunteers were killed in action. Captain Patrick Murphy commanded the local unit during the assault. He was severely wounded by gunfire as he advanced over open ground near the town's handball alley, which stood at the junction of Iveragh Road and Upper Bridge Street, near the site of the modern library, and died of his wounds a short time later.[4] The other Republican casualty was Con Looney of Kenmare. The Free State commander, Dan Lehane, was also killed in action.[5]

The site of Paddy Murphy's death is now marked by a plaque near the town's library which was unveiled in 1998 by his comrade Dan Keating, who was the last surviving veteran of the Tan and Civil Wars.[6] Captain Patrick Murphy was buried in the family plot at the scenic Ballinakilla Cemetery near Glenbeigh, where his grave is marked by an impressive Celtic cross.

4   Con Casey papers, Kerry County Library Archive.
5   Ernie O'Malley interview with Madge Clifford, UCD Archives.
6   Information from Dan Keating, Ballygamboon, Castlemaine.

Joe Taylor

Seoʀaṁ Ċáilliúʀa[1]

Joseph Taylor was a native of Glencar in the heart of the Iveragh Peninsula. The Taylor family was one of several families of Welsh miners that had originally come to this remote area in the eighteenth century to work the local copper mines, which were later to prove unprofitable. By the early decades of the twentieth century, the Taylor family was to the forefront of Ireland's fight for freedom. While Joseph Taylor's family were farmers at Lyranes, Glencar, he was the postman for the parish.

Following the 1916 Rising a meeting was called in Glencar by local Republican activist Liam Scully, with an agenda to reorganise the Irish Volunteers in the parish. About ten local men established the Glencar Company and in 1917, with the formation of the 6th Battalion, Kerry No. 1 Brigade, Joseph Taylor was appointed O/C of this company, comprising three sections. Based as it was on a few families, the Glencar Company was well organised and closely knit and became active very early in the Tan War. In the summer of 1918 both Taylor and Chris Scully were arrested and charged with illegal drilling and both were imprisoned in Cork and Belfast Gaols. As a result of an ambush on an RIC patrol in Glencar on 16 July 1920, the local barracks was evacuated and this gave Captain Joe Taylor's men freedom of movement in a large area of mountainous countryside.

On Saturday 26 February 1921 the 6th Battalion planned an ambush on an RIC patrol which routinely left its Killorglin Barracks. The battalion staff had planned the attack on the road from Killorglin to Milltown, at a point near Dromavalla Cemetery and about a mile from the town centre. Fourteen Volunteers from the Glencar Company, including Taylor, arrived at the ambush site, avoiding Killorglin town by travelling to the south and then crossing a ford on the River Laune at Dungeel. They waited at the ambush position for several hours, expecting the patrol to leave the town-centre barracks and to

---

1   There is no known photograph of Joe Taylor.

proceed down the main street and over the bridge, heading towards Milltown. However, unknown to the ambush party, the RIC had turned right having left their barracks and headed, in civilian clothes, towards Glencar, ten miles to the south-west. The IRA scouts failed to detect the change in the RIC's expected journey and, having waited several hours, the Volunteers dispersed, returning to their homes in the early hours of a moonlit night.

The crown forces patrol of fifteen men was composed of Black and Tans and regular RIC in civilian clothes. Among the group were the RIC men who had been stationed in Glencar Barracks before its evacuation. They were acting on accurate information as they raided several locations that were regularly used by the Glencar Company. One section of the patrol captured three local Volunteers, who were surprised by the RIC men in civilian attire. Another section went to the Taylor house, where Joe had just arrived following his long march from the ambush site. Leaving his rifle outside, he went into the house and placed his ammunition on the table and, while his sister was preparing a fire, he fell asleep. Suddenly the RIC stormed through the door and captured him. They brought him back to where the three other prisoners they had taken earlier were being guarded. There one of the RIC men fired at least three shots at Joe Taylor and wounded him in the region of the thigh, causing him to bleed profusely. Another RIC constable did attempt to stop the haemorrhage, but they soon left the scene, leaving Taylor and two of their prisoners behind but taking Chris Scully with them.[2]

Joe Taylor was carried by local people on a door used as a stretcher to a nearby house and made comfortable. Bertie Scully, V/C of the 6th Battalion, who lived near Taylor and who had travelled with him from the ambush that night, heard the fatal shots. He rushed to where Joe was taken, but it was clear that the wound was severe. A Dr Anistar who was staying at the nearby Glencar Hotel was sent for, as was Dr Dodds of Killorglin. However, the blood loss was considerable and within an hour Joe Taylor died. His Tricolour-draped coffin was brought to Incharoe Cemetery in Glencar by a cortège reported to be two miles long. His comrades from the Glencar Company fired a volley of shots as his remains were lowered into his grave.

2   Seán 'Bertie' Scully, BMH WS 788.

While a British bullet had killed Joe Taylor, it had not silenced his gun. On 1 June 1921 an RIC party cycling from Tralee to Killorglin was ambushed by men of the 6th Battalion at Ballymacandy, Castlemaine. Bertie Scully had given fellow officer Dan Mulvihill of Castlemaine the repeating shotgun that belonged to Taylor. With this gun RIC Constable Joseph Cooney was fatally injured – he was one of the group that had taken Taylor prisoner earlier that year. However, Cooney, in his dying declaration to a priest, denied he had fired the shots that killed Taylor.[3]

Captain Joe Taylor died on Sunday 27 February 1921 when he was twenty-eight years old. He is buried with his brother Séamus, who was killed in the Civil War, at Shronahiree Cemetery, Incharoe, Glencar. In 1933 a large Celtic cross memorial was erected by public subscription over the grave. He is also remembered by a roadside monument at the location where he was shot at Lyranes, near his Glencar home.

---

3   Ernie O'Malley, *The Men will Talk to Me – Kerry Interviews* (2012), interview with Seán 'Bertie' Scully.

Séamus Taylor

Séamus Táilliúra

Courtesy of the Martin Moore collection.

The Taylor family were from Lyranes, Glencar, and it was there that Séamus was born on 13 June 1897. Séamus was four years younger than his brother, Joe. Both were members of the Glencar Company of the IRA. While Joe was captain of the company during the Tan War and was killed while a prisoner on 27 February 1921, Séamus was the company's lieutenant when he too was killed in custody, but by Free State forces in March 1923. The Taylor family home was the centre of Republican activity during both conflicts and so it is not surprising that both brothers were taken prisoner by enemy forces at their homestead.

Much of the story of the final days of Séamus Taylor comes from evidence gathered in 1924 by Dorothy Macardle when she interviewed his family. Séamus was arrested in the family home at Glencar in March 1923. Undoubtedly his captors were aware that his brother had been murdered two years previously, but this did not influence the brutal treatment meted out to Séamus Taylor by a group of Free State officers in their barracks in Killorglin. While a captive there, Séamus was visited by his sister Sheila, who brought him a coat. It was reported that the pockets of the coat were filled with bullets by his captors before being passed to him. The Free State soldiers who planted the ammunition would have been aware that to be found in possession of ammunition carried a death sentence. Some of the Free State troops who were guarding Séamus Taylor did not condone the torture meted out to their prisoner by their officers and a priest was called as Taylor's injuries were so severe.[1]

---

1   Dorothy Macardle, *Tragedies of Kerry* (1924), p. 41.

Séamus Taylor was to be transferred to Tralee Barracks and was placed under the custody of Captain William (Johnny) Wilson of the Dublin Guard for the seventeen-mile journey. The Free State version of what happened next is that Captain Wilson's convoy was ambushed at Ballyseedy, three miles from Tralee and the scene of a massacre of prisoners seven days previously. At the time the road from Tralee to Killorglin passed through the townland of Ballyseedy. The convoy reported that a prisoner named Lawlor had been shot dead by a Republican ambush party. However, no engagement between the IRA and the Free State Army at Ballyseedy took place on that day and the man who had been killed by his captors was, in fact, Séamus Taylor. Local people contend that he had been killed before leaving the barracks in Killorglin.[2]

Taylor's bullet-riddled body was returned to his family and he was buried beside his brother, Joe, in Glencar's Shronahiree Cemetery. The funeral was attended by huge crowds, testament to the family's contribution and sacrifices in the struggle. Free State officer Michael 'Stanley' Bishop attempted to infiltrate the crowd by dressing his men in civilian clothes from captured Republican prisoners. As he and his men made their way from Beaufort to the funeral their ruse was detected and Captain Bishop thought better of appearing in Glencar that day.

Séamus Taylor was twenty-six years of age when he died on 14 March 1923. The place where his remains were found at Ballyseedy is marked by a traditional white roadside cross. He is also recalled by a monument at Lyranes, near his family home and where his brother Joe was killed in 1921.

---

2 Information from Catherine McGillycuddy of Glencar, whose father was on active service with Séamus Taylor.

Kerry No. 3 Brigade

South-west Kerry was the home of Kerry No. 3 Brigade. It is a geographically sparsely populated area and compared to the larger two brigade areas, it saw little action during the Tan War. However, men from the area were prominent throughout the county and further afield. Dinny Daly and Con Keating of Cahersiveen and Fionán Lynch of Ballinskelligs all played prominent roles in the 1916 Rising. Seán Ó Ceallaigh (Sceilg) of Valentia Island was a senior figure in Sinn Féin. James Sugrue was O/C of the 6th (Listowel) Battalion, while Tom Clifford, another South Kerry native, was O/C of the 2nd (Ardfert) Battalion. Tomás O'Donoghue of Reenard was V/C of Kerry No. 1 Brigade. Having been the only district in the county to come out in open rebellion during the Fenian Rising of 1867, there was a strong Republican tradition in this area of the Iveragh Peninsula, but lack of arms and few enemy to engage meant that the contribution the brigade made to the fight against the forces of the crown was not as significant as the county's other two brigades.

In 1919 the brigade was led by Diarmuid O'Connell of Cahersiveen. However, he was replaced by his deputy Jeremiah (Jerome) Riordan that year. The V/C was 1916 veteran Denis (Dinny) Daly, and his fellow Cahersiveen man Muiris Ó Cleirigh was both the adjutant and intelligence officer. The quartermaster was Muiris Breatnach of Knopogue, Mastergeehy.

The brigade was not divided into battalions until late in the Tan War. Before this it was composed of companies based in the scattered townlands from Kells to Castlecove. In May 1921 four battalions were created. The 1st Battalion (Cahersiveen and Foilmore) had as its commanding officer Michael Griffin and it was composed of companies from Kells, Coonana, Cahersiveen, Killoe, Foilmore and Ballycarbery. The 2nd Battalion (Valentia and Prior parishes) was commanded by Patrick Lynch and had five companies: Valentia, Portmagee, The Glen, Ballinskelligs and Fermoyle. Mike Walsh (Mícheál Breatnach) of Mastergeehy was O/C of the 3rd Battalion (Dromod and Lohar) and his companies were from Gortatlea, Doora, Baslicon, Killagurteen, Lohar, Tullig and Moulnahone. Finally the 4th Battalion served under Jack Teehan of

Sneem and was composed of companies from Glenlough, Sneem, Castlecove, Caherdaniel and Rath.

The brigade had two active service units: one in the Cahersiveen area under the command of Michael Griffin and another in the southern area commanded by former RIC man Mícheál Breatnach.

During the Tan War engagements between the Volunteers and crown forces were not common, although Mícheál Breatnach and his Volunteers from Mastergeehy ambushed an RIC patrol at Bunaderreen on 29 September 1920. Despite the low level of Republican activity, the RIC abandoned their barracks at Portmagee, Caherdaniel and Ballinskelligs but maintained garrisons at Waterville, Cahersiveen and Valentia.

The debate regarding the Treaty with Britain brought no significant division among the fighting men of South Kerry. The Kerry No. 3 Brigade was united in its opposition to the disestablishment of the Republic that it had fought for. While Ballinskelligs man Fionán Lynch held high positions in the Free State government and its army, he had long since lost any influence that he might have had with the Volunteers of his native place.

The Civil War came suddenly to the South Kerry peninsula. On 23 August Free State forces landed unexpectedly at Reenard Pier and quickly made the two mile journey to Cahersiveen without meeting any resistance. Republican forces hastily retreated to the east of the town and regrouped to fight the oncoming conflict in their familiar guerrilla fashion. The Free State Army quickly garrisoned Cahersiveen town and in October it occupied the district's large workhouse at Bahaghs, two miles to the south-east. Further garrisons were placed in Waterville and Valentia to protect British interests at the transatlantic cable stations located at these places. Republican fighting forces were divided into two active columns. Over the autumn and winter, neither side could gain an upper hand. The Free State Army had the advantage of vastly superior numbers of troops and weapons, while the Republicans had the benefits of suitable terrain and local support.

The early spring of the following year saw the deadlock broken as Free State forces began to summarily execute their Republican captives and adopt the tactic of sweeping the countryside with large columns of troops. In one such sweep the five men who were to be killed at Bahaghs were captured. In another, a week later, on 5 March 1923, an IRA column was encircled at Gurrane, but it battled its way out in a day of intense fighting. Outgunned and hunted in their own mountains and glens, Republican resistance stubbornly continued until the ceasefire in April 1923.

Dan Clifford

Domnall Ó Clubáin

Daniel Clifford was born on 15 April 1897 and lived in Old Road, Cahersiveen. He followed the profession of his father and brother and worked as a blacksmith. He was also a Volunteer in the 1st Battalion of Kerry No. 3 Brigade, which was centred on his native town. The trade that he practised was put to use when he was appointed battalion engineer. Following the signing of the Treaty he remained in the Republican Army.

Courtesy of Stephen Kelleghan.

When the Free State Army arrived by sea, in August 1922, they quickly moved the two miles from Reenard Pier to the lightly defended Cahersiveen town. Within a short time they had taken the town, while the Republican defenders evacuated in good order to Derrymore, three miles to the east. From there they engaged in a guerrilla war with the numerically superior and better equipped pro-Treaty forces.

The Kerry No. 3 Brigade had two flying columns. The No. 1 column was under the command of Mike Griffin and was composed mainly of men drawn from the 1st Battalion area. It operated from a base in the area of Gurrane, seven miles to the east of Cahersiveen in the foothills of the mountains to the south of the Killorglin road. Dan Clifford was a member of this unit. The No. 2 column operated from the mountainous area further to the south and was commanded by Michael Walsh. Its Volunteers were mainly from the 3rd and 4th Battalions and they had their operating base near Lough Derriana, several miles to the south of Gurrane.

Early on a dark and wet morning, 5 March 1923, three large columns of Free State troops converged on the townland of Gurrane. One had come from Cahersiveen and the other two from Sneem and Waterville. With several hundred men they encircled the No. 1 Republican column. Fighting began at 8 a.m. and lasted all day. In a house in Gurrane, now occupied by the O'Connell family, several senior Republican officers were besieged and were forced to surrender. These included the column commander and battalion O/C, Michael Griffin. Also captured were Dinny Daly, a veteran of the GPO in 1916 and V/C of Kerry No. 3 Brigade; John (Seán) Ryan, another IRA officer; Dan O'Connor, the brigade quartermaster; and Patrick O'Connor. Peter Brady of Derrynane, who had been a medical student in Cork and was the medical officer for the column, was injured when being detained. Dan Clifford, the battalion engineer, was also captured, apparently unarmed, in a cow house at the O'Connell farm. He was then shot dead under circumstances that have never been explained.[1]

The capture of their officers was a blow to the encircled column, but the Free State troops had to bring their prisoners down from Gurrane and back to Bahaghs workhouse. In doing so, the encircling ring was broken. Meanwhile, alerted by the gunfire to the north, the No. 2 column advanced towards their beleaguered comrades and outflanked the attacking enemy troops. Free State soldiers had to be re-deployed to relieve their men who had been cut off from the main force and, with the aid of an armoured car, they withdrew from the slopes of Gurrane. Meanwhile the main body of the No. 1 column had retreated in good order to the mountains in the east where they linked up with Bertie Scully's 6th Battalion column in Glencar.[2]

While three Free State soldiers were killed in the day-long encounter, Dan Clifford was the only Republican casualty. He is buried in the Republican Plot in Kilnavarnogue Cemetery in his native Cahersiveen.

---

1   Michael Teehan, BMH WS 961.
2   Ernie O'Malley, *The Men Will Talk to Me – Kerry Interviews* (2012), interview with Denis Daly.

Michael Courtney

Mícheál Ó Curnáin

Michael Courtney was a native of Spunkane, a townland adjacent to Waterville village. He was born on 19 April 1893. He was probably more commonly known as Mícheál Cournane, Courtney and Cournane both being the English translations of the Irish surname Ó Curnáin – the native language was still spoken in this area of South Kerry during his childhood. His father was employed in the Waterville transatlantic cable station where he worked as a livery man.[1] Young Michael Courtney was a gifted fife player and his music books still exist.[2]

Courtesy of Phil O'Shea and Stephen Kelleghan.

The area of the 3rd Battalion, Kerry No. 3 Brigade, was centred in the Dromod and Lohar districts and stretched from around the village of Waterville to deep within the Inny Valley, some fifteen miles to the east. Its commander was Mícheál Breatnach (Mike Walsh) who had resigned from the RIC and joined the Irish Volunteers early in the Tan War. He also commanded the No. 2 flying column of the brigade, which was based in the valley. It was with this column that Michael Courtney fought during the Civil War.

Courtney was taken prisoner while attending a wake at Curravoola in the remote foothills at the top of the valley. The house where the wake was held on that fateful day has long been abandoned, but its walls still stand. Earlier Courtney had called to the home of fellow column member, Dan Shea of Islandboy, and the pair walked to the wake house carrying their rifles on their shoulders. They and the other three IRA column men who went to this social event probably expected that the remote location of Curravoola would give

1   Information from Phil O'Shea, niece of Michael Courtney.
2   Information from Stephen Kelleghan, local historian.

them a degree of security. However, a large raiding party of Free State soldiers had been informed that several IRA Volunteers were attending the funeral there. Mike Courtney, Dan Shea, John Sugrue, Eugene Dwyer and Willie Rearden were taken prisoner and marched off across the hills to Bahaghs workhouse, where the Free State Army had a barracks. There the five men were brought before a military tribunal and convicted of waging war on the Free State government.

They were still in custody in Bahaghs when a group of Dublin Guards under Commandant James Delaney arrived from Tralee. Delaney was accompanied by Patrick Kavanagh, a native of North Kerry who was attached to Colonel David Neligan's Intelligence Unit in the Dublin Guard's headquarters in Ballymullen Barracks in Tralee. Delaney and his men were referred to as 'The Visiting Committee'.[3]

It will never be known whether this detachment came from Tralee to kill the prisoners who had been captured during the fight at Gurrane on 5 March 1923, in which there were several Free State casualties, or whether their mission was to kill men selected for no other reason than that they were Republican soldiers. In any event, the Gurrane prisoners had already been taken by an escort of soldiers on foot to Killarney when Delaney and Kavanagh arrived at Bahaghs. So the five prisoners taken at Curravoola were selected and were told that they were being taken out to remove barricades along the road. Courtney must have expected that they would not return, as he took his rosary beads with him.

Although clearly similar to the massacres at Ballyseedy and Countess Bridge five days earlier, in Cahersiveen there were no survivors to relate exactly what happened on that dark March morning as the Free State Army exacted revenge on the Kerry No. 3 Brigade for its continued resistance in South Kerry. The bodies of the victims were removed from the scene of the killing and placed in coffins by the soldiers. Despite the thoroughness of Delaney's men, Courtney's red rosary beads remained on the roadside as testament to the dreadful deed.[4]

Mike Courtney was buried with his four comrades in the Republican Plot in Kilnavarnogue Cemetery, Cahersiveen.

3   Information from the National Archives, Department of Justice files H197/52.
4   Information from Phil O'Shea, niece of Michael Courtney.

Eugene Dwyer

Eogan Ó Dubuidir[1]

Eugene Dwyer was born into a large family at Coomatlockane, an isolated townland between Derrynane and Waterville, on 3 March 1900. It was there his father had a small mountainside farm. The ruins of the house remain but the farm has long been abandoned, its fields repossessed by the mountain and its family scattered, like so many, away from the district. Eugene was a Volunteer in the 3rd Battalion, Kerry No. 3 Brigade. He was a member of the brigade's No. 2 flying column, which was based in the Mastergeehy area of the Iveragh Peninsula.

Young Eugene Dwyer remained in the Republican Army following the acceptance of the Treaty in 1922. Though greatly outnumbered by the large Free State garrisons in Waterville and Cahersiveen, No. 2 column continued to fight on and was aided by the largely sympathetic population in this mountainous area of South Kerry.

In the long and cold winter evenings of early March, the revelry that was part of a funeral wake being held in Curravoola provided a welcome diversion for young men on the run. Eugene Dwyer, John Sugrue and Willie Rearden were later joined by Dan Shea and Mike Courtney at the wake house in its mountainside location.

Curravoola is a remote and sparsely populated townland deep in the Inny Valley and was some fifteen miles from the nearest Free State garrison, and this may have lulled the five Volunteers into a false sense of security as they journeyed by foot to the house. There they joined the crowd celebrating with traditional revelry the life of the dead man. However, further down the valley a large Free State column was advancing towards Curravoola, having been made aware of the presence of the five men by a local informer. Though they were armed, there was no hope of escape when the Free State soldiers surrounded the house and arrested Dwyer and his four comrades. They were brought across

---

1 There is no known photograph of Eugene Dwyer.

the mountain to the large workhouse at Bahaghs where the Free State Army had a garrison.

On 9 March 1923 Dwyer was convicted of possession of a weapon when he was brought before a Free State military court in Bahaghs workhouse. However, he was not sentenced, nor were his comrades on that day. On 12 March he was taken by officers of the Dublin Guard to a site a mile from their place of detention. There, Dwyer, John Sugrue, Willie Rearden, Mike Courtney and Dan Shea were shot in the legs and placed near a landmine which the soldiers then detonated. The five men were killed on the roadside where a memorial now stands.

The five bodies were then returned to the workhouse, but the intervention of a local priest ensured that the mangled remains were returned to the five families. The coffins were opened and amongst the horrific wounds caused by the explosion, the bullet holes in the legs of the victims were clearly visible. Initially the remains were brought to the Market House in Cahersiveen and the following day all five Volunteers were buried in a single grave in Kilnavarnogue Cemetery.[2]

Eugene Dwyer was twenty-three years old when he died at the hands of Free State forces at Bahaghs on 12 March 1923.

---

2   Information from Mary Lehane, Cahersiveen.

Con Keating

Conċubaɼ Ó Céitinn

Cornelius 'Con' Keating was born in the townland of Reenard, between Cahersiveen and Valentia Island, on 13 March 1893. He was educated at the local Christian Brothers School and later went to the Agricultural College at Glasnevin's Model Farm which is now the site of Dublin City University. However, after a single college year in Dublin he returned home in the summer of 1914 and enrolled in the Atlantic College of Wireless Telegraphy in his native Cahersiveen. He and his brother Dan both achieved first class certificates in radio operation and signed up for work on ships to gain practical experience in their new profession.

Courtesy of the Martin Moore collection.

However, in October 1915 Con Keating had again returned to Cahersiveen, perhaps because he found that he was unsuited to life on the high seas, or because he had become involved with the growing Irish nationalist movement in Ireland. There was a strong Fenian tradition in the Keating family and it was not surprising that he was sworn into the IRB at about that time. By December 1915 he had come to the attention of the British authorities, who revoked his radio operator's licence due to his political activities.

From early April 1916 Con Keating was not seen in his native Reenard. He had travelled to Dublin where the Military Council of the IRB was secretly planning the Easter Rising. Paramount to the staging of the rebellion was the landing and distribution of an arms shipment from Germany. This enormous cache of weapons was on board the German ship, *Aud*, which was due to dock in Fenit on Easter Saturday night 1916. Radio contact with the ship would allow for an efficient landing of the vital cargo and to this end it was planned to take a radio set from the Atlantic Wireless College in Cahersiveen and to transfer it to Tralee. However, unknown to the Military Council the *Aud* did not carry radio equipment, so even if the mission Keating was sent on had been successful, the ship could not have been contacted by radio. A five-man unit, led by Cahersiveen native Denis 'Dinny' Daly, travelled from Dublin to Killarney and then planned to complete their journey to Cahersiveen in two cars. There Con Keating, one of the team, would remove the radio equipment from his former college and bring it to Ballyard, just outside Tralee, and reassemble and operate the transmitter from John O'Donnell's house.

Arriving in Killarney, the five-man unit divided into two groups as they travelled in cars driven by Tommy McInerney and Sammy Windrim, both of whom had driven from Limerick city. Dinny Daly and Colm Ó Lochlainn travelled with Windrim in the lead car while Tommy McInerney's vehicle contained Donal Sheehan and Con Keating in the back seat and Charlie Monaghan in the passenger seat. All five who had travelled from Dublin were armed and carried the necessary tools to complete their task at Cahersiveen.

On the initial stage of the journey from Killarney to Killorglin, McInerney's car fell behind and soon lost contact with Windrim's vehicle. As McInerney was suspicious that the first car had been intercepted, he travelled to Killorglin on an alternate route through Beaufort and arrived in Killorglin from an unexpected direction, confusing not only the driver but also Con Keating, the only Kerryman in the car. It is likely that they would not have wished to proceed up the town's main street as the RIC barracks was sited at its far end and so they attempted to seek an alternative route around the town centre. While Con Keating would have been in Killorglin many times, in an age where rail travel was a more common mode of transport, he may not have been familiar with the roads around the town. In any case, Charlie Monaghan was delegated to seek directions from a local lady, Lily Taylor, as to what was the most suitable way from where they were to Caragh Lake, which was on the Cahersiveen side of Killorglin. It is probable that he misinterpreted the information that he was given and so his driver, Tommy McInerney, took the road to Ballykissane rather than turning left at the Catholic church in the direction of Cahersiveen.

The road that the men had taken carried them the two miles to Ballykissane. There the paved road ended as it ran directly onto the unlit pier. Travelling at speed, McInerney attempted in vain to stop the car once he realised he was on the short unguarded pier. In the high tide and the darkness of the evening the car sank into the estuary of the River Laune. While McInerney managed to get safely ashore, the other three men drowned, weighted down by great coats laden with arms, ammunition and tools. The body of Donal Sheehan was recovered the next afternoon in the nets of a local fisherman who was dragging the river for the bodies. Shortly afterwards the remains of Con Keating were recovered. The two unidentified bodies were brought by the RIC to Killorglin, where they were laid out on benches in the courthouse. Tommy McInerney, now a prisoner in Killorglin Barracks, was brought there by the police to identify the victims of the drowning. He denied he knew their names but said that they were definitely the men who had 'hired his car as tourists' the day before.[1]

Con Keating was formally identified by his father, Jeremiah, at an inquest at Killorglin courthouse two days later, Monday 24 April. The remains were released to the Keating family and were brought back to his native Cahersiveen by train later that evening. He was buried in the family plot in Kilnavarnogue Cemetery the following morning. Con Keating was first Kerryman to die in the cause of Irish freedom in the twentieth century, but Kilnavarnogue Cemetery witnessed many more Republican funerals pass through its gates in the succeeding turbulent years.

1   Xander Clayton, *Aud* (2007). The author gives an excellent account of the events at Ballykissane on Good Friday 1916.

Jeremiah 'Romey' Keating

Diarmuid Ó Céitinn[1]

Jeremiah 'Romey' Keating was from High Street in Cahersiveen and was born on 16 December 1899. His father, Michael, had been a member of the RIC and had retired to Cahersiveen. Though christened Jeremiah, his name in Irish was Diarmuid and it could be translated into English as either Jeremiah or Jerome. It was from the shortened version of the latter that he became known as 'Romey'. He was an active Volunteer in the 1st Battalion, Kerry No. 3 Brigade. During the Civil War he was a member of an IRA column that was active in the Cahersiveen area. On Monday 4 September 1922 he took part in a large ambush on Free State forces at Ohermong between Cahersiveen and Waterville. In that engagement he was the 'auxiliary' gunner to John 'Gilpin' Griffin. His role was to aid the Lewis gunner during the attack by carrying ammunition pans and feeding these to the rapid firing weapon, as well as providing protection to the gunner. It is likely that Keating played a similar role when both he and Gilpin were members of the Iveragh contingent that took part in a large-scale attack on the Free State garrison in Killorglin four weeks later.[2]

In late September 1922 the O/C of Kerry No. 2 Brigade, John Joe Rice, attempted to repeat the success that he had had earlier that month when he recaptured Kenmare from the Free State forces occupying his home town. In the last week of that month a significant force of Republican soldiers converged on Killorglin. These men were largely drawn from Rice's brigade, but were supplemented by Volunteers from the Kerry No. 3 Brigade, including 'Romey' Keating.

The men from Cahersiveen entered Killorglin along the Iveragh Road and, linking up with other Republican units, were quickly in control of the streets. The Free State forces were composed of men from the 1st Western Division

---

1 There is no known photograph of Jeremiah Keating.
2 Unpublished account of the Ohermong Ambush, Cahersiveen, by Michael Christopher (Dan) O'Shea (private collection).

under the command of Daniel Lehane, whose father and brother were killed by crown forces during the Tan War. Lehane's men were garrisoned in the RIC barracks, the Carnegie Library, the Protestant church tower and other strongly defended buildings in the town. Gunfire raged throughout Killorglin for over twenty-four hours but the Republicans failed to dislodge their enemies. At that stage the IRA was forced to disengage, as a heavily armed Free State column began to arrive from their headquarters in Tralee, seventeen miles distant. Fighting a rearguard action, the Republicans retreated, but Captain Patrick Murphy of Cromane and Volunteer Con Looney of Kenmare had been killed in action. Free State Captain Dan Lehane was also fatally wounded. The Kerry No. 3 Brigade Volunteers headed westwards, taking their injured men with them. The wounded men were attended to by their 'Red Cross' man, Peter Brady of Caherdaniel, a medical student in Cork who had left his studies to join the Republican forces in South Kerry. The most seriously injured among the retreating IRA column was 'Romey' Keating.

The wounded Volunteers were brought back to Bahaghs workhouse three miles to the east of Cahersiveen where there was a rudimentary hospital. The workhouse was taken over by Free State forces in early October and used as a garrison, but in September it was in an area still controlled by Republican forces. It was there that 'Romey' Keating died of his wounds on 2 October 1922. He was buried in Kilnavarnogue Cemetery.

Keating's final journey is recorded in song:[3]

> *Killorglin Town I shall ne'er forget, did I live for six full score,*
> *There for hours we fought in its shot swept streets, 'til Romey fell wounded and sore,*
> *Bleeding and broken, we bore him back but by Bahaghs braes he died*
> *And the farewell volleys o'er his bier were heard by the Caol Óg's side.*

---

3 'John's by the Caol Óg's Side' composed by Dónal Ó Curnáin of Málainn.

Tadhg Keating

Tadg Ó Céitinn

Tadhg (Timothy) Keating was born on 27 June 1902 in Dungegan, Ballinskelligs. He was the second son of James Keating and Ellen Goggin, who had a small public house in the little village and also farmed a smallholding in the locality.

Tadhg Keating was a lieutenant in the Ballinskelligs Company of Kerry No. 3 Brigade's 2nd Battalion and he remained on active service with the Republican forces during the Civil War.

Waterville, Valentia Island and Ballinskelligs were sites of the transatlantic cable stations which relayed the bulk of the telegraph messages from Britain to the United States. The security of these stations was of strategic importance to the British government and so the Free State government made a determined effort to crush Republican resistance in this geographically remote corner of Ireland. Large garrisons of pro-Treaty forces were posted in Cahersiveen and Waterville, with smaller posts in Valentia and Ballinskelligs.[1]

Courtesy of Stephen Kelleghan.

On the evening of 23 March 1923, Tadhg Keating and his friend and IRA comrade Paddy 'Maukie' O'Sullivan were walking home from a wedding which had taken place over the hill in a townland called The Glen. As they approached Keating's home they encountered a Free State Army patrol. O'Sullivan was a marked man and would not have expected to survive if he had been captured. On seeing the soldiers, Keating turned and ran in an attempt to reach his house. O'Sullivan, who was armed with a rifle, stood his ground. The Free State soldiers, who included some local men, opened fire and directed their shots at the man who was fleeing. Keating was scrambling over a stone wall when he

---

1 Information from George Rice and Stephen Kelleghan.

was hit in the lower back. He fell, mortally wounded, and died within minutes. In the confusion, O'Sullivan took the opportunity to escape and fled through the fields, evading capture on that occasion.[2]

Lieutenant Tadhg Keating was buried in the family plot in Ballinskelligs' Abbey Graveyard. He is remembered by a prominent roadside cross between Dungegan and Ballinskelligs. His name is inscribed on the Kerry No. 3 Brigade memorial on Cahersiveen's main street and on the monument that stands over the Republican Plot in the town's Kilnavarnogue Cemetery. He was twenty years old when he died of wounds received in the service of the Irish Republican Army.

---

2   Information from William Goggins, Ballinskelligs, a relative of Tadhg Keating.

Patrick Lynch

Pádraig Ó Loinrigh[1]

Patrick Lynch was born into a farming family in Moyrish, The Glen, in the parish of Ballinskelligs. He was the third oldest of his eight siblings. The family home overlooks the Skelligs from its cliff-top location. A farmer by profession, he was married to Mary Murphy, who came from the other side of the beautiful St Finian's Bay. The couple had one daughter, Nancy, who was aged only fifteen months when her father was killed.

Patrick Lynch was a Volunteer in the IRA during the Tan War and when the Kerry No. 3 Brigade was reorganised in May 1921 he was appointed captain of the Ballinskelligs and Valentia Company, which was one of five companies which made up the 2nd Battalion of that brigade. Dorothy Macardle, who interviewed his family in the summer of 1924, records that Lynch had become O/C of the 2nd Battalion during the Civil War. His wife, Mary, was O/C of the local Cumann na mBan.[2]

When the Free State Army arrived in Valentia Harbour on Wednesday 23 August 1922, they quickly captured the only town in the brigade area, Cahersiveen. They installed garrisons in Waterville and Valentia where the transatlantic cable stations were of strategic importance, especially to British interests.[3] However, the mountains and glens of the Iveragh Peninsula provided a safe haven for the Republican Army, which by the autumn of 1922 had returned to the guerrilla tactics that were successful in the war against the British.

At 2 a.m. on 4 November 1922 a Free State raiding party arrived suddenly at the Lynch home. Patrick Lynch was asleep upstairs. His captors brought him down from the loft while an officer who was upstairs looking down with a gun in one hand and a candle in the other gave an order to shoot the prisoner. Just then Lynch's sister lunged at the Free State officer and knocked the candle

---

1   There is no known photograph of Patrick Lynch.
2   Dorothy Macardle, *Tragedies of Kerry* (1924), p. 36.
3   Unpublished account of Ohermong Ambush, Cahersiveen, by Michael C. (Dan) O'Shea (private collection).

from his hand. In the darkness and chaos that ensued, Patrick Lynch ran out the door and into the familiar countryside and thus managed to evade his pursuers.

From then onwards, he was a man 'on the run' and lived in a dugout or in the caves at the foot of the nearby cliffs. Over three weeks later, on 30 November, Lynch came home to plough the fields of his small farm. Following the day's work he went to his house to rest, being slow to return to the dugout in the cold and damp winter's evening. He was resting by the fire with his brother when, at about 7 p.m., a shout came through the door ordering the men to come out with their hands up. Lynch passed his revolver to his wife and he and his brother went out the front door with their arms raised. The house had been surrounded by Free State soldiers who were acting on accurate information supplied by one of their number who had been an officer in the local IRA before joining the pro-Treaty forces. While walking out on the pathway in front of the small house, the Lynch brothers were being covered by a soldier with a rifle who backed down the yard before them. Mrs Lynch went back into the house to get her husband's coat and to hide his revolver. When she was inside, gunfire erupted in the yard and she quickly ran out. Her husband was lying dead in the grass while her brother-in-law had managed to jump the wall and escape into the darkness of the November night. The Free State soldiers brought the bullet-riddled body of Captain Patrick Lynch back into his house where they put it on the floor.[4]

The remains of forty-year-old Lynch were buried in the family plot at the nearby An Gleann old graveyard. A roadside cross was erected by local subscription near the church at An Gleann on the road to Cahersiveen and less than a mile from where he was killed. This was unveiled by local IRA leader, Seán Ryan, on 4 December 1932, in front of a crowd of 1,200 people who had gathered to honour the memory of Captain Patrick Lynch.

Following the murder of her husband, Mary Lynch and her infant child Nancy left the family farm and moved away from the area. Many years later she married a local man, Batt Murphy, and the couple returned to settle at St Finian's Bay.[5]

4   Dorothy Macardle, *Tragedies of Kerry* (1924), p. 36.
5   Information from Mary Murphy, daughter-in-law of Mrs Mary Lynch Murphy.

Dan Shea

Domhnall Ó Seaġḋa

Courtesy of Mary Lehane.

Daniel Shea was born in Islandboy. This is a small townland on the northern slopes of the Inny Valley that stretches for almost twenty miles from Ballinskelligs Bay near Waterville to the Pass of Bealach Oisín. It was in this remote place the Shea family had a small farm. Dan, born in 1902, was the second eldest child in the large family of James and Mary Shea. Mrs Shea was a first cousin of Dinny Daly, the second in command of Kerry No. 3 Brigade.[1] In 1916 Daly had led the attempt to secure radio equipment from The Atlantic College in Cahersiveen which ended in the tragedy at Ballykissane. On returning to Dublin, he was part of the GPO garrison during the Easter Rising.

Despite their young age, Dan Shea and his brother Diarmuid (Jerry) joined the Irish Volunteers in 1917. In May 1921 their IRA company and others in the Dromod and Lohar parishes in the Waterville and Inny Valley districts were designated the 3rd Battalion of Kerry No. 3 Brigade. Its commander was Mike Walsh (Mícheál Breatnach) and his deputy was Mike Hallisey, Dan Shea's future brother-in-law. The company was involved in the Bunaderreen ambush on 29 September 1920, one of the few engagements in the brigade area during the Black and Tan War. During the Civil War, Dan Shea maintained his allegiance to the Irish Republic and fought in the mountains and glens of South Kerry with one of the brigade's two active service units.

With the arrival by sea at Reenard of a large Free State force on 23 August 1922, the Kerry No. 3 Brigade quickly ceded Cahersiveen, Waterville and Valentia to their enemies, regrouping in the mountains that dominate the

---

1 Information from Mary Lehane, Cahersiveen, niece of Dan Shea.

peninsula. From there they engaged in a guerrilla war against the numerically superior Free State forces that were garrisoned in coastal towns. The mountainous terrain of their native countryside favoured the local men and this forced the Free State Army to only venture out of their strongholds in large columns. Unknown to Dan Shea and his comrades, one of these columns was engaged in a sweep of the Inny Valley on the day in early March that they decided to attend the wake of a local person in a house at the extreme end of the valley. The remoteness of the house where the wake was being held should have ensured that the five local IRA Volunteers could not be surprised but, acting on accurate information that they had received, a detachment of Free State soldiers raided the house. John Sugrue, Willie Rearden, Michael Courtney and Eugene Dwyer were quickly identified and arrested. A girl sat on Dan Shea's lap and tried to shield him from the searching soldiers, but they had information that he too was in the cottage and soon he was their fifth prisoner.

The five men were brought to Bahaghs workhouse, a large walled building three miles from Cahersiveen, where the Free State Army had their headquarters. All five were convicted by a military tribunal of waging war against the Free State, but their sentence was not indicated to the men. Their execution was to be 'unofficial' and on 12 March 1923 the five were brought to a spot on the road a mile from the workhouse. There their Dublin Guard escorts shot the five prisoners in the legs and then the injured men were killed by a mine that was detonated remotely.

Later that Monday, as word of the killings spread, Dan's father, James Shea, made his way over the hills to Bahaghs workhouse. He had heard one of the men killed was named Shea and he had his fears realised when the sentry's description of the clothing of one the dead men matched what Dan had been wearing. He was not permitted access to his son's remains. This had become the Free State Army's policy following the angry scenes outside Tralee's Ballymullen Barracks five days earlier when the coffins of the Ballyseedy victims were released to their relatives. Soon word reached the families of the other four slain Volunteers and it was only following the intervention of Dromod parish priest, Fr Sheehan, that the five coffins, nailed closed, were handed to their relatives.

Dan Shea's parents were distressed by the fact that their son had not been given the opportunity to receive the sacrament of confession before his death at the hands of his captors. However, they received some solace from Fr Courtney of Ballinskelligs, who told the grieving relatives that the men 'had died without sin' as he had heard their confessions when he had travelled into the valley to meet with them a short time before they were captured.

Dan Shea, Willie Rearden, Eugene Dwyer, John Sugrue and Michael Courtney were buried in a common grave in the Republican Plot in Kilnavarnogue Cemetery near Cahersiveen. Dan Shea's sister later married Michael Hallisey, an active IRA Volunteer, who had had a leg amputated following injuries received in action against Free State forces near where his brother-in-law was captured.

It was to the Shea home in Islandboy that Dorothy Macardle travelled in 1924 in order to document the evidence of the Bahaghs massacre as she wrote her book, *The Tragedies of Kerry*.

John Tadhg O'Sullivan

Seán Tadhg Ó Súilleabáin[1]

John O'Sullivan was born on 24 March 1897 in the townland of Killurley East, three miles from Cahersiveen to the north of the Killorglin road. His father's name was Timothy and so he was commonly called John Tadhg. He was a Volunteer in the 1st Battalion, Kerry No. 3 Brigade, and he and his friend Patrick Coffey from nearby Cloghanelinaghan were members of its active service unit. Coffey was an experienced fighter, having served in the British Army during the Great War.[2]

Following the action at Gurrane on 5 March 1923, where a large Free State force had encircled their column, O'Sullivan and Coffey had been among those who had evaded capture. Most of the IRA column had retreated to the east in order to reach the safety of the mountains, where they regrouped. However, both John O'Sullivan and his neighbour Patrick Coffey had returned to briefly visit their families on Tuesday 6 March 1923 and then set out to rejoin their column in the Glencar area. They travelled on foot and were armed with rifles. Their route took them along the modern road and by the railway viaduct at Gleensk. There they encountered a Free State patrol at a bend in the road. Fire was exchanged and the two Republicans attempted to escape. Coffey managed to get off the road and escaped through the rough fields, but his comrade was captured as he ran, probably wounded by the gunfire. From a safe distance Coffey could see the wounded man standing in a field surrounded by the four Free State soldiers who had taken him prisoner.

At Bahaghs workhouse, three miles east of Cahersiveen, the Free State Army had a garrison and it was there local captured Republicans were held before their transfer to Tralee or Killarney. Two nurses visiting prisoners at Bahaghs were told by a Free State soldier that there was an IRA man lying wounded in Gleensk, some seven miles away. They set out by car to find the casualty, but on arriving at the scene they found the victim either dead or dying

---

1   There is no known photograph of John Tadhg O'Sullivan.
2   Information from Padraig Garvey, Cahersiveen.

on the roadside. They reported that he had bullet wounds in his leg, chest and arm. The nurses brought his body back to his home in Killurley.[3]

Today a roadside monument stands at Gleensk, several hundred metres east of the viaduct on the main road. It was unveiled in 1982 by Thady O'Sullivan at the spot where his brother was killed. A roadside Celtic cross had previously been erected at the site in 1924 but was destroyed by suspected Free State elements on 23 August 1925.[4]

Volunteer John Tadhg O'Sullivan of Killurley was buried in Kilnavarnogue Cemetery in Cahersiveen, where his name is inscribed on the Republican memorial. He is also remembered on the town's monument to the Republican dead of South Kerry.

---

3 Dorothy Macardle, *Tragedies of Kerry* (1924), p. 40.
4 *The Kerryman*, 5 September 1925.

WILLIE REARDEN

Liam ÓRíogbardáin[1]

William Rearden was born in 1904 in Reenard two miles west of Cahersiveen, though the family originally came to the district from Glencar. His father worked as a labourer and Willie was the third boy of a large family. The family name was spelled Rearden, though later the spelling Riordan was also used. Like his older brothers Pete and Pat, he was a Volunteer with Kerry No. 3 Brigade and during the Civil War he was on active service with one of the two IRA columns that operated in the brigade area. His unit was based in the Inny Valley to the east of Waterville village.

In the first week of February 1923, Rearden was in the Inny Valley and was 'on the run' from the Free State forces who garrisoned Waterville and Cahersiveen. However, the mountainous hinterland of Iveragh was still under the control of the Republican Army. The military advantage lay with the men who operated in their native hills and glens. In a determined effort to capture such IRA Volunteers, Free State soldiers combed the countryside with large enough numbers of troops to deter ambush by the small Republican units that still fought on despite the odds. One such sweep occurred in the Inny Valley on the first week of March, when it was reported that up to 250 soldiers were involved.

Willie Rearden was one of five IRA Volunteers who attended a funeral wake at the upper, remote end of the valley, unaware that the Free State forces were about to comb the valley looking for them. The social activities associated with such wakes were a welcome diversion on a bleak March evening for young men 'on the run'. While searching through the glen, the troops had received accurate information concerning the whereabouts of their quarry. They surrounded the house at Curravoola and captured Rearden, Eugene Dwyer, John Sugrue, Dan Shea and Michael Courtney. All the men were armed but offered no resistance as they were taken from the crowded

---

1 There is no known photograph of Willie Rearden.

house. They were brought to Bahaghs workhouse, the Free State headquarters three miles east of Cahersiveen.[2]

The five prisoners were brought before a military tribunal on 9 March and convicted of possessing weapons. The penalty for such an offence was death but the actual sentence was never conveyed to Rearden and his comrades. Three days later all five were brought about a mile from their place of imprisonment, shot in the legs and then blown up with a mine detonated by a Free State unit commanded by Commandant James J. Delaney, a senior officer in the Dublin Guard.

The remains of the five men were then brought from the scene. Initially they were denied to their families, but the intervention of a local priest allowed proper funerals to be held in Cahersiveen. Willie Rearden and his four comrades were buried together in the Republican Plot in Kilnavarnogue Cemetery a short distance from Cahersiveen. They are remembered on the impressive Republican monument in the town and the site of the massacre at Bahaghs is marked with a roadside memorial.

---

2   Information from Stephen Kelleghan and Dan Shea.

John Sugrue

Seán Ó Siocfrada[1]

John Sugrue was born in Canuig near Ballinskelligs in 1902. His parents, John Sugrue and Ellen Fitzgerald, had a small farm there and John was the eldest of their large family. He worked on the family farm which mainly consisted of marginal land overlooking the scenic Ballinskelligs Bay.[2]

As a young man he joined the Irish Volunteers and was a member of the Ballinskelligs Company of the 2nd Battalion, Kerry No. 3 Brigade. The commanding officer of the battalion was Patrick Lynch, who came from over the mountain in An Gleann. Like John Sugrue, he too died in the Civil War. During the Black and Tan War the brigade was relatively inactive, but that changed during the Civil War. Being the site of several transatlantic cable stations this area of Kerry was of strategic importance to British interests. To protect these vital communication centres, which relayed telegraphic messages between Europe and America, Free State forces established strong garrisons in Cahersiveen, Waterville, Ballinskelligs and Valentia. This resulted in an intense and bloody war of attrition between pro-Treaty forces under Commandant Jeremiah Griffin and the Republican troops of Kerry No. 3 Brigade under Jerome Riordan.

John Sugrue went on full-time active service in 1922 and was a member of the No. 2 IRA column that operated in the brigade area south of Cahersiveen. It was commanded by Mike Walsh (Mícheál Breatnach). In one recorded incident, Sugrue was a member of a group of Republican soldiers operating a checkpoint on a road near Waterville. They searched a car driven by the wife of a local Free State officer who had deserted from the IRA. She was aggrieved by her treatment and promised retribution on Sugrue. Though a wanted man, this incident probably had nothing to do with Sugrue's eventual death in captivity.

In the first week in March, Sugrue was operating in the Inny Valley to the east of Waterville. He and four of his companions went to the funeral

1   There is no known photograph of John Sugrue.
2   Information from William Goggin, Ballinskelligs.

wake of a local person deep in the upper reaches of the glen, fifteen miles from the nearest Free State outpost. However, a large Free State raiding party with accurate information on the whereabouts of the five men was making its way up the valley. The men were captured at the house in Curravoola and, though armed, they had no opportunity to offer any resistance before they were brought north over the hills to Bahaghs workhouse.

A military court tried the five Volunteers with bearing arms against the Free State and though this was a capital offence, no sentence was conveyed to the men following their conviction. They were detained in the workhouse and expected to be transferred to captivity in Tralee. However, this was not to be.

In the early hours of 12 March 1923, Captain James Delaney, Lieutenant Patrick Kavanagh and several other members of the Dublin Guard arrived in Cahersiveen and were billeted in a hotel in the town. They had with them a landmine ready for use. The group, who were known as the 'Visiting Committee', then travelled to Bahaghs. When they reached the large workhouse, which was situated four miles outside the town, they asked the duty sergeant to bring five prisoners from the cells, which he initially refused to do. However, bowing to Delaney's threats, the five prisoners captured at Curravoola were released into his custody.

The prisoners were marched out of the grim workhouse building and brought along the road to Cahersiveen. Approximately a mile into the journey, they halted by a flimsy barricade that was blocking the road and there the prisoners were shot in the legs as was evidenced when the remains were examined subsequently. The men were then blown up by a mine placed amid the rubble on the road, which the soldiers remotely detonated. The remains of John Sugrue, Willie Rearden, Eugene Dwyer, Michael Courtney and Dan Shea were quickly removed from the scene.

Initially the bodies of the men were refused to the families, but the intervention of a local priest persuaded the commander of the workhouse to allow the remains to be released for a Christian burial. The five coffins were brought to the Market House in Cahersiveen where the bodies were prepared for burial.[3] Volunteer John Sugrue of Canuig and his four comrades were

---

3   Information from Mary Lehane, Cahersiveen.

buried the next day in a single grave in Kilnavarnogue Cemetery, a mile from Cahersiveen.

Dying for the Cause Elsewhere

While within the county of Kerry there were a large number of Republican casualties during the fight for independence, there were also a significant number of Kerrymen who died for the cause elsewhere in the country. In the fighting in Dublin at Easter 1916, four Kerry Volunteers died on the capital's streets. An Irish Volunteer captain in County Galway, Jack O'Reilly of Tralee, died as result of imprisonment following the Rising. In 1917 Thomas Ashe of Kinard died on hunger strike in Dublin having commanded the 5th Battalion of the Dublin Brigade in 1916. In 1918 Thomas Russell of West Kerry was one of the first Republicans to be killed in the post-1916 period when he died in Kilrush, County Clare. Later, Tom Healy died in the same county when on active service with the Clare IRA. Seán O'Leary, William O'Brien and Jim Hickey all lost their lives in their adopted county of Tipperary. Liam Scully of Glencar was attached to the East Limerick Brigade when he was killed in the attack on Kilmallock Barracks in May 1920. During the Civil War, Charlie Daly, Tim O'Sullivan and Dan Enright were executed in Donegal while serving with the 2nd Northern Division of the IRA. During the 1940s IRA chief of staff Charlie Kerins and staff captain Maurice O'Neill were executed in Mountjoy Gaol while serving in Dublin. In this chapter their stories are told.

Thomas Ashe

Tomás Agar

Courtesy of Mercier Archive.

Thomas Ashe, the son of Gregory Ashe and his wife Ellen Hanafin, was one of ten children. He was born in Kinard, near Lispole, on 12 January 1885 into a family steeped in the Irish culture of Corca Dhuibhne. He was a pupil in Ardmore National School near Lispole and remained there as a monitor until he was eighteen. He was then accepted at the De La Salle teacher training college in Waterford city where, after two years of study, he qualified as a national schoolteacher. His initial teaching post was in Minard Castle National School, several miles from his home. However, after six months he successfully applied for the post of principal in the Corduff primary school in North County Dublin. It was there that he was to spend the next eight years as a teacher, until his participation in the 1916 Rising ended his career as an educator.

Living in Corduff, he became immersed in local Irish cultural and sporting activities. In 1913 he was on the executive committee of the Gaelic League. The Gaelic League was at this stage an organisation that was increasingly divided on political policy and Ashe sided with the progressive separatist elements against the conservative group. At this time Ashe was also a member of the IRB and was head of the secret revolutionary organisation's circle in his local parish.

The Irish Volunteers were founded on 25 November 1913 and Ashe, being an IRB member, joined the organisation in Corduff. However, his involvement was interrupted when, in January 1914, he and Diarmuid Lynch went to America on a fund-raising mission in support of the Gaelic League. On his return in October of the same year, he threw himself enthusiastically into building up the Irish Volunteers, who had by this stage suffered a split, with the vast majority following John Redmond into the National Volunteers which supported the British war effort. In February 1915 Ashe was appointed commandant of the 5th (Fingal) Battalion of the Dublin Brigade, which was composed of units in North County Dublin, including Lusk, Skerries, Swords, Donabate and Santry, at the time a country village. Being a high ranking officer and an IRB member, he was aware of the plans for a rising on Easter Sunday and had mobilised his men for manoeuvres on that day, but due to Eoin MacNeill's countermanding order the rebellion was delayed for twenty-four hours. Patrick Pearse's orders to Ashe were that the Fingal Volunteers were to rise at 1 p.m. on Easter Monday and this they did.

The battalion mobilised at Knocksedan Bridge, two miles west of Swords at 10 a.m., with Ashe going from company to company on his motorbike to gather his men for the fight that was to come. By the day's end he was in command of about seventy Volunteers who were armed with only fifteen modern rifles and an assortment of other weapons. All had bicycles and later they commandeered a bread van. Their orders were to disrupt enemy communications in North County Dublin. They blew up a bridge, cutting the Dublin to Belfast railway line and captured weapons from the RIC barracks at Swords and Donabate. Moving swiftly through North County Dublin, they destroyed all telephone lines, thus hampering enemy communications. On Wednesday Ashe's guerrilla force was weakened as James Connolly asked that some of the men from Fingal be transferred to the garrisons at the Mendicity Institution and the GPO.

On Friday morning of Easter Week, Ashe led his men to Ashbourne with the aim of capturing its RIC barracks. At 9.15 a.m. his column was divided in two in order to surround the barracks whose garrison had been increased. An initial call to surrender was met with a volley from within and so the attack started. Two explosions from home-made grenades rocked the building and the defenders then hung out a white flag. Just as they were in the process of surrendering to Ashe, a convoy of twenty vehicles with about eighty RIC men were spotted by scouts on a road near the barracks. The Volunteers quickly took up positions to attack the relieving party and a five-hour battle raged until the RIC column surrendered to the numerically inferior Fingal Battalion. Eleven RIC men had been killed and two Volunteers also lost their lives. With a haul of over ninety rifles the Volunteers withdrew from the area and rested the next day, which was Saturday. On Sunday morning an RIC car bearing a white flag was stopped by one of the sentries and thus the order to surrender was conveyed to the Volunteers of Fingal. Ashe and his gallant band surrendered at Swords and were brought in lorries to Dublin's Richmond Barracks.

Thomas Ashe was tried by court martial on 9 May 1916 on the same day as Seán MacDiarmada and Éamon de Valera. All three were sentenced to death by firing squad, but Ashe and de Valera had their sentences commuted to penal servitude for life. At the time, the attorney-general, Lord Glenavy, who was later chairman of the Irish senate, strongly objected to Ashe's reprieve. Within days he was transferred from Kilmainham Gaol to Mountjoy and from there to incarceration in Dartmoor in England on 23 May 1916. Before Christmas 1916 many of the internees from Frongoch were released, but the sentenced men from Dartmoor, including Ashe, were transferred to Lewes Prison near Brighton. At about this period he was appointed president of the Supreme Council of the IRB, the secretive revolutionary body that had been behind the failed rebellion, having organised it from within the ranks of the Irish Volunteers without the knowledge of it chief of staff, Eoin MacNeill.

Failure to be granted political status caused the captives to agitate for recognition as prisoners of war within the jail. The prison authorities decided to move the leaders of the revolt and so Ashe, chained to Piaras Béaslaí, was transferred to Portland Gaol in Dorset. However, anxious to placate growing unrest in Ireland and Irish-American protests, Bonar Law announced the convening of an 'Irish Convention' to air Irish grievances and defuse the political situation. As a gesture towards this aim, Irish prisoners in England were to be released and so Ashe was transferred to Pentonville Prison in London in preparation for release and within days was on the boat to Ireland.

On 20 June 1917, after midnight, Thomas Ashe, Austin Stack and Tadhg Brosnan arrived in Tralee to a tumultuous welcome. Staying in John O'Donnell's house in Ballyard that night, Ashe and Stack set out for West Kerry the next morning. At Lispole Ashe addressed a large welcoming party, before going to his home in Kinard. Later that evening he travelled on to Dingle where, arriving after midnight, he was again greeted by an enthusiastic crowd.

Later that day a telegram reached him in Dingle, summoning him to Clare to canvass for de Valera in the forthcoming by-election. While in Lewes Prison,

Ashe had been selected by the prisoners to stand in this election which had been caused by the death on the Western Front of William Redmond MP, John Redmond's brother. However, it would appear that a vocal influential clique supported de Valera's candidature. Ashe was reluctant to cause disunity and so suggested Clare man Peadar Clancy as a more suitable candidate. However, de Valera won out and his election in the East Clare by-election on 10 July 1917 marked an important milestone in the resurgence of the Republican movement.

Over the next month Ashe travelled the country giving increasingly defiant speeches, as the tide of opinion in Ireland turned in favour of the Republican position and away from Redmond's dominant Irish Party. On 5 August 1917, a year after Casement's execution, a crowd of 10,000 from all over Kerry gathered at McKenna's Fort near Ardfert to hear Ashe give an oration. However, this was to be one of his last public speeches, as a warrant for his arrest had been issued following a seditious speech he had made in Ballinalee, County Longford, in the previous month. Now a wanted man, he stayed in the home of wealthy Brosna-born property developer Batt O'Connor in Donnybrook, Dublin. On 18 August 1917, after just eight weeks of freedom, he was arrested and placed in detention in the Curragh Camp. His sentence for the crime of 'causing disaffection' under the Defence of the Realm Act (DORA) was announced on 11 September and he began to serve two years of hard labour in Mountjoy Gaol. There he was placed in a cell with common criminals and given the task of sewing mail bags. There was to be no political status despite the political nature of the offences which he had been convicted of. A battle of wills began between prisoners like Ashe and the Dublin Castle authorities, who sought to criminalise the Republican struggle.

Following the failure of other methods of agitation, forty Republican prisoners in Mountjoy commenced a hunger strike on 20 September 1917. Three days later the prisoners were being force-fed. This involved being strapped hand and foot in a chair, the mouth being forced open with a wooden spoon and a tube being inserted into the stomach. This process was repeated twice daily. On 25 September Ashe was brought down to the room where Dr Lowe began the ten-minute process of force-feeding, but there was an initial difficulty as the prisoner complained that the tube had gone down the wrong way. However, Dr Lowe denied that the feeding tube was inserted into the trachea in error and recommenced the procedure. Following the end of the process, Ashe was extremely weak and had to be removed to the gaol's hospital in a state of collapse. There was bruising around his neck and mouth, suggesting that the tube had been inserted with undue force. At 2 p.m. Dr Dowdall examined Ashe and found him to be extremely weak. He promised to have him released immediately and two hours later, the prisoner was transferred across the road to the Mater Hospital. There his condition continued to rapidly deteriorate and his family was sent for. A crowd gathered outside the hospital as news spread, with Constance Markievicz and Michael Collins being admitted to visit their dying comrade. At 10.30 p.m. on 25 September in St Raphael's Ward, Thomas Ashe died.

His body was removed to the Pro-Cathedral for requiem mass and from there to the City Hall where it was to lie in state until Sunday 30 September, the day of the burial. Thousands filed past the coffin with its guard of Irish Volunteers. On Sunday the huge funeral procession consisting of armed Irish Volunteers and Citizen Army units, numerous bands and thousands of mourners reached Glasnevin Cemetery at 4 p.m. The oration was due to be given by Fr Dominic, one of the Capuchin friars who attended the 1916 leaders before their executions. However, after the grave was filled and the volley of shots was fired, a relatively unknown Michael Collins stepped forward and announced that 'Nothing additional needs to be said. That volley we have just heard is the only speech which is proper to be made above the grave of a dead Fenian'.[1]

Thomas Ashe is remembered in Kerry by a monument at his birthplace in Kinard. His name is inscribed on the memorials in Dingle and Ballyseedy, and a street and the town's most prominent public building bear his name in Tralee.

In the words of his own poem, Thomas Ashe had 'carried his cross for Ireland'.

---

1   Seán Ó Luing, *I Die in a Good Cause* (1970), p. 175.

Charlie Daly

Cormac Ó Dálaigh

Courtesy of Mercier Archive.

Charles Daly was born in Knockaneculteen, Firies, on 10 August 1896. The Daly family were immersed in the Fenian tradition and in 1913 Con Daly and his three sons founded the Irish Volunteer company in the nearby village of Currans. At Easter 1916 Charlie Daly and his brothers, Tom and Willie, were assigned to blow up the railway bridge at Currans, but this never came to pass as the months of planning for a nationwide rebellion unravelled.[1]

In 1917, as the Volunteer movement was reorganising, Charlie Daly was arrested in Currans following a confrontation with the local RIC. He was detained under the Defence of the Realm Act by RIC Constable Patrick Buckley, who was later killed by Free State forces at Ballyseedy a week before Charlie Daly met a similar fate in Donegal. He was again arrested in 1918 and served a year in Cork Gaol. On his release he became a full-time Volunteer organiser and travelled throughout his native county recruiting and setting in place the structures of a guerrilla army. By late 1919 his efforts were coming to fruition as the Volunteers in Kerry began to attack rural RIC posts and Daly himself was prominent in the attack on the Gortatlea RIC Barracks on 25 March 1920. Shortly afterwards he was brought to Dublin by GHQ to continue his organisational activities there. Again in Dublin he was detained by the police, but was released after he gave a false name and it was only shortly after he was freed that his captors realised their error.

In early 1920 GHQ in Dublin appointed Charlie Daly as an organiser in the County Tyrone district, which had seen little activity in the Tan War as the IRA units there were scattered, ill-equipped and operating in hostile territory.

---

1   Uinseann Mac Eoin, *Survivors* (1980), interview with May Dálaigh, p. 363.

However, the success of his efforts was limited, as there was little enthusiasm for the fight amongst the nationalist population in Tyrone.

When the 2nd Northern Division was formed in April 1921, it was placed under the command of Eoin O'Duffy rather than the more popular Daly, who had been active on the ground for nearly twelve months. However, when O'Duffy became the director of organisation in GHQ later that year, Daly took his place as O/C of the 2nd Northern Division, which included County Tyrone and south County Derry.

While the Truce brought a cessation of warfare in the twenty-six counties, the situation in the six northern counties was different. The RIC had now become the Royal Ulster Constabulary (RUC), and an auxiliary paramilitary section of this force, the B Specials, was also established. They pursued a campaign of harassment and intimidation against the nationalist population to consolidate British control in the north-east. In the spring of 1922 an offensive was planned, whereby IRA units throughout the six counties would attack the crown forces. However, by this time the IRA had begun to divide. Senior figures within the GHQ staff, including Richard Mulcahy and Eoin O'Duffy, supported Michael Collins' pro-Treaty position, while the majority of IRA commanders in the field remained determined to achieve a thirty-two county Republic. As Charlie Daly was implacably opposed to the Treaty, O'Duffy removed him as O/C 2nd Northern Division and replaced him with the ineffectual Tom Morris. Severe dissensions within the staff of the northern divisions arose and, in an attempt to re-establish unity, Seán Lehane of Cork was appointed O/C of the 1st and 2nd Northern Divisions, with Charlie Daly as his deputy.

In May 1922 the general offensive that had been planned in the six counties took place, but in a fragmented and largely ineffectual manner. The IRA units within the six counties had divided; GHQ was financing and arming those units which remained loyal to the new Free State Army, while those serving under the IRA executive command were more determined to confront the crown forces but were short of arms and ammunition. And so, with depleted forces, the IRA units in Tyrone under the command of Charlie Daly took the war to the enemy. However, Daly's meagre forces were soon defeated by the RUC and the active units of the 2nd Northern Division were forced to retreat to the relative safety of Donegal.

Lehane and Daly had augmented their northern forces with almost thirty experienced officers and men from Cork and Kerry. They then began attacking targets across the border on a regular basis. When explaining his position on the Treaty to the officers of the 2nd Northern Division in Dublin, Michael Collins had said that the Treaty might look like an acceptance of partition, but the Free State government would make it impossible for partition to continue in existence by assisting the IRA in its cross-border campaign. However, by late spring, Michael Collins' enthusiasm for supporting a policy of insurrection in the six counties seemed to have waned. The army's GHQ had appointed Joe Sweeney as its O/C in Donegal and his enemies were not the British forces occupying the neighbouring counties, but the IRA units using Donegal as a base to attack the crown forces across the border. Collins' words were beginning to sound hollow.

With the attack on the Four Courts in Dublin on 28 June 1922, the Civil War began. The war quickly spread to Donegal, and with the county's population largely hostile and their men ill-armed and few in number, the IRA units were quickly driven into the hills by Sweeney's superior forces. In small columns they survived in the bogs and hills of the county until October 1922. Republican leader Ernie O'Malley, who commanded the Northern and Western divisions, ordered the Cork and Kerry men to return south, accepting that further resistance in Donegal was futile. On 2 November 1922, when they reached Dunlewy at the foot of Errigal Mountain, Daly's column had dwindled to just eight men. Hungry and exhausted after a march across mountainous boggy terrain, they did not place a sentry when they settled in two houses that evening, as no one was considered fit for the task. In the darkness, at 7 p.m., alerted to the presence of the column by a local informer, a large force of Free State soldiers arrived unexpectedly. Tim O'Sullivan, James Lane, Daniel Coyle, Frank Ward and Charlie Daly were found in one house while Seán Larkin, Dan Enright and James Donaghy were arrested in another nearby. The eight exhausted prisoners were taken to Drumboe Castle at Stranorlar. Lehane and his men reached Donegal town and subsequently managed to escape southwards, reaching Sligo on a commandeered boat.[2]

2   Liam Ó Duibhir, *Donegal & the Civil War* (2011), p. 211.

On 30 November the men captured at Dunlewy were convicted of the possession of weapons before a military tribunal at Drumboe. Subsequently they were sentenced to death by firing squad when brought before the tribunal again on 18 January 1923. Following the killing of a Free State officer in Creeslough in West Donegal, the Free State GHQ ordered that four men – Kerrymen Charlie Daly, Dan Enright and Tim O'Sullivan and Seán Larkin of Derry – be executed. On Wednesday 14 March the four were given the opportunity of a reprieve if they signed a document recognising the Free State's authority and promising not to take up arms against it. All four refused and were taken to the spot near Drumboe Castle, where the monument to the men now stands. There they were executed by a firing squad composed of ex-British soldiers.

Their remains were interred near the scene of their execution. In 1924 the bodies were disinterred and removed to Athlone Military Barracks and over a year after their executions, the remains of the three Kerry Republicans were returned to their families. Charlie Daly was buried in the family plot at Kiltallagh church near Castlemaine in August 1924.

Dan Enright

Domhnall Mac Ionnraċtaiġ

Courtesy of Mercier Archive.

Dan Enright was a native of Listowel, where his father was a cooper. He was born on 18 September 1899 and lived in Charles Street. He was a member of the Listowel Company of the 4th Battalion, Kerry No. 1 Brigade. Late in the Tan War he became a full-time member of the battalion's column, which had been depleted by the deaths of several Volunteers including those killed at Gortaglanna in May 1921. His comrade, Tim O'Sullivan, a native of Aughatubrid near Cahersiveen, but who was living in Listowel, also joined the column at this time. Both men died in front of a Free State firing squad less than two years later, at Drumboe Castle in County Donegal.

The resistance to British rule was fiercest in the counties of Munster. IRA units throughout the province had pushed the British garrison from the countryside and by July 1921 the rule of the crown was only in force in the larger towns and cities. The guerrilla army had become proficient and confident after two years in the field. However, in the northern counties there was a very different military situation prevailing. Poor organisation, lack of local leadership and a hostile environment meant that the IRA had made little impact on British rule in the province of Ulster. Following the Truce of 11 July 1921, IRA GHQ in Dublin turned its attention towards the northern province. Charlie Daly of Kerry was O/C of the 2nd Northern Division and Seán Lehane of West Cork was appointed O/C of the 1st Northern Division, which mainly encompassed the county of Donegal. Lehane and Daly supplemented their meagre and inexperienced fighting forces with thirty hardened Volunteers from the 1st Southern Division.[1] Approximately twenty

---

1   Liam Ó Duibhir, *Donegal & the Civil War* (2011), p. 84.

Volunteers went from Kerry to join Daly and Lehane's efforts to build an army sufficient to continue the war against the British in the six counties. These men mainly came from North Kerry, as the O/C of Kerry No. 2 Brigade, John Joe Rice, was not enthusiastic about sending his best men north, suspecting that the attitude of GHQ was becoming increasingly partitionist despite its public utterances.[2] The Kerry Volunteers who went to aid the northern divisions included Listowel men Dan Enright, Martin Quille, Tim O'Sullivan and Michael McElligott, Christy Broderick of Duagh and Patrick Clifford of Ballymacelligott.

Michael Collins and GHQ, with support from Liam Lynch and the anti-Treaty IRA forces, planned an offensive in May 1922 whereby there would be synchronised attacks on the crown forces throughout the six counties. However, GHQ support was at best half-hearted and the disjointed actions soon caused the offensive to collapse. Charlie Daly's men of the 2nd Northern Division were forced to leave Tyrone and to seek shelter in Donegal. However, the political climate within the twenty-six counties had changed and the Free State Army in Donegal was becoming increasingly hostile to Republican activity in the county. With the outbreak of the Civil War, the IRA was quickly placed on the defensive as Joe Sweeney's Free State forces quickly overcame any sustained Republican resistance. Seán Lehane, Charlie Daly and what few Republican soldiers remained were forced to divide into small columns that sought refuge in the mountains and bogs of a countryside that was mostly hostile or apathetic.

By early November 1922, with little local support and no hope of any meaningful resistance, Ernie O'Malley, IRA commander for the northern and eastern divisions, authorised Lehane and Daly to evacuate Donegal and head south with what little of their command remained. Daly's column was to move to Dromkeen and there link up with Lehane's men, then head south to Sligo. Two local Donegal men on the column had arranged for Daly and his small band to stay in two cottages at Dunlewy. Daly, Tim O'Sullivan, James Lane of Clonakilty, and Frank Ward and Daniel Coyle, both of Donegal, stayed in one house. In the other house nearby were Seán Larkin, Dan Enright and James

---

2   Ernie O'Malley, *The Men Will Talk to Me – Kerry Interviews* (2012), interview with Bertie Scully.

Donaghy. That evening, 2 November 1922, acting on information received from a local informer, the column was captured by Free State forces.

Enright and the others were placed in a lorry and brought to Falcarragh Barracks and the next day they were transferred to Drumboe Castle, a large period house on the outskirts of Stranorlar. The captured Republicans were tried before a military tribunal on 30 November 1922. They were convicted and on 18 January 1923 a sentence of death by firing squad was passed on the eight men. Following an incident in Creeslough Barracks in which a soldier was killed in unexplained circumstances on 10 March, the Free State Army GHQ ordered that four men be executed in reprisal. Enright, Daly, O'Sullivan and Larkin were chosen to die. When presented with a document to sign accepting the legitimacy of the Free State government on the day of their execution, 14 March 1923, the four men refused to compromise their principles and declined to sign it, though it would have brought them a reprieve. They went to face a firing squad composed of former British soldiers serving under General Joe Sweeney, the Free State military commander in Donegal.[3]

Dan Enright and his three comrades were buried near where they were executed but their remains were disinterred in August 1924 and brought to Athlone Military Barracks. From there Enright's remains were returned to his native town, where they now lie in the Republican Plot in Listowel Cemetery.

Today Daly, Enright, O'Sullivan and Larkin are remembered by a monument in Drumboe, which to this day remains the focus of Republican commemoration in County Donegal. The Drumboe Martyrs are immortalised in the iconic Republican ballad of the Civil War 'Take It Down from the Mast', in the lines:

> *For we stand with Enright and Larkin,*
> *With Daly and Sullivan, the bold,*
> *We'll break down the English connection*
> *And bring back the nation you sold.*

---

3 Liam Ó Duibhir, *Donegal & the Civil War* (2011), p. 228.

Tom Healy

Tomás Ó hÉalaigthe[1]

Tom Healy was from Lios an Iarla, a townland three miles to the north of Tralee. As a young man he had joined the RIC and during the Black and Tan War he was stationed in Ennis, County Clare, where he was a clerk to the district inspector of the RIC. Being sympathetic with the Republican cause he passed information to the local Volunteers and this proved to be extremely valuable in their fight with the crown forces. Eventually his sympathies and clandestine activities came under suspicion from his colleagues and as a result he defected from the RIC to the local Mid-Clare Brigade of the IRA.

Local reconnaissance had noted that the RIC regularly sent a patrol through the grounds of Carrigoran House near Newmarket-on-Fergus. Acting on this information, on Friday 17 June 1921 a column of twenty Volunteers commanded by Jim Hannon from Quin prepared an ambush at the gate of the demesne for this large patrol. On the day of the proposed attack, the IRA scouts lying in wait a little distance from the ambush site at Carrigoran were surprised by the RIC patrol which opened fire on them. Hearing the shooting in the distance, the ambush party hurriedly withdrew from their positions, firing on the RIC as they disengaged. Having retreated from Carrigoran, they arrived at Craggalough in Rossroe, some two miles away. However, there they were intercepted by a detachment of Black and Tans who had come from Sixmilebridge, having been alerted by the Newmarket-on-Fergus RIC of the attack that had occurred earlier. A firefight developed as the Tans pursued the IRA column while it retreated up the sloping fields, the Volunteers shooting as they went. One of the Tans was wounded as they advanced up the hill, whereupon his comrades broke off the engagement. IRA Volunteer Tom Healy, though not wounded by gunfire, died during the retreat and was suspected of having a heart attack. His body was taken to John Moloney's farm nearby, a strongly Republican household. Then the column commander, Jim Hannon, marched his men off in the direction of Quin.[2]

1   There is no known photograph of Tom Healy.
2   Pádraig Óg Ó Ruairc, *Blood on the Banner – The Republican Struggle in Clare* (2009), p. 254.

The next day, Saturday 18 June 1921, Tom Healy's remains were brought to Ennis cathedral. There was a concelebrated funeral mass attended by a large crowd. The chief mourners were his wife and two young children. On the following Monday the coffin was brought by train to Tralee and laid to rest in the family grave at Clogherbrien, two miles from Tralee on the Fenit road.

In the 1940s a fund was established to erect a monument at Meelick in County Clare to remember three local IRA Volunteers. This collection was oversubscribed and in recognition of Tom Healy's services and sacrifice in the fight for Irish freedom in his adopted county, the Clare committee decided that the surplus be used to place a monument over the grave of their comrade at Clogherbrien.[3] This was unveiled on Sunday 1 August 1948 by Charles Turner, following a parade led by a pipe band from Tralee's Ashe Memorial Hall. Tom Healy's niece, Kathleen Healy, laid a wreath during the ceremony, which was attended by many of his comrades from the East Clare Brigade.[4] Today this small monument stands over his grave indicating his rank and where this Volunteer died in action on Friday 17 June 1921.

---

3   Information from Pádraig Óg Ó Ruairc, author of *Blood on the Banner*.
4   *The Kerryman*, 24 July 1948 and 7 August 1948.

Jim Hickey

Séamus Ó hÍceada

The townland of Ballinatin lies in the parish of Knocknagoshel and along the Castleisland to Abbeyfeale road. Half hidden by trees and long since abandoned lies a cottage and it was to this refuge that Ireland's most wanted men arrived in the summer of 1919.[1] On 21 January that year Dan Breen, Seán Treacy, Seán Hogan and six others ambushed and killed two RIC men at Soloheadbeg in County Tipperary. They captured the policemen's weapons and the explosives that they had been escorting to a quarry near Tipperary town. This episode is generally taken to be the start of the Black and Tan War and it resulted in an intensive manhunt for the Volunteers involved. One of them, Seán Hogan, was captured and brought to Thurles RIC Barracks. On 13 May 1919, as he was being transferred from there to Cork by train and under armed guard, he was rescued at Knocklong Station by Dan Breen, Seán Treacy and six other Volunteers. The search for the South Tipperary men became even more intense and having been wounded in the rescue, Breen and Treacy left their native area, wanted men with a price on their heads. Travelling across south County Limerick, they found refuge in the Hickey farm in Ballinatin, Knocknagoshel. This was the childhood home of James Hickey and it was there that Breen recuperated from his wounds and went on to continue what he would later describe in his book as *My Fight for Irish Freedom*.[2]

Courtesy of Martin O'Dwyer.

Jim Hickey was born in this house in 1893, but as a young man he went to earn his living as a draper's assistant in the Arcade in Tipperary town. There he lived at 31 Main Street. In his adopted home he joined the Irish Volunteers and

1   Information from James Hickey, Ballinatin.
2   Dan Breen, *My Fight for Irish Freedom* (1924), p. 105.

in May 1918 he is recorded as being the captain of 'B' Company, one of two IRA companies in his adopted town which were attached to the 4th Battalion of Tipperary's 3rd Brigade, one of the most active units in Ireland during the Tan War. Thus he came in contact with the men who sought shelter in his parents' farm in the summer of 1919.

As a result of his Republican activities he was arrested just before Christmas 1920 and held in the large military barracks in Tipperary town. While in custody he was killed, apparently being stabbed with a bayonet by his captors. A British Army enquiry into his death reported that he had attacked the soldiers guarding him in an attempt to escape. This explanation was often used to explain the deaths of men who were killed in military custody. The same excuse was offered by the British military when William O'Brien from near Rathmore met the same fate in the same barracks later in the Tan War.

Captain Jim Hickey died in Tipperary, far from his Knocknagoshel home, on St Stephen's Day 1920. His remains were released to his family and brought back to Ballinatin. The funeral mass was held in Abbeyfeale and Captain Hickey is buried in the family plot in Dysert Cemetery, two miles south of Castleisland.[3] He is remembered on the Tipperary 3rd Brigade memorial in Saint Michael's Cemetery in Tipperary town and on a plaque on the remaining wall of the demolished military barracks in the town.

3   *The Freeman's Journal*, 2 January 1921.

Charlie Kerins

Cathal Ó Céirín

Charles Kerins was born in Caheranne in the Strand Road district of Tralee on 23 January 1918. His father, Tom Kerins, was a builder in the town and his mother, Johanna Griffin of Blennerville, died when Charlie was still very young. He was educated by the Christian Brothers and was awarded a scholarship. He used this to complete a commercial course and worked in Fennell's radio shop in Ashe Street, Tralee. An excellent footballer, he won a county championship medal with O'Rahilly's Gaelic Football Club in 1939.

From a Republican family, twenty-two-year-old Charlie joined the IRA in the town in 1940. In May 1942 he was appointed to the headquarters staff in Dublin and he left his employment to go and live in the capital. In 1932 Republicans had had high hopes following the election of what was described as 'a slightly constitutional' Fianna Fáil party, which replaced the pro-Treaty party that had prosecuted a bloody civil war a decade previously. However, as de Valera consolidated political power during the 1930s, his initial Republican policies were significantly diluted and he adopted broad populist economic policies, thereby maintaining his political power within the twenty-six counties. His enemies became not the British or their Free State allies, but those Republicans who would not accept partition and remained outside his control. An Emergency Powers Act was passed which introduced draconian measures, censoring the media and suppressing public protest. Following the outbreak of the Second World War, internment without trial was introduced and hundreds of Republicans were incarcerated in the Curragh as they had been in the Tan War by the British and during the Civil War by the Free State government. De Valera was to ensure that England's difficulty was not again to prove Ireland's opportunity.

Courtesy of Declan Horgan.

With little public support and hounded by the Broy Harriers, a special force of gardaí that de Valera had recruited from former IRA Volunteers from the Tan War, the ranks of the Republican Army quickly dwindled. Mountjoy, Arbour Hill and Portlaoise Gaols were filled with political prisoners, as was the internment camp in the Curragh. With few active Republicans still at liberty, Charlie Kerins rose quickly through the ranks and was appointed chief of staff of a depleted and scattered army in 1942.

Charlie Kerins' fate will always be linked to that of Dublin-born Denis O'Brien, a veteran of the 1916 Rising, and the Tan and Civil Wars. His brother, Paddy, had been a senior officer in the Four Courts garrison in 1922 and was subsequently killed by Free State forces in Enniscorthy in July of that year. Denis (Dinny) O'Brien initially worked as a clerk but was recruited into the Garda Síochána in 1933 as part of a group of IRA veterans under the command of Éamonn Broy. Broy, with David Neligan, had been one of those detectives who had supplied information from Dublin Castle to Michael Collins during the Tan War and he subsequently joined the IRA. He was placed in command of a special police unit which was ostensibly set up to counter the threat of the fascist Blue Shirt movement, but de Valera subsequently directed its attention to the unit's former comrades in the remnants of the IRA, which was uncompromising in its aim of ridding Ireland of the British presence. O'Brien, who had been a member of the IRA until he was recruited by Broy, quickly gained a reputation based on the vigour with which he pursued Republican activists. He was implicated in the shooting of several IRA members and the ill-treatment of political prisoners. Such was his reputation that a four-man group of IRA Volunteers took the unusual step of setting out to shoot him, although he was a member of the twenty-six county police force.

On the morning of 9 September 1942, Detective Dinny O'Brien left his home in his car and was heading towards Ballyboden in South Dublin. He was ambushed by four armed men and although he managed to get out of his car, he was fatally wounded in the shooting that ensued and died on the roadside. The four attackers left the scene on bicycles and evaded capture, despite a massive manhunt. Subsequently, Listowel Republican, Michael Quille, who had been captured by the RUC in Belfast, was handed over to the Free State government to face trial before a military court for the killing of O'Brien.

However, the evidence of a garda witness did not stand up to scrutiny and Quille was acquitted. Following this the military court rules were amended to make convictions easier.

At 5 a.m. on 15 June 1944, acting on information from an informer, Charlie Kerins was arrested at the home of Dr Kathleen Murphy in the Upper Rathmines Road. Before a special military tribunal on 2 October he was charged with the killing of Detective Dinny O'Brien two years earlier. The only evidence produced against him was that his fingerprint was found on a bicycle located near the scene of the ambush. However, it could not be shown that the bicycle was connected with the shooting. The bullets found at the scene were not from Kerins' gun and none of the witnesses who had seen the attackers flee could identify him. Charlie Kerins refused to recognise the military tribunal and he was convicted on the merest of circumstantial evidence of a killing that he had no part in. He was sentenced to death by hanging and refused leave to appeal.[1]

A groundswell of support to prevent the unjust execution was dealt with harshly on the street, by the censored media and in Dáil Éireann. The accepted opinion was that de Valera was determined that somebody would pay for the death of O'Brien, and Kerins was the obvious victim as he was the IRA chief of staff. Grounds for clemency were overwhelming, but the case fell on deaf ears, which was rather ironic as de Valera had himself been the beneficiary of British clemency when he was to be executed following a similar trial by military court in 1916. Charlie Kerins was hanged on Friday 1 December 1944 in Mountjoy Gaol by the English executioner Albert Pierrepoint, who was brought from Britain to carry out the task. He was accompanied to the gallows by Fr John Moloney, who later recalled the fortitude of the young patriot as he went to his death. Like Kevin Barry twenty-four years earlier, he had been refused a soldier's death by firing squad as this would have been seen to give legitimacy to the Republican cause.

Just as the British did in the case of the executed Kevin Barry, the de Valera government refused to give the remains to Kerins' family for a proper burial. Instead he was buried in the grounds of Mountjoy Gaol until the Fianna Fáil

---

1   Uinseann Mac Eoin, *The IRA in the Twilight Years 1925–1948* (1997).

government fell in 1948. The coalition government, of which the republican party, Clann na Poblacta, was a member, returned the remains to his family. On 18 September 1948 large crowds lined the towns and villages along the road from Dublin to Kerry as the remains of Charlie Kerins and Cahersiveen man Maurice O'Neill, who had been executed in 1942, made their way home. The hearses finally reached Tralee at 10 p.m. that evening and were brought to St John's parish church to repose overnight. The next day a huge funeral procession followed Charlie Kerins' coffin to the Republican Plot in Rath Cemetery. There proceedings were presided over by John Joe Sheehy, with Kerins' comrade Michael Quille of Listowel reciting a decade of the rosary. The oration was given by Tomás MacCurtain, who had also been sentenced to death by the de Valera government. Significance was given to the fact that Kerins' remains were laid in the north-eastern corner of the plot, as Kerins had died to free the northern-eastern part of Ireland.

A monument, erected in 1947, now stands in his honour in a public park on Strand Street, Tralee, and later the town's council named a housing estate in his honour. The local GAA club amended its name to Kerins O'Rahilly's to commemorate their former player.

MICHAEL MULVIHILL

Mícéál Ó Maoilmicíl

Michael Mulvihill was born in Ardoughter near Ballyduff in 1879. His father was the principal teacher in the Ballincrossig National School near Ballyduff, while his mother, Mary O'Connor, came from Kilmore, Ballyduff. Michael was one of nine children born into this family, which had a very strong Fenian tradition. His father's political convictions ran contrary to those of the parish priest and a dispute forced John Mulvihill from his teaching post in 1903.[1]

Courtesy of the Martin Moore collection.

Michael finished his primary education and, as was common at the time, he left for London in search of a job commensurate with his educational achievements. While employed in a number of posts there, he went to evening classes and eventually passed the civil service examination, thus securing a public service appointment in London. He was deeply involved in the Irish cultural and political movements that were flourishing in that city from the turn of the century. He became a member of the London Corps of the Irish Volunteers on their foundation and there he kept company with Dinny Daly of Cahersiveen, Austin Kennan of Dublin who was his brother-in-law, Michael and Seán McGrath of Longford, and Michael Collins of County Cork. Michael Mulvihill returned home to Ardoughter each year to visit his family.

With the expectation of a rising in 1916, many members of the London-Irish Volunteers returned to Dublin and were billeted in Larkfield Manor, Kimmage. The Plunkett family had leased a large mill and considerable surrounding land there and they established a training camp for the Volunteers. Those men who had come to Larkfield from the Volunteer companies in British cities were

---

1   Cecilia Lynch, *From the GPO to Clashmealcon Caves* (2003), p. 226.

termed the 'Kimmage Garrison'. Michael Mulvihill had decided to remain in London for some time after many of his Volunteer comrades there had moved to Dublin. However, with the threat of conscription hanging over him, Mulvihill did return to Ireland for a holiday at Easter 1916 and stayed in Dublin at the Kincora Hotel under his mother's maiden name to avoid detection by the police. Mulvihill and another Irish Volunteer who had come from England, Austin Kennan, did meet Dinny Daly, a Cahersiveen man in the London Volunteers staying at Kimmage, but there was no definite plan for a rising and so the pair decided not to stay in Kimmage with the rest of the London Volunteers but remain in their city centre lodgings. The countermanding order on Easter Sunday caused further confusion and it was only when Mulvihill and Kennan saw the rebel army marching up O'Connell Street on Easter Monday that they entered its ranks. Apparently Dinny Daly saw them as they walked along the footpath and shouted to them 'This is revolution.' The pair joined the ranks immediately and became part of the GPO garrison. They were posted in the front central area of the roof and were under continuous fire until Thursday, when the bombardment became too intense. Austin Kennan and Michael Mulvihill were then given different positions on the ground floor. However, the following day, Friday, the GPO was ablaze and Patrick Pearse gave the order to evacuate the building.

Kennan and Michael McGrath went with 'The O'Rahilly' as he attempted to break through the British lines at the upper end of Moore Street but, unlike the Ballylongford man, both of them survived. Michael Mulvihill was with a different unit in the same area and how exactly he was killed is not recorded. His body was found at the junction of Moore Lane and Henry Place and identified by an RIC officer from his native Ardoughter, the same man who had identified the body of 'The O'Rahilly'.[2]

Michael Mulvihill's remains were interred in the 1916 Plot in St Paul's Cemetery, Glasnevin, where he is listed with the London Corps of the Irish Volunteers. Today his old home in Ardoughter bears a plaque in his honour. The local Ballyduff GAA Club also commemorates him in their official name: The Ballyduff Michael Mulvihill Hurling Club.

2   Ray Bateson, *They Died by Pearse's Side* (2010), p. 226.

Seán O'Leary

Seán Ó Laoġaire

Seán O'Leary was born in Ballydribeen, Killarney, in 1899. His father worked as a clerk with the Mental Health Board in what is now St Finian's Psychiatric Hospital. For a short period Seán O'Leary worked with the Mental Health Board in Killarney until he took up a post with the Munster and Leinster Bank in Kilkenny in 1917. He was subsequently transferred to County Clare where he became involved in the Irish Volunteers. A year later his employment with the bank took him to Nenagh, Co. Tipperary. From a nationalist family, O'Leary was active in the Nenagh Company of the Tipperary No. 1 Brigade from 1919 onwards. In January of that year he was one of six Volunteers who destroyed a British lorry at a garage in the town and subsequently commandeered an RIC 'Black Maria', which they later destroyed. By 1920 suspicion had fallen on him and on 25 October his lodgings were searched by armed masked men who were probably an RIC unit that had begun to use such methods to kill Republican activists. He was not at the house when it was raided and subsequently, fearing for his life, he went 'on the run', joining the active service unit of the Tipperary No. 1 Brigade. This column of about eighteen men was responsible for many attacks on the crown forces in the North Tipperary area.[1]

Courtesy of Mercier Archive.

On Holy Saturday 1921 plans were made to free IRA Volunteer Paddy McCarthy from Nenagh Hospital. McCarthy was from near Kilmallock and had come to live in Nenagh a short time previously. He had told the local IRA that he was a senior officer in County Limerick, which was later found to be an exaggeration. He had been arrested and brought to Nenagh RIC Barracks.

---

1 Edward John Ryan of Nenagh, BMH WS 1392.

While a prisoner there, McCarthy claimed to be ill and was taken to the local workhouse hospital. It was from there that the Nenagh IRA Company planned to rescue him. A military guard was expected to be posted at the hospital to prevent the patient escaping. That night Seán O'Leary, Edward Ryan, Christopher Gaynor and Jim O'Meara managed to get McCarthy out of the hospital before sentries could be organised. They brought him to Laughton, near Moneygall, ten miles to the east. They stayed in a dugout that night and the next day went to the home of the Mangan family who were Republican sympathisers. From there, O'Leary, with Joe Mangan, Ryan, the ill McCarthy and Tom Waters, walked off to visit Pat O'Brien. O'Brien, from Silvermines, was a leading IRA officer in the North Tipperary area and a member of the active service unit. He was a teacher by profession and following the Civil War he made his home in Tralee.

Tom Waters, from Cork, had been working in the shipyards in Belfast. He had been on active service in the Belfast area and soon became a wanted man in his adopted city. He therefore moved to Nenagh, where he worked installing electricity in the town until one day he narrowly avoided being captured by the same undercover RIC unit that came for Seán O'Leary. Like the Killarney man, Waters subsequently went 'on the run' and joined Ned O'Leary's Tipperary No. 1 Brigade column.[2]

At Easter 1921 Pat O'Brien was recuperating from pneumonia in a house near Moneygall. Apparently Seán O'Leary was suffering from toothache and Waters knew a dentist in Nenagh and had arranged that the dentist would treat O'Leary in Moneygall on Easter Sunday afternoon, while the others met with O'Brien nearby.

The five men travelled without their weapons as they were aware that the area was regularly patrolled by the crown forces. As they made their way to the dentist that Easter Sunday, Joe Mangan, O'Leary, Waters, Edward John Ryan and McCarthy, who 'was not as ill as he had pretended', were surprised by three lorries containing Auxiliaries as they walked past the village's medical dispensary.[3] This Auxiliary patrol had entered Moneygall from Roscrea, travelling along the main Dublin to Limerick road. The convoy spotted the

2   *Nenagh Guardian*, 2 January 1938. Tribute to Seán O'Leary by Tom Waters.
3   Edward John Ryan of Nenagh, BMH WS 1392.

five-man group as they ran for cover. The only shelter was the ditch beside the dispensary and three of the men ran towards this while Waters and O'Leary ran into a field on the other side of the road. The Auxiliaries fired on the fleeing men and O'Leary and Waters were wounded as they ran through the field. Ryan and McCarthy were captured, but Joe Mangan escaped.

As O'Leary and Waters lay injured in the field, some of the Auxiliaries wanted to kill their prisoners, but the officer in charge ordered that they be medically treated and first aid was then administered. Waters had been shot in the hip but O'Leary's wounds were more severe. The Auxiliaries brought them to the Nenagh RIC Barracks where they were verbally abused by a Wexford RIC constable named Kane, who triumphantly declared that 'We have got ye at last.' The wounded men were transferred to Nenagh Hospital, where O'Leary died of his wounds later that day. Waters survived, though his injuries invalided him for the remainder of his life.

The remains of Volunteer Seán O'Leary were brought to his native Killarney, where he is buried in his family grave in Muckross Abbey. It was to this scenic graveyard that the men from the 1st Tipperary Brigade came on 9 April 1922, during the Truce, to pay their last respects to their comrade. Before they departed on the long journey home that Sunday evening, they fired a volley of shots in salute.[4]

Today the bridge over the River Flesk on the Muckross Road on the outskirts of Killarney town, which was opened in 1968, is named in honour of Seán O'Leary, who died of his wounds in Nenagh on 30 March 1921. He is also recalled on the North Tipperary Republican monument in Nenagh, which was unveiled by Frank Ryan in 1931.

4   *Nenagh Guardian*, 15 April 1922.

Maurice O'Neill

Muiŗir Ó Néill

Courtesy of Declan Horgan

Maurice O'Neill was born in 1917 at Letter, two miles south of Cahersiveen. He was from a strongly Republican family and enlisted in the local IRA company; he was later appointed its captain. Though the Republican Army was only a pale shadow of what it was in the Black and Tan War, it was still inspired by the ideals of 1916 and the necessity of removing the British presence from all of Ireland's thirty-two counties. In 1939 IRA activists travelled to Britain and initiated a campaign of bombing military and commercial targets, but this caused its ranks to become severely depleted due to widespread arrests and, as the clouds of war gathered in Europe, the IRA's campaign failed in its aims. In 1940, as the Second World War progressed, there were widespread arrests and internment of Republicans both north and south of the border. Despite this, the belief that Britain's difficulty was Ireland's opportunity still prevailed among certain elements and in 1942 plans were made to launch an offensive along the border with the six counties.

IRA activists were brought to Dublin from throughout the twenty-six counties to support the planned campaign. On 2 September 1942 Maurice O'Neill arrived in the city and was attached to the IRA headquarters staff. This small band of Republicans was constantly on the run from the special branch. Initially O'Neill was not known to the police and could move about the city freely, but it is probable that his absence from Cahersiveen was noted by the local garda and it would seem that eventually his movements in Dublin were monitored. In mid-October 1942 he was staying in a safe house belonging to the Kelly family in 14 Holly Road, Donnycarney, on Dublin's north side. With him was Harry White, a senior IRA officer from Belfast whom the special branch were anxious to capture or kill. O'Neill and White had been staying in the house for only five days when a Republican courier, Maggie O'Halloran, came to warn them late on the evening of 29 October that the house was no longer safe. Unknown to her, the Kelly family home was already surrounded by detectives and there was also a detachment of soldiers in support of the armed police. White and O'Neill left to collect their bicycles at the lane to the rear of the house, unaware that there were armed special branch officers hidden there also. As they entered the narrow lane there was a shout to halt and then, without warning, the fleeing IRA officers were fired upon. Harry White returned fire and jumped into a neighbouring garden, while Maurice O'Neill, who had fired five shots from his Webley revolver, retreated towards the Kellys' house. In the front of the house Superintendent Seán Gantly and Detectives Mordaunt, Gill and Foley had waited until Maggie O'Halloran had come out through the front door before they rushed in. Detective George Mordaunt rushed through the house and into the back garden and then into the neighbouring gardens as he pursued White. O'Neill, unable to escape via the back lane, was arrested by Gantly when he reached the house. Meanwhile, White made his way through a neighbouring house and out onto the main road, where he was fired on by a detective with a machine gun. He continued to run and escaped into Clontarf Golf Club, narrowly evading his captors.[1]

The next day one of the detectives returned to the scene to locate a fountain pen that he had dropped during the incident. While searching for it in a neighbouring garden, he discovered the body of Detective Mordaunt, who had been shot through the head.

Maurice O'Neill was charged with firing a gun while resisting arrest when he was brought before a special court composed of military officers in Collins Barracks on 2 November 1942. O'Neill was given only three days to prepare a defence for the capital charge, a period which was wholly inadequate. His lawyer, Seán MacBride, argued that his client had only fired to preserve his own life when he was shot at by unidentified gunmen. It became apparent that whoever shot Mordaunt, a former Free State soldier who had joined the special branch, it was not Maurice O'Neill. Although a regular court would, on balance, have come to a different verdict, the object of this specially constituted

1   Uinseann Mac Eoin, *Harry* (1986), p. 118.

tribunal was to subvert natural justice and so O'Neill was sentenced to be shot by firing squad in Mountjoy Gaol. The perception was that O'Neill was to be executed for a killing that he could not have carried out, but he was to pay the price that the Fianna Fáil government demanded. An appeal went to de Valera, the taoiseach, who rejected it, and so Maurice O'Neill was executed by firing squad on the morning of 12 November 1942 by soldiers of the Irish Army under the command of a Captain Fitzgerald who was from Kerry. The Fianna Fáil government then refused to release the remains to the O'Neill family and so his coffin was buried in Mountjoy. In a further act of cruelty, his last letters were not allowed to be delivered to his family in Cahersiveen.

In 1948 Fianna Fáil lost power and a coalition government in which O'Neill's lawyer, Seán MacBride, was a minister, released the remains of the two Kerrymen executed by the de Valera administration. Large crowds lined the villages and towns as the hearse carrying the remains of Maurice O'Neill and Charlie Kerins made its way from Dublin to Kerry. Just before midnight on 18 September the funeral reached Cahersiveen and the remains reposed in the parish church overnight. The next day, Sunday 19 September 1948, thousands attended O'Neill's burial at Kilnavarnogue Cemetery, where armed IRA Volunteers fired three volleys over their comrade's grave.

Captain Maurice O'Neill was twenty-five years old when he was executed. His name is inscribed on the Cahersiveen monument to local soldiers of the Republic who died for the cause of Irish freedom. He is also remembered in a popular ballad recalling his life. A North Kerry hurling club was named Crotta O'Neills in his honour, as is the large bridge linking Valentia Island to the mainland near Maurice O'Neill's home.

Michael Rahilly (The O'Rahilly)

Míceál Ó Raṫaille

Michael Rahilly was born in Ballylongford on 22 April 1875, the son of Richard Rahilly, a prosperous merchant in the town, and his wife, Ellen Mangan of Shanagolden, County Limerick. Richard Rahilly was a justice of the peace and a constitutional nationalist. Michael Rahilly's initial education was in the local national school, where he was taught by Patrick O'Connor, a native of Dingle and an Irish language enthusiast. In 1890 Michael Rahilly went to Clongowes Wood College in County Kildare for three years. This Jesuit-run boarding school catered for the sons of the professional and business families of the emerging prosperous Catholic middle classes of post-famine Ireland. The ethos of the school was unashamedly West British. From there he went to study medicine in Dublin, but ill health forced him to return home to Ballylongford and he abandoned his university education. In 1899, while in New York, he married Nancy Browne, the daughter of a wealthy Irish-American businessman. The couple had met when she visited Ballylongford some years earlier while on a tour of Europe. Initially settling in Dublin, the Rahilly family subsequently moved to Philadelphia, where Michael worked in his father-in-law's business. They returned to Ireland in 1909 and bought a house in the fashionable Herbert Park in Ballsbridge, Dublin.

In the early years of the century Michael Rahilly's political views began to change and he wrote a series of articles for the separatist newspaper *The United Irishman*. On his return from Philadelphia he threw himself wholeheartedly into the fledgling Sinn Féin movement. At this stage he had taken an interest in the old Irish clans and their coats of arms. As a counter to the awarding by the crown of titles to its Irish subjects, some prominent nationalists in the era

Courtesy of Mercier Archive.

of the Young Irelanders had taken on old Gaelic titles. Following this fashion, Michael Rahilly declared himself 'The O'Rahilly' and used the title consistently from 1909. He joined the Gaelic League and was appointed to its *coiste gnótha* or executive council and in 1913 he took over the running of the League's increasingly political newspaper *An Claidheamh Soluis*. In November 1913 it was he who sent out the invitations to the meeting in Wynn's Hotel that resulted in the formation of the Irish Volunteers two weeks later at a rally at the Rotunda. On its foundation, The O'Rahilly was appointed national treasurer to the Irish Volunteer movement and retained that post until his death during the 1916 Rising.

The Irish Volunteers quickly grew to a force of around 180,000, but John Redmond's demand in 1914 that the organisation become part of Britain's war effort caused a split. About 10,000 remained loyal to the Irish Volunteers, but the vast majority broke away to form the National Volunteers under Redmond's leadership and many of these died in the war with Germany. The O'Rahilly, though on the executive of the Irish Volunteers, was not a member of the secretive IRB, which was gaining an increasingly influential role within the movement.

By late 1914 an IRB group within the Irish Volunteers, led by Patrick Pearse, Seán MacDiarmada, Joseph Plunkett and Tom Clarke, were planning for the rebellion that would occur eighteen months later. In April 1916, with an arms shipment due to arrive from Germany, the Irish Volunteers were ready to rise on Easter Sunday. However, the chief of staff of the movement, Eoin MacNeill, and executive members Bulmer Hobson and The O'Rahilly were all opposed to the rebellion taking place and they were largely unaware of the plan for the insurrection devised by the IRB clique within the leadership. When, in the days immediately before the Rising, MacNeill, essentially a figurehead in the Volunteers, was made aware of the proposed rebellion, he set about trying to thwart the plans of the military council. On Easter Saturday he issued a countermanding order which was delivered to the Volunteer units throughout the country and it was also carried in the national newspapers. At 2 a.m. on Easter Sunday The O'Rahilly set out for Limerick, arriving there with MacNeill's countermanding order at 5 a.m. From there, Lieutenant Patrick Whelan brought the order to the Kerry Volunteers. The O'Rahilly then

Michael Rahilly (The O'Rahilly)

returned to Dublin and visited Liberty Hall, convinced despite all the activity there that the Rising was not to be. That evening, exhausted, he returned home to Herbert Park, but was woken the following morning by Desmond Fitzgerald with news that the Irish Volunteers had mobilised in open rebellion. Putting his allegiance to the Irish Volunteers ahead of his personal loyalty to MacNeill, he hurriedly drove to Liberty Hall, where he was greeted by a surprised Pearse and Connolly. His car was then loaded with weapons and brought to the GPO, where he was given command of the roof section of the garrison.

By Friday evening the situation in the GPO was hopeless, as flames had begun to spread to the inside of the building. This necessitated its evacuation, and at 8 p.m. the advance party left a side entrance in an attempt to proceed up Moore Street. The O'Rahilly volunteered to lead this group, which also contained Paddy Shortis of Ballybunion and Dinny Daly of Cahersiveen. On reaching the bottom of the Moore Street they found that the other end of their escape route had a barricade manned by British soldiers with machine guns. The O'Rahilly's group divided into two sections, each advancing up towards the barricade along the two sides of the street. Moving swiftly, the Volunteers had reached about halfway along Moore Street when they were met by fierce gunfire from the barricade some fifty yards in front of them. The O'Rahilly and his men sheltered in doorways and subsequently emerged to charge up the street again towards the enemy, who were only thirty yards away. He survived a second burst of machine-gun fire and found shelter at the doorway of 24 Moore Street, Kelly's fish shop, near to the entry of what is now called O'Rahilly Parade. Drawing his sword and with a pistol in his other hand, he emerged with his men behind him to launch a final charge on the British position. As he did the gunfire gravely wounded him in the hip and killed his comrades, Paddy Shortis from Ballybunion and Harry Coyle of Dublin. Despite his injuries, he managed to crawl the few yards to the entrance of Sackville Lane. He could go no further and while lying there further shots from the soldiers hit him in the abdomen.

A fellow Volunteer, Tom Crimmins, managed to crawl to his side but was unable to help or move him and so The O'Rahilly told him to move back to a safe position. Suffering from an extensive loss of blood and barely conscious, The O'Rahilly managed to write a final message to his wife on a piece of paper and he put it in his chest pocket. At midnight, nearly four hours later, a woman in a nearby house attempted to come to his aid, but she was shot at by the military. The next day, at 3.45 p.m., Patrick Pearse and Nurse Elizabeth O'Farrell passed the unconscious O'Rahilly as they went to surrender to General Lowe.

When peace had returned to Moore Street, a British Army ambulance came by to remove the dead from the street. On board was a Dublin man who had volunteered to assist the ambulance crews. When this man approached The O'Rahilly, he was still barely alive, but the assistant was ordered by the military to leave the unconscious man there as they would prefer him to be dead rather than have to deal with a grievously injured Volunteer officer. However, unknown to the soldiers, the Dubliner removed the note that the dying man had placed in his pocket and saw that it was delivered to Nannie O'Rahilly at 40 Herbert Park. The British officer removed The O'Rahilly's chain, watch and seal ring and kept these for himself. A short time later, the Ballylongford man died, some twenty-four hours after being shot.

The O'Rahilly was the only member of the executive of the Irish Volunteers to be killed in action during the Rising. His family initially wished him to be buried in his native Ballylongford. However, some senior rebel leaders who were still at large persuaded them to have him buried in Glasnevin, as he was the only figure amongst the leadership of the Volunteers who might be buried there, as the bodies of the other soon to be executed leaders would not be released to their families for public funerals.[1]

Today The O'Rahilly is remembered in Moore Street by an impressive large bronze plaque which is a replica of his dying letter to his wife. In Ballylongford his birthplace is commemorated by a plaque on his family home and in Tralee his memory is kept alive in the name of one of the town's GAA teams, Kerins O'Rahilly's.

---

1 Áine Rahilly, BMH WS 333. Part of the sentence of executed men at this time was that their remains would be buried in prison grounds.

Tim O'Sullivan

Tadg Ó Súilleabáin

Tim O'Sullivan's parents met in New York. His father, Michael O'Sullivan, was from Aghatubrid near Cahersiveen, while his mother, Nora Kennedy, was a native of Asdee. They returned to Aghatubrid and bought a small farm where they lived with their nine children. Tim was the oldest boy and was born in 1900. However, on the death of Michael, economic necessity required that the farm be sold and Nora O'Sullivan bought a house at 44 William Street, Listowel, where she raised her large family. Tim O'Sullivan, having attended the local national school, got employment in Gibson's drapery shop in the town. There he became acquainted with the Irish Volunteer leader in Listowel, James Sugrue, who was from the same area of South Kerry where O'Sullivan had spent his early years. Immersed in the nationalist tradition, young Tim O'Sullivan attended Irish language classes in the Carnegie Library, which were taught by Tomás O'Donoghue, who was from Reenard, a mile from Aughatubrid. O'Donoghue became a senior officer in the Kerry No. 1 Brigade, eventually becoming its V/C. Tim O'Sullivan joined the Listowel Company of the 4th Battalion of that brigade and was appointed a section commander.[1]

During the Tan War O'Sullivan was arrested on a Listowel street by two RIC constables, Cahill and Redmond, and received a severe beating. In late May 1921, following this incident, he went on full-time active service with the battalion flying column.[2] During the Truce, from July 1921, he attended the brigade training camp but volunteered for active service in the northern counties in March 1922.

Courtesy of the Martin Moore collection.

---

1 Donegal Martyrs Memorial Committee, *The Story of the Drumboe Martyrs* (1956).
2 Patrick Joseph McElligott, BMH WS 1013.

During the Tan War, Republican activity in the northern counties was hampered by lack of arms, leadership and a hostile environment, as well as a general neglect by GHQ. As part of an effort to maintain army unity following the ratification of the Treaty, Liam Lynch and Michael Collins agreed a joint strategy on the six counties whereby the IRA units there would be armed and trained so that they could continue the fight against the British and gain total independence for the country. However, what was lacking were experienced fighting men. Volunteers were sought from the Cork and Kerry brigades to go north to aid Seán Lehane of West Cork, the O/C of the Donegal-based 1st Northern Division and Charlie Daly of Firies, who commanded the Republican forces of the 2nd Northern Division which operated in Tyrone and South Derry. Tim O'Sullivan was one of twenty or so Kerry IRA Volunteers who went north to Donegal and Tyrone in the spring of 1922.

While Lehane's and Daly's units waged war on the crown forces in Derry and Tyrone, the divisions in the twenty-six counties caused by the Treaty deepened. Within days of the start of the Civil War, the IRA who were fighting the British from their bases in Donegal were attacked by Free State forces and quickly forced to adopt guerrilla tactics to survive in the hostile environment of Donegal. With little local support and no hope of any meaningful resistance the remnants of the few IRA columns still in the field were authorised to withdraw from the county. O'Sullivan was one of the seven men captured with Charlie Daly at Dunlewy on 2 November while they were billeted in two cottages in this remote location.

Tim O'Sullivan, Charlie Daly and Dan Enright of Kerry, Jim Lane of Clonakilty, Seán Larkin and James Donaghy of Derry, and Donegal men Frank Ward and Dan Coyle faced a military court on 30 November 1922. They were convicted of armed resistance to the Free State but their death sentences were not passed until 18 January 1923. The capture of this IRA unit effectively ended Republican resistance in Donegal. General Joe Sweeney also held a number of other prisoners under sentence of death and these became hostages to ensure that there would be no resurgence in Republican activity.

On the night of 10 March, at Creeslough Barracks in mid Donegal, Captain Bernard Cannon was shot dead. The circumstances of his killing were never satisfactorily explained, but there was no IRA activity in the district and it would seem that he died as the result of a dispute. However, the initial explanation put forward was enough to direct blame onto Republican forces and on receiving a report of the incident from Joe Sweeney, the Free State GHQ sanctioned the executions of Tim O'Sullivan, Dan Enright, Charlie Daly and Seán Larkin.[3]

General Joe Sweeney, a veteran of fighting the British in 1916, had his four prisoners brought to a site at the edge of a wood near where they were detained at Drumboe Castle, Stranorlar. There they were executed by a firing squad composed of former British troops in Sweeney's command. He refused to release the remains to the men's families and had them interred in unconsecrated ground at Drumboe Barracks. When the barracks was being evacuated in 1924, the remains of the four executed men were transferred to Athlone Military Barracks. In August 1924 Tim O'Sullivan was finally laid to rest in the Republican Plot in Listowel.

---

3   Liam Ó Duibhir, *Donegal & the Civil War* (2011), p. 227.

Jack O'Reilly

Seán Ó Raġallaiġ[1]

John (Jacko) O'Reilly was the son of a successful building contractor and was born in Moyderwell, Tralee, on 20 June 1878. A noted singer, he became involved in the national movement at an early age. He was appointed a technical instructor in Tralee Technical School but soon afterwards emigrated to New Zealand. There he qualified as a civil engineer and spent two years as a teacher in Tonga, where he reputedly became friendly with the island's royal family. In 1913, on returning home to Ireland via America, he successfully applied for the civil service position of technical instructor for County Monaghan.

Following a short period in Monaghan, he transferred to the same post in County Galway and subsequently he became principal in the Technical School in Ballinasloe. He joined the Volunteers there and was appointed a captain in the East Galway Brigade of the Irish Volunteers. Following the Rising, he was arrested and was one of the over 320 Volunteers from County Galway to be interned. He was initially imprisoned in Richmond Barracks in Dublin and subsequently transferred to Wandsworth Gaol in England. No charges were brought against him. Later he was interned in Frongoch. In Frongoch Camp he was placed in charge of the fumigator, which was used to disinfect the prisoners' clothes. However, his health began to fail while incarcerated and he was released on 25 July 1916 for medical reasons.[2]

He returned to Kerry but died eight weeks later on Saturday 30 September 1916 in the County Infirmary, High Street, Tralee. His coffin was draped with the national flag and his funeral was attended by an enormous crowd as sympathy was now firmly on the side of the Irish Volunteers following the executions of the leaders of the Rising. His burial in his native town became the first public display of Republican support in Kerry following the events of Easter Week.

1   There is no known photograph of Jack O'Reilly.
2   *The Kerryman*, 2 September–7 October 1916. The correspondent notes that the account has been passed by the government censor.

He was buried the next day, 1 October, in the family plot in Rath Cemetery, Tralee, following the sounding of the Last Post. On 14 October 1916 a letter was published in *The Kerryman* newspaper which was sent by those Kerry Volunteers who were interned in Frongoch and stated that they were happy to know that their comrade had been buried 'in a fitting and worthy manner'.³

---

3   *The Kerryman*, 14 October 1916.

Thomas Russell

Tomás Rúiréal

Courtesy of the Martin Moore collection.

Thomas Russell was born in the West Kerry parish of Ballyferriter in 1897. As a young man he had a keen interest in the native culture that he was nurtured in. He was employed as a teacher by the Gaelic League in Carrigaholt, West Clare and it was there that he joined the Irish Volunteers.

Captain William Glass had orders to prevent drilling by the Irish Volunteers in the Carrigaholt district of West Clare. On Sunday 24 March 1918 he received information from Sergeant Moynihan of the RIC barracks in the village that members of the Irish Volunteers had marched to a local hall and he suspected that these men were illegally drilling. A detachment of British soldiers went by boat to the village from Kilrush, while their officer, Captain Glass, went by car. Arriving at the village he ordered the arrest of the local Volunteer leader, Michael Keane, and commanded him to call off the meeting in the hall. However, Keane would not accede to the request of a British officer and so the troops were ordered to proceed to the hall to enforce the captain's order.[1]

Over fifty men were in the hall and they were attending a Sinn Féin Club cultural session rather than engaged in drilling as the RIC had mistakenly suspected. When the troops arrived, they ordered Edward Fennell, the organiser of the meeting, to have the hall emptied, but Fennell asked them to delay a few minutes until one of the readers had finished his lecture. Annoyed at this, Sergeant Duff entered the hall with five soldiers who had bayonets fixed to their rifles. About fourteen of the troops remained outside. The soldiers, having entered the building, aggressively ordered everybody to leave and this

---

1   Pádraig Óg Ó Ruairc, *Blood on the Banner* (2009), p. 79.

caused panic amongst the men inside as they headed towards both the main and rear exits. Four men were injured by the soldiers as they attempted to leave the building as ordered. Thomas Russell was stabbed with a bayonet in the lower back and this perforated his bladder. Russell and the other injured men were brought to a local hotel owned by the Behan family and there they were treated by a doctor who dressed their wounds. Initially, Russell's condition improved but the next day he developed septicaemia and was transferred to St Joseph's Hospital in Kilrush. There he died of his wounds on Wednesday 27 March 1918. An inquest jury later declared that he died of injuries inflicted 'by a deliberately thrust bayonet'.[2]

On Good Friday his remains were brought by rowing boat across the Shannon and then on to Tralee where they reposed overnight in St John's church before making the journey to Dingle the next day. A large crowd accompanied the coffin, which was draped with the Tricolour, from Dingle's railway station to the parish church, where requiem mass was held the following day. The funeral procession then made a two-hour journey to Kilmalkeadar churchyard where he was buried.[3]

Today Volunteer Thomas Russell's grave is marked by a Celtic cross just inside the boundary wall of the medieval church which commands a striking view over his native Baile na nGall. The name of Tomás Ruiséal is inscribed on the West Kerry Republican memorial on The Mall in Dingle.

---

2   *The Freeman's Journal*, 29 March 1918 and 8, 13 April 1918.
3   *The Kerryman*, 6 April 1918.

Liam Scully

Liam Ó Scolaide

Courtesy of the Martin Moore collection.

Liam Scully was born in Shanacashel, Glencar, in 1892 where his father, Seán Scully, was a teacher in the local primary school. The Scully family were very nationalist in their outlook and several members of the family were prominent in Ireland's struggle for freedom. One brother, Bertie, was V/C of the 6th Battalion; another, Chris, was a Volunteer; and their sister Lily (Ellen) was a member of Cumann na mBan and is remembered for her care of wounded Volunteers.[1]

Liam Scully followed his father's footsteps and qualified as a national teacher, and his first post was in the national school that stood in Tralee's Strand Street. There he became a member of the IRB and an acquaintance of Austin Stack, O/C of the Irish Volunteers in Kerry. Before the Rising in 1916 Scully was an active figure in the preparations in Kerry. His brother, Bertie, recalled him cycling from Glencar to Cahersiveen on Easter Thursday with a communication, the contents of which he never revealed. Returning home, he departed for Dublin on Easter Saturday, but never reached his destination and apparently went to Thurles, though what his mission in Tipperary was he never explained.[2]

Liam Scully's career as a teacher was short and soon he was appointed a full-time organiser for the Gaelic League in North Kerry. As such, he was able to combine his cultural nationalism with his political and military roles in the resurgent Republican movement. The Kerry Irish Volunteer command made him their organiser in the North Kerry area. He was based in Ballylongford and was attached to the Volunteer company in this village. There, in 1918, he was also treasurer of the anti-conscription campaign, which used its funds to buy rifles

---

1 Information from Liam Scully, Tralee, nephew of Liam Scully.
2 Seán 'Bertie' Scully, BMH WS 788.

for the local Volunteer battalion. With the reorganisation of the Volunteers in Ballylongford now completed, Liam Scully then moved to County Limerick. There he was attached to the East Limerick Brigade and was one of the men who took part in the capture of the RIC barracks in Ballylanders on 27 April 1920. This was the first significant attack in the county and ended successfully with the destruction of the barracks and the surrender of its RIC garrison. The confidence gained there, as well as the haul of guns and ammunition, spurred on the East Limerick Brigade to identify another RIC barracks that might fall in a similar assault and so, on 28 May 1920, an IRA force converged on the south Limerick town of Kilmallock. The RIC barracks there had withstood an attack in 1867 during the Fenian Rising and this added to the significance of a proposed assault for the Limerick IRA.

Following the Ballylanders attack the brigade was short of ammunition. To obtain the necessary munitions for an attack on Kilmallock Barracks, Nicholas O'Dwyer and Liam Scully travelled to Dublin, where they received two bags of bullets and grenades. They returned by train to Knocklong, sharing a carriage with an unsuspecting detachment of British military.

The barracks at Kilmallock, the site of which is now a bank, was situated on the main street. The neighbouring building was a storey higher and this allowed the attackers to gain access to the roof. Slates were removed and petrol was poured into the upper story of the fortified building. As the building blazed, a fierce battle developed with the defenders under the command of Sergeant Tobias O'Sullivan, who bravely refused to surrender. Two RIC men were killed, but still their comrades fought on. Eventually, the blaze was such that the garrison decided to evacuate the building and take shelter in a fortified outhouse at the rear of the barracks. It would seem that there was a brief lull in the firing and, believing that the RIC had already evacuated the main building, Scully left his cover. To aid in their retreat from the barracks building, the remaining RIC men fired intensely to cover their evacuation and it was one of these shots that hit Liam Scully in the neck. He was removed from the scene by his comrades and was given first aid by a local nurse.[3]

With the sun rising and the barracks destroyed, though with the garrison

---

3   Seán 'Bertie' Scully, BMH WS 788 and James Roche, BMH WS 1125.

still resisting in the fortified outhouse, the IRA withdrew, fearing the arrival of RIC reinforcements from Limerick city. The Volunteers headed to the west as this was the only direction in which the roads were not barricaded and allowed for the easy withdrawal of the attacking force. Nurse O'Sullivan accompanied the mortally injured Scully in one of the cars in the three-vehicle convoy that headed towards West Limerick. However, at Lisanisky near Castlemahon, Scully died of his wounds. The small convoy then halted at Tournafulla. Pat Mulcahy, an officer from nearby Monegay and a carpenter by trade, made a coffin and Liam Scully was waked at O'Gorman's of Killikilleen. Later that night the funeral party travelled to Templeglantine Cemetery as it was deemed too hazardous to complete the journey to Kerry with the remains. At 11 p.m., under torchlight, the secret funeral was held and was attended by a local priest, IRA officers Seán Finn, Donnacha O'Hannigan and Tomás Malone, and by several of Liam's comrades from the Limerick brigades. Tomás Malone travelled on to Glencar to inform the Scully family of Liam's death.[4]

A large Celtic cross was erected over his grave and Austin Stack unveiled it on 4 September 1927.[5] Both the East and West Limerick Brigade memorials carry the name of the Glencar patriot. A plaque at the site of the Kilmallock RIC also recalls his sacrifice.

The sergeant of the Kilmallock RIC garrison, Tobias O'Sullivan, was in a position to identify some of the Volunteers involved in the attack and this was a cause of concern for the Limerick IRA. As a consequence of his actions in the defence of his barracks, he was promoted to the rank of district inspector in Listowel. However, his knowledge of the identities of the Kilmallock attackers made him a significant threat should any of those Volunteers fall into crown force custody. Acting under orders from GHQ, an IRA unit composed of men of the Moyvane Company – Con Brosnan, Jack Ahern, Dan O'Grady and Jack Sheehan – shot O'Sullivan dead in Listowel on 20 January 1921.

4   Nicholas O'Dwyer, BMH WS 680.
5   *Limerick Leader*, 5 September 1927 and 10 September 1927.

Paddy Shortis

Pádraig Seoirtur

Patrick Shortis was born in Ballybunion on 6 July 1892. His father, William Shortis, was originally from Carrick-on-Suir and came to the area as the manager of the Lartigue Railway which linked Ballybunion to Listowel. He later established a business on Ballybunion's main street. As a child Paddy Shortis attended the local national school and then went as a boarder to St Brendan's Seminary in Killarney. From there he attended All Hallows College in Drumcondra, Dublin, where he studied for the priesthood. However, on realising that he did not have a strong vocation he abandoned his ambition to enter religious life, but still achieved a BA degree.

Courtesy of the Martin Moore collection.

Subsequently he attended the Atlantic Wireless College in Cahersiveen, where he passed the examination but was not awarded a certificate of competence by the governing body which suspected his political allegiances. Shortis went to work in London, where he became involved in Irish political and cultural movements and joined the London detachment of the Irish Volunteers. Many of the London Volunteers and others from cities in Britain returned to Dublin early in 1916 in preparation for the Rising. There these men were billeted in Larkfield Manor in Kimmage, in a large flour mill surrounded by extensive grounds. The Plunkett family, who played a prominent role in the Rising, leased the property. Larkfield was also the base for the 4th Battalion of the Dublin Brigade of the Irish Volunteers before the rebellion. Those Volunteers who had returned from Britain in preparation for the Rising were termed the Kimmage Garrison and Paddy Shortis held the rank of lieutenant in this detachment.[1]

---

1 Ann Matthews, *The Kimmage Garrison, 1916* (2010), p. 61.

During the Easter Rising Paddy Shortis was attached to 'F' Company of the 2nd Battalion and this unit formed part of the GPO garrison. He was also in action in the Henry Street and Jervis Street areas of central Dublin. As the British encirclement around the GPO garrison tightened, the besieged garrison made a last determined effort to break through. Led by The O'Rahilly of Ballylongford, a group of Volunteers, including Shortis and Dinny Daly of Cahersiveen, charged down Moore Street and were met by a hail of bullets from the British rifles and machine guns at the other end of the street. Paddy Shortis was killed and his body lay near the junction of Moore Street and Henry Place until it was removed after the surrender.

His remains were identified by Áine Rahilly who had also identified the body of her brother, Michael. Lieutenant Paddy Shortis was buried in the 1916 Plot at St Paul's Cemetery, Glasnevin. His is remembered in his native Ballybunion by a plaque on the wall of the building where he was born.[2]

Paddy Shortis' brother, Dr Liam Shortis, was an active Volunteer in the University College Galway Company of the IRA and was interned for his Republican activities in the Civil War.

---

2   Ray Bateson, *They Died by Pearse's Side* (2010), p. 221.

'The Others'

While generally most of those who gave their lives in the fight for Irish freedom can be categorised by the units within the county to which they were attached and those Kerrymen who died on active service outside the county, a small group defy such artificial and arbitrary classification. William Brosnan of Castleisland is named in some sources as a Republican casualty but not in others. William O'Brien was from the parish of Rathmore in East Kerry, but was born in Nohoval Daly, a townland that lies within County Cork. Liam Hegarty was from Ballyvourney, but was buried in his family grave in Kilgarvan, County Kerry. Charles Monaghan of Belfast and Donal Sheehan of County Limerick drowned at Ballykissane on Good Friday 1916 and are buried in Killorglin. Giles Cooper of Droum, Headford, was not killed in action, but his comrades considered his death to be due to his time on active service and he was listed amongst the Republican dead on the 5th Battalion memorial in Rathmore. Similarly Brendan Doherty of Currow who died in 1983 was considered to have died as a result of his service in the cause of Irish freedom and his name is recalled in the Republican Plot in Kilbannivane Cemetery, Castleisland. Austin Stack, who is buried in Glasnevin, Dublin, is commemorated on the Ballyseedy monument roll of honour and in the Republican Plot in Rath Cemetery, Tralee. He died prematurely of natural causes, perhaps arising from imprisonment and hunger strikes during the Tan and Civil Wars. Though many more would have gone to their graves at a young age as a result of the hardships they endured, his comrades considered Austin Stack to be worthy of admission to the 1st Brigade's roll of honour. When John Joe Sheehy, the post-Civil War O/C of the Kerry IRA, was compiling a list of the of Republican casualties for North Kerry he included Stack's name. This was due to Stack's stature within Kerry's Republican movement and the fact that he had endured several hunger strikes which may have led to his premature death. Thomas Leane and Michael Lynch both died of natural causes, but their deaths were attributed by their comrades to their roles in the armed struggle and they are buried in the Republican Plot in Gale Cemetery.

WILLIAM BROSNAN

Liam Ó Brosnacháin[1]

On 3 December 1922 William Brosnan and a companion were walking up Castleisland's broad Main Street when shots were fired at them by a Free State patrol. Brosnan was fatally injured when a bullet hit him in the head and he died at the scene. Local lore suggests that the incident occurred a minute after the 9 p.m. curfew began. William Brosnan and his friend were unarmed and there was no suggestion of any Republican military activity in the town when the unprovoked shooting took place.[2]

Brosnan was born on 4 June 1896 and was a butcher by trade. He was the son of Denis Brosnan, a cattle dealer and victualler, and his wife Hanna Griffin. The family lived on Main Street and were known as the 'Denny Mike' Brosnans.

William Brosnan is listed among the thirteen men from the 7th Battalion that senior IRA officer David McCarthy counted as Republican Volunteers who were 'killed in action or murdered by FS forces in 1922 and 1923'.[3] The remainder of this list, which David McCarthy included in a statement to the Military Pensions board, is accurate and for this reason William Brosnan's death is recorded in this volume. However, he is not listed amongst the 7th Battalion dead on the Ballyseedy monument.

---

1 There is no known photograph of William Brosnan.
2 *The Cork Examiner*, 8 December 1922
3 David McCarthy, report of Civil War Casualties of 7th Battalion, Kerry No. 1 Brigade, Irish Military Archives MA/MSPC/RO95, p. 12.

GILES COOPER

Giles Cuipéaɼ

Giles Cooper was born on 14 February 1895 in Droum, a townland midway between Glenflesk and Barraduff in East Kerry. A noted athlete in his youth, he was a member of the Glenflesk GAA team that rose to prominence in the second decade of the twentieth century.[1] He was known on the sporting fields of East Kerry as 'Giles the Rock'. On the reorganisation of the Irish Volunteers in East Kerry in 1917, he enlisted and was attached to the Bealnadeaga or 'C' Company of the 5th Battalion, Kerry No. 2 Brigade. James Daly was the company captain.

Courtesy of Seán S. Ó Suilleabháin, Ráth Mór.

Giles Cooper saw active service from early in the Tan War. When the RIC barracks in Rathmore was attacked in May 1920, he was one of the assault party. Though ultimately the attack was unsuccessful, it was the first major attack of an enemy post in East Kerry. On 3 March 1921 Cooper was one of the large number of men who waited in vain to attack a British Army convoy at The Bower between Barraduff and Rathmore. On 21 March he was one of the Volunteers who took part in the Headford Junction ambush with the Kerry No. 2 Brigade column. He was posted on the north embankment at the station during the attack, as was Jim Baily, who was killed during the fighting that day. Cooper and his company captain, Jim Daly, were among the last of the attackers to leave the ambush site. They maintained their firing positions as a second train arrived with British troops. These troops came to the rescue of the Royal Fusiliers, who had suffered terrible casualties as they exited the train which had brought them from Kenmare. When all hope of capturing the military's Vickers gun had gone, Daly and Cooper escaped

---

1   Seán S. Ó Súilleabháin, *Aililiú Rathmore* (1990).

northwards into their native countryside, while the remainder of the flying column fled to the south. That evening the two men volunteered to return to the railway station to recover any arms or ammunition that may have been discarded during the fight. The next month the brigade column was disbanded and battalion columns were organised, whereupon Giles Cooper became a member of the 5th Battalion's active service unit.

As with the other battalions in the Kerry No. 2 Brigade, the officers and Volunteers of the 5th Battalion remained united in their opposition to the Treaty which partitioned the country. Cooper remained on active service with the battalion column as they fought a guerrilla war in East Kerry against the numerically superior Free State Army which had garrisons in Killarney and Rathmore. Life became very difficult for Cooper and his comrades as they lived from day to day, sleeping at night in dugouts constructed in ditches and on mountain slopes. Refusing to surrender, they fought on until the Republican leaders declared a ceasefire in April 1923. However, life 'on the run' had taken its toll on the physical health of Cooper and he died in February 1925 as a result of the hardships that he had suffered on active service in the defence of the Irish Republic.[2]

Lieutenant Giles Cooper was buried with military honours by his comrades in the defeated Republican Army in Kilquane Cemetery near Barraduff. There he lies in the little graveyard's Republican Plot with Michael McSweeney and Mick O'Sullivan. His name is inscribed on the 5th Battalion's monument in Rathmore, where it is recorded that Giles Cooper 'died as a result of active service'.

2   Jeremiah Murphy, *When Youth Was Mine* (1998), p. 303.

Brendan Doherty

Breandán Ó Dochartaigh

Brendan Doherty was born in Currow in 1948. He was from a family with a long history of service to the cause of Irish freedom. His granduncle was Phil O'Connor, who was a noted Moonlighter during the Land Wars and who served a five-year prison sentence in Mountjoy Gaol as a result of his activities in opposing the tyranny of the landlords. His uncle, John Doherty from Dromroe, was an active volunteer and was a member of the Kerry No. 2 Brigade flying column.[1]

Courtesy of the Houlihan Family, Dromroe, Currow.

It was in this Republican tradition that Brendan Doherty was raised. When the Troubles erupted in the six counties in 1969, young men and women from all over Ireland rallied to the cause once again. Several IRA Volunteers from Kerry were on active service against the crown forces in the six counties. Much of the work of the Kerry command of the IRA was to support their comrades in the north of Ireland. This included raising finance to purchase arms and maintain Volunteers who were on full-time active service. The county was also a base for the training of IRA activists, storing and importing weapons.

Volunteer Brendan Doherty was arrested following the robbery of a large amount of cash from a post office van in Tralee on 27 September 1974. He was charged with the possession of weapons and was brought before a non-jury special court in Dublin. He refused to recognise the court's authority to try him. In doing so he was following the example of the legendary Tadhg Brosnan of Castlegregory who, following his arrest after the 1916 Rising, was

---

1 Information from John Houlihan and Margaret Houlihan, sister of Brendan Doherty.

the first Irishman to refuse to recognise the authority of a court to try an Irish Republican seeking to free his native land. A guilty verdict was passed, based on an alleged confession obtained during his interrogation. His mother described him as being unrecognisable when she visited him while he was in custody. This was the era of the Heavy Gang, whose task it was to obtain convictions from Republican suspects. Doherty was sentenced to eight years in prison.

He was subsequently charged with another armed robbery at Farranfore on 16 August 1974. A search of his land led to the seizure of several rifles, pistols and explosives, and he was sentenced to another six years in prison. When he began his sentence the conditions within the prison were described as not being too oppressive and the inmates were treated as political prisoners. However, by 1977 beatings, degradation and flooding of the cells were the order of the day in Portlaoise Gaol. When all other avenues had failed, volunteers for a hunger strike were called for and Doherty and nineteen of his comrades began a fast that lasted forty-seven days. Martin Ferris and Danny O'Sullivan of Kerry were also among the hunger strikers. The protest eventually ended in a negotiated settlement. In 1981 Doherty was released and, returning home, resumed his activities on behalf of the Republican cause.

However, the effects of the brutality he suffered as a prisoner and the forty-seven-day hunger strike had severely damaged his physical and mental health. Three years after his release he died, on 3 June 1984. Volunteer Brendan Doherty of Dromroe, Currow, was thirty-six years of age. He is buried in Kilbannivane Cemetery in Castleisland and his name is inscribed on the Republican Plot, where he was honoured by the National Graves Association for his contribution to the cause of Irish freedom.

Liam Hegarty

Liam Ó hÉigeartaig[1]

On 6 September 1920 a procession of men left the West Cork Gaeltacht town of Ballymakeera bearing on their shoulders the coffin of their comrade Liam (Bill) Hegarty. The previous day Hegarty had been killed in action by a detachment of British military near his native village of Ballymakeera. His final journey would be over fifteen miles through the Derrynasaggart Mountains to his father's home parish of Kilgarvan in County Kerry.

John Hegarty was a boot maker from Kilgarvan and he and his Kerry-born wife had made their home in Ballymakeera. Liam was their eldest child and he followed in his father's profession in the village. He was the quartermaster in the Ballyvourney Company of the IRA, which was attached to the 8th Battalion, 1st Cork Brigade.

By the summer of 1920 the quiet Muskerry Mountains had become an active area of rebellion against the British crown. The RIC barracks which lay between the twin villages of Ballymakeera and Ballyvourney had been garrisoned by regular British troops. Earlier that summer Captain Eyrie had been killed and several of his men wounded as they travelled the main Killarney to Cork road near Ballyvourney.

On Sunday 5 September 1920 two lorries containing British soldiers travelled through Ballymakeera towards Macroom, having left the RIC barracks which lay about half a mile to the east of the church from where parishioners were exiting after mass. They passed through the village but stopped about a half mile outside, at a place on the road that was hidden from view. There, one of the lorries was parked and the impression given was that it had stopped due to mechanical problems and so had been abandoned by the soldiers. Children nearby saw the vehicle and soon word had reached the Volunteers of Ballymakeera that the British had abandoned one of their vehicles a short distance away. The soldiers had covered the rear of the lorry with a canvas sheet

---

1   There is no known photograph of Liam Hegarty.

and apparently driven away towards Macroom, nine miles to the east. Liam Hegarty was the section commander of the local Volunteers and he decided to delay a journey that he had planned and went instead to investigate the vehicle. Hegarty and Dan Healy, a fellow Volunteer, thought it might to better to shoot on the seemingly abandoned vehicle, suspecting that there may be trap prepared by the soldiers, but no weapon was readily available so they decided to directly investigate what the children had reported.

With the intention of burning it before the soldiers returned to retrieve it, several local Volunteers walked to where the lorry was. Dan Healy went to the rear of the vehicle while Liam Hegarty approached it from the front. When Healy pulled off the canvas cover which occluded the back portion, he was met with a hail of gunfire but miraculously escaped unscathed, reaching the cover of the ditch on the other side of the road. Liam Hegarty, it seems, was wounded, but still managed to get to the cover of the small ditch on the side opposite to where Healy sought shelter. Hegarty scrambled over the ditch but could go no further, probably because of his wounds. He was followed over the hedge by a soldier who coldly shot him in the head as he lay on the ground. He died instantly.

The shooting caused the children to scatter and the remainder of the Volunteers, who were further from the lorry, escaped uninjured. However, a local man, Michael Lynch, who lived a few hundred yards further east along the road, heard the shots and came to his front door to investigate. He too was shot dead, though he had no involvement with the incident and had two brothers in the RIC.[2]

Micheál Ó Súilleabháin, a local Volunteer and author of *Where Mountainy Men Have Sown*, records that the funeral procession that accompanied the remains of Liam Hegarty was a mile long. At Kilgarvan village he was buried in the Hegarty family plot and his comrades from the 8th Battalion fired a volley over the grave of their fallen comrade.[3] The grave lies inside the ruins of the medieval church which lies in Kilgarvan's old graveyard. Perhaps a Cork man in life and a Kerry man in death.

Today, a large Celtic cross marks the site a mile from Ballymakeera village

---

2   Daniel Harrington, BMH WS 1532 and Patrick O'Sullivan, BMH WS 794.
3   Micheál Ó Súilleabháin, *Where Mountainy Men Have Sown* (2013).

on the Macroom road where Liam Hegarty gave his life for Irish freedom. He was twenty-seven years old when he was shot dead on 5 September 1920.

Thomas Leane

Tomás Ó Laiginn[1]

Thomas Leane (or Leen) was the eldest son of a widow who farmed a smallholding in Knockenagh to the north of Listowel. He was born on 28 August 1897 and was to be one of the earliest IRA Volunteers to die in North Kerry. He was attached to the Ballydonoghue Company of the 3rd Battalion. His brother Jerry was a member of the battalion's active service unit.

Tom Leane was a member of the force which attacked Ballybunion RIC Barracks in March 1920. Following this assault on the barracks he walked that night through the rain to his home in Knockenagh, near Lisselton. As a result of the wetting he received on the journey, he contracted pneumonia from which he died shortly afterwards.[2]

Though he is not recalled on the Ballyseedy monument, he is buried in the Republican Plot in Gale Cemetery, and when the monument was unveiled at the grave in 1932, he was noted to have died as a result of his actions in the service of the IRA.

---

1   There is no known photograph of Thomas Leane.
2   *The Kerryman*, 23 April 1932.

Michael Lynch

Mícéál Ó Loinriġ[1]

Michael Lynch was born in Urlee, Lisselton, on 3 February 1901. He was a Volunteer in the 6th Battalion, Kerry No. 1 Brigade, and was widely known by his nickname 'Griffin'. He was on active service during the Civil War and was captured by Free State forces. He was imprisoned in Limerick Gaol initially and later in Tintown Camp in the Curragh. As a result of ill treatment, his health failed and he died prematurely. The exact circumstances of his death are not recorded. His remains were buried in the Republican Plot in Gale Cemetery, where he lies with five other Volunteers of the 6th Battalion. A memorial was erected over the grave in 1932.[2]

---

1 There is no known photograph of Michael Lynch.
2 *The Kerryman*, 23 April 1932.

Charles Monaghan

Caṫal Ó Monaċáin

Courtesy of the Martin Moore collection.

Charlie Monaghan was born in the Short Strand area of East Belfast in 1880. He was the great-grandson of a United Irishman who had fought in the 1798 rebellion. He was educated in the Christian Brothers School at Oxford Street and later trained as a wood cutter. As a young man Charlie Monaghan was a member of the Gaelic League and played Gaelic games in his native city. He moved to Dublin when about twenty years of age to work as a wood-cutting machinist. He later trained as a mechanic and took a particular interest in the new wireless technology which he went on to study. Economic hardship at home caused him to emigrate to America and there he worked as a motor mechanic. With the outbreak of the Great War he returned to Ireland and lived in Dublin, where he was sworn into the IRB and enlisted in the newly formed Irish Volunteers. He was attached to the 2nd Battalion of the Dublin Brigade.

Before the Rising at Easter 1916, Monaghan was chosen to travel from Dublin with IRB men Donal Sheehan, Con Keating, Colm Ó Lochlainn and under the command of Dinny Daly to Cahersiveen Wireless School. From there they were to obtain a radio set to be used to contact the expected arms ship *Aud* as it arrived into Tralee Bay that weekend. The five men travelled from Dublin by train on Good Friday and were met at Killarney railway station by Limerick men Tommy McInerney and Sammy Windrim, who had driven two cars from Limerick city. They collected the five Volunteers and drove towards Killorglin on their way to Cahersiveen, with Dinny Daly and Colm Ó Lochlainn in the lead car driven by Windrim. McInerney, Keating, Sheehan and Monaghan were in the second car.

Shortly after leaving Killarney, McInerney had lost sight of the first car. While Windrim's car drove through Killorglin, McInerney's lagged behind and then took an alternative route through Beaufort to Killorglin, fearing that the first car had been stopped by the RIC. Reaching Killorglin, they were directed through the town by a local girl, Lily Taylor, from whom Monaghan was delegated to ask for directions around the town. Mistaking her instructions, the car drove off on a straight route, missing the turn at the town's church, and heading instead along the road to Ballykissane Pier. As the car plunged from the pier into high tide in the darkness of that Good Friday evening, Monaghan was in the front passenger seat of McInerney's car. Keating and Sheehan were seated in the rear and the three passengers had their coat pockets laden with ammunition and equipment that prevented their escape from the sinking vehicle. Only McInerney successfully freed himself from the car after it entered the water.

The bodies of Con Keating and Donal Sheehan were recovered in the afternoon of the following day. It was not until 30 October, six months after he had been drowned and following a flood on the river, that a farmer walking the shore discovered the partial remains of Charlie Monaghan. However, the police failed to identify the decomposed body. The bones were taken to the courthouse for examination and on 31 October 1916 they were interred in the same grave as the remains of Donal Sheehan in Dromavalla Cemetery just outside Killorglin. Over three months later, at low tide on 3 February 1917 and 400 yards from the pier, a local man discovered some more of the skeletal remains belonging to Charlie Monaghan. Nearby was a belt with a pistol and ammunition. These bones too were interred in the grave at Dromavalla.[1]

Today, a large granite cross stands over the grave of Charles Monaghan and Donal Sheehan at Dromavalla Cemetery and an obelisk was erected at Ballykissane Pier in 1939 to mark the spot where the first casualties of the 1916 Rising died.

---

1   Xander Clayton, *Aud* (2007), p. 257. This book contains an excellent account of the events at Ballykissane at Easter 1916.

WILLIAM O'BRIEN

Liam Ó Briain

Courtesy of Martin O'Dwyer

William O'Brien was a native of Nohoval Daly, a townland between the County Cork village of Knocknagree and the larger village of Rathmore in Kerry, to which parish it belongs. He was the son of a stonemason and he followed in his father's profession.[1]

In 1920 he was living in Tipperary town and was a Volunteer in one of the two companies of the IRA which were attached to the 4th Battalion, 3rd Tipperary Brigade. In 1921 he had become a lieutenant of that company. He was arrested and held prisoner in the Tipperary Military Barracks and it was there, on the afternoon of 30 May 1921, that he was shot dead.[2]

It is reported that William O'Brien and another prisoner, Martin Purcell of Dundrum, County Tipperary, had attempted to escape from the military barracks where they were being detained. While in the exercise yard, these two men approached the sentries guarding them and tried to overpower them. William O'Brien managed to grab one of the sentries, but after a brief struggle the soldier freed himself, pushing O'Brien to the ground. When the prisoner got to his feet he again tried to disarm the soldier, who then fired at him. The first shot missed and as William O'Brien continued to approach the sentry, he was hit by two bullets from the soldier's rifle. Meanwhile the other sentry, whom eighteen-year-old Martin Purcell had tried to disarm, had also opened fire and killed the young Tipperary man. William O'Brien of Nohoval Daly

1   Although born and buried in Nohoval Daly, a townland in County Cork, it is on the border with County Kerry and within the parish of Rathmore. Volunteers from this townland were attached to the Rathmore Company and so William O'Brien is included amongst the Kerry casualties for purposes of this book.
2   Martin O'Dwyer, *Tipperary's Sons and Daughters 1916–1923* (2001), p. 191.

and Martin Purcell were two of six IRA Volunteers to be killed in that barracks during the Tan War, including James Hickey of Knocknagoshel.[3]

William O'Brien is remembered on the 3rd Tipperary Brigade memorial in St Michael's Cemetery in Tipperary town. The large military barracks in Tipperary town was later demolished, but one of the remaining walls bears a plaque commemorating O'Brien and those other Volunteers who gave their lives for Ireland within its walls.

It is ironic that some of the stone from the demolished Tipperary Military Barracks where William O'Brien was killed was used in the construction of the Roger Casement Memorial at Banna Strand some fifty years later.[4]

Lieutenant William O'Brien is buried in the family plot at the old cemetery at Nohoval Daly Graveyard which overlooks Rathmore village.

---

3   Information from Martin O'Dwyer, Cashel, County Tipperary, relative of Martin Purcell.
4   Information from Seán Seosamh Ó Conchubhair, Banna Memorial Committee member and local historian.

John O'Connor

Seán Ó Concubair

Courtesy of Aidan Larkin.

John O'Connor was the only son of Edmund O'Connor of Droum, Glenbeigh, and Hanora Curtin of Brosna. Edmund O'Connor was a member of the RIC, having joined the force in 1885. He was subsequently posted to Counties Galway, Clare, Limerick and eventually to County Cork. John O'Connor was born on 4 January 1896 in Mountcollins, near Brosna, where his mother's sister lived. At this juncture his father was stationed in White Gate, Co. Galway. In 1897 Constable O'Connor was transferred to Innishannon, County Cork and he remained there until his retirement in 1911. It was there that John O'Connor grew up.[1]

As a young man John O'Connor joined the Royal Navy and in the Great War he served as a stoker aboard the battleship, HMS *Victorious*.[2] On demobilisation in 1919 he returned to Innishannon and subsequently joined the Irish Volunteers. He was attached to the Innishannon-based 'G' Company of the 1st (Bandon) Battalion of the 3rd Cork Brigade.

He was employed as a fireman on a ship that sailed between Cork and Liverpool. This placed him in an ideal position to smuggle arms from Britain into Cork city. His chief contribution to the Republican cause was as an arms smuggler. In 1919 he married Eileen Walsh in Liverpool. The couple's first child, Kathleen, was born in 1920.[3]

---

1 Information from Aidan Larkin, Dublin, grandson of Volunteer John O'Connor.
2 For this information I am indebted to Dan King, Tralee, who researched the episode and wrote of it in an article entitled 'A Short Visit to Fenit – John O'Connor and Ballyseedy', which was published in *Innishannon Candlelight* (2010).
3 Kathleen O'Connor was christened Christine but was called Maureen by her mother. She later became known as Kathleen, the name she uses to this day. At the time of writing Kath-

Following the division caused by the Treaty O'Connor remained in the Republican Army and was listed as being attached to the Innishannon Company at the start of the Civil War. Most of the Liverpool Volunteers sided with the pro-Treaty faction and this curtailed O'Connor's gun-running activities. In late 1922 he told his wife that he was going on a voyage to America, probably to protect her from the fact that he was leading a precarious life as a Republican activist in Ireland, which was then in the midst of a Civil War.

On 22 January 1923 he signed on as a crew member on the SS *Cumbria*, a ship belonging to the City of Cork Steam Packet Company. The next month, on 27 February, at Liverpool port he joined the crew of the SS *Cahiracon* where he worked as a stoker. This was a cargo ship owned by the Limerick Steamship Company and it sailed from Liverpool to Limerick via Fenit. Captain Jack Hanrahan of Limerick took command of the ship on 2 March 1923 in Liverpool port and set sail.

The ship arrived in Fenit, the deep water port for Tralee seven miles from the town, on 5 March. When the SS *Cahiracon* entered Fenit harbour, there was a grain ship already there being unloaded by the local dock workers. Colonel James Hancock of the Dublin Guard and a local Free State lieutenant, Patrick Kavanagh, from near Ardfert, arrived with a detachment of soldiers. Both officers were later implicated in many of the atrocities of the Civil War in Kerry. The troops crossed over the grain ship to board the newly arrived SS *Cahiracon* and began to search the vessel. It was obvious that they were acting on definite information. No weapons were found but John O'Connor was taken into custody by Hancock. The Free State officers also carried away a life buoy which bore the ship's name as proof that they had boarded the vessel. As he was being brought ashore, the dockworkers described how Lieutenant Kavanagh, who was holding a Peter the Painter pistol to his prisoner, physically abused O'Connor. As he exchanged greetings with the station master at Fenit, Kavanagh described O'Connor as another '1000 rounds man', i.e. an arms smuggler.[4]

> leen Larkin is the only surviving child of those who died for the Irish Republic in Kerry during the Civil War.

4 Witnesses Dan Crowley, Dan King, William Crowley, Daniel Clifford and Michael Ferris were working on Fenit pier that day and were interviewed by Dan King of Tralee. His father was one of those present that day.

The lorry carrying John O'Connor and his captors broke down at the corner of the road near the old railway station in Fenit. Witnesses related how they saw O'Connor among the soldiers pushing the vehicle and eventually they got it to restart. The prisoner was then brought to the Free State headquarters in Ballymullen Barracks. There he was imprisoned with the large number of Republicans being held in the large military complex. The other prisoners reported that they had no idea who he was, as he was not a native of the county and had not been on active service in Kerry.

In the early hours of the next day, five Free State soldiers were killed at Barranarig, Knocknagoshel, by a landmine as they were searching for local IRA Volunteers. This precipitated a mass killing of prisoners by Free State forces throughout the county. In Ballymullen Barracks, on 6 March 1923, Colonel David Neligan, the chief of intelligence for the Free State Army in Kerry, selected the prisoners he would send to their deaths at Ballyseedy in the early hours of 7 March. Why John O'Connor was chosen is beyond explanation, as he was not captured under arms and was not on active service in Kerry during the Civil War. One report at the time suggested that a prisoner from Derrymore was selected but he had been so badly beaten that he was unable to be taken from his cell and that a man in the next cell was taken instead. This may have been John O'Connor.

In the darkness of that night John O'Connor and eight others were brought by Captain Ned Breslin to Ballyseedy Cross on a convoy of lorries. There he and seven other prisoners were killed, with only Stephen Fuller escaping to testify to the horrific facts of the massacre.

John O'Connor had given an address at West Terrace in Liverpool, which was fictitious, and stated that his next of kin was his father. This was probably to protect his young family in Liverpool. It was Edmund O'Connor who told his daughter-in-law of her husband's death. At this time his wife, Eileen, was pregnant with their second child. She had presumed that her husband had gone to America as he had told her that was what he had planned. It was only following his death that she learned he was still in Ireland and she immediately travelled to Tralee to make arrangements for his burial.

While in Tralee for the funeral she was cared for by members of Cumann na mBan. She was befriended by Cis and Jo Power, who produced a Republican newspaper called *The Invincible* using only a typewriter. The Power sisters were anxious to acquire a duplicator to increase the production of their newssheet. Mrs O'Connor agreed to carry the letter to Dublin requesting one from Republican headquarters. When detained at Tralee railway station on her way back to Liverpool, the incriminating letter was found in her hat and she and the Power sisters were arrested and sent to Kilmainham Gaol. Mrs O'Connor had told the Power sisters that her dead husband had promised their daughter a doll and so they had procured one for her and had clothes made for it by a local dressmaker. Eileen O'Connor carried the doll with her to Kilmainham.[5]

While in prison, perhaps because she was pregnant, she became ill and was released to return to her Liverpool home. There she lived with her daughter at 1a Lyon Street. Later the couple's second daughter, also called Eileen, was born and the family returned to Ireland.

Volunteer John O'Connor is buried in the Republican Plot in Rath Cemetery, Tralee. His name is inscribed on the Ballyseedy monument together with those of his comrades who died there in defence of the Irish Republic on 7 March 1923.

---

5   Sinéad McCoole, *No Ordinary Women* (2003), p. 105.

Thomas Prendiville

Tomás de Prendibile[1]

Thomas Prendiville was a farmer from Kilcusnan, about three miles to the north-east of Castleisland town. He was a married man with four children. He was a known Republican sympathiser and perhaps activist. Little is known of his involvement with the IRA in the Civil War, but when he was recognised by Free State officers in Castleisland early on the morning of 18 January 1923 he was detained.

On that Thursday morning, at about 1 a.m., Thomas Prendiville and Dan Daly were arrested by Lieutenant James Larkin of the 1st Western Division on Main Street, Castleisland, about thirty yards from the barracks. The two local men had attended a fair in the town the previous day and it was late when they began the journey home. Lieutenant Larkin, who had been drinking heavily, noted that Prendiville's address was where they had been searching for an IRA arms dump the previous day. Larkin took his two prisoners to the Free State Army headquarters in the town, which was further up Main Street at Hartnett's Hotel.

Dan Daly was the first to be questioned by Larkin in the guardroom. He subsequently brought Prendiville in to interrogate him in this room also. Witnesses who later testified at an inquiry gave evidence that Larkin put Thomas Prendiville standing against the wall and asked him questions regarding local Republicans and their arms dumps. When the prisoner failed to answer, Larkin initially hit him with his fist and said that he would shoot him if he didn't divulge the information. He then shot the prisoner at close range in the chest with his pistol and while Prendiville was lying wounded on the floor Larkin shot him again. The officer then left the room. Another officer, Sergeant O'Loughlin, was also present and fearing further bloodshed, he took the gun from his commanding officer. The inquiry was told that O'Loughlin and Larkin had been drinking all day and were in no fit state for duty, but as

---

1 There is no known photograph of Thomas Prendiville.

Larkin was O/C of the post, nobody dared to question his fitness to carry a loaded weapon. Following the killing, Larkin was transferred to the Free State barracks in Tralee and later to Claremorris, where he continued to serve until he was tried for the murder of Thomas Prendiville.[2]

The cold-blooded murder of Thomas Prendiville could not be covered up as it occurred in the presence of Free State officers and these witnesses were willing to testify about the facts of the killing. James Larkin was tried as a civilian in November 1924 and convicted of the manslaughter of Thomas Prendiville for which he was sentenced to eight years' imprisonment.

Though not recorded in *The Last Post*'s list of Republican dead, historian Uinseann Mac Eoin states that this is an oversight.[3] Certainly Thomas Prendiville was taken prisoner as he was a known Republican and killed while in captivity.[4] In a letter to the Military Pensions Board, senior Republican officer David McCarthy names Thomas Prendiville as one of the thirteen IRA Volunteers from the 7th Battalion area to have been killed by Free State forces during the Civil War period.[5]

Thomas Prendiville is buried in a family tomb in Kilbannivane Cemetery, Castleisland.

---

2   *The Southern Star*, 21 June 1924; *The Freeman's Journal*, 29 January 1923 and 8 November 1924; *Irish Independent*, 30 January 1923, 16 June and 8 November 1924.
3   Uinseann Mac Eoin, *The IRA in the Twilight Years 1923–1948* (1997), p. 104.
4   Thomas Prendiville may not have been a member of the IRA and may have been mistaken for Maurice Prendiville, an IRA Volunteer, also from Kilcusnan. However, he was arrested because of his Republican sympathies and was killed during interrogation for failing to give information. Therefore he is included in this volume as it is more fitting to include his name than to omit him.
5   David McCarthy report of Civil War Casualties of 7th Battalion Kerry No. 1 Brigade, Irish Military Archives MA/MSPC/RO95, p. 12.

Donal (Dan) Sheehan

Domhnall Ó Síoccáin

Courtesy of the Martin Moore collection.

Donal Sheehan was a native of Ballintubrid in the parish of Monagea, near the County Limerick town of Newcastle West. He was educated in Killoughteen National School and later at the Courtenay School in Newcastle West. As a young man he developed a keen interest in the Irish language and the GAA. From 1909 he was employed in the British civil service in London but later worked as a bookkeeper in the Savoy Hotel in that city. While living in London he was involved in the Irish societies, including the Gaelic League, which promoted the revival of Irish culture and language amongst Irish immigrants in the city. He became a member of the IRB and in 1914 he returned to Ireland as the threat of conscription loomed in Britain for young men resident there. He got a job in Geary's Biscuit Factory in Limerick city and while there he joined the Irish Volunteers and achieved the rank of captain. In early April 1916 he left his job and moved to Dublin, where planning for the Easter Rising was at an advanced stage.

He was chosen to be one of the four Volunteers to accompany Dinny Daly in the mission to secure a radio transmitter from the Atlantic Radio and Telegraphy College in Cahersiveen and to use this to contact the arms ship *Aud* as it entered Tralee Bay.

Sheehan was a back seat passenger in the second of the two cars that left Killarney on the mission to Cahersiveen. When the car plunged over the pier at Ballykissane, his position in the car and the weight of the ammunition, pistol and equipment in the pockets of his great coat gave him no chance of reaching the surface as the vehicle sank into the high tidal water of the estuary of the River Laune. Like Con Keating and Charlie Monaghan, he drowned on that

Good Friday night. The following morning at 9 a.m., when the tide was at its lowest, local fishermen began trawling the river estuary with their nets in an attempt to recover the bodies. The initial efforts were fruitless, but later one of the men on the boat felt the net catch on something and so the net was cast again and soon the body of Donal Sheehan was lifted on to their boat. It was brought ashore and put in a cart and then transferred to Killorglin courthouse. Con Keating's remains were recovered later that day and were laid out on straw beside that of Donal Sheehan. The driver, Tommy McInerney, was brought there to identify the two bodies and said that he recognised the remains as his passengers. However, he did not divulge their names as he claimed he had only met the drowned men because they had hired his car as tourists.

And so the mortal remains of thirty-year-old Donal Sheehan remained unidentified in Killorglin courthouse for some weeks, though the RIC was aware that this stranger was involved in the activity connected with the subsequent Rising. The relatives of Con Keating sought permission to bury the body of Sheehan with their son in Cahersiveen but the RIC refused.[1] He was eventually buried in Dromavalla Cemetery on the outskirts of the town where months later the shattered remains of Charlie Monaghan were also laid to rest. A large granite cross marks the grave of these first victims of the Rising and the site where they drowned at Ballykissane Pier has a large monument to commemorate their sacrifice on that Good Friday night.

---

1 *The Kerryman*, 24 April 1933, article by Máirín Cregan.

AUSTIN STACK

Aibirtín de Staic

Courtesy of Mercier Archive.

Austin Stack was the most prominent figure from Kerry during the revolutionary period. Following his premature death from natural causes in 1929, such was his stature that his comrades from the period inscribed his name amongst the patriot dead on the Republican memorial at Rath Cemetery in Tralee and on the Ballyseedy monument.

Austin Stack was born in Ballymullen, Tralee, on 7 December 1879. His father was a solicitor's clerk and had served prison sentences for Fenian activities and later for his involvement with the Land League. Austin Stack was educated by the Christian Brothers in the town and leaving school at the age of fourteen, he went to work for John O'Connell, a solicitor in Nelson Street (now Ashe Street). There he trained as a law clerk and lived in Upper Rock Street. He remained with the O'Connell legal firm until his arrest in April 1916. In 1901 he and Maurice McCarthy founded the John Mitchel's GAA club in Tralee. He both played and managed the team which became exceptionally successful. As a result, Stack went on to play in the All-Ireland-winning Kerry teams, being the captain of the team that won the 1904 championship. He was secretary of the GAA Kerry County Board from 1904 until 1908 and its chairman from 1914 until his arrest. In 1909 he was sworn into the IRB by Cathal Brugha and was its head centre in Kerry from 1910. He attended the inaugural meeting of the Irish Volunteers in Tralee on 10 December 1913 and within six months he had become O/C of the Kerry Brigade. The majority of the Volunteers in the county remained loyal to Stack's leadership after the split in 1914. Stack's command of the IRB and Irish Volunteer movement in Kerry strengthened as the military council planned for a rebellion at Easter 1916. Arrangements for the landing and distribution of a large arms shipment from Germany were entrusted to Stack by Patrick Pearse, Tom Clarke and Seán MacDiarmada.

On Good Friday 1916 the German arms ship, *Aud*, failed to land its cargo and Roger Casement was captured near Banna Strand. Having been informed of Casement's arrival by Robert Monteith, Stack went in a car with three others in an unsuccessful attempt to find him. However, Casement had already been arrested and was soon in custody in Tralee's RIC Barracks. In circumstances that have never been satisfactorily explained, Stack went to the barracks and was arrested there in possession of incriminating documents. He was imprisoned by the British until June 1917. Although he was cleared of any incompetence by an Irish Volunteer inquiry led by Cathal Brugha in 1917, the shadow of Holy Week in Tralee hung over Stack's otherwise heroic career.

Arrested again in 1918, he became the leader of the Republican prisoners who successfully protested for political status in Crumlin Road Gaol in Belfast. He became Sinn Féin TD for North Kerry and West Limerick in the 1918 election and was then appointed Minister for Home Affairs in the First Dáil in January 1919. As the minister in charge of local government, he began a campaign to subvert the British civic administration and to replace it with a system of Republican or Dáil courts, a policy that was largely successful and complemented the armed actions that made Ireland ungovernable for the British crown.

He vehemently opposed the Treaty and was removed from office by pro-Treaty elements, allowing for the disestablishment of the Dáil courts system of justice and the disbandment of the Republican Police. Their replacement was a new justice system dominated by a Redmondite legal establishment and a new police force, the Civic Guard, highly influenced by elements of the RIC. Stack was appointed a minister in the shadow Republican government that emerged during the Civil War and he was also the vice-president of the now defunct and defeated Republic.

In April 1923, in the final weeks of the Civil War, Austin Stack was captured in Tipperary and imprisoned in Arbour Hill. While in captivity he participated in the long hunger strike which began in November 1923, and this adversely affected his health. In 1924 he was one of the last prisoners to be released by the new Free State regime.

Following his release he worked tirelessly to build up the shattered Republican movement. He remained committed to Sinn Féin and its abstentionist policy, refusing to accept the legitimacy of the new Free State. He refused to follow de Valera into Fianna Fáil and constitutional politics and remained a stalwart figure in a Sinn Féin party whose influence was on the wane.

He remained hugely popular in Kerry and was elected one of its TDs in every election until his death. His last public address was in Cahersiveen where he ended his speech by saying that Irish nationality was 'an undying thing and would never be lost as long as Ireland possessed her martyred dead'.

Two weeks later he was admitted to the Mater Hospital, Dublin, where he was operated on for appendicitis. He died of complications the next day, 27 April 1929. Following a large funeral in which he was given full military honours by the IRA, he was buried in Glasnevin Cemetery's Republican Plot. He was survived by his widow, Úna, who remained faithful to the Republican cause until her death in 1950.[1]

---

1 J. Anthony Gaughan, *Austin Stack – Portrait of a Separatist* (1977).

Timeline of Events in Kerry

1913

28 November: In Killarney Kerry's first company of Irish Volunteers is formed.

10 December: Establishment of Irish Volunteers in Tralee.

1914

April: Irish Volunteers organise in Castleisland.

September: Split in Irish Volunteers as John Redmond forms National Volunteers to support British war effort.

1915

1 August: Funeral of O'Donovan Rossa in Glasnevin attended by many Kerry Volunteers.

4–11 September: Kerry Irish Volunteer officers attend training camp in Coosane, Athlone.

September: Fenit selected as port where German arms would arrive.

1916

21 April: Death of Volunteers at Ballykissane, scuttling of *Aud* arms ship, capture of Roger Casement at Banna.

23 April: Volunteers arrive in Tralee for proposed Rising.

24 April: Easter Rising in Dublin. Four Volunteers from Kerry killed in action during the fighting.

29 April: Jim Riordan fires the only shots of the Rising in Kerry as he shoots two RIC constables in Firies village.

May: Widespread arrests of Irish Volunteers in Kerry; some are sentenced while others are interned in Frongoch, Wales.

3 August: Roger Casement hanged in London.

30 September: Captain Jack O'Reilly, a former Frongoch prisoner and veteran of the 1916 Rising, dies in Tralee.

December: Final release of prisoners from Frongoch Camp. Celebrations on arrival of released Volunteers in Kerry.

1917

5 August: Thomas Ashe addresses a large Volunteer gathering at Banna on anniversary of Casement's execution.

11 July: Volunteer Dan Scanlon shot dead in Ballybunion during victory parade for de Valera's election in Clare by-election.

25 September: Thomas Ashe dies on hunger strike in Dublin's Mater Hospital.

1918

27 March: Thomas Russell of Ballyferriter dies of wounds inflicted by British military at Carrigaholt, County Clare.

13 April: First attack on Gortatlea RIC Barracks, two Volunteers die.

16–17 May: Widespread arrests of leading Volunteers, including many in Kerry, in response to 'The Second German Plot'.

14 June: Ballymacelligott Volunteers shoot two RIC constables in Tralee's main street.

14 December: Sinn Féin candidates win all four (uncontested) parliamentary seats in the general election in Kerry constituencies.

1919

21 January: Dáil Éireann established in Dublin. Austin Stack appointed Minister for Home Affairs.

21 January: Tipperary Volunteers kill two RIC constables in Soloheadbeg when raiding for explosives.

19 February: Captain Patrick Casey of the Black Valley shot dead.

April: Three IRA brigades formed in Kerry in a reorganisation of the original command structure.

24 June: RIC patrol is attacked and disarmed near Camp.

1920

15 January: Sinn Féin candidates successful in urban council elections in Tralee, Killarney and Listowel.

19 February: Large-scale attack on Camp RIC Barracks.

13 March: Attack on Ballybunion RIC Barracks.

25 March: Gortatlea Barracks destroyed in a second attack.

31 March: Scartaglin Barracks attacked and later abandoned.

3 April: Vacated RIC barracks destroyed throughout the county.

3 May: RIC Sergeant Francis McKenna killed at Gale Bridge.

11 May: Michael Nolan of Kilmoyley killed in ambush on Magistrate Wynne near Causeway.

14 May: Cannons removed from Ross Castle by Ballymacelligott IRA.

28 May: Liam Scully of Glencar killed in assault on Kilmallock RIC Barracks.

5 June: Failed assault on Brosna RIC Barracks with capture of Duagh Volunteers en route to the attack.

18 June: Brosna Barracks attacked again.

14 June: Sinn Féin candidates control rural district councils following elections.

19 June: Constable Jeremiah Mee and several other members of the RIC mutiny at Listowel Barracks over shoot to kill policy.

11 July: First Black and Tan killed in Ireland dies in an attack on Rathmore Barracks.

13 July: Two RIC men die at Kilmore, Cloghane, in an ambush led by Tadhg Brosnan.

16 July: Attack on the RIC at Ahabeg, Lixnaw.

16 July: Two RIC constables wounded in Glencar.

18 August: Annascaul ambush of military lorry. First attack in Ireland where landmines were used.

1 September: Cashen coastguard station captured.

25 October: Lord Mayor Terence MacSwiney, Cork, dies on hunger strike in Brixton Prison, London.

31 October: RIC Constable George Morgan killed in Ballyduff.

31 October: Two Black and Tans killed in Abbeydorney.

31 October: Two RIC constables killed at Hillville, Milltown.

5 November: Attack on Causeway RIC Barracks.

5 November: Crown forces raid Ardfert village.

9 November: Two Black and Tans killed at Ballybrack Station.

10 November: Frank Hoffman killed at Farmer's Bridge.

12 November: Auxiliaries attack Ballymacelligott Creamery killing two IRA Volunteers.

24 December: Mossy Reidy and John Leen killed by Major McKinnon in Ballydwyer, Ballymacelligott.

1921

1 January: John Lawlor dies of injuries received the previous day when assaulted by crown forces in Listowel.

20 January: Moyvane IRA unit kill DI Tobias O'Sullivan in Listowel.

28 January: Toureengarrive ambush claims the life of Major General Philip Armstrong Holmes, divisional commander of the RIC.

21 February: Attack on Ballybunion RIC Barracks.

22 February: Two RIC constables killed in Ballylongford.

27 February: Captain Joe Taylor captured and killed at Glencar.

5 March: Second attack on Causeway RIC Barracks.

5 March: Clonbanin ambush.

13 March: Kerry No. 1 Brigade column attacks RIC barracks in Killorglin.

21 March: Headford Junction ambush.

22 March: Lispole ambush.

15 April: Major John McKinnon, Commander of 'H' Company of the Auxiliaries, killed in Tralee.

24 April: 1st Southern Division formed at Kippagh, near Ballydaly. Com-

manded by Liam Lynch, it includes the three Kerry brigades.

26 April: Attack on British military at Glenbeigh Station.

4 May: Bog Road ambush near Rathmore kills eight RIC constables.

12 May: Paddy Dalton, Jerry Lyons (Duagh) and Paddy Walsh are killed at Gortaglanna, Knockanure.

21 May: Attack on RIC at Ballyduff.

June: Andy Cooney appointed temporary O/C of Kerry No. 1 Brigade, replacing Paddy Cahill.

1 June: Large ambush at Ballymacandy, Castlemaine.

4 June: Failed attempt to derail train at Ballymacelligott.

10 July: Eve of Truce attacks in Castleisland, Killorglin and Tarbert.

11 July: Truce between Republican and crown forces.

August: Humphrey Murphy appointed O/C of Kerry No. 1 Brigade and John Joe Rice becomes O/C of Kerry No. 2 Brigade.

October: Court of inquiry by GHQ held into the sacking of Paddy Cahill.

6 December: Anglo-Irish Treaty signed in London.

1922

7 January: Dáil approves Treaty and it comes into force on 14 January.

14 January: Last Kerry IRA prisoners of Tan War released from Cork Gaol. Those held in British jails also freed.

February: Pro-Treaty Free State Army under Tom Kennelly garrisons Listowel.

3 March: Humphrey Murphy disarms large Free State detachment at Lixnaw station as they travel by train to form garrison at Ardfert.

26 March: Convention of IRA rejects Treaty at a meeting in the Mansion House attended by Kerry IRA commanders.

22 April: Michael Collins receives a hostile reception in Killarney and next day in Tralee as he visits the county promoting the Treaty.

20 May: Political pact formed between pro and anti-Treaty parties to jointly contest June general election. This is repudiated by Collins on the eve of

the election, probably under pressure from the British.

16 June: Pro-Treaty parties win a majority in the Third Dáil and Republican TDs later refuse to take their seats. Kerry votes to support the Republican cause.

28 June: Free State forces shell Dublin's Four Courts to begin the Civil War.

29 June: Fighting in Kerry as Republican forces quickly capture Listowel.

30 June: IRA units from Kerry advance on Limerick city.

4 July: Liam Lynch and Free State commanders call a ceasefire in Limerick in an attempt to halt the Civil War.

11 July: Free State forces, having been reinforced, break Limerick ceasefire and capture the city after ten days of heavy fighting.

21 July–5 August: Kerry IRA columns led by Tadhg Brosnan, Tom O'Connor and Tom McEllistrim involved in fighting in south County Limerick.

2 August: Free State forces land in Fenit and capture Tralee after fierce fighting.

3 August: Free State Army's 1st Western Division land in Tarbert and march south to capture Listowel.

11 August: Free State forces under Tom O'Connor Scarteen capture Kenmare, having landed by ship from Limerick.

13 August: Free State Army enters Killarney unopposed.

22 August: Michael Collins killed at Béal na Bláth, County Cork.

22 August: Tom Daly, Dan Mulvihill, Con O'Leary and Will Patrick Fleming, senior officers in Kerry No. 2 Brigade, captured in Kilcummin.

23 August: Free State forces land at Reenard Pier, near Cahersiveen.

24 August: Cahersiveen captured by Free State Army in early hours as Republican forces retreat to the countryside.

4 September: Ohermong ambush, near Cahersiveen.

9 September: Republican forces under John Joe Rice capture Kenmare after intense fighting.

27 September: IRA forces repel a landing party from HMS *Barrington* at Lackeen Pier, Blackwater and fire is exchanged with the warship.

Timeline of Events in Kerry

27 September: Intense fighting in Killorglin as IRA attempt to capture the town.

20 October: Senior IRA leader in the Causeway area, Captain Paddy O'Connor, is captured.

31 October: Jack Lawlor shot dead in custody in Ballyheigue.

2 November: Mick O'Sullivan killed at Knockane, Headford.

6 December: Free State forces retake Kenmare.

19 December: Con Casey, Dermot O'Connor, Matthew Moroney and Tom Devane sentenced to death in Ballymullen Barracks.

1923

20 January: James Hanlon, James Daly, Michael Brosnan and John Clifford executed in Ballymullen Gaol.

22 February: Michael Pierce's IRA column surrenders.

28 February: Tom O'Driscoll's IRA column surrenders.

5 March: Intense fighting at Gurrane near Cahersiveen as IRA column fights its way out of encircling Free State troops.

6 March: Landmine at Knocknagoshel kills five Free State soldiers.

7 March: Massacre at Ballyseedy by Free State forces kills eight Republican prisoners, with Stephen Fuller escaping.

7 March: Massacre at Countess Bridge, Killarney, by Free State forces kills four Republican prisoners, with Tadhg Coffey escaping.

12 March: Five Republican prisoners shot and blown up at Bahaghs, Cahersiveen.

14 March: Charlie Daly, Dan Enright and Tim O'Sullivan of Kerry and Seán Larkin of County Derry executed at Drumboe, County Donegal.

6 April: Fighting at Derrynafeena, Glencar.

10 April: General Liam Lynch, IRA chief of staff, killed in Knockmealdown Mountains in County Tipperary.

14 April: Austin Stack taken prisoner near Lismore, Co. Waterford.

16 April: Clashmealcon Caves siege begins.

18 April: Clashmealcon Caves siege ends.

25 April: Reg Hathaway, Jim McEnery and Ned Greaney executed in Ballymullen Gaol.

30 April: IRA declares unilateral ceasefire.

24 May: IRA units ordered to dump arms by new chief of staff, Frank Aiken.

29 May: Commandant Jeremiah O'Leary killed in custody in Castleisland.

November: Hunger strike undertaken by thousands of Republican prisoners.

December: Free State begins to release Civil War prisoners.

1924: Last of Civil War prisoners released in July.

1926: Foundation of Fianna Fáil after Éamon de Valera leaves Sinn Féin.

1927: General elections in June and September see Fianna Fáil as the dominant party in County Kerry.

1929: Austin Stack dies on 27 April.

1932: De Valera becomes taoiseach as Fianna Fáil win the general election, backed by the IRA.

1936: IRA declared illegal by Fianna Fáil government and arrests of Republicans begin.

1939: Several Kerry IRA Volunteers take part in Seán Russell's IRA bombing campaign in Britain which is based on a similar campaign by the Fenians in the 1880s.

1940: Fianna Fáil government interns over 500 Republican suspects and jails a further 600 under Offences Against the State Act, including a large number from Kerry.

1942: Execution of Cahersiveen Volunteer Maurice O'Neill.

1944: Execution of IRA Chief of Staff Charlie Kerins of Tralee.

1956: IRA Volunteers from Kerry active in 'Border Campaign'.

1957: John Joe Rice elected Sinn Féin TD for South Kerry but Fianna Fáil remain the dominant party in the county.

Timeline of Events in Kerry

1962: 'Border Campaign' ends as IRA call a ceasefire.

1969: 'Troubles' begin in the six counties and IRA becomes increasingly active in the war against crown forces.

1975: Kerry IRA Volunteer Brendan Dowd captured in England while on active service. He is released in 1999 having served twenty-five years, the longest period of incarceration served by a Kerryman in the cause of Irish freedom.

1977: Brendan Doherty of Currow, Martin Ferris of Churchill and Danny O'Sullivan of Barrow are among twenty IRA prisoners who take part in a hunger strike in Portlaoise Gaol that lasts forty-seven days.

1984: Large arms shipment from America aboard the *Marita Ann* destined for IRA units in the six counties is captured off the Kerry coast.

1997: Provisional IRA declares ceasefire.

2005: Death of Volunteer Dan Keating of Ballygamboon, Castlemaine, the last survivor of the Tan and Civil Wars. He remained an uncompromising, unreconstructed Republican throughout his 105 years and his death marked the end of an era. There was no official recognition of his passing.

Bibliography

Abbott, Richard, *Police Casualties in Ireland 1919–1922* (Mercier Press, 2002)
Barrett, J. J., *In the Name of the Game* (Dub Press, 1997)
Bateson, Ray, *They Died by Pearse's Side* (Irish Graves Publications, 2010)
Bourke, Marcus, *The O'Rahilly* (Anvil Books, 1967)
Breen, Dan, *My Fight For Irish Freedom* (Talbot Press, 1924)
Clayton, Xander, *Aud* (GAC Publications, 2007)
De Bhulbh, Seán, *Sloinnte na h-Éireann – Irish Surnames* (Comhar-Chumann Íde Naofa, 1997)
Donegal Martyrs Memorial Committee, *The Story of the Drumboe Martyrs* (1956)
Doyle, Tom, *The Civil War in Kerry* (Mercier Press, 2008)
Doyle, Tom, *The Summer Campaign in Kerry* (Mercier Press, 2010)
Gaughan, J. Anthony, *Listowel and its Vicinity* (Mercier Press, 1973)
Gaughan, J. Anthony, *Austin Stack – Portrait of a Separatist* (Kingdom Books, 1977)
Hanley, Brian, *The IRA 1926–1936* (Four Courts Press, 2002)
Harnett, Mossie, *Victory and Woe* (University College Dublin Press, 2002)
Harrington, Niall C., *Kerry Landing* (Anvil Books, 1992)
Lynch, Cecilia, *From the GPO to Clashmealcon Caves* (privately published, 2003)
Lynch, Robert, *The Northern IRA and the Early Years of Partition* (Irish Academic Press, 2006)
Macardle, Dorothy, *Tragedies of Kerry* (Emton Press, 1924)
Mac Eoin, Uinseann, *Survivors* (Argenta Press, 1980)
Mac Eoin, Uinseann, *Harry* (Argenta Press, 1985)
Mac Eoin, Uinseann, *The IRA in the Twilight Years 1923–1948* (Argenta Press, 1997)
Mac Ciarnáin, Séamus (ed.), *The Last Post* (National Graves Association, 3rd edition, 1985)
MacEvilly, Michael, *A Splendid Resistance* (De Burca, 2011)
Matthews, Ann, *The Kimmage Garrison, 1916* (Four Courts Press, 2010)
Matthews, Ann, *Dissidents – Irish Republican Women 1923–1941* (Mercier Press, 2012)

McCoole, Sinéad, *No Ordinary Women* (O'Brien Press, 2003)
Monteith, Robert, *Casement's Last Adventure* (privately published, 1932)
Murphy, Jeremiah, *When Youth Was Mine* (Mentor, 1998)
O'Callaghan, John, *The Battle for Kilmallock* (Mercier Press, 2011)
Ó Concubhair, Brian (ed.), *Kerry's Fighting Story 1916–1921* (Mercier Press, 2009)
Ó Concubhair, Seán Seosamh, *Kilmoyley to the Rescue* (privately published, 2000)
O'Connor, Séamus, *Tomorrow Was Another Day* (Anvil Books, 1970)
O'Connor, Tommy, *Ardfert in Times Past* (Foilseacháin Bréanainn, 1999)
O'Donoghue, Florence, *Sworn to be Free – IRA Jailbreaks 1918–1921* (Anvil Books, 1971)
Ó Duibhir, Liam, *The Donegal Awakening* (Mercier Press, 2009)
Ó Duibhir, Liam, *Donegal & the Civil War* (Mercier Press, 2011)
O'Dwyer, Martin (Bob), *Tipperary's Sons and Daughters 1916–1923* (Cashel Folk Village, 2001)
O'Dwyer, Martin (Bob), *Seventy-Seven of Mine Said Ireland* (Deshaoirse Publications, 2007)
O'Dwyer, Martin (Bob), *Death Before Dishonour* (Cashel Folk Village, 2010)
Ó Luing, Seán, *I Die in a Good Cause* (Anvil Books, 1970)
O'Mahony, Seán, *Frongoch – University of Revolution* (FDR Teoranta, 1987)
O'Mahony, Seán, *The First Hunger Striker – Thomas Ashe 1917* (Elo Publications, 2001)
O'Malley, Ernie, *The Men Will Talk To Me – Kerry Interviews*, edited by Cormac O'Malley and Tim Horgan (Mercier Press, 2012)
Ó Riordáin, John J., *Kiskeam Versus The Empire* (privately published, 2010)
Ó Ruairc, Pádraig Óg, *Blood on the Banner – The Republican Struggle in Clare* (Mercier Press, 2009)
Ó Ruairc, Pádraig Óg, *The Battle for Limerick City* (Mercier Press, 2010)
Ó Súilleabháin, Micheál, *Where Mountainy Men Have Sown* (Mercier Press, 2013)
Ó Súilleabháin, Seán S., *Aililiú Rathmore* (privately published, 1990)
Pinkman, John A., *In the Legion of the Vanguard* (Mercier Press, 1999)
Toomey, Thomas, *The War of Independence in Limerick 1912–1921* (privately published, 2010)

INDEX

A

Abbeydorney 82, 83, 86, 87, 93, 103, 105, 121, 211, 450
Abbeyfeale 161, 174, 198, 200, 209, 215, 216, 217, 247, 391, 392
Acres 132
Active service units/flying columns 22, 28, 29, 38, 40, 54, 58, 60, 64, 66, 73, 78, 83–86, 93, 96, 103, 131, 137, 154, 158, 163, 171, 174, 178, 185, 189, 194, 200, 221, 222, 230, 235, 237, 239, 242, 248, 253, 255, 259, 261, 265, 267, 269, 271, 274, 278, 279, 281, 293, 307, 313, 328, 329, 333, 349, 351–353, 355, 366, 369, 399, 400, 409, 424, 425, 430
Aghadoe 320
Aglish (Ballyhar) 239, 283
Aglish (Lispole) 138
Ahabeg 84, 449
Ahane 48
Ahaneboy 200, 201, 224
Ahern, Jack 174, 189–191, 418
Ahern, Michael (Ballycleave) 331, 332
Ahern, Michael (Ballydonoghue) 184
Aiken, Frank 23, 219, 454
Allman, Dan 235, 238, 239, 278, 281–283, 307
Allman, Paddy 239, 278, 283
Alohert 294
Anabla 193, 291, 307
Anistar, Dr 344
Annagh 65, 81, 143, 322
Annascaul 56, 128, 129, 132, 133, 137, 140, 141, 203, 449
Arabella 235, 268
Arbour Hill prison 394, 445
Archer, Edmond 86
Archer, Florence 86
Archer, John 86
Archer, Richard 86
Archer, Thomas 86–88, 122
Archer, William 86
Ardea 269
Ardfert 38, 39, 50, 69, 70, 78, 82, 83, 91–93, 108, 113, 115–117, 119, 120, 195, 196, 348, 380, 437, 450, 451
Ardoughter 84, 85, 397, 398
Armstrong Holmes, Major General Philip 450
Asdee 153, 155, 190, 409
Ashbourne 131, 378
Ashe, Gregory 56, 132, 142, 377
Ashe, Thomas (Kinard) 142, 376, 377–381, 448
Ashe, Thomas M. (Lispole) 55, 56, 131, 132
Ashill 233
Athea 106, 158–160, 174–176, 185
Athlone 385, 388, 411, 447
Aud 21, 27, 278, 357, 432, 442, 445, 447
Aughacasla 73, 74, 128, 135, 136, 151
Aughatubrid 386, 409
Auxiliaries 22, 28, 57, 59, 62, 83, 105, 109, 119, 121, 230, 248, 249, 253, 255, 256, 260–262, 265, 266, 268, 279, 315, 316, 400, 401, 450

B

Bahaghs 338, 349, 352, 354, 356, 361, 367–369, 372, 374, 453
Baile na nGall 415
Bailey, Bill 40, 41, 42, 167, 252
Baily, James (Jim) 237, 238, 239, 255, 282, 283, 423
Ballinacourty 132, 141

INDEX

Ballinahunt 56
Ballinakilla 342
Ballinalee 380
Ballinasloe 412
Ballinatin 391, 392
Ballinbranhig 93, 123
Ballincrossig 397
Ballineanig 148, 149
Ballinoe 233, 249, 250
Ballinskelligs 348, 349, 362–364, 366, 368, 373
Ballintubrid 442
Balloonagh 48
Ballyard 358, 379
Ballybeg 230
Ballybrack 59, 60, 255, 279, 450
Ballybunion 84, 85, 113, 123, 125, 153, 155, 157, 158, 165, 175, 178, 184, 185, 187, 188, 407, 419, 420, 430, 448–450
Ballycarbery 251, 348
Ballycarty 76, 77, 235, 240, 241
Ballycleave 331, 332
Ballydavid 55, 128
Ballydonoghue 84, 154, 161, 163, 165, 171, 183, 184, 430
Ballydribeen 399
Ballyduff 84, 85, 95, 97, 100–102, 107, 110, 112, 113, 125, 128, 135, 153, 163, 397, 398, 450, 451
Ballydwyer 235, 255, 256, 261, 262, 265–268, 450
Ballyferriter 128, 143, 146, 148, 149, 414, 448
Ballygamboon 66, 68, 455
Ballyhar 239, 278, 279, 283
Ballyheigue 82, 83, 86, 93, 96, 98, 103, 104, 118, 123, 453
Ballykissane 21, 328, 339, 358, 366, 421, 433, 442, 443, 447
Ballylanders 417
Ballylongford 153, 155–158, 161, 174,
184, 190, 398, 405, 408, 416, 417, 420, 450
Ballymacadam 205
Ballymacandy 64, 129, 345, 451
Ballymacelligott 19, 20, 57, 59, 60, 172, 181, 193, 205, 207, 221, 231, 233–237, 239–244, 247, 251–253, 255, 257–259, 261, 262, 265–268, 281, 283, 387, 448–451
Ballymacthomas 235
Ballymakeera 427, 428
Ballymullen 29, 31, 36, 39, 41, 48, 62, 63, 69, 74, 78, 79, 81, 94–99, 106, 108, 111–114, 121–123, 126, 127, 142, 166, 167, 179, 199, 201, 202, 205, 213, 214, 243, 252, 291, 292, 337, 341, 354, 367, 438, 444, 453, 454
Ballyrobert 83
Ballyroe 27, 29, 33
Ballyseede Castle 336, 337
Ballyseedy 16, 41, 49, 59–61, 71, 81, 88, 90, 95, 107, 112, 113, 119, 121, 122, 127, 139, 144, 152, 167–169, 199, 202, 214, 225, 240, 241, 255, 336, 337, 347, 354, 367, 381, 382, 421, 422, 430, 438, 439, 444, 453
Ballyvourney 421, 427
Banna Strand 21, 27, 38, 70, 82, 195, 234, 435, 445
Barleymount 300, 303
Barraduff 283, 297, 306, 307, 314, 319, 321, 324, 423, 424
Barranarig 201, 202, 210, 211, 438
Barrett, Dick 52
Barrett, James 221
Barrett, John 164
Barrow 46, 69, 73
Barry, James 89, 90
Barry, Paddy 28
Baslicon 348
Beale 153, 155
Bealnadeaga 307, 324, 423

Beara peninsula 269
Béaslaí, Piaras 379
Beasley, M. 188
Beaufort 233, 278–280, 286, 287, 289, 293–296, 329, 331, 332, 347, 358, 433
Bedford 153
Beheenagh 244, 247, 248
Behins 153
Belfast 322, 325, 343, 378, 394, 400, 402, 421, 432, 445
Benson, Head Const. Francis 28
Bishop, Michael Stanley 294–296, 347
Black and Tans 22, 50, 51, 59, 60, 64, 83, 87, 91, 92, 101, 105, 115, 116, 154, 156, 159, 160, 164, 169, 171, 176, 177, 190, 191, 195, 196, 198, 255, 262, 279, 307, 323, 344, 389, 449, 450
Black Banks 218, 297
Black Valley 278, 279, 288, 448
Blackwater 269, 452
Blennerville 27, 29, 41, 393
Blue shirts 394
Bog Road ambush 222, 307, 310, 451
Boherbue 27, 57, 62
Bonane 269
Bower, The 222, 229, 307, 423
Boyle, Sgt 244–247, 257, 258
Brackhill 176, 249, 328
Brackloon 274
Brady, Peter 352, 361
Brandon 144, 145
Breahig 221, 222
Breen, Dan (Causeway) 117
Breen, Dan (Tipperary) 391
Breen, J. 188
Brennan, Michael 161, 162, 198
Brennan's Glen 208
Breslin, Ned 122, 127, 167, 202, 438
Brian Houlihan Barracks 31, 126
Brick, William 118
Broderick, Christy 'Broder' 174, 175, 387

Broderick, Denis 240, 241
Brosna 193, 198, 200, 215, 216, 218, 221, 229, 247, 297, 380, 436, 449
Brosnan, Con 163, 174, 189–191, 211, 216, 418
Brosnan, Fr 284, 292
Brosnan, Jack 242
Brosnan, Michael (Ballymacelligott) 97, 242, 243, 251, 252, 291, 453
Brosnan, Michael (Castleisland) 92, 195, 196
Brosnan, Seán 144
Brosnan, Tadhg 28, 64, 66, 75, 128–130, 132, 133, 135, 139, 140, 144, 145, 147, 203, 379, 425, 449, 452
Brosnan, Thomas 212
Brosnan, William 421, 422
Brown, Danny 164
Browne, Fr 320
Browne, John (Ballymacelligott) 244, 245–248, 257, 258
Browne, John (Firies) 250
Browne, Paddy 244
Browne, Peter 204
Browne, Richard 212
Browne, Robert (Bob) 244, 246–248
Broy, Éamonn 394
Broy Harriers 394
Brugha, Cathal 444, 445
Bruree 38, 66, 171, 181
Buckley, Patrick 197–201, 214, 382
Buckley, Stephen 284, 285, 292, 299–301, 304
Bunadereen 349, 366
Bunyan, Dick 172
Burke, Fr 212
Burke, James 336
Byrne, Joe 178, 179
Byrne, John (Ballymacelligott) 57, 234, 244, 259, 267, 268
Byrne, Patrick (Castleisland) 219
Byrne, Patrick (Tralee) 31, 32

C

Caher 242, 251
Caheranne 393
Caherbarnagh 282
Caherdaniel 349, 361
Cahersiveen 16, 20, 49, 82, 178, 214, 242, 251, 252, 275, 338–340, 348, 349, 351, 352, 354–375, 386, 396–398, 402, 404, 407, 409, 416, 419, 420, 432, 442, 443, 446, 452–454
Caherslee 57, 63
Cahill, Const. 409
Cahill, Fr John 106, 111
Cahill, Michael 339
Cahill, Paddy 27–29, 43, 54–56, 58, 64, 71, 73, 75, 82, 131, 137, 174, 178, 189, 235, 327, 329, 451
Callinafercy 327
Camp 73, 128, 129, 139, 142, 145, 151, 179, 192, 448, 449
Cannon, Bernard 410
Cantillon, John 91, 92, 195, 196
Canuig 373, 374
Caragh Lake 327, 331, 358
Carey, Dr Ned 296
Carey, Jeremiah 309
Carhooearagh 190
Carmody, Edmund (Eddie) 156, 157
Carmody, James 262
Carmody, Maurice (Mossy) 237, 241, 244, 245, 247
Carmody, Tom 174
Carnahone 296
Carrahane 38, 39, 69, 70, 78, 79
Carrantuohill 67, 333
Carrigaha 151
Carrigeens 308
Carrigoran 389
Carroll, Jack 163
Carroll, Tim 163, 175
Casement, Roger 21, 22, 27, 39, 40, 78, 82, 195, 234, 237, 265, 325, 380, 435, 445, 447
Casey, Con 36, 251, 453
Casey, Jeremiah (Jerry) 286, 287
Casey, John 133, 134
Casey, Maurice (Mossie) 233, 249, 250
Casey, Patrick (Pat) 288, 289, 448
Cashen 84, 123, 184, 449
Castlecove 348, 349
Castlegregory 56, 65, 66, 73–75, 128, 129, 133–136, 139, 140, 144–147, 151, 152, 425
Castleisland 20, 76, 155, 181, 182, 192–196, 198–202, 204–207, 209, 211–227, 230, 232, 234, 235, 237, 238, 240, 244, 247, 253, 256, 261, 262, 281, 282, 391, 392, 421, 422, 426, 440, 441, 447, 451, 454
Castlemahon 418
Castlemaine 64, 66, 68, 129, 176, 263, 328, 329, 336, 345, 385, 451, 455
Cathair Chaoin 148
Causeway 82, 83, 86–90, 93, 96–99, 106, 110, 111, 113, 116–118, 123, 195, 243, 449, 450, 453
Charleville 36
Childers, Erskine 181
Churchill 29, 45–47, 69, 70, 78, 80–82, 455
Churchtown 287
Clancy, Peadar 380
Clann na Poblacta 396
Clare 187, 197, 198, 205, 215, 224, 286, 324–326, 341, 376, 379, 380, 389, 390, 399, 414, 436, 448
Claremorris 441
Clarke, Jim 122, 202
Clarke, Tom 406, 445
Clashmealcon Caves 82, 84, 85, 94, 95, 97, 99, 100, 106, 107, 110, 111, 113, 114, 123–125, 127, 454
Clifford, Daniel 351, 352
Clifford, Dinsy (Denis) 331, 332

Clifford, Jim 266
Clifford, John (Jack) 97, 242, 243, 251, 252, 291, 453
Clifford, Patrick 387
Clifford, Tom 82, 91, 115, 348
Clifford, Vol. 69, 78
Cloghane 128, 129, 140, 146, 147, 203, 449
Cloghanelinaghan 369
Clogher 247, 260, 261, 266, 268
Clogherbrien 390
Clonbanin 194, 222, 230, 307, 310, 450
Clonmel 140
Cloonnafinneela 86
Clounalour 265
Clounts 306
Coffey, Dr Brian 245
Coffey, David 204
Coffey, Jerry 294, 295
Coffey, Jim 279, 282, 283
Coffey, John 278
Coffey, Johnny 295
Coffey, Mike 294, 295
Coffey, Patrick 369
Coffey, Tadhg 285, 300, 302–304, 453
Coilbee 189, 190
Colgan, Const. 184
Collins, Jimmy 198
Collins, Michael 23, 25, 97, 224, 291, 381, 383, 384, 387, 394, 397, 410, 451, 452
Collins, Tom (Ballydonoghue) 165
Condon, Michael 152
Connolly, James 378, 407
Conor Pass 135
Considine, Const. 245, 257
Conway, Dan Joe 31
Conway, John 'Sonny' 31, 32
Conway O'Connor, Charlie 333, 334
Conway O'Connor, William 68, 333, 334
Coolard 162, 175

Coolmagort 293
Coomatlockane 355
Coombs, Major 226
Coonana 348
Cooney, Andy 28, 29, 84, 177, 179, 193, 226, 235, 237, 278, 281, 306, 311, 451
Cooney, Const. Joseph 345
Cooper, Giles 421, 423, 424
Cordal 193, 203, 204, 218, 219, 221, 222, 227, 231, 235
Corduff 377
Cork 23, 33, 51, 60, 76, 118, 151, 152, 188, 222, 229, 231, 239, 276, 306, 307, 309, 310, 319, 322–325, 329, 340, 343, 352, 361, 383, 384, 386, 391, 397, 400, 410, 421, 427, 428, 434, 436, 437, 449, 452
Cork Gaol 66, 69, 221, 382, 451
Corridon, Paddy 184
Corry, Lt 273
Costello, Jim 172
Cotton, Alf 27
Countess Bridge 280, 285, 292, 296, 300, 302, 304, 305, 354, 453
Countess Road 285
Courtney, Fr 368
Courtney, Michael (Mícheál Cournane) 353–356, 367, 368, 371, 374
Coye, Patrick 215–217
Coyle, Daniel 384, 387, 410
Coyle, Harry 407
Crag 241
Craggalough 389
Creeslough 385, 388, 410
Crimmins, Tom 407
Cromane 361
Cronin, Batty (the Smith) 310
Cronin, Denis (Castlegregory) 135
Cronin, Denis (Din Batt) 310
Cronin, Jack (Castlemaine) 328
Cronin, James (Castlemaine) 328
Cronin, Jimmy (Castlegregory) 135, 136

Cronin, John 59, 181, 234, 235, 237, 240, 244, 245–247, 255, 257, 258, 265
Cronin, Michael 135
Cronin, Patrick (Pat) 310
Cronin, William (Bill) 310, 311
Crossroads 269, 270, 271, 276, 277
Cuas 128
Culhane, Maurice 211, 224
Cumann na mBan 40, 132, 166, 201, 210, 218, 229, 297, 364, 416, 438
Cumming, General Hanway 222, 230
Curragh 30, 49, 81, 148, 206, 243, 322, 380, 393, 394, 431
Curraghatoosane 165
Curraheen 27, 29, 64, 65
Currans 197, 231, 233, 382
Curravoola 353–355, 371, 374
Currow 192, 193, 203, 218, 229, 230–233, 291, 421, 425, 426, 455

D

Dáil Éireann 22, 27, 315, 395, 445, 448, 451, 452
Dalton, Patrick (Paddy) 158–160, 174–177, 185, 186, 451
Daly, Charles (Charlie) (Firies) 68, 230, 233, 376, 382–388, 410, 411, 453
Daly, Charles (Gortatlea) 231
Daly, Con 382
Daly, Dan (Castleisland) 440
Daly, Dan (Killorglin) 33, 34, 35
Daly, Denis (Dinny) 338, 339, 348, 352, 358, 366, 397, 398, 407, 420, 432, 442
Daly, James (Jim) (Knockeendubh) 97, 243, 252, 284, 290–292, 453
Daly, Jim (Castlegregory) 56
Daly, Jim (Headford) 423
Daly, John (Jack) 199, 200–202, 214
Daly, Julia (née OConnor) 35
Daly, Michael 307
Daly, Paddy 29, 32, 34, 42, 74, 94, 97, 98, 111, 121, 122, 167, 208, 209, 213, 224, 235, 252, 291
Daly, Tom (Firies) 208, 209, 233, 382, 452
Daly, Willie (Firies) 382
Darcy, Martin 216
Dartmoor 379
Dawros 269
Deasy, Liam 93
Dee, Con 155, 158–160, 174–177, 185, 186
Deegan, Peter 157
Deelis 139, 151
Delaney, James J. 354, 372, 374
Dempsey, Jim 224, 296
Dennehy, Dan 306, 314, 324
Dennehy, Mick 293, 306, 324
Denning, Const. 245, 257
Derk 248
Derrig, Tom 309
Derry (Listowel) 174
Derry county 233, 383, 385, 410, 453
Derrycunnihy 279, 288, 289
Derrymore 43–45, 47, 66, 70, 81, 179, 185, 351, 438
Derrynafeena 67, 68, 328, 333, 334, 453
Derrynane 352, 355
De Valera, Éamon 24, 25, 187, 379, 380, 393–396, 404, 446, 448, 454
Devane, Michael 278
Devane, Patrick 278
Devane, Tom 251, 453
Dillane, Brian 156, 157
Dingle 44, 54–56, 58, 65, 81, 128, 129, 131, 133, 135–143, 147–149, 379, 381, 405, 415
Dodds, Dr 344
Doherty, Brendan 421, 425, 426, 455
Doherty, Flossie 327
Doherty, John 230, 425
Dominic, Fr 381
Donaghy, James 384, 387, 410

Donegal 149, 154, 376, 382–388, 410, 453
Donnelly, Dan 117
Donoghue, Denis 58
Dooks 332
Doonferris 185
Doora 348
Dowdall, Dr 381
Dowd, Brendan 455
Dowling, Joseph 325
Downey, Mick 187
Doyle, Michael 28
Dromavalla 35, 60, 332, 337, 343, 433, 443
Drombeg 163
Dromerrin 190
Dromkeen 94, 96, 98, 387
Dromod 348, 353, 366, 367
Dromroe 229, 230, 425, 426
Droum 261, 262, 421, 423, 436
Drumboe 384–386, 388, 411, 453
Drummond, Thomas 36, 37
Drummond, Tim (Taidhgín) 69, 78
Duagh 153, 159, 172, 174, 175, 177, 248, 387, 449, 451
Dublin 20, 23, 27, 52, 80, 91, 97, 133, 142, 144, 161, 162, 169, 178, 180, 193, 197, 205, 206, 209, 224, 233, 256, 262, 271, 278, 291, 296, 306, 317, 318, 320, 324, 325, 338, 354, 357, 358, 366, 376–380, 382, 384, 386, 393, 394, 396–398, 400, 402, 405, 407, 408, 412, 416, 417, 419–421, 425, 432, 439, 442, 446–448, 452
Dublin Guard 23, 29, 31, 41, 44, 46, 68, 74, 79, 80, 99, 122, 142, 202, 205, 208, 211–214, 219, 224, 225, 231, 252, 269, 280, 291, 296, 303, 308, 314, 338, 347, 354, 356, 367, 372, 374, 437
Duff, Sgt 414
Duhig, Michael 129, 144

Dún Chaoin 128
Dungeel 327, 343
Dungegan 362, 363
Dunlewy 384, 385, 387, 410
Dunloe 286, 287
Dunne, Michael 202
Dún Síon 142
Dunworth's Cave 110, 113, 123, 124
Dwyer, Eugene 354–356, 367, 368, 371, 374
Dysert 168, 207, 238, 281, 392

E

Easter Rising 21, 22, 24, 27, 52, 80, 82, 131, 133, 144, 145, 153, 156, 183, 192, 197, 233, 234, 237, 244, 249, 267, 278, 306, 312, 317, 318, 322, 324, 327, 328, 338, 339, 343, 348, 352, 357, 366, 376–378, 381, 382, 394, 397, 398, 406–408, 411, 412, 416, 419, 420, 421, 425, 432, 433, 442–445, 447
Egan, Timmy 105, 163, 164
English, Patrick 216
Ennis 389, 390
Enniscorthy 394
Ennismore 174
Enright, Dan 154, 174, 376, 384–388, 410, 411, 453
Eyrie, Captain 427

F

Faha 146, 281
Fahadubh 213
Fahamore 139
Falcarragh 388
Faley, John 158
Fallon, Const. 244–247, 257, 258
Fallon, Joseph 216
Farmer's Bridge 27, 37, 59–61, 71, 222, 251, 336, 450
Farnlow, Const. 190, 191

Index

Farranfore 59, 60, 197, 207, 229, 230, 233, 234, 238, 258, 282, 426
Favier, Joe 320
Feale's Bridge 215, 216, 218, 247
Fenit 21, 23, 29, 33, 43, 45, 46, 64, 66, 69, 73, 74, 78, 115, 129, 181, 192, 205, 235, 280, 290, 306, 308, 357, 390, 437, 438, 447, 452
Fennell, Edward 414
Fermoyle 348
Ferris, Dr 56
Ferris, Martin 426, 455
Ferriter, Mike 148
Fianna Fáil 24, 393, 395, 404, 446, 454
Fianna, Na 38, 40, 48, 50, 51, 54, 64, 65, 69, 71, 75, 76, 78, 146, 178, 187, 207
Fingal 378, 379
Finn, Seán 418
Finuge 153, 166
Firies 20, 60, 193, 197, 226, 230, 233, 235, 249, 250, 281, 382, 410, 447
Fitzgerald, Anthony 38
Fitzgerald, Capt. 404
Fitzgerald, Desmond 407
Fitzgerald, Eugene 38, 39
Fitzgerald, James 56, 128, 132, 137
Fitzgerald, Maurice 137, 138
Fitzgerald, Paddy Paul 29, 43, 47, 74
Flavin, Dan 98
Flavin, Jack 44
Fleming, John Joseph (Jackie) 40–42
Fleming, May 40
Fleming, Michael (Mick) 28, 40
Fleming, Tom 203, 204, 232
Fleming, Will Patrick 208, 209, 452
Flood, Ed 97, 122, 202, 243, 252
Flood, Frank 181, 243
Flying columns. *See* Active service units/flying columns
Flynn, Jack 222, 227, 237, 244–246, 253, 254, 257, 258
Flynn, Michael (Aughacasla) 151, 152

Flynn, Michael (Mickey Joe) (Tralee) 43–45
Flynn, Neilus 87
Flynn, Thomas 46, 47
Foheraghmore 138
Foilmore 20, 348
Foley, Daniel 48, 49, 71, 75
Foley, Detective 403
Foley, John 48
Foley, Thomas 28
Foley, Timmy 48, 49
Foran, Patrick (Paddy) 161, 162
Fossa 278, 295, 296
Four Courts 23, 154, 161, 180, 384, 394, 452
Foxfort 86
Frongoch 234, 244, 268, 278, 379, 412, 413, 447, 448
Fuller, Seán 113, 123
Fuller, Stephen 121, 122, 126, 127, 167, 438, 453
Fullerton, Alf 132
Fybough 28, 54, 64, 178, 328

G

Gaelic Athletic Association 20
Gaelic League 20, 27, 377, 406, 414, 416, 432, 442
Gaffney, Jeremiah 211, 212
Gale Bridge 84, 184, 449
Gale Cemetery 162, 164, 165, 172, 173, 186, 421, 430, 431
Gallagher, Const. 157
Galvin, John (Jack) 113, 163, 335–337
Galvin, Michael (Mick) 163–165, 184, 202
Galvin, Mossy 222, 227
Galvin, Murt 163
Galway 37, 215, 224, 325, 376, 412, 420, 436
Galwey, John 230
Galworthy, Private 37

Gantly, Superintendent Seán 403
Gap of Dunloe 238, 278, 281, 286, 293, 296
Garrahadoo 335
Garrynagore 105–107
Garvey, Paddy 28, 58, 74, 179
Gaynor, Christopher 400
Germany 21, 22, 59, 325, 357, 406, 445
Gill, Detective 403
Glanageenty 19
Glanteenasig 56
Glass, William 414
Gleann na nGealt 142
Gleensk 369, 370
Glenbeigh 129, 320, 327, 328, 331, 338, 340, 342, 436, 451
Glencar 48, 49, 64, 67, 181, 294, 327–329, 333, 334, 343–347, 352, 369, 371, 376, 416, 418, 449, 450, 453
Glenflesk 208, 283, 306–308, 319, 423
Glenlahern 218, 221
Glenlough 56, 269, 349
Glen, The (An Gleann) 348, 362, 364, 365, 373
Glountane 203, 204, 231, 232
Gneeveguilla 299, 306, 307, 309, 310, 315, 316
Gormanston 30, 205, 206
Gortaglanna 154, 155, 159, 160, 164, 175–177, 185, 186, 386, 451
Gortalassa 271, 276, 277
Gortatlea 22, 221, 231, 233–235, 237, 242, 244, 246, 247, 253–255, 257, 258, 267, 288, 348, 382, 448, 449
Gortclohy 126
Gortdromagowna 175
Gortnahaneboy 313
Gortnaminch 166, 167
Gortnaskehy 187
Gortroe 217
GPO 317, 339, 352, 366, 378, 398, 407, 420

Grady, Frank 320, 338, 339, 340
Grady, Stephen 84
Greaney, Edward (Ned) 93–95, 98, 99, 106, 111, 112, 114, 454
Greaney, Thomas (Greany) 139
Great Southern Hotel Killarney 208, 209, 279, 280, 285, 299–301, 303, 305
Greer, Mr 69, 78, 79
Griffin, David 193
Griffin, Denis 142, 149, 150
Griffin, Jack 132
Griffin, Jeremiah 373
Griffin, Jerome 288
Griffin, John 'Gilpin' 360
Griffin, Michael (Aughacasla) 151, 152
Griffin, Michael (Cahersiveen) 348, 349, 351, 352
Gurrane 338, 350–352, 354, 369, 453
Gurrane Bridge 171
Gurranemore 253
Gurteen 141

H

Hallisey, Michael (Mike) 366, 368
Hamilton, Capt. 135
Hancock, James 99, 111, 142, 437
Hanlon, James 94–99, 112, 243, 252, 291, 453
Hannafin, Jerry 51
Hannafin, Michael 51
Hannafin, Ned 172
Hannafin, Percy (Patrick) 48–51, 71, 75
Hannon, Jim 389
Hanrahan, Jack 437
Harnett, Mossy 198
Harrington, Michael 132
Harrington, Niall 126, 127
Harrington, William 52, 53
Hartnett, Mary Ann 166
Hartnett, Moss 166
Hartnett, Patrick (Pat) 166–168
Hartnett's Hotel (Castleisland) 194,

199, 201, 207, 212, 219, 220, 224, 230, 440
Hathaway, Reginald 95–100, 106, 111, 112, 114, 454
Hawley, Thomas (Tommy) 54–56, 132
Hayes, Edmund (Eddie) 156, 157
Headford 282, 283, 307, 319, 321, 421, 453
Headford Junction 194, 203, 235, 238, 239, 271, 276, 282, 283, 307, 310, 423, 450
Healy, Con 57, 58, 62, 265
Healy, Danny (Ballymakeera) 428
Healy, Dan (Tralee) 28, 29
Healy, James 57, 62, 63
Healy, Paddy 113, 123
Healy, Philip 116
Healy, 'Sailor' Dan 272
Healy, Tom (Ardfert) 116
Healy, Tom (Clare) 376, 389, 390
Hegarty, Denis 269
Hegarty, Liam (Bill) 421, 427, 428, 429
Herbert, Arthur 229
Herlihy, Paddy 255, 256, 261
Herlihy, William 262
Hickey, Ben 325
Hickey, Cornelius 207, 209
Hickey, Eily 201
Hickey, Jim (James) 376, 391, 392, 435
Hickey, Kathleen 201
Hickey, Laurence (Larry) 312
Hillville 281, 327, 450
Hobson, Bulmer 406
Hoffman, Frank 59, 60, 61, 450
Hogan, Michael 113, 336, 337
Hogan, Seán 391
Hollywood, Sgt 323
Home Rule 20, 21
Horan, Neddy (Éamonn) 63, 337
Hostages 37, 92, 195, 207, 208, 230, 231
Houlihan, J. 188
Houlihan, James 101

Houlihan, John (Seán) 101, 102
Houlihan, Willie 101
Hunger strikes 24, 28, 54, 69, 91, 101, 115, 130, 131, 152, 206, 322, 325, 376, 380, 426, 445, 448, 449, 455

I

Incharoe 344, 345
Inchycullane 291
Innishannon 436, 437
Inny Valley 353, 355, 366, 367, 371, 373
Irish Republican Brotherhood (IRB) 21, 27, 73, 269, 317, 357, 377–379, 406, 416, 432, 442, 444
Islandboy 353, 366, 368
Iveragh Peninsula 49, 67, 343, 348, 355, 364

J

Johnston, Edward 60, 61

K

Kane, Const. 401
Kane, Dr 56, 132
Kavanagh, Patrick 354, 374, 437
Kavanagh, Seán a Chóta 143
Keane, Maurice 128
Keane, Michael (Clare) 414
Keating, Cornelius (Con) 21, 348, 357–359, 432, 433, 442, 443
Keating, Dan (Ballygamboon) 68, 342, 455
Keating, Dan (Cahersiveen) 357
Keating, Jeremiah 'Romey' 360, 361
Keating, Tadhg (Timothy) 362, 363
Keel 28, 58, 64, 233, 251, 329
Kelliher, Michael 230
Kells 348
Kelly, Michael 295, 296
Kelly, Paddy 58
Kenmare 23, 238, 269–277, 279, 282,

288, 289, 336, 342, 360, 361, 423, 452, 453
Kenmare, Lord 279
Kennan, Austin 397, 398
Kennedy, James 144
Kennedy, Jerry 306
Kennedy, Patrick (Paddy) 140, 141
Kennedy, Tadhg 108, 140
Kennedy, Tom Bawn 132
Kennelly, Thomas (Tom) 84, 85, 154, 158, 161, 163, 174, 178, 183, 185, 190, 248, 451
Kenny, Patrick Gerald (Eric) 205, 206
Kenny, Tomeen 106
Kerins, Charlie 24, 376, 393–396, 404, 454
Kerins, Seán 219
Kerry Head 82, 86
Kevins, John 293–296
Kevins, Thomas 293
Kilbane 265, 266
Kilbannivane Cemetery 182, 196, 199, 202, 204, 206, 209, 214, 220, 223, 225, 228, 231, 421, 426, 441
Kilbreanmore 299
Kilcummin 208, 209, 278, 284, 291–293, 296, 300–302, 304, 452
Kildrum 143, 149
Kilfenora 46
Kilflynn 82, 83, 86–88, 106, 121, 122, 126, 127
Kilgarvan 269, 273, 277, 421, 427, 428
Kilgobnet 327
Kilkenny 108, 399
Killagurteen 348
Killahenny Cemetery 188
Killarney 21, 48, 59, 76, 208, 214, 229, 238–240, 243, 271, 274, 276, 278–285, 288–290, 292, 293, 295–303, 305, 306, 308, 312, 313, 319, 320, 324, 331, 332, 336, 354, 358, 369, 399–401, 419, 424, 427, 432, 433, 442, 447, 449, 451–453

Killeagh 230
Killeen Cemetery 340
Killeentierna 229, 231
Killerisk 41
Killikilleen 418
Killiney 74, 134, 136, 139, 145, 152
Killoe 348
Killorglin 15, 33, 35, 48, 66, 153, 235, 272, 273, 279, 281, 294, 295, 327–329, 331–333, 335–338, 340, 341, 343–347, 351, 358–361, 369, 421, 432, 433, 443, 450, 451, 453
Killoughteen 442
Killurley 369, 370
Killury 90
Kilmainham Gaol 30, 40, 206, 379, 439
Kilmalkeadar 415
Kilmallock 38, 64, 66, 162, 180, 181, 189, 235, 263, 327, 329, 376, 399, 417, 418, 449
Kilmaniheen 215
Kilmeany 163, 165
Kilmorna 158, 163, 165, 175, 177
Kilmoyley 82, 83, 117, 449
Kilnabrack 338
Kilnanare 250
Kilnavarnogue 252, 352, 354, 356, 359, 361, 363, 368, 370, 372, 375, 404
Kilquane 297, 314, 321, 424
Kilrush 376, 414, 415
Kiltallagh 68, 233, 263, 385
Kiltomey Cemetery 109
Kimmage Garrison 398, 419
Kinard 131, 132, 376, 377, 379, 381
Kippagh 450
Kissane, John 295
Kissane, Mick 183
Knockaderry 212
Knockalougha 217, 248
Knockane 212, 217, 246, 248, 259, 453
Knockaneculteen 226, 230, 233, 382
Knockanes 320, 321

Knockanish 78
Knockanure 153, 159, 160, 163, 175, 190, 451
Knockavinnane 267
Knockeen 231
Knockeendubh 243, 284, 290, 291
Knockenagh 183, 430
Knocklong 391, 417
Knocknageeha 309
Knocknagoshel 106, 193, 201, 202, 210–215, 217, 218, 244, 246–248, 391, 392, 435, 438, 453
Knocknagree 309, 434
Knockrour 193
Knopogue 348

L

Lacca 296, 301
Lackeen 452
Laide, Richard 244–247, 254, 257, 258
Landers, Bill 67, 333
Landers, Paddy 153, 166
Lane, James (Jim) 384, 387, 410
Larkin, James 440, 441
Larkin, Seán 384, 385, 387, 388, 410, 411, 453
Laughton 400
Lauragh 269
Lawlor, David 169, 170
Lawlor, Dr 119
Lawlor, John (Jack) 103, 104, 453
Lawlor, John (Listowel) 169, 450
Leahy, Dave 211
Leahy, Tim 51, 204
Leam 84
Leane (or Leen), Jerry 430
Leane (or Leen), Thomas 421, 430
Leen, John 57, 259, 260, 265, 267, 268, 450
Lehane, Dan 341, 342, 361
Lehane, Seán 383, 384, 386, 387, 410
Lerrig 118

Letter 402
Lewes Prison 379
Limerick 23, 29, 38, 59, 64, 66, 75, 76, 93, 96, 105, 129, 158, 161, 162, 171, 176, 180, 181, 185, 189, 194, 197, 198, 207, 219, 234, 235, 242, 263, 264, 272, 290, 293, 309, 329, 358, 376, 391, 400, 405, 406, 417, 418, 421, 431, 432, 436, 437, 442, 445, 452
Limerick Gaol 30, 106, 183
Linnane, John (Jack) 155, 165, 171–174
Lios an Iarla 389
Lisanisky 418
Lisardboola 59
Liscahane 119
Liscannor (Clare) 324–326
Lisheenbawn 229
Lismore 453
Lisodigue 46, 80, 81
Lispole 54–56, 64, 128, 129, 131, 132, 137, 138, 328, 377, 379, 450
Lisselton 158, 172, 430, 431
Lissivigeen 278
Listowel 38, 78, 84, 85, 87, 89, 93, 101, 105, 129, 153–156, 158–161, 163–166, 169, 171–181, 183–186, 189, 190, 209, 216, 235, 247, 248, 329, 348, 386–388, 394, 396, 409, 411, 418, 419, 430, 449–452
Listowel, Lord 183
Listry 233, 278, 279, 281
Liverpool 436–438, 439
Lixnaw 82, 84, 85, 101, 105, 108, 109, 122, 126, 153, 168, 184, 248, 449, 451
Lohar 348, 353, 366
Longfield 197
Longford 293, 380, 397
Looney, Cornelius (Con) 15, 17, 270–273, 275–277, 342, 361
Lough Acoose 67, 68, 333, 334
Lough Derriana 351
Lowe, Dr 380

Lowe, General 408
Lydon, Sgt Jack 68, 80
Lynch, Dan (Cork) 33, 34
Lynch, Diarmuid 377
Lynch, Fionán 348, 349
Lynch, Liam 23, 29, 161, 162, 176, 180, 219, 329, 387, 410, 451–453
Lynch, Mary (née Murphy) 364, 365
Lynch, Michael (Ballymakeera) 428
Lynch, Michael (Lisselton) 421, 431
Lynch, Patrick (Maharees) 139
Lynch, Patrick (Moyrish) 348, 364, 365, 373
Lyne, Fr 132
Lyne, John 288
Lyons, Bridie 211, 212
Lyons, Con 212
Lyons, Const. 188
Lyons, Dan 47
Lyons, Jerry (Duagh) 159, 160, 174–177, 185, 186, 451
Lyons, Jerry (Knockalougha) 217
Lyons, Mary Ellen 230
Lyons, Michael Tiny 320, 338–340
Lyons, Timothy 'Aero' 83, 94, 98, 99, 105–107, 110, 111, 113, 114, 122–124, 127
Lyranes 343, 345–347
Lyre 193, 218, 229, 230
Lyreacrompane 193, 259, 267
Lyreatough 297, 298

M

MacBride, Seán 112, 162, 179, 403, 404
MacCurtain, Tomás 396
MacDiarmada, Seán 379, 406, 445
MacNeill, Eoin 237, 306, 312, 378, 379, 406, 407
Macroom 427–429
MacSwiney, Terence 28, 54, 91, 101, 115, 449
Magherabeg 144

Maharees 128, 139
Maher, John 157
Mahony, John 204
Mallow 238, 282, 283, 306
Malone, Tomás 418
Mangan, Joe 400, 401
Mannix, Jimmy 141
Markievicz, Constance 381
Mason, Mary 188
Mastergeehy 348, 349, 355
Maugha 211
Maunsell, Michael 151
McAuliffe, William 211
McCarthy, Dan 193
McCarthy, Daniel (Bob) 142, 143, 149
McCarthy, David 193, 231, 422, 441
McCarthy, Hannah Mary 297
McCarthy, Maurice 444
McCarthy, Ned 222, 227
McCarthy, Neilus 297
McCarthy, Paddy (Nenagh) 399–401
McCarthy, Patrick (Killarney) 297, 298
McCarthy, Richard 166
McCarthy, William 'Sonny' 108, 109
McCrohan, James 116
McElligott, Maurice (Mossy) 92, 195, 196
McElligott, Michael 387
McElligott, Michael Robert (Bob) 153, 178, 179, 185, 248
McElligott, Patrick Joseph (P.J.) 153, 179, 185
McEllistrim, Jack 255
McEllistrim, Richard 262
McEllistrim, Tom 59, 60, 234, 235, 237, 238, 240, 241, 244, 245–247, 255–259, 261, 267, 268, 278, 281, 283, 452
McEnery, Catherine 110
McEnery, James 95, 99, 106, 110–112, 114, 454
McEnery, Thomas 111
McGillycuddy Reeks 66, 293, 294, 333

Index

McGinn, Patrick 219, 231
McGlynn, Mick 74, 216
McGrath, Jim 99, 113, 114, 123, 124
McGrath, Michael 397, 398
McGrath, Seán 397
McGrath, Sgt 86, 87
McGrath, Thomas (Tom) 106, 113, 114, 123–125
McGuinness, Gerard 339
McGuinness, Jim 224
McGuire, Michael 115, 116
McInerney, Tommy 358, 359, 432, 433, 443
McKelvey, Joe 52
McKenna, Francis 184, 449
McKenna, Michael 144, 145
McKenna's Fort 39, 78, 380
McKinnon, Major John 22, 28, 57, 58, 62, 109, 249, 260, 261, 265, 266, 268, 450
McLoughlin, Thomas 234, 263, 264
McMahon, Bridget 159, 176
McMahon, John 255, 261, 262
McMahon, Matthew 27
McNamara, Mick 174
McSweeney, John 313
McSweeney, Michael 313, 314, 424
McSweeney, Pat 313
McSweeney, Tom 'Dundon' 313
Meath 131, 205, 206
Meehan, Tadhg 118
Mee, Jeremiah 449
Meelick 390
Meenascarthy 151
Meenoghane 110, 113, 123
Mein 216
Meinleitrim 200, 201, 216
Melinn, Joe 27
Mellows, Liam 52
Mícheál Breatnach. *See* Walsh, Mike
Milltown 128, 180, 233, 249, 279, 281, 327, 328, 331, 343, 344, 450

Minard 137, 377
Mitchel, Florence 230
Moll's Gap 269
Moloney, Fr John 395
Moloney, John 389
Monagea 442
Monaghan, Charlie 21, 358, 421, 432, 433, 442, 443
Monaghan county 412
Monaree 142, 149
Moneen 84, 174, 183
Monegay 418
Moneygall 400
Monteith, Robert 22, 234, 237, 445
Moonlighters 20, 133, 192, 197, 215, 221, 229, 234, 237, 259, 279, 293, 425
Mordaunt, Detective George 403
Morgan, George 101, 450
Moriarty, Bishop David 279
Moriarty, John (Seán) 57, 62, 63, 202, 338
Moriarty, Margaret 62, 63
Moriarty, Michael 128
Moriarty, Thomas 146, 147
Moriarty, William 62
Morley, Con 324, 325
Morley's Bridge 269
Moroney, Matthew 251, 453
Morris, Tom 383
Mortell, Michael 216
Moulnahone 348
Mountain Stage 338–340
Mountcoal 85
Mount Falvey 231, 232
Mountjoy Gaol 30, 52, 152, 206, 212, 243, 325, 376, 379, 380, 394, 395, 404, 425
Moyderwell 57, 64, 412
Moylan, Seán 222, 229, 239, 283, 310
Moynihan, Andrew 315, 316
Moynihan, Con 306
Moynihan, Manus 307

Moynihan, Maria 313
Moynihan, Sgt 414
Moyrish 364
Moyvane. *See* Newtownsandes
Muckross 278, 288, 289, 298, 401
Mulcahy, Pat 418
Mulcahy, Richard 94, 383
Mulcahy, Sgt 188
Mullaly, John (Jack) 172
Mullaly, Mick 50, 51
Mullins, Billy 27
Mulvihill, Dan 176, 208, 209, 249, 250, 328, 345, 452
Mulvihill, Michael 397, 398
Mulvihill, P. 188
Murhur Cemetery 157
Murphy, Bartholomew (Bertie) 207–209
Murphy, Daniel 210, 211, 212
Murphy, Den 'Gow' 310
Murphy, Humphrey 'Free' 29, 85, 96, 111, 155, 161, 192–194, 200, 210, 215, 216, 218, 222, 226, 227, 229–231, 233, 235, 252, 253, 278, 306, 451
Murphy, Jeremiah 314, 319, 320
Murphy, Dr John 258
Murphy, John 'Coffey' 210, 211, 216
Murphy, Dr Kathleen 395
Murphy, Patrick (Ennismore) 174
Murphy, Patrick (Killorglin) 341, 342, 361
Murphy, Tim (Tadhg/Timothy) 284, 285, 299–301, 304
Murphy, W. R. E. 96, 97, 213, 251, 252, 291
Muskerry 427
Myles, Jerry 64
Myles, William (Billy) 45, 64, 65, 71, 75

N

Nagle, George 66–68, 333, 334
National Volunteers 21, 144, 378, 406, 447

Neligan, David 41, 81, 122, 126, 127, 149, 167, 199, 202, 208, 209, 214, 235, 354, 394, 438
Neligan, Jack 164
Neligan, Tim 165
Nenagh 399–401
Newbridge 30, 49
Newcastle West 161, 216, 442
Newmarket-on-Fergus 389
Newtownsandes (Moyvane) 153, 154, 157, 163, 174, 175, 189–191, 211, 418, 450
Nohoval (Ballymacelligott) 262
Nohoval Daly 307, 421, 434, 435
Nolan, Fr 341
Nolan, Martin 219
Nolan, Maurice 118
Nolan, Michael (Mike) 117, 118, 449

O

Oakpark 27, 58
Oates, Sgt Barney 151
O'Brien, Denis (Dinny) 394, 395
O'Brien, Molly 67
O'Brien, Paddy 394
O'Brien, Pat 400
O'Brien, Tim 67
O'Brien, William 376, 392, 421, 434, 435
Ó Ceallaigh, Seán 348
Ó Cleirigh, Muiris 348
O'Connell, Diarmuid 348
O'Connell, J. 151
O'Connell, Michael 213, 214
O'Connell, Sarah 116
O'Connor, Batt 380
O'Connor, Dan (Cahersiveen) 352
O'Connor, Danny (Headford) 320
O'Connor, Dave Ned 231
O'Connor, Denis (Denny) 212, 215–217
O'Connor, Denis (Rathmore) 317
O'Connor, Dermot 251, 453

INDEX

O'Connor, Edmund 436, 438
O'Connor, Eileen (née Walsh) 436, 438, 439
O'Connor, James Joseph 69, 70, 78, 79
O'Connor, John (Innishannon) 436–439
O'Connor, Johnny (Farmer's Bridge) 36, 59, 71
O'Connor, Laurence 202
O'Connor, Fr Maurice 231
O'Connor, Ned 89
O'Connor, Paddy 224
O'Connor, Pat 200, 201
O'Connor, Patrick (Cahersiveen) 352
O'Connor, Patrick (Dingle) 405
O'Connor, Patrick (Dromavalla) 58, 60
O'Connor, Patrick (Dromavalla) 61
O'Connor, Patrick (Paddy) (Causeway) 83, 86, 87, 89, 96, 116, 453
O'Connor, Patrick (Paddy) (Rathmore) 306, 317, 318
O'Connor, Patrick (Patie Pats) 201, 202
O'Connor, Phil 425
O'Connor, Roger 175
O'Connor, Rory 52
O'Connor, Séamus 106
O'Connor, Thomas (Ballydonoghue) 184
O'Connor, Thomas (Milltown) 180, 281, 327–329, 331, 452
O'Connor, Thomas (Scart) 234, 244, 262, 267
O'Connor, Timothy 193
O'Connor, Toss 211
O'Connor, William Den 217
O'Connor Scarteen, John 272
O'Connor Scarteen, Tom 269, 271, 272, 452
O'Donnell, Capt. 219
O'Donnell, John 358, 379
O'Donnell, Tom 56, 327
O'Donoghue, Dan 284, 285, 296, 299–302, 304

O'Donoghue, Jeremiah 285, 300, 302–305
O'Donoghue, Jeremiah (Lacca) 296
O'Donoghue, Patrick 302
O'Donoghue, Tomás 153, 348, 409
O'Dowd, Thomas 148, 149
O'Driscoll, Daniel 119
O'Driscoll, Tom 83, 93, 121, 123, 453
O'Duffy, Eoin 383
O'Dwyer, Nicholas 417
O'Farrell, Elizabeth 408
O'Grady, Brian 156, 174
O'Grady, Dan 174, 189–191, 418
O'Grady, Donailín 163
O'Halloran, Maggie 403
O'Hanlon, Charlie 180–182
O'Hannigan, Donnacha 418
Ohermong 360, 452
O'Higgins, Kevin 272
O'Leary, Con 181, 208, 209, 307, 452
O'Leary, Jer (Knockanes) 320
O'Leary, Jeremiah (Scartaglin) 181, 193, 194, 198, 215, 218, 219, 220, 454
O'Leary, Mike 76
O'Leary, Ned 400
O'Leary, Seán 298, 376, 399–401
Ó Lochlainn, Colm 358, 432
O'Loughlin, Sgt 440
O'Mahony, Abel 144
O'Mahony, Dan 192, 193, 306
O'Mahony, John 193
O'Mahony, Nurse 56
O'Malley, Ernie 40, 71, 384, 387
O'Meara, Jim 400
Ó Murchú, Seán 340
O'Neill, James 124
O'Neill, Maurice 24, 376, 396, 402–404, 454
O'Reilly, Jack 376, 412, 447
O'Riordan, George 34
O'Riordan, John 58
O'Shea, Dan (Castlegregory) 144

O'Shea, Dan (Glencar) 67, 333
O'Shea, George 83, 105, 106, 121, 122, 126, 127
O'Shea, Michael (Mike) 113, 123, 125
O'Shea, Patrick (Pat) (Clashmealcon) 106, 114, 123–125
O'Shea, Patrick (Pat) (Killarney) 278
O'Shea, Richard 'Starry' 248
O'Shea, Timothy (Tim) 274, 275
O'Shea, Timothy (Tim) 270
O'Shea, T. P. 184
Ó Siochfrada, Pádraig 128
Ó Súilleabháin, Mícheál 428
O'Sullivan, Bishop Charles 44, 231, 279
O'Sullivan, Dan (Ballineanig) 148
O'Sullivan, Danny 426, 455
O'Sullivan, Donal Bill 174
O'Sullivan, Edward 278
O'Sullivan, Humphrey (Fredy) 306
O'Sullivan, Jeremiah (Jerry) 71, 72, 75
O'Sullivan, John (Aughacasla) 46, 73, 74
O'Sullivan, John (East Commons) 119
O'Sullivan, John Joe 87
O'Sullivan, John Tadhg (Killurley) 369, 370
O'Sullivan, John (Tralee) 109
O'Sullivan, Michael J. 278
O'Sullivan, Michael 'Mick Cud' 319, 320, 424, 453
O'Sullivan, Mick Flor 295
O'Sullivan, Nurse 418
O'Sullivan, Paddy Maukie 362, 363
O'Sullivan, Paddy Rua 328
O'Sullivan, Patrick (Ned) 277
O'Sullivan, Tadhg 322, 323
O'Sullivan, Thady 370
O'Sullivan, Tim 154, 174, 376, 384–388, 409–411, 453
O'Sullivan, Tobias 189, 417, 418, 450
O'Sullivan, Tom (Ballineanig) 148, 149
Oysterhall 74

P

Pallas 331
Parsons, Joseph 52, 53
Passage West 23
Pathé 256, 262
Pearse, Patrick 82, 378, 398, 406–408, 445
Pelican, Thomas 164, 248
Pentonville Prison 379
Pierce, Michael 83, 86, 87, 93, 94, 96, 98, 99, 103, 110, 116, 121, 123, 453
Pierson, Henry 124
Pinkman, John 181
Plunkett, Joseph 406
Poff, Sylvester 221
Pollard, Hugh 256, 262
Portland Gaol 379
Portlaoise Gaol 152, 394, 426, 455
Portmagee 348, 349
Power, Cis 438, 439
Power, Jo 438, 439
Prendiville, Denis 221, 222, 254
Prendiville, John (Jack) 221–223, 227, 440
Prendiville, Thomas 440, 441
Prior 348
Purcell, Martin 434, 435
Purtill, Mick 163

Q

Quille, Denis 84, 154, 158, 171, 172, 174, 177, 185, 190
Quille, Martin 174, 387
Quille, Michael 394–396
Quin 389
Quirke, Edward 164
Quirke, Thomas 164
Quirke, Tim 44

R

Rabbett, Const. 184
Radrinagh 284, 299, 301, 302

Rahilly, Áine 318, 420
Rahilly, Denis (Dinny) 231, 249, 250
Rahilly, Michael (The O'Rahilly) 398, 405–408, 420
Rath 292, 349
Rath Cemetery 32, 37, 39, 42, 45, 49, 51, 53, 56, 58, 63, 65, 70–72, 75, 77, 79, 246, 248, 252, 254, 258, 396, 413, 421, 439, 444
Rathanny 237, 265
Rathea 84
Rathela Cemetery 95, 97, 100, 102, 112
Rathkeale 59
Rathmore 16, 222, 229, 238, 282, 293, 306–319, 322–326, 392, 421, 423, 424, 434, 435, 449, 451
Rathoneen 195
Reaboy 310
Rearden, Pat 371
Rearden, Pete 371
Rearden, Willie 354–356, 367, 368, 371, 372, 374
Redmond, Const. 409
Redmond, John 21, 133, 144, 156, 324, 378, 380, 406, 447
Redmond, Capt. William 324
Redmond, William 380
Reen, Jerry 313, 314
Reenard 153, 348, 349, 351, 357, 366, 371, 409, 452
Reidy, John (Jack) 265, 266
Reidy, Maurice (Mossy) 57, 237, 244, 259, 260, 265, 267, 268, 450
Reidy, Paddy (Ballymacelligott) 227, 265
Reidy, Patrick (Paddy) (Lisselton) 163
Reidy, Patrick (Paddy) (Tralee) 71, 75
Reidy, Phil 266
Republican Police 198, 199, 293
Rice, John Joe 24, 45, 161, 233, 269, 270, 272, 280, 319, 329, 336, 360, 387, 451, 452, 454

Richmond Barracks 144, 379, 412
RIC (Royal Irish Constabulary) 22, 28, 40, 54, 59, 60, 64, 82–93, 101, 102, 108, 109, 115–119, 121, 128, 129, 133, 135, 139, 140, 144–147, 151, 153, 154, 156, 157, 164, 166, 169, 170, 174, 178, 183–185, 187–190, 193–199, 203, 221, 222, 227, 229, 230, 233, 234, 237, 238, 244–247, 253, 255, 257, 258, 263, 265, 267, 269, 276, 279–282, 288, 293, 297, 307, 315, 322–325, 327–329, 335, 336, 341, 343, 344, 345, 349, 353, 358–361, 378, 379, 382, 383, 389, 391, 398–401, 409, 414, 417, 418, 423, 427, 428, 430, 433, 436, 443, 445, 447–451
Rinn 333
Riordan, Jeremiah (Jerome) 348, 373
Riordan, Jim 197, 233, 447
Riordan, Pat (Paddy) 197, 233, 235
Roche, Patrick 88
Rockfield 281
Rock Street, Tralee 27, 28, 33, 38, 40, 69, 75, 444
Rohan, Dan 129
Roscrea 400
Rossboy 271
Rossdohan 270, 274, 275
Roughty Valley 269, 271
RUC (Royal Ulster Constabulary) 383, 394
Rundle, John (See John Conway) 31
Rusheen 156
Russell, Seán 24, 454
Russell, Thomas 376, 414, 415, 448
Ryan, Edward 400, 401
Ryan, Frank 401
Ryan, John (Seán) 352
Ryan, Seán 92, 119, 273, 277, 365
Ryle, Michael Joseph 71, 75, 76

S

Sammy's Rock (Tralee) 46, 73, 74
Savage, John (Seán) 224, 225
Scanlon, Dan 187, 188, 448
Scannell, Mick 159, 175, 176, 185
Scart 234, 262, 267
Scartaglin 181, 193, 194, 198, 204, 208, 212, 214, 218, 220, 221, 227, 229, 235, 238, 242, 253, 449
Scully, Bertie (Seán) 67, 181, 327, 328, 329, 330, 333, 334, 340, 344, 345, 352, 416
Scully, Chris 343, 344, 416
Scully, Liam 189, 343, 376, 416–418, 449
Scully, Lily 416
Scully, Nancy 56, 132
Shanacashel 416
Shanahan, Dr 261, 262
Shanahan, Jack 226
Shanahan, John 121, 126, 127
Shanahan, Richard (Dick) 193, 222, 226–228, 254
Shannow Bridge 83, 105, 121, 122
Shannow River 121
Sharry, John 324, 325, 326
Shea, Dan 353–356, 366–368, 371, 374
Shea, Diarmuid 366
Sheahan, Patrick Pats 295
Sheehan, Denis 190
Sheehan, Donal (Dan) 21, 358, 359, 421, 432, 433, 442, 443
Sheehan, Fr 367
Sheehan, Jack (Moyvane) 174, 189, 190, 191, 418
Sheehan, Michael 274
Sheehan, Patrick 115
Sheehy, John Joe 24, 28, 29, 58, 94, 396, 421
Sheehy, Tommy 73
Shortis, Liam 420
Shortis, Patrick 407, 419, 420
Shronahiree Cemetery 345, 347
Shrone 313, 314
Sinn Féin 24, 80, 134, 135, 183, 184, 187, 324, 335, 348, 405, 414, 445, 446, 448, 449, 454
Sinnott, Annie 79
Sinnott, Michael 69, 70, 78, 79
Sixmilebridge 197, 198, 389
Sliabh Luachra 306
Sliabh Mish Mountains 43, 60, 65, 80, 178, 328
Slieveadara 110
Sligo 263, 293, 384, 387
Sneem 269, 274, 349, 351
Soloheadbeg 234, 391, 448
South Dublin Union 30, 79
Spa, The 43, 46, 47, 68, 69, 73, 74, 78, 80, 81, 91, 115
Spillane, Dominic 306
Spillane, Margaret (Maggie May OLeary) 320
Spillane, Michael (Aughacasla) 151
Spillane, Michael (Killarney) 278, 281
Spillane, Timothy 151, 152
Spindler, Karl 21
Spunkane 353
Stack, Austin 21, 22, 27, 237, 296, 300, 302, 315, 325, 379, 416, 418, 421, 444–446, 448, 453, 454
Stack, J. 188
Stack's Mountains 248
Stapleton, Ed 202
Strand Street, Tralee 27–29, 31, 36, 43, 50, 52, 396, 416
Stranorlar 384, 388, 411
Sugrue, Daniel 304, 305
Sugrue, Denis 136
Sugrue, James 84, 153, 171, 174, 178, 184, 348, 409
Sugrue, John 354–356, 367, 368, 371, 373–375
Sullivan, Alexander M. 265

Sullivan, Dan 27
Sullivan, J. 188
Sullivan, Tadhg Crón 294
Sutton, Charles 316
Swayne, George 339
Sweeney, Joe 384, 387, 388, 410, 411

T

Tahilla 269, 274
Tangney, William Duffer 36
Tarbert 23, 85, 153, 155, 158, 163, 171, 181, 190, 191, 451, 452
Taylor, Joseph 343–347, 450
Taylor, Lily 358, 433
Taylor, Séamus 294, 345–347
Taylor, Sheila 346
Teampaillín Bán 164
Teehan, Jack 348
Templeathea Cemetery 160
Templeglantine 209, 418
Templenoe 269
The Bower 313
Thurles 391, 416
Tipperary 23, 29, 36, 76, 93, 129, 181, 237, 290, 293, 298, 325, 376, 391, 392, 399–401, 416, 434, 435, 445, 448, 453
Togherbane 118
Toureenamult 307, 315
Toureengarrive 310, 450
Tournafulla 197, 418
Tralee 21, 22, 27–34, 36–41, 43, 44–54, 56–76, 78–83, 87, 89, 96–99, 103, 105, 108, 109, 113, 117, 118, 119, 121–124, 126, 131, 133, 137, 140–144, 151, 160, 161, 166–168, 174, 177, 179, 181, 184–186, 188, 195, 199–203, 205, 207, 208, 213, 214, 221, 234, 237, 240, 242, 245–248, 250–252, 254–256, 258–262, 265, 267, 268, 280, 284, 290–292, 294, 300, 302, 304, 308, 315, 316, 329, 336, 338, 341, 345, 347, 354, 357, 358, 361, 367, 369, 374, 376, 379, 381, 389, 390, 393, 396, 400, 408, 412, 413, 415, 416, 421, 425, 432, 437–439, 441, 442, 444–452, 454
Treacy, Seán 391
Trieneragh 172
Truce 22, 50, 51, 80, 83, 153–155, 157, 171, 190, 194, 199, 204, 249, 253, 269, 279, 280, 286, 293, 297, 307, 329, 331, 383, 386, 401, 409, 451
Tubrid 91
Tullamore 84, 89, 161
Tullig 348
Tuohy, Denis 270, 271, 273, 275–277
Tuomey, Tim 107, 121, 122, 126, 127
Tuosist 269
Turner, Archibald 255
Turner, Charles 390
Twiss, John Joe 221
Tyrone 233, 382, 383, 387, 410

U

Union Hall 23

V

Valentia 20, 348, 349, 357, 362, 364, 366, 373, 404
Ventry 128, 142
Vicars, Sir Arthur 163, 175
Victoria Barracks (Cork) 60, 323

W

Wade, Martin 272
Walsh, Edmond 184
Walsh, Fr Bill 232
Walsh, James (Jim) (Lisodigue) 46, 80, 81
Walsh, James (Séamus) (Currow) 229–232
Walsh, Jeremiah 230
Walsh, John (Lyre) 184, 193, 229

Walsh, Kathleen 201
Walsh, Michael (Currow) 231
Walsh, Mike (Mícheál Breatnach) (Dromad) 348, 349, 351, 353, 366, 373
Walsh, Ned Joe 84
Walsh, Nora 229
Walsh, Paddy (Patrick) 158–160, 164, 165, 175–177, 183–186, 451
Walsh, Tim 255
Wandsworth Gaol 412
Ward, Frank 384, 387, 410
Waterford 23, 29, 66, 78, 96, 129, 180, 184, 235, 293, 296, 308, 324, 329, 377, 453
Waters, Tom 400, 401
Waterville 349, 351, 353, 355, 360, 362, 364, 366, 371, 373
Watson, J. B. 164
Wexford 78, 308, 401
Whelan, Patrick 406
White, Harry 402, 403
White, Mikey 274
White, Dr Vincent 324
Williams, Pat Belty 48, 50, 51, 310
Wilson, William John 69, 79, 303, 304, 347
Windrim, Sammy 358, 432, 433
Wynne, E. M. P. 117, 118, 449

MERCIER PRESS
IRISH PUBLISHER - IRISH STORY

We hope you enjoyed this book.

Since 1944, Mercier Press has published books that have been critically important to Irish life and culture.

Our website is the best place to find out more information about Mercier, our books, authors, news and the best deals on a wide variety of books. Mercier tracks the best prices for our books online and we seek to offer the best value to our customers, offering free delivery within Ireland.

A large selection of Mercier's new releases and backlist are also available as ebooks. We have an ebook for everyone, with titles available for the Amazon Kindle, Sony Reader, Kobo Reader, Apple products and many more. Visit our website to find and buy our ebooks.

Sign up on our website or complete and return the form below to receive updates and special offers.

www.mercierpress.ie
www.facebook.com/mercier.press
www.twitter.com/irishpublisher

Name: _____

Email: _____

Address: _____

Mobile No.: _____

Mercier Press, Unit 3b, Oak House, Bessboro Rd, Blackrock, Cork, Ireland